JUDITH R. WALKOWITZ is Professor of History at The Johns Hopkins University. She is the author of the prize-winning *Prostitution and Victorian Society: Women, Class and the State* and has published many articles on the history of feminism and sexuality. She has been active in numerous feminist organisations. She lives in New York City.

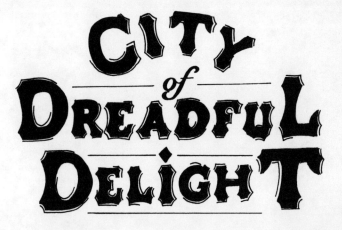

CITY
of
DREADFUL
DELIGHT

NARRATIVES OF SEXUAL DANGER IN LATE-VICTORIAN LONDON

JUDITH R. WALKOWITZ

A *Virago* Book

Published by Virago Press 1992

Reprinted 1994, 1998, 2000

First published in the USA by The University of Chicago Press, 1992

Copyright © Judith R. Walkowitz, 1992

The moral right of the author has been asserted

A CIP catalogue record for this book is available from the British Library

ISBN 1 85381 517 9

Printed and bound in Great Britain by Creative Print and Design (Wales), Ebbw Vale

Virago Press
A Division of
Little, Brown and Company (UK)
Brettenham House
Lancaster Place
London WC2E 7EN

For Danny and Rebecca

CONTENTS

Illustrations follow p. 134.

SERIES EDITOR'S FOREWORD

ack the Ripper has an entry in *The Dictionary of Cultural Literacy,* that long list of what every American needs to know. It simply states, "Jack the Ripper—A criminal in LONDON in the late nineteenth century apparently responsible for several ghastly murders by slashing. His identity is unknown."[1] The *Dictionary* fails to note that the mutilated victims were all women, a perverse lacuna for even a short note about a notorious figure who seemed to prefer killing women, especially if they were prostitutes, to men. However, as *City of Dreadful Delight,* Judith R. Walkowitz's brilliant, fertile, and original new book shows, our stories about Jack the Ripper have often been wayward and cross-grained.

City of Dreadful Delight does not "solve" the mystery of the Ripper's identity. Nor does it pretend to do so. For Walkowitz, the author of one greatly influential text about the nineteenth century, *Prostitution and Victorian Society: Women, Class, and the State* (1980), is exploring a far more labyrinthine and vital mystery, the identity and meaning of late nineteenth-century England itself, especially of London, its capital. So doing, Walkowitz tells of a number of vivid figures: W. T. Stead, the journalist who in 1885, three years before the Ripper murders, wrote the "Maiden Tribute," his sensational series about vice; Karl Pearson, who, in the same year, formed the "Men and Women's Club," a group of freethinkers, among them the bold New Women, who met to talk about sex; Georgina Weldon, the plucky and iconoclastic spiritualist who campaigned against the efforts of her husband and doctor to incarcerate her in an insane asylum; the working-class men and women who scripted the public spectacles of marches and protests; the women of all classes who insisted on occupying public space—be it music hall, department store, civic office, or a prostitute's bit of street and corner.

In turbulent London, on this rich and multileveled stage, Walkowitz deftly and lucidly locates a crucial moment in which our "feminist sexual politics" and narratives of "sexual danger" were formed. They were insep-

1. E. D. Hirsch, Jr., Joseph H. Kett, James Trefil, *The Dictionary of Cultural Literacy* (Boston: Houghton Mifflin, 1988), p. 215.

arable from representations of the city that sharply contrasted proper worlds with teeming underworlds; from the emergence of modern norms of sex and gender; and from the powerful discourses of law, science, and medicine that helped to forge these norms. Feminist sexual politics and narratives of sexual danger were also tied to each other as tightly as doctor to disease. To be sure, the activities of Jack the Ripper set off many anxieties and fears, exacerbated because the fact that he was never caught made any definitive, common labels for him impossible. Anti-Semitism, for example, transmogrified Jews into possible Rippers. However, the Ripper became a pervasive, bloody symbol for violence against women that feminists and other women had to face daily.

Some of the fascination of *City of Dreadful Delight* lies in the drama of Walkowitz's setting and subjects. Some of it also lies in the care of her thinking about history. Maturely, judiciously, she balances deep archival research with a variety of sophisticated approaches to the history of culture in general and women in particular. She retains a commitment to history as the study of human agency, action, and experience in a material world. To this, she adds a poststructuralist interest in the ways in which we organize meaning for ourselves and others; interpret and control our experience through language and narrative; ransack past and present for a language and narrative. W. T. Stead, for example, called on the generic traditions of melodrama and pornography when he wrote the "Maiden Tribute." In brief, history is the story of our stories, full of contradictory, shifting, and contested meanings. Walkowitz also draws on the ideas of Michel Foucault about Victorian sexuality and power, "a dispersed and decentered force that is hard to grasp and possess fully." One tool that her men and women have for displaying power is some degree of control over the narratives about sex and gender. However, her realism also maps the inequalities produced by class and gender, interlocking socioeconomic structures and processes.

During and after 1888, stories about Jack the Ripper proliferated, many of them variants of the theme of male violence and female helplessness before it. In 1980, Madame Tussaud's wax museum in London installed a Jack the Ripper exhibit, still another cultural narrative about him and his city. Walkowitz reads this significant effusion carefully, but in an Epilogue she focuses on a twentieth-century English mass murderer, the "Yorkshire Ripper," whom the media between 1975 and 1981 represented as a son of Jack. Walkowitz suggests that the twentieth-century discourses of law and medicine were as inadequate as those of the nineteenth century in their attempts to explain and codify the monstrous. However, she shows contemporary feminists differing from their nineteenth-century predecessors. They organized patrols. They fought against the glorification of sexual violence in films and bias against women in the press and law enforcement. So doing, feminists rejected a representation of women as passive victims who might, despite their passivity, have provoked a man's violence.

Walkowitz respects these efforts. Once again, however, her realism and scrupulous intelligence are at work. For the feminist response, virtuous in its resistance to violence, bold in speaking of both sexuality and violence, risks reducing our gender identities, which multiply in time and change over time, to two unchanging monoliths: the aggressive and violent male, the passive and violated female. Such a reduction establishes women's sexuality as perpetual dread, never delight. Inevitably, the feminist response to male violence extends to pornography. Consistently aware of complexities, Walkowitz sees no single discourse of pornography, but several that collide and clash, one advocating the most militant of antipornography campaigns, another asking if such campaigns really empower women or instead create a counterproductive "politics of fear, frustration, and rage."

The stories of Jack the Ripper and his heirs, like pornography, confront us with these questions: Can we realize that women are in danger on our streets and in our spaces? Can we simultaneously rip apart representations of women that project them only as victims in need of a protection that drifts inexorably towards control and repression? Because of its own narrative, because it asks such questions, *City of Dreadful Delight* should shape our cultural literacies.

CATHARINE R. STIMPSON

ACKNOWLEDGMENTS

his book took many years to write and is the result of joint intellectual labors. Over the years, I have incurred many debts. Let me begin by thanking those institutions, foundations, and granting agencies that helped to underwrite the research and writing of this book: Rutgers University, Johns Hopkins University, the American Council of Learned Societies, the Center for the Critical Analysis of Contemporary Culture, the Institute for Advanced Study, the National Endowment for the Humanities, the National Institutes of Health, the New York Institute for the Humanities, and the Rockefeller Foundation.

Librarians on both sides of the Atlantic greatly assisted me in my research. I would like to thank the staff of the British Library, British Library of Political and Economic Science, British Newspaper Library, Brunel University Library, Fawcett Library, Guildhall Library, Madame Tussaud's Archives, the Oral History Archives at the University of Essex, Public Record Office, Salvation Army Archives, Tower Hamlets Library, Manuscripts Room of the University College Library, and the Wellcome Institute. In the United States, I received assistance from the staff of the Milton S. Eisenhower Library, Johns Hopkins University; Alexander Library, Rutgers University; Beinecke Library, Yale University; Bobst Library, New York University; Law Library, Harvard University; New York Public Library; Firestone Library, Princeton University; and the Library of the Institute for Advanced Study.

Many students and former students assisted me in my research and shared their own work with me. Thanks to Polly Beals, Johannah Bradley, Anna Clark, Dina Copelman, Joy Dixon, Kali Israel, Jan Lambertz, Erika Rappaport, Jennifer Tucker, and Pamela Walker. When members of my graduate seminars at Johns Hopkins University and at Rutgers University read my work-in-progress, they invariably offered me sound advice about strategies of presentation and interpretation. The Hopkins undergraduates in a 1991 seminar on Victorian London, co-taught by Mary Poovey and myself, directed me to many subtle features of the media coverage of the Jack the Ripper murders. Laura Larson of the Women's Studies program of

Johns Hopkins was invaluable in assisting me in the final preparation of the manuscript.

Dozens of friends and colleagues have read all or parts of this text as it has evolved over a decade. My thanks to Thomas Bender, Gillian Brown, Ed Cohen, Dina Copelman, Anna Davin, Nicholas Dirks, John Gillis, Temma Kaplan, Thomas Laqueur, Ruth Leys, Alex Owen, Judith Newton, Deborah Nord, Rayna Rapp, Mary Ryan, Elaine Showalter, Carroll Smith-Rosenberg, Ruth Richardson, Herb Schreier, Eliott Shore, Joan Scott, Ann Snitow, Judith Stacey, and Martha Vicinus. I owe a special debt to Martha Howell, Mary Poovey, and Laura Engelstein, who read and edited numerous versions of each chapter. Cora Kaplan and Ellen Ross, who joined me at the Chelsea Gallery for our Friday mornings "rescue group," not only gave me practical advice and personal support, but offered acute readings of numerous chapters.

Friends in London offered astute commentary, wonderful conversation, and spectacular hospitality. In this regard I would like to thank Michele Barrett, Mary McIntosh, Ruth Petrie, and Barbara Taylor, who housed me at various times for weeks on end. Jerry White deserves special thanks for introducing me to the pensioner "luncheon clubs," where I acquired gripping family stories of "Mother meets Jack the Ripper." The following individuals shared their personal archives with me: J. O. Baylen, Anna Davin, and Mandy Merck. In general, I want to thank my London friends for introducing me to the multiple and conflicted agendas of contemporary feminism in Britain.

I would like to thank Karen Wilson and John McCudden, from the editorial staff of the University of Chicago Press, for their patience and meticulous care. Catharine Stimpson has been behind this project from the start, and I deeply appreciate her support and intellectual guidance.

Finally, I want to thank Daniel and Rebecca Walkowitz, who made considerable intellectual contributions to this work, besides offering material and emotional support for its undertaking. To these two feminists, I dedicate this book.

INTRODUCTION

n April 1980, Madame Tussaud's wax museum in London installed a new exhibition in its Chamber of Horrors: the Jack the Ripper street. With the aid of concealed refrigerators that brought the temperature down to that of a "foggy winter's night," it set about literally making the "blood run cold." Newspapers around the world excitedly reported what might be in store for the intrepid visitor. After passing a wall plastered with Victorian tabloid illustrations of the Ripper murders and their locale, the visitor "finds himself stumbling over cobbles, past green slime-covered walls, his way barely illuminated by flickering gas lamps." On the left the effigy of Mary Kelly, the "last victim" of Jack the Ripper, waits for custom at the door of her "sordid" room. Meanwhile,

> Boisterous singing from a nearby pub does little to dispel the sense of malice and foreboding. Suddenly there is a shadow on the wall, the sound of running feet, and then a hideous scream. Nervously, the visitor presses on—only to wish he hadn't. In a back alley, lies the disfigured woman with her throat cut. . . . It is horribly realistic.

Yet the star of the new installation, Jack the Ripper, was "nowhere to be seen"—only a disappearing shadow, whose "signature" was the mutilated body of a woman.[1]

The Ripper street transports the visitor back into a Victorian "Carnival of the Night" of mean streets, menacing obscurity, and drunken raucous laughter. Newspaper accounts of Tussaud's street represent it as a movie set designed from the male point of view, despite the fact that women and children also walked through the exhibit. As the spectator abruptly observes the prone body of the murdered Catherine Eddowes, he/she becomes complicit in the act of looking, forced into an uneasy alliance with the disappearing shadow of the Ripper.[2] The power of the "male gaze" does not go unchallenged, however; it is met by the blunt, frontal stare of the prostitute Mary Kelly, standing at her door; audacious, unflinching looks, like these, or so cultural critics tell us, are a sure sign of the unchaste public woman whose sinful wages must lead to death.[3]

I

The installation of the Ripper street represents an important departure from tradition for Madame Tussaud. In keeping with its proud heritage of "authenticity" and "fact," the descendants of Madame Tussaud had steadfastly refused to include the notorious Ripper of 1888 in their exhibit, despite the frequent "surprise" of visitors on failing to find him there. For the Ripper had never been apprehended: "No one had caught a glimpse of his figure, or even a likely figure, let alone a face." And Tussaud's, while willing to apply illusionary techniques to a "setting," will not "invent a face."[4]

By 1980, however, Madame Tussaud's faced a dilemma: visitors (particularly children) were complaining that the Chamber of Horrors was not "horrible" enough. "People were just not finding it bloody enough." By installing the "Ripper street," Madame Tussaud "bowed" to demands for "more gore." To accommodate new tastes, modern sound and lighting effects were introduced to produce a realistic "setting," so that the "accuracy of likeness and presentation still prevail."[5]

The elusive identity of the murderer and the "authentic" setting so carefully represented in Tussaud's Ripper street were not facts but complex rhetorical structures, public fantasies containing contradictory and historically shifting meanings. In returning to London of the 1880s, *City of Dreadful Delight* examines the cultural dynamics and social struggles that informed these fantasies and originally produced Jack the Ripper in 1888 as a mythic story of sexual danger.[6] This study locates the Ripper story as part of a formative moment in the production of feminist sexual politics and of popular narratives of sexual danger. It examines the competing cultural elements incorporated into the Ripper narrative, as well as those elements that the Ripper story excluded and resisted, particularly those in which women were not silent or terrorized victims.

Tussaud's Ripper street condenses many elements of the original tabloid reporting about the murders, but it presents a far more stabilized account than media coverage offered at the time. In 1888, the narrative of the murders was assembled piecemeal and retrospectively during that year's "autumn of terror," when five prostitutes were brutally murdered within ten weeks (31 August to 9 November), some sexually mutilated as well. All but one murder occurred within the East London parishes of Whitechapel and Spitalfields (the exception occurred nearby, just within the boundary of the City of London). Although some prior homicides of prostitutes were retrospectively linked to the Ripper, only after 31 August did coroners and police suspect "something extraordinary." Only then did police authorities, newspaper readers, and the local population of Whitechapel come to interpret the cluster of five murders as the work of one unknown killer and to brace themselves for "more to follow." Like the disappearing shadow of Tussaud's installation, the murderer, who was never caught, was known only by his *modus operandi*—despite the concerted efforts of police and citizen action groups to hunt "him" down.[7]

A wide variety of stories circulated around the identity of the murderer and the meanings of his murders. As anxiety and interest in the case intensified, different constituencies assembled a convergent set of fantasies in relation to the figure of the murderer. Eventually some newspaper correspondents imagined the Ripper as a privileged, sexually dangerous man and publicity hound who, they believed, communicated with a mass audience through letters published in those very same newspapers. "His" sexual appetite was perverse and unbounded. "His" "lust murders" and sexual mutilations of prostitutes were, commentators claimed, unnatural alternatives to heterosexual copulation. "His" taste for clinical, sadistic practices also led to speculations that "he" was a mad, syphilitic doctor. Often imagined as a seasoned urban traveler, the Ripper could move effortlessly and invisibly through the spaces of London, transgressing all boundaries, committing "his" murderous acts in public, under the cover of darkness, exposing the private parts of "public women" to open view. While these compelling stories never cohered into a single version, for Londoners of the 1880s, these perceptions shaped the Ripper murders into a story of class conflict and exploitation and into a cautionary tale for women, a warning that the city was a dangerous place when they transgressed the narrow boundary of home and hearth to enter public space.

The popularity of Madame Tussaud's exhibit testifies to the symbolic potency of the Ripper murders as quintessential acts of transgression, evoking the repressed Victorian past, when a dangerous male sexuality—a sexuality that many experience as all too contemporary—found stark representation. In featuring Jack the Ripper, Tussaud's continued a well-established media fascination with the "world's ultimate sexist murderer."[8] No single criminal has appeared so tirelessly in literature, drama, opera, television, and motion pictures. "If a journalist cannot sell anything else in London he can always sell a story about 'Jack the Ripper,'" observed one author in the 1920s; the frequency with which "printed solutions" to the hundred-year old mystery have been turned into films, argues Christopher Frayling, is "a clear indication of their strong *resonance* in contemporary popular culture."[9] The Whitechapel murderer has been the subject of over one hundred literary and visual productions, from the dark "mental" fantasies of the expressionists, who situated the Ripper's acts of sexual violence in "someone else's nightmare," to the Hollywood thrillers of Alfred Hitchcock, featuring the "man-with-the-knife" and the deadly, controlling, murderous gaze.[10]

Renewed contemporary interest in the Ripper story may also account for Tussaud's decision to spotlight the Ripper. New trends in horror movies, the "real life" exploits of a contemporary Ripper operating in the north of England, and a revival of speculation about the historic Ripper, vastly increased general familiarity with the details of the Ripper story and provoked a consuming desire to re-enact and resolve the mystery. Post-1960s theories which identified the original Ripper as a homosexual member of the Royal Family and the Ripper's recent reincarnation as the proletarian Yorkshire Ripper testify to the Ripper story's capacity to play out an elaborate repertoire of contemporary anxieties—from heterosexual violence, to the "lavender menace," to the specters of imperial and domestic industrial decline. Yet Tussaud's refusal to "invent a face" capitalized on the most terrifying meaning of all: the myth of an "eternal" Ripper, "the never named, could-be-anyone killer," unifying past and present terror.[11]

Like the feature-length films and dozens of Ripper books churned out at the end of the 1980s to celebrate the centenary of Jack the Ripper, Tussaud's Ripper street adheres to a certain invention of the Victorian past, expressed through an overworld/underworld structure. This historical imagination recreates Victorian London as a geographically and class-divided city whose social boundaries were regularly transgressed by illicit acts of sex and crime. Whereas Tussaud's Ripper street provides the period setting for the "poetics" of transgression, other accounts of the Ripper frequently invent an "overworld" family identity for this supremely "undomesticated" killer. To the male fantasy of urban descent, advocates of a Royal Ripper theory, for instance, have attached a domestic melodrama, featuring the "highest" family in the land.[12]

The "overworld/underworld" structure of Ripper histories informs the political lessons drawn from them. Such a structure allows contemporary authors to articulate a longing for the secure world of our fathers, but also to penetrate the smug, hypocritical facade of that world to uncover a perverse sexual jungle. As Jeffrey Weeks notes, this historical imagination represents a certain projection into the past of current debates over the "constraints" of society and the "unruly energy of sex." Nostalgia for a "golden age of propriety" represents a retreat from contemporary challenges to the values and family life of the "neo-Victorian" fifties, challenges posed by the disruptive forces of the 1960s, the youth culture, and the women's and gay liberation movements. Yet piercing the nostalgia for sturdy Victorian values and stable family life is the belief that the Victorians themselves were wracked by anxieties and contradictions—that they too had "terrible secrets."[13]

Ripper productions may be symptomatic inventions of the past, but they are not, as one reviewer of the genre observes, critical interrogations of the Victorian culture "that created and succored" a figure like Jack the Ripper,[14] critical interrogations that *City of Dreadful Delight* proposes to undertake. This study treats the Jack the Ripper story, told in chapter 7, as a far less unified and bounded production than the depiction offered by Tussaud's installation and other popular renditions. To account for the Ripper narrative's power and instability, *City of Dreadful Delight* assesses the internal contradictions of the Ripper story and juxtaposes the Ripper narrative against competing narratives of gender and sexuality circulating in the late-Victorian metropolis.

City of Dreadful Delight maps out a dense cultural grid through which conflicting and overlapping representations of sexual danger circulated in late-Victorian London. Two newspaper scandals, W. T. Stead's 1885 exposé of child prostitution, the "Maiden Tribute of Modern Babylon," and the tabloid reporting of the Ripper murders in 1888, provide my chronological frame. Although they emanated from different political locations, both media scandals manipulated similar cultural themes and rhetorical strategies. Both produced contradictory and unanticipated effects. As catalyzing events, the "Maiden Tribute" and the media coverage of the Ripper murders forced a range of constituencies to take sides and to assert their presence in a heterogeneous public sphere. In the process, such narratives influenced the language of politics, fictional forms, and journalistic innovations in *fin de siècle* London.

Although *City of Dreadful Delight* observes chronological boundaries, it does not proceed in linear fashion. It moves synchronically, linking the narrative tradition of urban exploration and the dark labyrinthine city, found in media scandals like the Ripper or the "Maiden Tribute," to contiguous stories of sexual possibility and urban adventure, some of them located in different social spaces of the metropolis. Like the Ripper story, these other stories (presented in chapters 2, 5, and 6) introduce a wide panorama of social actors, who engaged in cultural contests over sexuality and gender that both echoed and inverted the theme of sexual danger and the social vision of the city that were featured in the Ripper story. In these alternative narratives of gender conflict, women appear as interlocutors as well as figures in the imaginary urban landscape of male spectators.

A conjunction of shifting sexual practices, sexual scandals, and political mobilizations provided the historic conditions in the late-Victorian period for the elaboration of such narratives. In their assessment of similar developments on the other side of the Atlantic, American historians John D'Emilio and Estelle Freedman contend that nineteenth-century sexuality acquired a privileged status as a primary identity precisely as sexual practices and meanings became disengaged from procreation in the United States, at least for the white middle-class portion of the population. This provoked a shift in "the dominant [i.e. middle-class] meaning of sexuality" from a "primary association of sexuality with reproduction within families" to an association with a more intimate, nonreproductive yet conflicted marital sexuality and to sex outside the family. To assuage a mounting anxiety that the erotic had lost its moorings and fixed identity in reproductive sexuality, they argue, cultural commentators marked off a range of sexual practices—same-sex relations, free love, commercialized sex—as dangerous and set about specifying a new heterosexual (nonprocreative) norm.[15]

A similar constellation of media scandal, anti-vice campaigns, and proliferating sexual categories and identities occurred in Great Britain in the second half of the nineteenth century. Out of this maelstrom, the narratives of sexual danger emerging in London in the 1880s developed. These narratives reverberated in courtrooms, learned journals, drawing rooms, street corners, and in the correspondence columns of the daily press. Diverse men and women employed a variety of competing social languages to interpret sexual experience, from the language of sexual bartering, to melodramatic newspaper representations, to the authoritative language of the law and medicine. In these discussions, gender transgression and sexual transgression continually overlapped, for as Thomas Laqueur observes, "almost everything one wants to *say* about sex already has in it a claim about gender."[16] As a consequence, concern over "dangerous" sexual practices focused on much more than disorderly sexual conduct: dangerous sexualities had as much to do with work, life-style, reproductive strategies, fashion and self-display, and nonfamilial attachments of urban men and women as with nonprocreative sexual activity.

Women as well as men participated in the debates and cultural exchanges around dangerous sexualities. In the two decades prior to the Ripper murders, female reformers had actively engaged in public discussions of sexual danger. Through the feminist politics of prostitution, middle-class women inserted themselves into the public discussion of sex to an unprecedented extent, using access to new public spaces and to new journalistic practices to speak out against men's double lives, their sexual diseases, and their complicity in a system of vices that flourished in the undergrowth of respectable society. Along with female antivivisectionists, who plastered the thoroughfares of London with the posters of mutilated and tortured bodies of innocent "feminized" laboratory animals, feminist opponents of regulated prostitution disseminated images and narratives of scientific sexual violence more widely than any other literary vehicles of the time, including pornography.[17]

These campaigns facilitated middle-class women's forceful entry into the world of publicity and politics, where they claimed themselves as part of a public that made sense of itself through public discourse.[18] These women were able to capitalize on the volatile political conditions of the 1880s, particularly the expansion of political opinion "out of doors," to gain access to a redefined public sphere.[19] As political actors, female moral reformers drew on traditions of radical political culture aimed at producing and consolidating public opinion against a privileged class of sexually dangerous men who preyed on the innocent. Women's presence in this public world provoked a heightened sense of sexual antagonism and reinforced assumptions of sexual difference, particularly the prevailing Victorian association of sexual desire with maleness. A number of historians, including myself, have criticized the "social purity" legacy of first-wave feminism for reinforcing women's subordination and sexual fear.[20] But these campaigns also opened up new heterosexual expectations for middle-class women, even as they set into motion repressive public policies, mostly directed against working-class women on the streets.

A number of factors inspired me to undertake a cultural history of this sort. In part, I am continuing to explore some interpretive questions suggested by, but left undeveloped, in my earlier study of the state regulation of Victorian prostitution. In *Prostitution and Victorian Society,* I was able to call into question certain myths about prostitution handed down from the Victorian era: that prostitution was a question of working-class supply and middle-class demand; that prostitutes were social outcasts, irrevocably cut off from a community of the laboring poor; that the wages of sin were death. Yet these myths compelled the attention of people across gender and class lines, forming a story that powerfully ordered people's experience and their own self-representations.[21]

This line of inquiry itself emanates from intellectual and political debates of the late twentieth century. The pornography debate among feminists in the early 1980s provoked me to confront thorny and unresolved problems about the power of representation and feminists' relation to cultural production. Equally provocative and unsettling were the epistemological challenges posed by poststructuralist critics, who insisted that historians pay closer attention to the "complex way meanings are constructed and cultural practices are organized," in particular, the rhetorical, linguistic means by which "people represent and understand their world."[22]

By considering these questions historically, this study engages in a productive dialogue with poststructuralists, reformulating their insights about cultural meanings to address analytic categories conventionally of interest to the historian: power, agency, and experience. This book also draws a cultural map that resists the conceptual oppositions that traditionally inform historical interpretation: representation and reality; elite and popular culture; the creation/reception and production/consumption of cultural texts. It posits instead a more complex interaction of cultural worlds.[23]

The events and stories narrated in this book illustrate the operation of power in a Foucauldian sense, as a dispersed and decentered force that is hard to grasp and possess fully. On the whole, my own narratives, in keeping with Foucault's insight, call into question old-fashioned assumptions about a centralized and stable hierarchy of power. Mindful of feminist critiques of Foucault's theory that have developed in the past few years, I have set out to illustrate simultaneously how different individuals and social groups had access to different levels and sources of power.[24] While challenging a picture of a fixed hierarchy of power, *City of Dreadful Delight* still tries to convey a sense of the inequality of power—along class and gender lines—and of the unequal power of different stories amidst the proliferation of cultural meanings.

In his last three books, Foucault came to believe that the discourse of sexuality was a privileged object of analysis, the essential place to grasp the working of power in modern Western societies.[25] Many of his insights into Victorian sexuality were already anticipated by feminist scholars, who also recognized that there was nothing natural or inevitable about sexual practices and meanings. Feminist historians such as Linda Gordon, Nancy Cott, and Carroll Smith-Rosenberg had already begun to outline the contested, heterogeneous, and pluralistic history of sexuality in the nineteenth century. They had come to recognize, in the words of Kathy Peiss and Christina Simmons, that sexuality was not an "unchanging biological reality or a universal natural force, but was rather a product of political, social, economic, and cultural processes. Sexuality, that is, had a history." Feminist scholars showed how sexuality was a contested site for other struggles and social divisions, particularly those of class, gender, and race.[26]

Even if it were not alone in historicizing sexuality, Foucault's *The History of Sexuality* helped to sharpen and focus the discussion of the politics of sexuality in some important ways. Foucault took the lead in repudiating the "repressive hypothesis" underlying Marcus's dichotomized and condescending psychic map of the Victorians. Far from repressing sexuality, Foucault argued, Victorian culture actually produced, multiplied, and dispersed it. This volubility led to the special privileging of sexuality as the core of a private identity, which was dangerous when made public. Through the incitement, prohibition, and normalization of desire, these discourses facilitated the policing of society, a policing that extends into the liberated twentieth century, when the "mechanisms of repression" deceptively seem to be loosening their grip: "We must not think that by saying yes to sex, one says no to power."[27]

Feminist scholars have called for a more complex picture of Victorian sexual politics and sexual practice than Foucault's paradigm allows, one that gives more attention to the material context of discursive struggle and to the specificity of women's experience in these struggles. They have not lost sight of the dominating role played by sexual danger in Victorian sexual discourses and of its implications for women. They have been sensitive to the difficulty faced by women of all classes in entering public discourse and to the deep sense of sexual vulnerability (because they *were* more vulnerable) that most women articulated when they claimed public space to speak on sexual matters.[28]

Foucault's insight that no one is outside of power has important implications for expressions from the margins. Just because women are excluded from centers of cultural production, they are not left free to invent their texts, as some feminist critics have suggested.[29] They are not innocent because they are on the sidelines. They are bound imaginatively by a limited cultural repertoire, forced to reshape cultural meanings within certain parameters. Women, for example, do not simply experience sexual passion and "naturally" find the words to express those feelings, nor do they experience sexual danger and naturally find the words to express the threat. In the simplest sense, women of different classes and races all have to rely on cultural constructs to tell their "truths," but the cultural constructs available in different social situations vary. London in the 1880s was a historic moment when middle-class women were enabled to speak publicly about sexual passion and about sexual danger, thanks to the new spaces, forms of social communication, and political networks available in a redefined public domain.

Foucault and other poststructuralists have called into question the authority of the subject as a free, autonomous author of a text. Yet, as Judith Newton has observed, the fact that subjects are culturally determined does not mean that "human agency in a changing world is for the most part illusory."[30] That individuals do not fully author their texts does not falsify Marx's insight that men (and women) make their own history, albeit under circumstances they do not produce or fully control. The historian's task still remains to explain cultural expressions in terms of "historically situated authorial consciousness"[31] and to track how historic figures mobilized existing cultural tools. In my account of late Victorian sexual scandals, figures like the journalist W. T. Stead and the feminist Josephine Butler acted as catalysts who made things happen. They were important historical actors, if not autonomous authors, even if the outcomes of their actions were not always or only what they had intended.

This book shows the narrative challenges raised by the new agenda of cultural history.[32] *City of Dreadful Delight* observes many conventions of historical writing, particularly those of social history; yet it has had to depart from a traditional historical narrative to convey the dynamics of metropolitan life as a series of multiple and simultaneous cultural contests and exchanges across a wide social spectrum. It has resisted, for example, providing narrative closure to some chapters, or organizing its historical account in terms of fixed gender and class polarities. It does not emphasize change over time so much as it highlights a shifting pattern of cultural and social perspectives, set in dynamic relationship to each other, that offered a range of social constituencies different incitements to self-expression and self-creation in a modern urban landscape.

On the whole, I analyze the cultural events of the 1880s from the critical standpoint of my generation of feminist scholars, but I start by identifying the systems of meaning articulated by social actors of the past. Their perspectives—on gender and power, on representations of the city and the self—constitute the conditions of possibility that allow me as a late-twentieth century feminist to examine Victorian social and sexual relations. That is to say, there is a family resemblance, if not complete identity, between the interpretive strategies available on sexuality and the social order in the 1880s and those available and contested today. Most notably,. the dilemmas that late-Victorian feminists confronted echo many of the dilemmas we feminists encounter today, with many of the same terms of agreement and disagreement operating inside and outside of feminist ranks. Contested terrain appropriately characterizes urban life and sexual politics of the 1980s and 1990s as it did the social world of the late-Victorian metropolis.

City of Dreadful Delight opens with two chapters that examine why London in the 1880s provided a fitting imaginative landscape for sensational narratives of sexual danger like the "Maiden Tribute" and the Ripper stories. The material and cultural features of late-Victorian metropolitan life helped to inspire a range of explorations into consciousness and identity as well as to shape the stories of sexual danger circulating in London at the time. Specifically, these two chapters look at the tradition of urban male spectatorship and the creation of a bifurcated imaginary urban landscape as a backdrop for personal adventure and self-creation. Throughout the Victorian period, it had been the prerogative of privileged men to move speedily as urban explorers across the divided social spaces of the nineteenth-century city, to see the city whole, and thereby to construct their own identity in relation to that diversity. However, in London in the 1880s, the prevailing imaginary landscape of London shifted from one that was geographically bounded to one whose boundaries were indiscriminately and dangerously transgressed.

In fact and fantasy, London had become a contested terrain: new commercial spaces and journalist practices, expanding networks of female philanthropy, and a range of public spectacles, from the Hyde Park "Maiden Tribute" demonstration of 1885, to the marches of the unemployed and the matchgirls in the West End, enabled workingmen and women of many classes to challenge the traditional privileges of elite male spectators and to assert their presence in the public domain. In so doing, they revised and reworked the dominant literary mappings of London to accommodate their own social practices and fantasies. The effect was a set of urban encounters far less polarized and far more interactive than those imagined by the great literary chroniclers of the metropolis.

W. T. Stead's reworking of melodrama and urban sexual adventure are the focus of chapters 3 and 4, centering on his newspaper exposé, the "Maiden Tribute of Modern Babylon." "Maiden Tribute" presented a distorted picture of youthful prostitution, whose very distortions and silences called attention to themselves within the text. Yet "Maiden Tribute" shifted the public discourse on sexuality, encouraged women to articulate publicly a new sexual subjectivity, and incited political movements that had a marked effect on class relations and the political economy of sex.

Tracking the progress of the "Maiden Tribute" through Victorian London is a dizzying exercise in the interaction and collision of cultural worlds: first originating in the newspaper, it was retold in the houses of Parliament, recast in the courts of law, heralded by feminists and socialists, read aloud in the slums of Marylebone. The wide circulation of the "Maiden Tribute" (estimated at one and a half million unauthorized copies) signaled a new stage in the expansion of a mass market that was simultaneously segmented into multiple reading publics. Thanks to this expanding market, the "Maiden Tribute" became a component of political culture, the everyday culture of work, family, and gender relations; the mass culture of the new journalism, the official culture of the law, and the high culture of intellectuals. In these different contexts, "Maiden Tribute" was taken up by different social constituencies and revised for a variety of political purposes. Stead himself had produced the "Maiden Tribute" by renovating an older melodramatic narrative of sexual danger, merging it with cultural products of the late-Victorian period. His story in turn was taken up by feminists and working-class radicals who resisted its innovations; meanwhile popular journalism quickly pounced on the new typology of sexual crime—and possibilities for sexual terrorism—that was packaged in the "Maiden Tribute" and that was fully elaborated three years later in the narration of the Ripper murders.

Chapters 5 and 6 move away from the narratives of urban descent and sexual crime to examine adjacent stories of sexuality and gender that existed in tension and conflict with the dark media scandals of the period. These two chapters highlight the role of positivist science as an epistemology and as an authoritative discourse on gender, but one that did not lead to a stabilized account of sexual difference. In these chapters, men and some women invoked sexual science and psychiatry to bolster diverse interpretations of female destiny, while others, mostly women, repudiated the claims of materialist medical science altogether in favor of competing systems of meaning, notably spiritualism, melodrama, and the law.

Chapter 5, on "The Men and Women's Club," shifts from the public discussions of sexual danger to the semiprivate debates of a discussion club of freethinking men and women, who were intent on exploring the history and future possibilities for heterosexual relations. This chapter explores the dialectic of sex in the 1880s; a dialectic between sexual possibility and sexual danger that reveals different attitudes towards masculinity and femininity, and especially towards heterosexuality, on the part of men and women of the professional middle class. It looks at the erotics of discourse developed in the labyrinthine relations of the club, where a dynamic, interlocking relationship existed between censorship, secrets, and sexual incitement. The chapter also explores the interaction between the earnest, lofty scientific language of the club and the sensational narratives of the "Maiden Tribute" and Jack the Ripper that frame its own history.

"Science and the Seance" continues the theme of sexual danger and modern science. It recounts the exploits of a plucky female spiritualist, Mrs. Weldon, in her successful adventures against the lunacy doctors in the 1880s. Mrs. Weldon's comic, populist tale contains elements also found in the Ripper narrative—particularly the sexual danger of contemporary medicine and the modern use of publicity. Her story also demonstrates what had been excluded and silenced in the Ripper episode. In contrast to the Ripper story, Mrs. Weldon's is a female success story of the 1880s, one that celebrates the possibilities, rather than the dangers, of urban life for enterprising middle-class women like herself.

Another theme linking chapters 5 and 6 is the growing antagonism of male professionals towards an expanding market culture, which they interpreted as sordid and feminized. In the Men and Women's Club, Pearson and his male friends went to great pains to mark off their scientific study of sexuality from the "feminine" emotionalism of Stead's "Maiden Tribute." Whereas men of science like Pearson believed that their intellectual capital elevated them above the commercial operations of the market, Mrs. Weldon willfully confounded these distinctions in her campaign against the mad doctors. Not only did she parody male professionalism in her legal performances, she used the spaces of commercial culture to pillory medical men as sordid "traders in lunacy."

These cultural contests and divisions also surfaced in the Jack the Ripper stories, where medical men emerged as primary experts and suspects in the case. Chapter 7, "Jack the Ripper," returns the reader to the cityscape of the obscure and mysterious labyrinthine city and to the media organization of sexual scandal. Building on long-standing cultural fantasies as well as capitalizing on the journalistic innovations of the "Maiden Tribute," press coverage highlighted new elements of late-Victorian conceptions of the self and of London's imaginary landscape. The Ripper story was produced out of a medley of Victorian cultural products—melodrama, the late-Victorian male Gothic, the medical literature of psychopathology—that with different emphases articulated the fears and antagonisms provoked by existing and contested gender, class, and ethnic relations. Diverse social constituencies responded to this media organization by weaving their own stories and superimposing them upon the emerging gestalt produced in the press. An epilogue, "The Yorkshire Ripper," explores the press treatment of the "Yorkshire Ripper" case in the north of England in the late 1970s and early 1980s, in conjunction with contemporary feminist campaigns against pornography and the representation of violence.

ONE

Urban Spectatorship

hen Henry James arrived in London in 1876, he found the city "not a pleasant place" nor "agreeable, or cheerful, or easy, or exempt from reproach." He found it "only magnificent . . . the biggest aggregation of human life, the most complete compendium in the world." It was also the "largest chapter of human accidents," scarred by "thousands of acres covered by low black houses of the cheapest construction" as well as by "unlimited vagueness as to the line of division between centre and circumference." "London is so clumsy and brutal, and has gathered together so many of the darkest sides of life," that it would be "frivolous to ignore her deformities." The city itself had become a "strangely mingled monster," the principal character in its own drama: an "ogress who devours human flesh to keep herself alive to do her tremendous work."[1]

Despite its brutalities, London offered James an oasis of personal freedom, a place of floating possibilities as well as dangers. Alone in lodgings, James first experienced himself in London as "an impersonal black hole in the huge general blackness." But the streets of London offered him freedom and imaginative delights. "I had complete liberty, and the prospect of profitable work; I used to take long walks in the rain. I took possession of London; I felt it to be the right place." As an artist, bachelor and outsider, James aestheticized this "world city," the "center of the race," into a grand operatic panorama of movement, atmosphere, labyrinthine secrets and mysteries. London's "immeasurable circumference," argued James, gave him a "sense of social and intellectual elbow room"; its "friendly fogs," which made "everything brown, rich, dim, vague," protected and enriched "adventure." For the "sympathetic resident," such as James, the social ease of anonymity was matched by an ease of access to and imaginative command of the whole: one may live in one "quarter" or "plot" but in "imagination and by a constant mental act of reference . . . [inhabit] the whole."[2]

James celebrated the traditional prerogatives of the privileged urban spectator to act, in Baudelaire's phrase, as *flaneur,* to stroll across the divided spaces of the metropolis, whether it was London, Paris, or New York, to experience the city as a whole. The fact and fantasy of urban exploration had long been an informing feature of nineteenth-century bourgeois male subjectivity. Cosmopolitanism, "the experience of diversity in the city as opposed to a relatively confined localism," argues Richard Sennett, was a bourgeois male pleasure. It established a right to the city—a right not traditionally available to, often not even part of, the imaginative repertoire of the less advantaged. In literary and visual terms, observes Griselda Pollock, "being at home in the city" was represented as a privileged gaze, betokening possession and distance, that structured "a range of disparate texts and heterogeneous practices which emerge in the nineteenth-century city—tourism, exploration/discovery, social investigation, social policy."[3]

A powerful streak of voyeurism marked all these activities; the "zeal for reform" was often accompanied "by a prolonged, fascinated gaze" from the bourgeoisie. These practices presupposed a privileged male subject whose identity was stable, coherent, autonomous; who was, moreover, capable through reason and its "science" of establishing a reliable and universal knowledge of "man" and his world.[4] It was these powers of spectatorship that Henry James ascribed to his "sympathetic resident" who, while residing in one quarter of town, was capable "in imagination" of inhabiting "the whole" of it.

At odds with this rationalist sensibility was the flaneur's propensity for fantasy. As illusionist, the flaneur transformed the city into a landscape of strangers and secrets. At the center of his art, argues Susan Buck-Morss, was the capacity to present things in fortuitous juxtapositions, in "mysterious and mystical connection." Linear time became, to quote Walter Benjamin, "a dream-web where the most ancient occurrences are attached to those of today." Always scanning the gritty street scene for good copy and anecdote, his was quintessentially "consumerist" mode of being-in-the-world, one that transformed exploitation and suffering into vivid individual psychological experience.[5]

James's affectionate portrait of London, that "dreadfully delightful city," is dominated by the flaneur's attention to the viewer's subjectivity and by the capacity of the city to stimulate. In James's "strangely mingled monster," activities of manufacture, trade, and exchange were overshadowed by rituals of consumption and display. Extremes of wealth and poverty aroused the senses, for "the impression of suffering was part of the general vibration," while London's status as repository of continuous culture and national heritage—its "great towers, great names, great memories"—served as a further stimulant to his own consciousness and memory: "All history appeared to live again and the continuity of things to vibrate through my mind."[6]

The literary construct of the metropolis as a dark, powerful, and seductive labyrinth held a powerful sway over the social imagination of educated readers. It remained the dominant representation of London in the 1880s, conveyed to many reading publics through high and low literary forms, from Charles Booth's surveys of London poverty, to the fictional stories of Stevenson, Gissing, and James, to the sensational newspaper exposés by W. T. Stead and G. R. Sims. These late-Victorian writers built on an earlier tradition of Victorian urban exploration, adding some new perspectives of their own. Some rigidified the hierarchical divisions of London into a geographic separation, organized around the opposition of East and West. Others stressed the growing complexity and differentiation of the world of London, moving beyond the opposition of rich and poor, palace and hovels, to investigate the many class cultures in between. Still others among them repudiated a fixed, totalistic interpretive image altogether, and emphasized instead a fragmented, disunified, atomistic social universe that was not easily decipherable.

Historians and cultural critics have linked this contest over and "crisis" in representation to a range of psychological and social crises troubling literary men and their social peers in the 1880s: religious self-doubt, social unrest, radical challenges to liberalism and science, anxiety over imperial and national decline, as well as an imaginative confrontation with the defamiliarized world of consumer culture "where values and perception seem in constant flux."[7] Equally crucial may have been the psychic difficulties produced by the imperatives of a "hard" physical manliness, first developed in the mid- and late-nineteenth century public schools and then diffused among the propertied classes of the Anglo-Saxon world. The hallmarks of this "virile" ethos were self-control, self-discipline, and the absence of emotional expression.[8] Whatever the precipitating causes, the public landscape of the privileged urban flaneur of the period had become an unstable construct: threatened internally by contradictions and tensions and constantly challenged from without by social forces that pressed these dominant representations to be reworked, shorn up, reconstructed.

Middle-class men were not the sole explorers and interpreters of the city in the volatile decade of the 1880s. On the contrary, as the end of the century approached, this "dreadfully delightful city" became a contested terrain, where new commercial spaces, new journalistic practices, and a range of public spectacles and reform activities inspired a different set of social actors to assert their own claims to self-creation in the public domain. Thanks to the material changes and cultural contests of the late-Victorian city, protesting workers and "gents" of marginal class position, female philanthropists and "platform women," Salvation Army lasses and match girls, as well as glamorized "girls in business," made their public appearances and established places and viewpoints in relation to the urban panorama. These new entrants to the urban scene produced new stories of the city that competed, intersected with, appropriated, and revised the dominant imaginative mappings of London.

Before tracking the progress of these new urban travelers and their social visions, let us first examine the tradition of urban spectatorship embodied in Henry James's alter ego, the "sympathetic resident." As a cosmopolitan, the "sympathetic resident" could take up nightwalking, a male pursuit immortalized in urban accounts since Elizabethan times, but one that acquired a more active moral and emotional meaning for intrepid urban explorers in the Victorian period. Whereas Regency dandies of the 1820s like Pierce Egan's characters, Tom and Jerry, had experienced the streets of London as a playground for the upper classes, and interpreted streets sights and characters as passing shows, engaged urban investigators of the mid- and late-Victorian era roamed the city with more earnest (if still voyeuristic) intent to explain and resolve social problems. Frederick Engels, Charles Dickens, and Henry Mayhew were the most distinguished among a throng of missionaries and explorers, men who tried to read the "illegible" city, transforming what appeared to be a chaotic, haphazard environment into a social text that was "integrated, knowable, and ordered." To realize their subject, their travel narratives incorporated a mixture of fact and fancy: a melange of moralized and religious sentiment, imperialist rhetoric, dramatized characterization, graphic descriptions of poverty, and statistics culled from Parliamentary Blue Books.[9]

As early as the 1840s, these urban explorers adapted the language of imperialism to evoke features of their own cities. Imperialist rhetoric transformed the unexplored territory of the London poor into an alien place, both exciting and dangerous. As Peter Keating notes, urban explorers never seemed to walk or ride into the slums, but to "penetrate" inaccessible places where the poor lived, in dark and noisy courts, thieves' "dens," foul-smelling "swamps," and the black "abyss." To buttress their own "eye of power," these explorers were frequently accompanied by the state representative of order, a trusty policeman: in the 1860s, the journalist George Sims made excursions to East End taverns frequented by sailors and prostitutes, accompanied by a detective or professional "minder." As a master of disguise, the journalist James Greenwood felt comfortable enough to dispense with this latter precaution: "A private individual," he insisted, "suitably attired and of modest mien, may safely venture where a policeman dare not show his head."[10]

The literature of urban exploration also emulated the privileged gaze of anthropology in constituting the poor as a race apart, outside the national community.[11] Mayhew, for example, introduced his investigation in *London Labour and the London Poor* by linking the street folks of London to the ethnographic study of "wandering tribes in general," arguing that, like all nomads, costermongers had big muscles and small brains, and were prone to be promiscuous, irreligious, and lazy;[12] even Engels, who went to great lengths to expose the "culpability" of the bourgeoisie for the slums, still retained, according to Peter Stallybrass and Allon White, "an essentialist category of the sub-human nomad: the Irish."[13]

Mid-Victorian investigators represented the urban topography of the "gaslight era" as a series of social juxtapositions of "high" and "low" life. Observers in the 1860s and 1870s frequently reproduced a Dickensian cityscape of dirty, crowded, disorganized clusters of urban villages, each with its own peculiar flavor and eccentricity, where the Great Unwashed lived in chaotic alleys, courts, and hovels just off the grand thoroughfares. In the 1860s, for instance, James Greenwood began his tour of "Low Life Deeps" with a visit to the "notorious Tiger Bay" of the East End's Radcliffe Highway, but he soon moved westward to "Jack Ketch's Warren" in Frying Pan Alley, Clerkenwell, and then to a "West End Cholera Stronghold." Henry Mayhew also moved from place to place in his study of the urban poor, although he noticed a difference between the laboring classes in the East and the West: "In passing from the skilled operative of the West-end, to the unskilled workman of the Eastern quarter, the moral and intellectual change is so great, that it seems as if we were in a new land, and among another race."[14]

Mayhew's observations portended an important reconfiguration of London as a city divided into East and West. Mid-Victorian explorations into the *terra incognita* of the London poor increasingly relied on the East/West opposition to assess the connecting links between seemingly unrelated parts of society. One of the most powerful and enduring realizations of this opposition, Doré and Jerrold's *London: A Pilgrimage* (1872), envisioned London as two distinct cities, not of capital and labor, but of the *rentier* and the impoverished criminal. It juxtaposed a West End of glittering leisure and consumption and national spectacle to an East End of obscure density, indigence, sinister foreign aliens, and potential crime.[15]

This bifurcated cityscape reinforced an imaginative distance between investigators and their subjects, a distance that many urban explorers felt nonetheless compelled to transgress. Cultural critics Stallybrass and White offer a Bakhtinian explanation of the cultural dynamics at work in this "poetics" of transgression. In class society, they argue, the repudiation of the "low" by the dominant "top" of society was paradoxically accompanied by a heightened symbolic importance of the "low Other" in the imaginative repertoire of the dominant culture.

> A recurrent pattern emerges: the "top" attempts to reject and eliminate the "bottom" for reasons of prestige and status, only to discover not only that it is in some way frequently dependent on the low-Other . . . , but also that the top *includes* that low symbolically as a primary eroticized constituent of its own fantasy life. The result is a mobile, conflictual fusion of power, fear and desire in the construction of subjectivity.

For this reason, Stallybrass and White argue, "what is *socially* peripheral is so frequently *symbolically* central. . . . The low-Other is despised, denied at the level of political organization and social being whilst it is instrumentally constitutive of the shared imaginary repertoire of the dominant culture."[16]

Urban investigators not only distanced themselves from their objects of study; they also felt compelled to possess a comprehensive knowledge of the Other, even to the point of cultural immersion, social masquerade, and intrapsychic incorporation.[17] James Greenwood, for example, prided himself on his improvisational skills, on being able to mingle as "one of the crowd": as "The Amateur Casual," he achieved journalistic fame for gaining admission to a workhouse casual ward dressed as a "sly and ruffianly figure marked with every sign of squalor."[18] In his investigations of the London poor, Henry Mayhew also played a number of roles, including stage manager and director/voyeur. At a public meeting, he encouraged impoverished needlewomen who had been forced by economic distress to resort to the streets to "tell their own tale." Each recounted "her woes and struggles, and published her shame amid the convulsive sobs of the others," while Mayhew and one other gentlemen observed the scene, "scarcely" visible in the "dimly lighted" meeting place.[19]

No figure was more equivocal, yet more crucial to the structured public landscape of the male flaneur, than the woman in public. In public, women were presumed to be both endangered and a source of danger to those men who congregated in the streets. In the mental map of urban spectators, they lacked autonomy: they were bearers of meaning rather than makers of meaning. As symbols of conspicuous display or of lower-class and sexual disorder, they occupied a multivalent symbolic position in this imaginary landscape.[20]

The prostitute was the quintessential female figure of the urban scene, a prime example of the paradox, cited by Stallybrass and White, that "what is socially peripheral is so frequently symbolically central." For men as well as women, the prostitute was a central spectacle in a set of urban encounters and fantasies. Repudiated and desired, degraded and threatening, the prostitute attracted the attention of a range of urban male explorers from the 1840s to the 1880s. Leonore Davidoff assesses the "close affinity" among a long line of urban voyeurs and social investigators who eroticized working women. There is the "sexual scoring" noted by Walter in his notorious diary, *My Secret Life*, the streak of voyeurism that can be sensed behind the work of a journalist such as Mayhew, the "detailed account of moral depravity in the pages of staid publications such as the *Journal of the Royal Statistical Society*," the "nocturnal wandering in search of conversation with 'women of the streets' which figure in the lives of men like Gladstone," and A. J. Munby's passion for collecting examples of muscular women at work. Uniting all these efforts was a similar "pattern of wandering from place to place in search of encounters, the emotional urgency and the sense of culmination with each 'find'."[21]

The public symbol of female vice, the prostitute established a stark contrast to domesticated feminine virtue as well as to male bourgeois identity:[22] she was the embodiment of the corporeal smells and animal passions that the rational bourgeois male had repudiated and that the virtuous woman, the spiritualized "angel in the house," had suppressed. She was also a logo of the divided city itself. When commentators detailed the social geography of vice, extending from the courtesans of St. John's Wood, to the elegantly attired streetwalkers who perambulated around the fashionable shopping districts, to the impoverished women—the "kneetremblers" and "Round-the-corner-Sallies"—committing "acts of indecency" in the ill-lit back alleys and courts of the city's slums,[23] they brought into relief the class structure and general social distribution of London. In these accounts, prostitution appeared in two guises: as disorderly behavior on the part of "soiled doves," sauntering down the city thoroughfares, dangerous in their collectivity; or as the isolated activity of the lone streetwalker, a solitary figure in the urban landscape, outside home and hearth, emblematic of urban alienation and the dehumanization of the cash nexus.[24] In both cases, they stood in stark opposition to the classical elite bodies of female civil statuary that graced the city squares: they were female grotesques, evocative of the chaos and illicit secrets of the labyrinthine city.

By the 1840s, literary accounts invested considerable emotion and anxiety in the lonely figure of the streetwalker; she had become both an object of pity and a dangerous source of contagion. This new concern found powerful expression in Dickens' fiction and in the illustrations accompanying his texts: when in *David Copperfield* (1849–50), David and Mr. Peggotty seek out the streetwalker Martha to help them in their search for the seduced Emily, they spot a "solitary female figure" walking towards the Thames. Contemplating the scene at the river edge, an environmental nightmare of "ooze" and "slush," dominated by the "blighting influence" of the "polluting stream," David mentally associates "the girl" with "the refuse it had cast out and left to corruption and decay."[25]

Dickens' elision of prostitution and excrement was symptomatic of a middle-class concern with immorality, city waste, pollution, and infection emanating from the "Great Unwashed." In the wake of devastating cholera epidemics of 1831 and 1849, sanitary reformers and writers on "moral statistics" used this fear to promote interest in their cause: they identified the prostitute literally and figuratively as the conduit of infection to respectable society—a "plague spot," pestilence, a sore. Like the slums from which she emanated, she carried with her, argues Alain Corbin, the "heavy scents of the masses," with their "disturbing messages of intimate life." She evoked a sensory memory of all the "resigned female bodies" who serviced the physical needs of upper-class men in respectable quarters: in 1888 these resigned but disorderly bodies included the servant girls and nannies who brought the dangers of the streets into the bourgeois home by spreading the latest newspaper account of the Whitechapel "horrors" across the nursery tables.[26]

As the permeable and transgressed border between classes and sexes, as the carrier of physical and moral pollution, the prostitute was the object of considerable public inquiry as well as the object of individual preoccupation for respectable Victorians. Official concern over prostitution as a dangerous form of sexual activity, whose boundaries had to be controlled and defined by the state, led to the passage of the first Contagious Diseases Act in 1864 (followed by the Acts of 1868 and 1869), which provided for a medical and police inspection of prostitutes in garrison towns and ports.[27]

Regulationists praised the supervision and inspection of prostitutes as a defense of public health, public decency, and public order. In pressuring for the medical inspection of prostitutes while refusing to impose periodic genital examination on the enlisted men who were their clients, architects of the acts reinforced a double standard of sexual morality, which justified male sexual access to a class of "fallen" women. They were confident about the physiological imperative of sexual desire for men but often hedged their bets in relation to women. On the one hand, regulationists condemned prostitutes as so "unsexed" that they exhibited "male lust"; on the other hand, they insisted that sexual desire on the part of prostitutes did not enter into the picture at all. A report of the Royal Commission in 1871 insisted that there was "no comparison to be made between prostitutes and the men who consort with them. With the one sex the offense is a matter of gain; with the other it is an irregular indulgence of a natural impulse."[28]

Regulationists also exhibited considerable enthusiasm for state intervention into the lives of the poor. Although such Acts were ostensibly passed as sanitary measures to control the spread of venereal disease, their local administration extended well beyond the sanitary supervision of common prostitutes. The Acts were part of institutional and legal efforts to contain the occupational and geographic mobility of the casual laboring poor, to clarify the relationship between the unrespectable and respectable poor, and specifically to force prostitutes to accept their status as public women by destroying their private associations with the poor working-class community.

Regulation would also contribute to public decency, its defenders argued, by checking the public spectacle of vice. Middle-class commentators repeatedly complained of the physical and visual aggressiveness of the "painted creatures," with their "gaudy dress," aggressive gaze, and provoking deportment.[29] For this reason, London Metropolitan police eagerly awaited the extension of the Acts to London, where they hoped to institute a system of *police de moeurs* to supervise and contain the street disorder of West End prostitutes.[30]

The Metropolitan police's dreams were shattered, however, when a successful opposition of middle-class moral reformers, feminists, and radical workingmen forced the repeal of regulation in 1886. This political campaign impinged on the imaginary cityscape of the flaneur in two ways. The repeal campaign brought thousands of respectable women, the "shrieking sisterhood," into the political arena for the first time, thus disturbing the public/private division of space along gender lines so essential to the male spectator's mental mapping of the civic order. Moreover, the repeal campaign and the social purity movement which it inspired significantly impinged on the public face of London prostitution. With regulation and confinement out of the question, London police found themselves increasingly under pressure from social purity and antivice groups to suppress the indoor resorts of West End prostitutes—Cremorne Gardens, the Argyll Rooms, the Holborn dancing casino, the infamous nighthouses at Haymarket—as well as to clear public thoroughfares and theaters of streetwalkers to make room for respectable women. For the next twenty years, the police would be forced to instigate periodic crackdowns which moved prostitutes temporarily to other quarters, or from sites of commercial sex into the streets, and subjected law enforcement authorities to outcries against the false arrests of respectable women. Crackdowns and ensuing scandals would keep prostitution before the "public" eye as a confusing and protean identity that invoked the larger question of women and civil society.[31]

By the 1880s, most of the salient features of London's imaginary landscape, which writers like Dickens, Mayhew, and Greenwood had helped to construct, had formalized into a conception of London as an immense world-city, culturally and economically important, yet socially and geographically divided and politically incoherent. Social and political developments of the mid- and late-Victorian period materially reinforced this complex image. London was the largest city in the world, totalling four million inhabitants in the 1880s. Since the first half of the nineteenth century, it had reclaimed its status as the cultural and nerve center of the nation and empire, overshadowing Manchester and Liverpool as the embodiment of the "modern city."[32]

In the second half of the century, the West End of Mayfair and St. James had undergone considerable renovation; from a wealthy residential area it had been transformed and diversified into the bureaucratic center of empire, the hub of communications, transportation, commercial display, entertainment, and finance. In the process, a modern landscape had been constructed—of office buildings, shops, department stores, museums, opera, concert halls, music halls, restaurants, and hotels—to service not only the traditional rich of Mayfair but a new middle class of civil servants and clerks, living in such areas as Bayswater and the nearby suburbs.[33] New figures appeared in this urban landscape, most significantly "girls in business," neither ladies nor prostitutes, but working women employed in the tertiary sector of the economy, there to assist the large numbers of "shopping ladies," attracted to the new feminized world of department stores that had been created for them in the center. In late-Victorian London, the

West End was not just the home and fixed reference of the urban flaneur; it had become a new commercial landscape, used by men and women of different classes.

Yet, in the 1880s, these commercial and institutional developments were imaginatively overshadowed by representations of urban pathology and decline. As the capital city, London epitomized the power of the empire but also its vulnerability. The disquieting effects of the Great Depression, the erosion of mid-Victorian prosperity, the decline of London's traditional industries, and international competition from the United States and Germany for industrial and military supremacy, all contributed to a sense of malaise and decline. This anxious mood was communicated through representations of London itself, particularly those involving political disorder, urban pathology, and physical degeneration.[34]

Despite its economic and social centrality, London lacked a clear political identity. "In London, there is no effective unity," complained John Morley, "interests are too varied and diverse." This great world-city lacked a unified or systematic water, sanitation, and public-health system, and it suffered from periodic plagues of typhus and typhoid. Until 1888, when the London County Council was established, it had no city government other than a Metropolitan Board of Works, dozens of little vestries and parishes, and forty-eight boards of guardians. In addition, there was no local control over the police force (the metropolitan police would remain under the control of the Home Office even after the establishment of the LCC). Debates over centralization at the time certainly intensified public consciousness that the capital of the Empire was "the worst governed city of the Empire."[35]

One apparent symptom of political disorder was London's vulnerability to international terrorism. In the mid-80s, middle-class Londoners were gripped by fears that assassination on the part of Continental anarchists and Irish Fenians was spreading as a political strategy. London was, in fact, a prime target of terrorist attacks. In March 1883 the Local Government Board Offices were blown up, and an unsuccessful attempt was made to blow up the offices of *The Times*. In October 1883, two underground railways were dynamited; in February 1884 a portion of Victoria Station was blown up; in May 1884 the offices of Scotland Yard were attacked.[36] Writing to a friend in January 1885, Henry James was appalled at the "gloomy, anxious" state of London:

Westminster Hall and the Tower were half blown up two days ago by Irish Dynamiters, there is a catastrophe to the little British force in the Soudan in the air . . . and a general sense of rocks ahead in the foreign relations of the country. . . . The possible malheurs—reverses, dangers, embarrassments, the "decline," in a word, of old England, go to my heart. . . . [37]

Accompanying this political malaise were equally striking social divisions and residential segregation. Slum clearance in the mid-Victorian period had successfully destroyed many of the "plague spots" and rookeries that had previously darkened the glittering landscape of the West End. In his tour of the wilds of London, Greenwood could rejoice that only one "West End Cholera Stronghold" remained after "hideous slums that once disfigured the district between Westminster and Pimlico had been routed and destroyed." Wide new roads cut through the slums, observes historian Jerry White, "letting in air, light and police, and, most important of all, disturbing the inhabitants from their old haunts." The effect of this demolition was to destroy some of the "fever strongholds" and to force the unrespectable poor into the few remaining rough areas, but overall to enforce a stricter residential segregation according to class.[38]

The opposition of East and West increasingly took on imperial and racial dimensions, as the two parts of London imaginatively doubled for England and its Empire. The West End, with its national monuments and government offices, served as a site for imperial spectacle: during her golden jubilee in 1887, Queen Victoria, elevated above politics as the mother of the nation, was carted around the major thoroughfares, escorted by an Indian cavalry troop. Meanwhile, another kind of imperial spectacle was staged in the East End. The docks and railway termini of the East End were international entrepôts for succeeding waves of immigrants, most recently poor Jews fleeing the pogroms of Eastern Europe. Gravitating to the central districts, the declining inner industrial rim, the "foreign element" had to compete with the indigenous laboring poor for housing and resources.[39]

In the last decades of the nineteenth century, journalistic exposés highlighted this geographic segregation, impressing on Londoners the perception that they lived in a city of contrasts, a class and geographically divided metropolis of hovels and palaces. A string of highly publicized events and scandals, between 1883 and 1888, sustained the problem of poverty as a subject of concern for the educated reading public. Startling revelations of "Outcast London" familiarized middle-class readers with the sordid and depressing living conditions of the poor and reminded them again, as had the literature of the 1840s, of the dangerous social proximity between vast numbers of casual laborers and a professional criminal class. In the established tradition of urban exploration, George Sims introduced his exposé of London slum housing, *How the Poor Live* (1883), as a "book of travel," a venture through "a dark continent that is within easy walking distance of the General Post Office." His "object," he explained was "to skim the surface lightly . . . to awaken in the general mind an interest in one of the great social problems of the day."[40]

Sims depicted a London of social extremes, where increased wealth and increased civilization merely intensified the "gulf between classes," a gulf that was moral, material, and biological. "It is the increased wealth of this mighty city," he insisted, "which has driven the poor back inch by inch, until we find them herding together, packed like herrings in a barrel, neglected and despised." As a late-Victorian London flaneur, Sims had moved his base of operations from the street to the interior dwellings of the London poor, shedding light on a domestic life that lacked the necessary accoutrements for privacy and "decency." Masquerading as a board-school visitor, Sims gained entrance to the homes of the poor by putting "a statistical question," yet he conveyed his experience through the descriptive language of moral environmentalism, in which he sensationally condensed images of poverty, dirt, immorality, and disease into a shocking picture of abject destitution. His "intimate" portraits of the poor were visual and specular, accompanied by little or no dialogue. Sims's eye of power cast a spotlight upon images of contagion and physical degeneration, as he detailed the "one-roomed helots" of slumdom, touching here upon a poor woman, "white and thin and sickly," carrying in her arms a young girl "with a diseased spine," and there upon inhabitants living in quarters "full of refuse; heaps of dust and decaying vegetables." Moving around London, Sims found it hard to inject the "picturesque" into his revelations; for "scene after scene is the same: rags, dirt, filth, wretchedness." The particularity of slum life had disappeared: "one room in this district is very like the other." Simultaneously, the presence of the "residuum" immensely expanded as a generalized problem: instead of a small number of idle and casual poor living in a few pockets of poverty, the chronically poor residuum now appeared to be a substantial portion of the population.[41]

Sensational depictions of inner London poverty also found their way into "The Bitter Cry of Outcast London." First published as a pamphlet in 1883, the "Bitter Cry" was then excerpted in the *Pall Mall Gazette* and ultimately found its way into parliamentary discussion and helped to provoke a Royal Commission on the Housing of the Working Class in 1884–85. Penetrating "courts reeking with poisonous and malodorous gases," Andrew Mearns, Congregationalist minister and author of the "Bitter Cry," discovered "pestilential human rookeries . . . where tens of thousands are crowded together." A "vast mass of moral corruption," reported

Mearns, was "seething" in the very "centre" of "our great cities." In these overcrowded slums, family life had disintegrated, "incest," was common.[42]

The threatening appearance of the poor in the "wrong" part of town, in the form of socialist-led demonstrations of the East End unemployed in the wealthy West End, exacerbated fears of "Outcast London." In 1886, one of these demonstrations ended in some stoning of fashionable Pall Mall clubs and in sporadic looting and rioting in London's principal shopping district. The response was hysterical. "King Mob" had emerged from the East to wreak havoc. Rumors spread of a mob advancing westward through Whitechapel from Commercial Road and of another march of "roughest elements" heading for the City from Bethnal Green Road. *The Times* reported that some hundreds of dock laborers planned to join others from the East End "in further attacks upon property in the West." For the next eighteen months, there was extensive concern over public order, and police forbade any further demonstrations. The tension peaked on 18 November 1887, "Bloody Sunday," when London's working classes tried to enter Trafalgar Square and were repressed by the police.[43]

The sense of a geographically and socially divided city was intensified by journalistic accounts and royal commissions that focused on the degraded work conditions in the East End. The East End suffered from declining male employment in the London docks and shipbuilding industries, from overcrowded and unsanitary living conditions, and from the noisome and sweated industries that mostly employed women and girls. The 1886 influx of East End Jews disturbed the precarious relations in East London trades and made "visible conditions of work" in the sweated trades that had existed for a long time. In 1888 and 1889, widespread publicity over wages and conditions in the sweated trades and docks accompanied the strikes of the match girls and the dockers. Both strikes involved unskilled and impoverished laborers and were heavily dependent on public sympathy and financial support. Among concerned middle-class reformers, these multiple occasions provoked a "consciousness of sin," to use Beatrice Webb's phrase, and stimulated a legion of philanthropic activities, including large increases in charitable donations to the London poor, religious missions, college settlement houses, housing reform, Peoples Palaces (cultural centers), and massive social surveys. The publicity campaign over poverty finally culminated in 1890 with the Salvation Army's "grandiose scheme for the rehabilitation of the down-and-outs," as imagined in General Booth's *Into Darkest England*.[44]

In this charged atmosphere fears of class conflict and social disintegration predominated over class guilt, despite the increase in charitable schemes. For many members of the propertied classes, the menacing presence of "King Mob" in their part of town threatened the imaginative boundaries erected to mark off and contain the poor. The demonstrations confirmed their worst fears of Outcast London as a vast, unsupervised underclass that could be readily mobilized into the revolutionary ranks of the new socialist movement. Governmental concern over public order certainly overshadowed any structural response to urban poverty. One member of Parliament deemed it in "bad taste [for] people to parade their insolent starvation in the face of the rich and trading portions of the town. They should have starved in their garrets." "After such a breakdown of police administration," wrote Octavia Hill during the 1886 demonstrations, "one feels as if one *might* meet violence *any* where."[45]

The crisis of the 1880s, experienced as a turning point by so many late-Victorian reformers, and shifting in some important ways the prevailing imaginary landscape of London from one that was geographically bounded to one whose boundaries were indiscriminately and dangerously transgressed, was not only a response to the material crisis of London employment and housing: it was also very much a product of bourgeois self-doubt and journalistic intervention. The moral and political panics of the period were heavily orchestrated from start to finish by W. T. Stead of the *Pall Mall Gazette*. Aside from his principal involvement in the sexual scandals of the period, to be investigated in some detail later, Stead also provided a platform for social criticism and social exposé of poverty in the *PMG*, and helped to initiate a public outcry over slum housing by publishing excerpts of "Outcast London" in 1883. Stead sustained the momentum of social criticism and the attention paid to social unrest when he opened the pages of his newspapers to socialist protesters and strike supporters. He was even alleged to have ghostwritten General Booth's "Darkest England" scheme in 1890. By addressing and constructing a national newspaper-reading public, Stead's New Journalism expanded and consolidated the social boundaries of the public sphere. After the *PMG* took the lead, other daily newspapers followed suit, in part because Stead's new journalism had shown how "good copy is oftener found among the outcast and disinherited of the earth, than among the fat and well-fed citizens."[46]

Most of the explicit anxieties and attention generated by Stead and others focused on the East End, a symbol of the social unrest born of urban degeneracy. The prosperity of the West End contrasted sharply with the urban crisis perceived to be brewing among an impoverished and immobilized proletarian East End, a "city" of one million people, which lacked a resident gentry and the official amenities and institutions of wealth to oversee the masses. The image of the East End as a separate territory, peopled by a degenerate class and species, gained clarity in the fiction and urban investigations of the early 1880s. Walter Besant located *All Sorts and Conditions of Men,* his tremendously popular "romance" of philanthropy and hopeless poverty, in East London. The journalistic exposés of "Outcast London" further elaborated the crisis and the sense of separateness. Although the "Bitter Cry" focused on South London, and Sims moved from place to place in his investigations of *How the Poor Live,* these melodramatic accounts of family disintegration, violence, biological degeneration, and undifferentiated, monotonous wretchedness were rapidly superimposed upon the East End. By the mid-80s, Whitechapel, with its last remaining rookeries of crime and vice, became the quintessence of inner London poverty, the "boldest blotch on the face" of the capital of the civilized world.[47]

Thanks to these literary outpourings, the middle-class reading public became emotionally invested in a set of representations about the poor that cast poor Londoners as central figures in narratives that divested them of any agency or ability to extricate themselves from their situation. Whereas earlier Victorian writings had emphasized pauperism as a failure of the moral will, these new writings relocated the locus of poverty, putting it within the homes and the bodies of the poor themselves. Whether victims of environmental or biological determinism, the poor would remain the poor, unless extricated from their fate by the transforming power of heroic investigators and reformers.[48]

Many of these imaginative tendencies found expression in the voluminous investigations of London poverty undertaken by Charles Booth and his assistants. The publication of *East London* (1889), the first volume of Booth's *Life and Labour of the People in London,* observes Peter Keating, "marks the culminating point in the discovery of the East End." Booth's study, expanded from two papers prepared for the Royal Statistical Society in 1887 to seventeen volumes after 1889, constructed an interpretive image of late-Victorian London that would continue to inform popular and scholarly studies of the metropolis into the late-twentieth century. Since Booth's study has set the parameters for knowledge of the late-Victorian metropolis for the past one hundred years, it is worth examining in some detail.[49]

Booth's study was both a challenge to and a confirmation of the image of East London as a place of extreme deprivation and violence. A Liberal Unitarian and wealthy shipbuilder from Liverpool, Booth began his study during the crisis of 1886, allegedly in response to the claim of H. M. Hyndman, leader of the Marxist Social Democratic Federation, that 25 percent of the London population was living in poverty.[50] Concentrating on East London, Booth found, to his surprise, that the extent of poverty

was greater than Hyndman's estimate, but that the danger was more localized. East London, he insisted, was much more heterogeneous than the
representations of "Outcast London" would suggest. Dividing the population into eight classes (A–H), he identified 35 percent of East Londoners as
living more or less in want, 22 percent as on the "line of poverty" (classes C
and D) and 13 percent (groups A and B) below it, a group for whom "decent life is not imaginable."[51] When he extended his research to the rest of
London, he uncovered an even more disquieting situation: many other
areas of London were equally poverty-stricken, with practically a third of
the inhabitants living in poverty. This was a "serious state of things," he
explained, "but not visibly fraught with imminent social danger or leading
straight to revolution."[52] Contrary to sensational accounts, the savage
"hereditary" criminal class prone to disorder amounted to little more than
1 percent of the population. In short, the "barbarian hordes do not exist."[53]

Unlike mid-Victorian reformers who tended to interpret poverty as a
failure of the will, a sign of thriftlessness or drink, Booth calculated that
inadequate employment (no work or low wages) was the reason for poverty
in 55 percent of all "very poor" families and in 68 percent of the "poor"
families. He further challenged prevailing wisdom by claiming that political discontent was a feature of the better-educated, better-paid and organized grades of workers, not of the residuum: it was among the
"aggravated idealism" of the skilled workers in class E, and not the "ruffia-
nism" of Class A or the "starvation" of Class B, that "we find the springs of
Socialism and Revolution."[54]

Booth employed a number of methods to convey these findings, including, in his phrase, a "wilderness of figures" on occupations, descriptions of
families, streets, and work conditions, and colored "maps of poverty" depicting London street by street (according to colored equivalents for his
eight classes, from the black streets of "savage" class A to the comfortable
middle-class enclaves of class H, painted gold). Using quantitative and
qualitative evidence, Booth constructed a new mapping of the social geography of London: instead of a stark opposition between East and West
London, he represented London in a series of concentric rings around the
City as the center. The inner ring was notable for its severe overcrowding
and extensive poverty in east, central, and south London, but not in the
west, an area of extreme wealth. The second ring was slightly less wealthy
in the west, slightly less impoverished elsewhere. The third ring was favored
by the lower middle classes, the fourth by wealthy railway commuters. To
explain this social geography, Booth formulated a theory of successive mi-
gration: overcrowding in the center forced the poor to move out to other

neighborhoods, thus precipitating a flight of respectable residents to the suburbs and more outlying areas. Booth also noted other ecological factors constructing the "poverty areas" that appeared as black and blue patches in his "Maps of Poverty": the customs and social character of the residents; the physical site; proximity or distance from "industrial elements"; and accessibility to other areas all contributed to the "peculiar" flavor of a locale. The edited volumes acquired further complexity from the multiple voices of the contributing investigators, which included the female voices of Beatrice Potter on East End Jews and of a "Lady Resident" on "Life in Buildings," as well as observations of working-class family life drawn from the notebooks of schoolboard visitors and the testimony of local police officers.

The imaginary map of London presented in *Life and Labour of the People in London* was considerably more subtle than the dichotomous juxtaposition of hovels and palaces featured in *How the Poor Live* or *London: A Pilgrimage*. Between the extremes of wealth and poverty, Booth and his researchers identified many social gradations, particularly in the respectable working classes and in the many social fractions of the suburbanized middle class. Booth's study vividly detailed the world of small masters and skilled artisans, and of an increasing number of clerks, teachers, shop assistants, and minor civil servants who populated the nearby suburbs.[55] Compared to earlier urban explorers, Booth and his host of researchers also accumulated more detailed empirical evidence about the poor, including a quantifiable "line of poverty." However, as E. P. Hennock observes, this assessment of poverty was highly "impressionistic," without any "comprehensive knowledge of household income." Nor did Booth explain how London worked as a system or why East London emerged as a poverty district.[56]

By focusing on the "problem" of poverty in the midst of "wealth," Booth also tended to ignore some of the urban dynamism of London life. Rather than describing the social geography of London in terms of a new urban consumer culture, one that opened up new public spaces that produced new kinds of class and gender interactions, Booth and his collaborators focused more exclusively on the relations of production operating in different locales. As Asa Briggs observes, Booth was more interested in the production of objects than in their advertising, display, and sale, or in the new urban panorama of leisure and consumption that resulted.[57]

Despite its innovations, Booth's seventeen-volume *Life and Labour of the People of London* by no means represented an imaginative break with the tradition of urban exploration pioneered forty years earlier by Engels and Mayhew, and adapted and continued in the mid-Victorian period by

Greenwood, Sims, and Mearns. On the contrary, Booth reproduced many key features of this literary genre; he recreated himself as an urban male spectator and flaneur within an imaginary landscape of the metropolis. Although he minimized the social danger of a geographically distinct "Outcast London," he did not obliterate the psychological oppositions that distinguished and distanced the Self from the low-Other. Despite his scientific pretensions, his study relied heavily on moralized impressions of social customs and conditions that reproduced familiar tropes of degeneration, contagion, and gender disorder, in order to mark off the dangerous from the respectable working class. Like his predecessors, he was personally caught up in the adventure of exploration: he constituted himself as the conqueror of the great unknown, a brave explorer of the "terra incognita" of the city, shedding light on "darkness" and calming "doubting hearts and ignorant unnecessary fears."[58] His efforts towards totalizing knowledge and self-creation also led to the exploration of multiple self-identities: to a desire to impersonate "the people," a masquerade that enabled him to gain command over his subject but that also articulated a questioning of his own class/gender position. In his own explorations, Booth enacted the blurring of boundaries between a falsely homogenized East and falsely homogenized West.

Booth's work belonged to the "grand tradition of English empiricism," which assumed that facts spoke for themselves, that they were perceived by the senses and gathered by an impartial mind. When Booth introduced his preliminary findings on East London to the Royal Statistical Society in 1887, he went to some pains to cultivate a "deliberate impersonalism," to quote Raymond Williams, to distinguish himself from the host of melodramatic chroniclers of "Outcast London." He presented himself instead as an Olympian master-intelligence manipulating an army of workers. He defended his reliance on the memory and notebooks of school-board visitors on the grounds that he wanted to avoid "personal investigation"; his object was "rather" to process "that which could be had from those whose life is spent amongst the people they describe." In the second half of his report, presented the following year to the Royal Statistical Society, he continued to uphold his study as disinterested truth, against the seductive attractions and mendacious sensationalism of "realist" fiction: "I am indeed embarrassed by the mass of my material, and by my determination to make use of no fact to which I cannot give a quantitative value. The materials for sensational stories lie plentifully in every book of our notes; but even if I had the skill to use my material in this way—that gift of the imagination which is called "realistic"—I should not wish to use it here."[59]

In fact, Booth did possess the "gift of the imagination" and extensively displayed this gift throughout his study. Booth's claims to science were based on a disinterested aloofness from the object of study and the use of "quantitative" fact instead of sensational narrative; but despite his tables and classifications, Booth could not resist the temptation to transform his findings into a story, with vivid characters, drama, and moral significance. "I cannot hope to make the rows of figures in this table as luminous and picturesque to every eye as they are to mine, and yet I am not content without making an attempt to do so." Each district, he explained, has its own "character." "One seems to be conscious of it in the streets. It may be in the faces of the people, or in what they carry . . . or it may lie in the sounds one hears, or in the character of the buildings."[60]

These sensory and moral variations were all testimony to the vitality of city life, to the "contagion of numbers," to quote his assistant Llewellyn Smith, that lured rural workers to the city. Taking into account all the problems of the city, declared Smith, it was "the sense of something going on . . . the difference between the Mile End fair on a Saturday night and a dark and muddy country lane which drew the young in particular into the 'vortex'."[61]

Booth himself was clearly attracted to the "sense of something going on" in working-class neighborhoods. He was impressed by the "brightness not extinguished by, and even appertaining to, poverty and toil, to vice, and even to crime." He was also attracted to the East End by, as one critic describes it, the "terrible Darwinian drama of survival in the streets." Here Booth witnessed, in his own words, "a clash of contest, man against man, and men against fate—the absorbing interest of a battlefield—a rush of human life as fascinating to watch as the current of a river." "The feeling that I have just described—this excitement of life which can accept murder as a dramatic incident, and drunkenness as the buffoonery of the stage—is especially characteristic of Whitechapel. And looked at in this way, what a drama it is!" With its furnished rooms, transients, street markets, and foreign population, Whitechapel was "Tom Tiddler's Ground, the Eldorado of the East," a "gathering together of poor fortune seekers; its streets are full of buying and selling, the poor living on the poor."[62]

The artificial excitement of life was coupled with disorderly social arrangements, including striking inversions of the sex/gender system: shiftlessness and lack of control on the part of the men; immodesty, physical aggression, public display on the part of the women; a general lack of privacy and domesticity. As they moved across London, Booth and his investigators employed a complicated but well-established moral and visual semiotics to identify the social character of streets as rough or respectable.[63] Signs of a "rough," unrespectable street could be found in children playing in the streets, women gossiping at the door, open doors, broken windows, violence in intimate relations, "a row always going on between warlike mothers," the presence of prostitutes and thieves.[64] Alternatively, flower pots, closed doors, lace curtains, scrubbed doorsteps, hanging bird-cages, almost empty streets were the hallmarks of a respectable neighbor-hood. When social investigators like Booth and his assistants used these visual signifiers to grasp the nature of gender relations among the unskilled poor, they found themselves in an "incomprehensible region," to quote historian Ellen Ross, "where women were neither ladylike nor deferential, where men struggled to hold on to their authority over them, where 'sexual antagonism' was openly acknowledged."[65]

To render the "incomprehensible" comprehensible, Booth and his in-vestigators applied Lamarckian and Spencerian evolutionary theory to the social world of the slums. They interpreted signs of gender and sexual transgression as symptoms of biological degeneracy. Over a number of gen-erations, they explained, slum-dwellers had acquired pathological charac-teristics that rendered them impoverished and incapable of better work. Llewellyn Smith, for example, posited an inverse relationship between poverty and immigration: the poorest areas were populated by slum-dwellers whose families had resided in London for generations. "It is the result of the conditions of life in great towns and especially in this the great-est town of all, that muscular strength and energy get gradually used up; the second generation of Londoner is of lower physique and has less power of persistent work than the first, and the third generation (where it exists) is lower than the second." When old residents of notorious rookeries find themselves forcibly displaced by "improvements," they "carry contamina-tion with them wherever they go," but so scattered, "they never again create . . . such hotbeds of vice, misery, and disease."[66]

Biological racism not only manifested itself in Booth's accounts of the indigenous casual laboring poor but also informed his depictions of the predominant foreign element of East London, the Jews. In the case of the Jews, however, the inconsistencies of Booth's racial theory—particularly his blurring of social and biological causation—revealed themselves in a series of paradoxes and contradictions. Like other "urban primitives," Jews bore the physical stigmata of racial Otherness. "It is not difficult to recognise the Jews," explained Booth: facial features, skin pigmentation, even posture and bearing denoted their racial type. Along the Whitechapel Road, wrote Llewellyn Smith, "the observant wanderer may note the high cheekbones and the thickened lips of the Russian or Polish Jews [and] the darker complexion and unmistakable nose of his Austrian co-religionist." Yet these marks of racial inferiority were not accompanied by a consistent pattern of social degradation—a lack of correlation that considerably complicated Booth's attempt to use physical "race" as a demarcation of difference and safeguard of his own distinct identity. For the social portrait of Jews that emerges from *Life and Labour of the People in London* is of a population who are neither rough nor respectable, who are clean in person but dirty in habits, who can be quarrelsome and noisy, yet possess the middle-class virtues of sobriety and industry. Jewish homes lacked the visual signifiers of respectability—clean curtains, wax flowers, closed blinds—yet Jews seemed to be a private, home-centered people not given to street brawls, wife-beating, or child neglect. The Jews, in short, were a peculiar people who eluded and challenged Booth's categories of class and gender Otherness.[67]

Booth's efforts towards totalizing knowledge and stable demarcations of otherness eventually led him to abandon his "deliberate impersonalism" and go to live anonymously in lodgings among the "people."[68] Booth's masquerade synthesized two practices: the investigative journalism of Greenwood and others, and the tradition of living among the poor pioneered in the 1860s by Edward Denison and even more extensively promoted by Octavia Hill. Booth's domestic adventure differed from Greenwood's sensational immersion in "lowlife deeps," but it also revised Hill's philanthropic project, which had called upon middle-class reformers to establish close personal contact between rich and poor in order to reform the habits of the poor. As Deborah Nord notes, Booth's objective was not to "reshape the lives of the poor, but to establish scientific knowledge of a class without exerting personal influence on individuals. In Booth's scheme, it was, in fact, the middle-class observer who would be transformed through contact with the working class, and would then go on to promote reform."[69]

Booth's description of his sojourn among the London working class in *East London* was notable for its conversational tone, gentle humor, and relaxed intimacy with the objects of study.[70] He was overwhelmingly pleased by what he found among the families of class E: "wholesome, pleasant family life, very simple food, very regular habits, healthy bodies and healthy minds, affectionate relations of husbands and wives, mothers and sons, of elders with children."[71] Both his notebook and published commentaries on these sojourns acknowledged a distinctive gender system operating within these households, but, unlike other sections of the London study, do not treat deviations from the bourgeois norm in a pathological light. These observations, which did not find much expression in the "scientific" *Life and Labour*, were more aural than visual,[72] more interactive than specular. Booth was clearly impressed with the powerful role of the working-class woman as household manager, whose authority could even extend to bullying and manipulating her menfolk. Mrs. Mayson, his first landlady, had contrived early in her marriage to convert her seafaring husband into a stable land-dweller. "To have her husband at the antipodes and to go back to her shop did not agree with Mrs. Mayson's idea of married life and she told him so when he next came home." "Thus appealed to he was willing to settle down" and live quietly at home with his wife.

> "But one never knows," she would say. "A restless fit might at any-time come over him," and she added that within a year of the time when she was speaking he had, on coming home one evening, announced his intention of taking train to Liverpool, there to find a ship.
> "Better wait till tomorrow," she had said; and when tomorrow came the idea had passed.[73]

As Mary Booth observed in her memoir of her husband, Booth was attracted to the public life of the poor as well as to their casual domestic arrangements. Not only did he find the Others of the East End observing many of the domestic values that he himself cherished, but he also found himself as much like them as they were like him. He enjoyed roaming the East London streets at night, eating in their coffee palaces, visiting their music halls and their missions. "He likes the life and the people and the evening roaming—and the food, which he says agrees with him in kind and time of taking better than of our class." Taking up rooms in poor households, thus establishing a greater social intimacy than female philanthropists had even ventured to do, enabled him to explore multiple self-identities and to question his class/gender position. As a detached, scientific explorer of the "terra incognita" of the London poor, Booth assumed a carefully constructed persona of a male narrator whose scientific knowledge of a class would shed light on "darkness." Nonetheless, Booth's personal adventures revealed his own self-doubts and fears: as Nord observes, his "deliberate impersonalism" could not disguise his own confusion and ambivalence "about his place in the social structure, his relationship to his family and vocation." Beatrice Webb recognized in Booth a man who had reconstructed himself after a severe breakdown, a man "who has passed through a terrible illness and weakness and who has risen out of it." Booth's preference for the food and "simple, natural" family life of East Enders highlighted his own discomfort with his role as paterfamilias and captain of industry, residing on a country estate, obliged to uphold a decorous position in society, encumbered by all the paraphernalia of conspicuous consumption.[74]

Booth's study both challenged conventional markings and boundaries of social difference and tried to erect new ones in their place. By presenting the East as a socially heterogeneous region and locating poverty areas elsewhere in London, Booth exposed the bifurcated cityscape of East/West London as reductive and illusory. He offered a complex, differentiated portrait of the "people" of London, while struggling to sustain a totalizing interpretive image of the city as a whole. If social geography offered no fixed boundary, race and biological difference could still establish some demarcations. But as his treatment of Jews shows, racial boundaries of natural differences were not reliable either. Finally, Booth's own masquerade and affinity for East Enders suggest one reason that his system of difference kept unraveling: as a scientific male observer, he set out to produce objective, totalizing knowledge, only to find himself the site of internal conflict and multiple selves.

Other writers on the city in the 1880s were far less sanguine about unlocking its mysteries and sustaining a fixed, unified gaze on its denizens. Instead, George Gissing, R. L. Stevenson, and Henry James produced meditations on London that emphasized fragmentation and introspection. All three articulated an epistemological crisis that precipitated changes in the visual image of the city that produced new representations of the self and the Other.

Gissing's urban sensibility was socially located in the lower middle-class milieu of Grub Street journalism and class-marginal clerkdom, in the world of the single room set against the chaos and inhospitality of the street. Although Gissing compulsively roamed the London streets, acquiring a local knowledge that commanded the respect even of Charles Booth (Gissing's *Demos* was the only piece of realist fiction recommended in *East London*),[75] he was still unable to project a confident mastery over that social terrain. Instead, Gissing's novels represent an embattled, defensive self, contending with an anomic social environment lacking coherence, meaning, or direction. As Adrian Poole observes, Gissing's city is "drained of epistemological excitement; the blank streets, the coarse sounds seem to provoke sullen resignation rather than vigilant expectancy."[76]

Other male writers of the period invented somewhat different strategies to represent what Poole characterizes as a growing "imbalance between an expanding world of consciousness" and a "narrowing and rigidifying world of peremptory self-assertion." Aesthete-decadents like Whistler, Symons, and Wilde accepted the disconnection between appearance and reality, fashioning an aristocratic, dandified aesthetic of surface impressions, of detached cosmopolitan observation. For many writers of the fin de siècle, the epistemological crisis intersected with and manifested itself as a crisis of gender and class identity. In Stevenson's *Strange Case of Dr. Jekyll and Mr. Hyde* (1886), the fragmentation of the social world seems to have precipitated a division of the self. The London streets of *Dr. Jekyll and Mr. Hyde* appear as a vast, empty wasteland; here the integrity of the inner self is threatened less by social disorder or external constraint than by a failure to reach expression. Part of the problem of self-definition resulted from the marginalization of women in this professional bachelor-dom: as Stephen Heath observes, women exist on the margins of the text, as observers and incidental victims of Jekyll's crime, or as threatening, ephemeral manifestations of the commercial city itself, but they have no effective embodiment as central characters. This virtual absence itself presents a problem in male self-definition: as critics like Eve Sedgwick have argued, to sustain the fiction of a unified heterosexual male subject, Western sexual narratives have traditionally required a female figure to serve as a contrasting sexual Other and mediator among men. The perils of excluding women from the picture are fully revealed in Jekyll's "closet" world: men rapidly disintegrate into split personalities when they turn their gaze on themselves.[77]

As a novelist, Henry James also retreated from a totalizing vision into a more constrained introspection, without necessarily invoking the same kind of psychic splitting suffered by the male persona in Stevenson's "shilling shocker." In his fiction of the eighties, Henry James was able to spare some of his female protagonists the "horror" of disintegration, when, as in the case of Isabel Archer, they remained relatively untouched by the disorienting effects of the market. Their gender, however, made them different spectators of the city. Although Isabel Archer learns "a great many things" from her few walks around London, in the end she is driven into introspection and relinquishes all claims to the urban pleasures of anonymity, movement, and imaginative command of the whole enjoyed by James and his alter ego, the "sympathetic resident."[78]

Social investigation, serious fiction, and "shilling shockers" of the 1880s all bear witness to a growing skepticism among men of letters about their capacity to read the city and to sustain a coherent vision of a structured public landscape. They expressed this unease by constructing a mental map of London marked by fragmentation, complexity, and introspection, all of which imperiled the flaneur's ability to experience the city as a totalizing whole. Forces inside and outside of bourgeois culture provoked this epistemological crisis: for while it undoubtedly mirrored the self-doubts of professional and literary men, the crisis was also precipitated by the actions and energies of different social actors making claims on city space and impinging on the prerogatives of privileged men.

TWO

Contested Terrain:
New Social Actors

n the 1880s, marginalized groups—working men and women of all classes—repeatedly spilled over and out of their ascribed, bounded roles, costumes, and locales into the public streets and the wrong parts of town, engaged on missions of their own. In their moves around the city, these new explorers drew on the well-established repertoire of the urban flaneur, imaginatively revamping certain features of urban spectatorship to accommodate their own social circumstances. The spectacle and enterprise of these social actors produced a social geography more complex than the opposition of East and West, instigating cultural exchanges more dynamic than those Gissing or Stevenson represented in their texts. In fact and fantasy, these developments rendered the streets of London an enigmatic and contested site for class and gender encounters.

Protesting Workers and Political Autobiographers

Among these new entrants were protesting workers, who made their presence known to West Enders in the mid-1880s through a series of spectacular demonstrations demanding unemployment relief. Building on a tradition of direct action transmitted by the Radical Clubs of London, they advanced to Trafalgar Square in 1886 and 1887, under the red flag of revolution. They also marched under the silken banners of trade unions and socialist societies that proclaimed workingmen's rights to civic participation, as producers of wealth and as respectable patresfamilias. Walter Southgate's father, a quill-pen maker and "radical" of the "Charles Bradlaugh school," remembered these demonstrations, particularly "Bloody Sunday" of 1887, as a short-lived but unique moment when he had helped to make history. From these heights, he had descended ten years later into an "armchair politician," pontificating eloquently from his corner of the kitchen, disparaged by his wife, the "linchpin" of the family, who had no time for his "polish ticks" and would plead, "For Gawd's sake Bill give it a rest."[1]

Echoing the mottoes of the trade-union banners, political autobiographers reminiscing about London in the 1880s also represented themselves within a civic discourse, as part of a national, sometimes international, community. They struggled against the limitations of localized or parochial identity, recognizing that "an attack on the localization of the working man's outlook was a prerequisite of any sort of class action."[2] Political organizers like Tom Mann, in fact, led a highly peripatetic urban existence, often commuting long distances to work, moving across London to address workingmen's clubs and street assemblies from Battersea to Tower Hamlets.[3] An educated workingman like Frederick Rogers could also imagine London as a place of opportunity, a site for self-development: "London," he explained, "was an education to those who could read the lessons which it taught." Once he gained the habit of reading, the tedium of life disappeared: "I realized I could live in so many worlds at once."[4]

Except for political autobiographers, however, a workingman was more likely to present himself as a "social atom," "one of the multitude." Few of them imagined that workingmen had a "right to the city," nor did they position themselves as centered, unified subjects or selves who could imaginatively inhabit the whole of the Imperial City. Most working-class writers exhibited a localized perspective on what constituted their own community, a vision largely restricted to the neighborhood.[5]

Without respectable attire, workingmen ran the risk of arbitrary arrest and conviction for nuisance activities if they ventured out of their own locale. Within their own neighborhood, they were still subject to police surveillance but nonetheless felt at home on the street. Music-hall songs and autobiographies regularly celebrated "life down our street" as a familiar place populated by a troupe of local "characters" who added color to the local scene. "So self-contained was that North Street community," remembered Walter Southgate of his Cambridge Heath neighborhood in the 1890s, "that even after sixty years, I was able to recall most of the names of neighbours and the men's occupations."[6]

Gents and Swells

This insularity was punctured, as we have seen, by a few spectacular demonstrations of the 1880s, but also by mass media fantasy. To transcend their social and cultural limitations, workingmen resorted to the fantasy of easy access—of being a "gent" or a "swell"—manufactured for them by the popular culture of the period, particularly the music hall and the comic magazines.[7]

. The "gent" or "swell" has a long and complicated class genealogy. First produced as a literary satire of pretentious upstarts, the image was ultimately appropriated by popular entertainers and aspiring young clerks and workingmen about town. Ellen Moers traces the gent's origins from a "second hand, shopworn imitation of the dandy" appearing in the 1830s and 1840s, drawn from the "very bottom of the respectable class, the scrubby clerks, apprentices and medical students," and satirized by Dickens and Thackeray, to *Punch*'s 1850s portrait of "'Arry," a lower-class rake of exuberant vulgarity. In the mid-Victorian period, argues Gareth Stedman Jones, the swell came to embody for men of letters the Cockney archetype, a genial but politically disquieting figure intrinsically connected with the attempt to discover and embody a form of national spirit in the city.[8]

The gent possessed three important attributes: flamboyant and self-conscious dress, rakishness, and counterfeit status. These literary portraits were patronizing caricatures, but, argues Peter Bailey, they inspired behavior that "became increasingly institutionalized as a self-sufficient and indigenously authentic style among the expanding lower middle class and more self-regarding members of the working class." In the 1870s, the heavy-swell performances of the comic male stars of the music halls, the "Lion Comiques," continued and extended the swell's popularity as a model of working-class masculinity. By the 1880s, the toff, the masher, and the cad had a "sizable constituency."[9]

The history of the gent thus reveals a complex process of exchange and negotiation between class cultures in late-Victorian society. However much working-class Londoners resisted middle-class moralizing (about thrift, temperance, work discipline), they were nonetheless susceptible to other influences from above, particularly the attractions of sartorial consumption and libertine dandyism. The swell image reveals a more general problem of working-class self-representation: working people's difficulty in presenting their own versions of themselves, when constantly confronted with "more imaginative and competing pictures of themselves in fiction."[10]

With its heavy emphasis on masculine display and prowess, the swell image may have also served as a compensatory fantasy for a troubled working-class masculinity. Some historians have argued that unskilled London working men experienced more difficulty in "manufacturing" a stable and satisfactory masculinity than either other regional working classes or other more privileged groups in London. The decline in apprenticeship, an early and prolonged submersion in a female domestic culture (resolved among the propertied classes by sending the boy away to public school), and the shaky parental status of casual laborers as unreliable breadwinners all tended to diminish the father-son tie and reduce the authority of the male head of household to an absent or decorative role, one highly vulnerable to parody as something of a "comic disaster." Music-hall songs, such as "We all Go to Work but Father," deprecated the "head" of the house as the "laziest man I ever yet did know," while autobiographies such as Southgate's routinely deflated the authoritative stance of the father as public representative of the family. Men clung all the more tenaciously to patriarchal prerogatives, including wife-beating, and younger ones seem to have compensated by aping the hyper-masculine leisure habits of a superannuated aristocracy, from the fantasies of a night on the town to the homosocial mystiques of boxing and gambling. The swell, observes Peter Bailey, extolled a "form of male behaviour in which women were merely accessories like the cane and the bottle" (a fantasy that would vindicate their masculinity in the face of highly effective and outspoken female counterparts).[11]

Equipped with a leer, sporting dress, and a tour-book knowledge of London's fashionable spots, music-hall gents and swells like George Leybourne's immaculately dressed "Champagne Charlie" or the cartoon character "Ally Sloper" reassured their masculine admirers that they too could confidently navigate the social difficulties of modern urban relations. Like his social betters, Sloper was "at home" in London; he comfortably moved through its social spaces and different locales, transgressing all the social boundaries. Yet, London as a contrast of extremes had no place in the social geography of *Ally Sloper's Half Holiday*. Instead, social oppositions were muted and reworked, both at the top and bottom. In Sloper's comic world, fashionable society lacked the license and abandon of earlier Regency fast sets. Cockney lowlife was similarly transformed; an opulent West End was not contrasted to a Whitechapel rookery but to the working-class suburb of Battersea and to the new seaside resorts available to "day trippers." The top and bottom of masculine society were no longer linked by an addiction to vice and crime, with their association of violence and abandon, as much as by boyish pranks and genial philandering.[12]

Women in the Halls

These male pretensions did not go unchallenged, particularly in the charged social atmosphere of the music halls, where female entertainers forcefully presented the woman's perspective to a mixed audience. As a new heterosocial space, the music hall (along with the theater, department stores, museums, libraries, and public transport) illustrates what Mary Ryan had called a major "civic project" of the nineteenth century: the provision of public space for women. It was an achievement that in turn provoked multiple and contradictory effects—it provided individuals with a "new source of freedom and pleasure" and it gave "legitimacy and definition to gender difference."[13]

The presence of women, as performers and members of the audience ready to rebut male pretensions, transformed the atmosphere of the halls, forcefully contributing to their multivocal effect. Whereas thirty or forty years earlier, observes Jane Traies, a "natural audience" for the swell performance existed "in the all-male clientele of the song-and-supper rooms," by the late 1870s the audience at most music halls would contain "not only workingmen, but their wives and girlfriends, not only a 'few fast clerks and midshipmen,' but respectable family parties." Such an audience, argues Peter Bailey, constituted a "volatile collectivity, dissolving and recomposing as members of other groups by nationality, age, gender and stratum as invoked in performance." No clearly hegemonic gender message emerged from these exchanges, nor did meanings remain fixed either at the point of production or consumption.[14]

Female comic singers used the particular dynamics of music-hall performance—the constantly shifting and heterogeneous audience and a performance style noted for parody and innuendo—to puncture holes in the "magnificent cheek" of aspiring swells. Nellie Power, a male impersonator of the 1860s and 1870s, pilloried the gent for his counterfeit style and effete manners: "And he wears a penny flower in his coat, lah di dah! /And a penny paper collar round his throat, lah di dah!"[15] Female coster stars were even more critical of the daily performances of men as husbands and family men.[16] Male costers responded by depicting their own view of marriage as an unfortunate but comic calamity, with Charles Coburn making an enduring hit by celebrating the virtues of wife-beating in "Two Lovely Black Eyes."[17]

Male and female singers were also of different minds about the independent working girl. Songs for women defended the shop assistant and milliner, who disdained the slavery of domestic service. Such a girl "could look after herself, knew her own mind and had her latch key, and was too worldly wise to be taken advantage of or 'got round'."[18] In her self-sufficiency, the independent working girl was reminiscent of feisty heroines of earlier popular ballads, with the added "knowingness" of the denizen of the modern metropolis. In many ways, she was the equivalent of the swell image for men: meticulously dressed, able to move beyond the confines of her neighborhood (and the social constraints imposed by the "local matriarchs") and to navigate the class distinctions of the West End. However, songs performed by male singers displayed a more ambiguous attitude towards the self-possessed workingwoman. Like his middle-class betters, the workingman mused about her commercial status: if she sold things, did she not sell herself? For men of all classes, the shopgirl, the barmaid, and other service workers occupied the "middle" ground of sexuality, women whose visual code was "glamour," argues Peter Bailey. Neither "ladies" nor "prostitutes," they appeared as "accomplished managers" of a "carefully channelled rather than fully discharged" sexuality, which they negotiated in a range of sites: behind the counter, in the street, on the omnibus, and at the new leisure resorts of London.[19]

Shopping Ladies

Entering public space placed women of all classes, whether shopgirls or shopping ladies, in a vulnerable position. Being out in public, observes Richard Sennett, was for a woman to enter an immoral domain "where one risked losing virtue, dirtying oneself, being swept into a 'disorderly and heady swirl'." By venturing into the city center, women entered a place traditionally imagined as the site of exchange and erotic activity, a place symbolically opposed to orderly domestic life, where, to quote Roland Barthes, "subversive forces, forces of rupture, ludic forces act and meet." This cityscape of strangers and secrets, so stimulating to the male flaneur, was interpreted as a negative environment for respectable women, one that threatened to erase the protective identity conferred on them by family, residence, and social distinctions.[20]

Nevertheless, expanded opportunities for shopping, philanthropy, civic participation, and an "independent" life in the 1880s generated a new urban female style of "being at home" in the city, a style that women had to diligently cultivate against male harassment. Middle-class women first established their urban beachheads around West End shopping and East End philanthropy. Both activities depended on new public services and transportation that facilitated the movement of respectable women across urban spaces. Ladies' kiosks, new cafés and teashops, the use of buses, department stores where women could meet their female friends unchaperoned were as "important," argues Leonore Davidoff, "in freeing middle-class women from strict social rituals as the slow erosion of chaperonage."[21]

Shopping emerged as a newly elaborated female activity in the 1870s, but it reinforced a public role traditionally performed by ladies as decorous indicators of social distance, visible signs of the social system. As consumers, ladies served as status symbols of their husbands' wealth, the "specialized personnel" whose social labor consisted in making a spectacle of themselves and participating in the "pageant of fashionable life." In Doré and Jerrold's *London: A Pilgrimage,* fashionable beauties were the objects of view and occupants of space in the West End. Conversely, when, thirty years later, Walter Besant condemned East London as a cultural wasteland, "unparalleled in the magnitude of its meanness and its monotony," he cited as evidence the absence of "public institutions and amenities" and, as telling, the absence of "ladies in the principal thoroughfares; there is not visible anywhere the outward indication of wealth."[22]

The expansion of the mass market and the retail revolution in the second half of the century extended this decorative role to a larger segment of middle-class women, the targeted clientele for the multistoried department stores, where shopping ladies were equipped with the paraphernalia of gentility, the ever-proliferating props for the drama of social life. Thanks to the department stores, many of the essential features of modern consumer culture were in evidence in London's West End by the 1880s: the radical division of production and consumption; the prominence of standardized merchandise with fixed, marked pricing; ceaseless introduction of new products; the extension of credit; and ubiquitous publicity.[23] These innovations transformed the terms and meaning of shopping: they extended the consumer role to a larger social group; they established new social interactions in shopping; and they marketed commodities to fill the needs of the imagination.

Signs of commercial transformation of the West End were evident in the 1860s and 1870s, when drapers' shops began to expand into multistoried department stores. Following the example of international expositions, the new emporia organized themselves as comprehensive displays of material production. Whiteley's, England's first department store, opened further west in Bayswater in 1863, a few months after the opening of the underground railway. It quickly expanded beyond drapery to include groceries, meat, ironmongery, dry cleaning, and the house-agency business. In the 1870s, Oxford Street drapers followed suit, transforming themselves into multistoried palaces of consumption, complete with plate-glass windows heralding a constantly changing exhibition of goods. Department store interiors were organized as a microcosm of the Workshop of the

World: the 1887 edition of *Modern London* lauded Whiteley's as "an immense symposium of the arts and industries of the nation and of the world; a grand review of everything that goes to make life worth living passing in seemingly endless array before critical and bewildered humanity." The new emporia also served as imperial expositions of the 'exotic' and 'sensuous' luxuries of the colonies, with Liberty's Eastern Bazaar leading the way in marketing the 'romance' of the East to metropolitan customers.[24]

Palaces of consumption like Whiteley's and Liberty's offered women an opportunity to become leisurely spectators in a new urban landscape, comfortably gazing, reviewing "everything that goes to make life worth living." In the controlled fantasy world of the department store, women safely reimagined themselves as flaneurs, observing without being observed, constructing dreams without being obliged to buy. To attract women into the city, department stores offered a series of services and comforts that would recreate a homelike atmosphere: restaurants, complete with soft carpets, music, china, and elegant waitresses; restrooms and writing rooms; and endlessly patient shopgirls. By the 1880s, a set of ancillary services outside the department stores—inexpensive teashops, eating establishments, public lavatories, and cheap public transportation—also serviced female consumers, allowing them to enter the city center and to enjoy the new public leisure of shopping.[25]

Historians, however, are of different minds about the effects of consumer culture on shopping women. The fantasy world of consumption, argue Jackson Lears and Jean Christophe Agnew, created a defamiliarized world of floating images, detached from material referents, where values and perceptions seemed to be in constant flux. The decline of stable referents, they argue, encouraged men and women to retreat into intense private experience and to seek emotional fulfillment through material consumption. Women were particularly vulnerable to the seductions of the acquisitive impulse, insists critic Rachel Bowlby. The new dream world of consumption was a "seduction of women by men," in which women were addressed as yielding objects, subordinate to a powerful male subject, who formed and informed their desires. In contrast, other historians of consumer culture stress the liberating effects of a new visual culture and environment, particularly for women and working people, who were traditionally deprived of imaginative stimulation. William Leach, for example, extols the "inventive surreal, multi-color, saturated texture of consumer life" and the "excitement of possibility" inherent in the commodity form. By refashioning the urban center as a place for female pleasure, he contends, the retail revolution served as a vehicle of individualist expression, expanding the female imagination, drawing it into the vortex of modernity, and overturning an older mentality of repression and self-denial.[26]

Victorians themselves were alert to the contradictory effects of the retail revolution on urban women's subjectivity. In an 1896 article, Lady Jeune assessed the ethics of shopping, noting the changes that had taken place since her youth. When she was young, she explained, shopping was a "somber and dreary affair": one bought "what was wanted and nothing more" from a solemn gentlemen in black and left as seriously as one arrived. Now "overwhelming temptations . . . besiege us at every point. We go to purchase something we want; but when we get to our shop there are so many more things that we never thought of till they presented their obtrusive fascination" on the vulnerable customer. Two developments, she explained, contributed to impulse buying. The gathering together under one roof of all the necessities of life incited new acquisitive desires: "[w]e look for a ribbon, a flower, a chiffon of some sort or other, and we find ourselves in a Paradise of ribbons, flowers, and chiffons, without which our life becomes impossible and our gown unwearable." The replacement of male assistants by females further enhanced the seductive and intimate atmosphere of shops: elegantly attired shopgirls were quicker to "understand" what other women "want" and to enter into the "little troubles" of their customers. Shopping had become a major form of female pleasure: "Many women go to shops for no reason beyond the desire of looking round and generally surveying things, they are possibly tempted and succumb before leaving."[27]

In the 1880s, numerous writers echoed Lady Jeune's assessment of the addictive qualities of the new world of shopping. Thanks to the increase in mainline railway tickets and the introduction of day returns, remarked the *Woman's Gazette*, "People think nothing of running up constantly to London. . . . and ladies travel alone and unattended for reasons, which would, in the eyes of their grandmothers, hardly have justified a jaunt into the nearest market-town." Female diarists and autobiographers recorded their own fascination with the shopping world of the West End, untroubled by the moral qualms that plagued Lady Jeune. Jeanette Marshall, the daughter of a prominent surgeon, lived with her family in Savile Row and made shopping an everyday practice. Her weekday morning walk combined exercise and shopping and focused on the Regent Street district. Hardly a week passed without a visit to Lewis's, Liberty's, and sundry cooperative stories. Mary Vivian Hughes, who lived with her mother in Canonbury during the 1870s and 1880s, always ventured into the West End when she wanted to purchase an important item. She also acquired "the Londoner's ability to enjoy things without buying them. . . . My delight was to walk down Regent Street and gaze in shop windows, pointing out all the things I would like to have."[28]

Sexual Harassment

Despite the effort of department stores to create a safe, comfortable environment for their female customers, women who ventured into the shopping district found themselves subject to the intrusive gaze of men. Shopping may have fulfilled women's social obligations as status symbols of their families' wealth, but immersion in the sensuous world of consumption still rendered them suspect. In the West End, the presence of perambulating prostitutes, window-shopping ladies, "girls in business," and idle male civil servants in one public area provoked territorial tensions and hostile social acts on the part of men towards women. As a consequence, the West End and the City were notorious areas for street harassment of women.

The polarization of womanhood into two categories, the fallen and the virtuous, observes Lynda Nead, ideologically depended on sustaining clear, visible differences between them. Faded looks, painted faces, gaudy, seedy clothes supposedly marked off the streetwalkers from respectable ladies, dressed in muted colors, tailor-made jackets and waistcoats. Nonetheless, in the mid- and late-Victorian period, even as police cleared the streets and theaters of prostitutes to make room for respectable women, these two categories constantly overlapped and intersected at the juncture of commerce and femininity. Although Victorians expected to see the vices and virtues of femininity "written on the body," confusions over identity frequently occurred. In the elegant shopping districts around Regent Street, prostitutes, dressed in "meretricious finery," could and did pass as respectable, while virtuous ladies wandering through the streets, "window gazing at their leisure," often found themselves accosted as streetwalkers.[29]

Cases of mistaken identity were so frequent that they became the stuff of jokes. In one lithograph in 1865 a well-dressed woman in the street is approached by an evangelical clergyman, who offers her a reforming tract. She rejects his attempt to rescue her and assures him, "you're mistaken. I am not a social evil, I am only waiting for a bus." This confusion was frequently blamed on the "fast" daughters of the upper middle class who imitated the sumptuary habits of the demimonde. Apparently seduced by the values of the market, these inveterate consumers seem to have repudiated the self-sacrifice of traditional reproductive womanhood in favor of the selfish pursuit of pleasure and self-display. As early as the late 1860s, cultural commentators railed against the "Girl of the Period," "a creature who dyes her hair and paints her face, whose sole idea of life is plenty of fun and luxury," a critique that was given wider scope in the 1880s by professional and literary men who condemned "shopping dolls" as embodiments of a debased market culture.[30]

"Male pests" persistently dogged women who tried to experience the freedom of the city and to enter the palaces of consumption organized for their pleasure. Overwhelmingly, the culprits appeared to be "not tradesmen or errand boys who could be ignored" but "gentlemen . . . [who] crowded the streets of the West End, released from their desks by the short working hours of Victorian officialdom." Individual women responded differently to masculine attention of this sort. Jeannette Marshall accepted verbal advances as "entertaining challenges" and compliments to her outfit: "more than the usual number of 'creatures' glared me out of countenance at crossings and corners, wh. is somewhat embarrassing, though I am pretty used to it." As a newcomer to London, Elizabeth Robins was unnerved by harassments in the street and in other public spaces. Two gentlemen who helped her over a dangerous crossing "said things that frightened me." The situation had not changed in the mid-1890s, when C. S. Peel, then a dress editor for *Hearth and Home*, recalled: "Although I was quietly dressed, and I hoped looked what I was, a respectable young woman, scarcely a day when I, while waiting for an omnibus, was not accosted."[31]

Women adopted a series of strategies to deal with this situation, assisted by the prudential advice of parents and magazines. Early in her adolescence, a girl had to learn to free herself of unwanted admirers. In her gestures, movements, and pace (always dignified and purposeful), she had to demonstrate that she was not available prey. Jeannette Marshall always made sure to take no notice, however intensely men "stared": "I had to go home *tout-seule* and was spoke to by a disgusting man. I never looked at him and took no notice." The *Girl's Own Paper* advised its correspondents to organize their gaze along similar lines: "avoid strolls where you are annoyed, and always look straight before you, or on the opposite side when passing any man. Never look at them when near enough to be stared at in any impertinent and abrasive way."[32]

Some women devised personal maps and proscribed zones to organize their walks around the West End. At eighteen or twenty, Jeannette Marshall may have been imprecise about the specific danger of each forbidden zone, but "she knew exactly which route should be avoided." She regularly promenaded, chaperoned, along the edge of Green Park, carefully avoiding the "masculine" territory of clubs and bachelor chambers on the north side

of the street. The "heavenly" Burlington Arcade, one of her shopping desti-
nations but also a renowned resort of streetwalkers, was forbidden from
lunchtime on.[33]

Mothers who allowed their daughters to walk freely in their local neighborhoods often forbade them to venture into the center unchaperoned. Undoubtedly, many daughters meekly obliged, although some clearly balked
at this restriction. In her autobiography, Helena Swanwick, née Sickert,
cited this maternal prohibition as an example of the unnecessary constraints
placed on her freedom by a fearful and possessive mother.

> My mother had said that I could not go into town alone, because I
> might be "spoken to" by some man. I replied that I had already been
> "spoken to" and had been very angry with the fool, but I could not
> see that it had done me any harm. She then said a girl as young as I
> would be taken for a "bad woman" if she went about Piccadilly or
> Oxford Street unaccompanied. . . .
>
> She didn't explain what she meant by a "bad woman" and I had
> not the least idea, but I can remember hotly saying that if more well-
> behaved girls went about Piccadilly on their business, alone, it would
> improve the state of Piccadilly.

Women's publications heartily endorsed this sentiment, and hoped that harassment would decline as women became "more in the habit of moving
about." Champions of female independence had to confront the popular
prejudice that when a woman met with a "certain order of disagreeable-
ness," she "brought it on herself—if only by leaving home." Some strong-
minded women even advocated appropriating the gaze of men as a form of
resistance: Lady Grey, a friend of Elizabeth Robins, counselled her to stare
back at men who glared at her, to subdue accosters with the "strength of
fearlessness." "Any woman who doesn't lose her head," she insisted, "can
make it so inconvenient for [the pleasure seeker who does not want "trouble"] he will go about his business."[34]

Charity Workers

Whatever their discomfort at being under the scrutiny of privileged men,
middle-class women did not relinquish their claim to public space. Not
only did they continue to shop, but as philanthropists they increasingly
traveled into different regions of the city in search of adventure and self-
discovery. Female charity workers who ventured into the slums of the East
End often enjoyed greater social freedom than ladies trying to navigate the
"male pests" of the West End. "The streets of the slums, away from upper-

class men's eyes, were theirs," observes Vicinus. Some respectable women treated shopping and charity work as roughly equivalent recreational activities appropriate to their station. Certainly this was the perspective of Margot Asquith, when she sought diversion in London streets to distract her from her private grief over the death of her sister Laura. When she was not slumming "in the East End of London," she "wandered about looking at shop-windows in the West." Both pursuits established Asquith's right to look, to assume a mask of anonymity without relinquishing the privileges of class.[35]

In 1886, Asquith marched into the office of a Whitechapel box-factory owner and secured his permission for her to visit his factory girls. The owner, Cliffords, "Never asked my name and I visited his factory three days a week for eight years [until her marriage]." In the pages of her autobiography, the Whitechapel poor appeared as picaresque Others to be observed in their natural habitat, humorous foils for her urban adventures: they "talk in funny accents, solemnly transcribed into funny spelling, and follow very closely the stereotypes depicted in the pages of *Punch*," as one recent commentator notes. Like Booth and Greenwood, Asquith was not the least curious about what the people of Whitechapel thought of her, or self-conscious about her intrusion into their lives. Like Greenwood and many others, Asquith's adventures into "lowlife deeps" extended to impersonation; it even extended to active participation in the disorderly conduct of female proletariats. Asquith regularly accompanied her factory girls to the local pub, where she sat in the corner, eating her sandwich and smoking her cigarette. One day she stepped out briefly; when she returned, she observed her protégé, the "beautiful cockney" Phoebe, hitting another woman "like a prize fighter." She tried to intervene in the fight: "before I could separate the combatants, I had given and received heavy blows." Unexpected help came from a Clifford's packer, and Asquith, "feeling stiff all over," returned home to Grosvenor Square. Cliffords, "who was an expert boxer, invited me into his room on my next visit to tell him the whole story and my shares went up." Asquith's complete sense of superiority and physical security was not even threatened by the Whitechapel murders which took place near the factory in 1888: "the girls and I visited what journalists call 'the scene of the tragedy'. It was strange watching crowds of people collected daily to see nothing but an archway."[36]

Asquith was part of an army of intrepid women of the upper and middle classes who went "slumming" in search of adventure, self-discovery, and meaningful work. By the late nineteenth century, Louisa Hubbard estimated that at least twenty thousand salaried and half-a-million voluntary women were at work befriending "the homeless, rootless, and handicapped."[37] This female army numbered many self-indulgent amateurs like Asquith, who fitted charity work in between social engagements. However, by the late decades of the century, a new spirit of professionalization also prevailed, one that demanded charity workers be trained, disciplined, and businesslike, with considerable organizational skills. Women "have developed an unexpected capacity for organization," observed Octavia Hill, "an enterprise in arduous undertaking, and an enthusiasm for difficult, disagreeable, and unpromising work."[38]

Much of this change was due to the influence of Octavia Hill herself. Although middle-class women had visited the poor since the 1790s, Hill had advanced a more ambitious project of female slum supervision in the 1860s. With the help of John Ruskin, Hill purchased London tenements and oversaw their improvement by the tenants, from whom she collected the rents. She also became a founding member of the Charity Organization Society (COS), dedicated to the systematic coordination of charity giving and assessment of individual cases in the dispensing of alms to the deserving poor. The ideology of Hill's philanthropic projects rested on the assumption that poverty was a moral, not a structural, problem, and that through personal relations between rich and poor the deserving poor could be weaned out of habits of dependence and thriftlessness.[39]

Hill looked to an army of female district visitors to carry out the task of social reconciliation and domestic supervision. District visitors, Hill insisted, should regard "the poor primarily as husbands, wives, sons and daughters, members of the household, as we are ourselves," rather than as "a different class." Hill's rent collectors were obliged not only to collect rents but also to supervise the welfare of the people and the conditions of their homes. They had to offer spiritual uplift and discipline to "tenants who through flabbiness of will required continual bracing lest they should fall hopelessly behind." This "most excellent way of charity" involved detailed knowledge of the domestic state of the poor as well as the ability to teach them domestic virtues, skills at which middle-class matrons excelled.[40] Building on a long-standing tradition of home inspection carried on by slum clergymen, public health inspectors, the Ladies Sanitary Association, and Ranyard Bible women, Hill's rent collectors began to consolidate some new social meanings around this philanthropic activity.[41]

As Frank Mort has observed, Hill and her protégés regularly collaborated with male professionals in an enterprise of social regulation and class discipline. Able to penetrate the homes of the poor and their neighborhoods, female philanthropists took careful note of abusive husbands, alcoholism, gossiping women at doorsteps, dirty children, open doorways—all conventional signs of social, sexual, and moral disorder. To frame their impressions of the poor, female memoirists and investigators relied on the same distancing literary conventions as their male counterparts, drawn from the sensational literature of urban exploration or the comic scenarios of *Punch*. The same monotonous and sensational slum scene featured in *How the Poor Live* reappears in the memoirs and writings of socialist feminists and charity organization visitors: in "noisy courts," crowded rooms, and "sodden alleys" of the slums, children "swarmed," the noise was "deafening," the crowd "bewildering," the whole humanity reduced to a "hustling, jostling, restless, struggling, noisy, tearing existence."[42]

Although many female philanthropists would persist in constituting themselves as controlling observers in the "country" of the poor, by the 1880s some charity workers had begun to shift their ideological stance towards poverty and their own self-definition as female philanthropists. As Patricia Hollis observes, Hill had trained a whole generation of able women in "professional 'scientific' philanthropy, based on careful enquiry, detailed observation, and personal casework." Her students went on to be district visitors, rent collectors, sanitary inspectors, poor-law guardians, and settlement house workers in Bermondsey, Lambeth, and the East End. As they applied their organizational skills, ability to address public meetings, and fundraising talents to settlement house work and local government, they superimposed considerable bureaucratic skills and perspectives on the particularism and personalism that traditionally characterized "female philanthropy." They began to relax their commitment to classical political economy and to look to the state for various interventions. Like male socialists and New Liberals, they increasingly came to reject a view of poverty as moral failure in favor of a more structural explanation, focused on unemployment, underemployment, and insufficient wages. Unlike male reformers of the time, female philanthropists linked this emerging perspective on poverty to a close observation of domestic patterns among the poor gained from COS work or rent collecting.[43]

Increasingly, female philanthropists constituted themselves as people who saw more than men, because they saw the domestic side of poverty. In their effort to moralize the poor into paragons of domestic virtue, they came to recognize the centrality of women to family and neighborhood. The writings and observations of rent collectors testify to women's role as household managers and controllers of the family wage economy, who ordered internal relationships within the family and acted as chief representatives to the outside world. Appreciation of the power of the mother led some female observers to blame mothers for the conditions of the slums and slum-dwellers, while provoking others, mainly socialist feminists, to champion the cause of the mother in demands for the "endowment of motherhood."[44]

Because of their distinctive social location, middle-class women also produced some new social meanings, new "truths," from their urban explorations. Unlike male investigators, whose accounts, in the words of one Victorian female philanthropist, gave "the impression of the outsider who makes official visits during the business hours,"[45] these women spent many hours among women and children, their principal informants,[46] listening to their stories. Their characteristic mode, insists historian Ellen Ross, was "aural" rather than "visual." As incipient urban ethnographers, they may well have been influenced by the studies of folklore or by the work of evolutionary anthropologists such as Morgan and Bachofen who focused on systems of kinship and marriage; both folkore and ethmography may have predisposed them to see the life of the poor in terms of patterns and continuities, rather than urban chaos.[47]

In sum, a keen appreciation of working-class domestic arrangements coexisted with a cultural repertoire replete with condescending and distancing stereotypes of the poor. Beatrice Webb was a notable exemplar of this doubled consciousness; in the mid-1880s, while she was dividing her time between rent collecting in Katherine Buildings, Whitechapel, and society hostessing at her father's estate, her diary entries frequently recorded a sense of the hopelessness of the East End. She deplored the "low level of monotonous and yet excited life, the regular recurrence of street sensations in quarrels and fights, the greedy street bargaining." Yet her own detailed observations of family and tenant relations, as well as her account of workplace relations in the tailoring trade, belied this relentless and unredeeming pessimism. Despite her injunctions to tenants, "Don't meddle with your neighbours," Webb acknowledged that the "bright side of East End life is the sociability and generous sharing of small means." "I enjoy the life of the people at the East End," she wrote in her diary, "the reality of their efforts and aims; the simplicity of their sorrows and joys; I feel I can realize it and see the tragic and comic side."[48]

Another lady resident of a model dwellings building in Whitechapel offered a less grudging, more sympathetic portrait of female domestic networks. Shared facilities and duties in "Buildings," she argued, created the material conditions for collective life. Communal balconies, stairs, and washhouses might lead to "endless contention" among female neighbors, but they also served as the basis for mutual support. Living in the buildings, the lady resident was privy to the movements, visits, activities, conversations, and disputes of the inhabitants. The "advantages of living in

Buildings," she concluded, "far outweigh the drawbacks." Above all, "the impossibility of being overlooked altogether, or flagrantly neglected by relatives in illness or old age," seem to be "the great gains." Even the disadvantages—loss of privacy and increased facility for gossiping and quarreling—had a bright side, introducing "a constant variety of petty interest and personal feeling into the monotony of daily life."[49]

Female charity workers also revised the position from which the meanings of urban exploration and bourgeois spectatorship could be articulated. This "new breed of governing and guiding women,"[50] as Beatrice Webb characterized the female philanthropists of the 1880s, did not simply fit themselves into an imaginary landscape of male public space, but reimagined the cityscape of London, particularly the slums, as a place appropriate for women in public. They felt compelled to justify their position as public actors and observers in distinctly feminine ways, stressing, as Martha Vicinus notes, an ethos of service, self-sacrifice and bodily control.[51] Yet female philanthropists also seemed to have experienced considerable pleasure in the new social freedoms and prerogatives they had acquired.

Like male urban explorers, female charity workers interpreted the slum as a backdrop for their own personal drama, a place to test their moral fiber or to enjoy the passing show. Like James's "sympathetic resident," they assumed that they could observe without being observed. At home on the street (perhaps more at home than male investigators), they could enjoy the spectacle of characters and "moving pictures." The slum street acquired the ludic qualities traditionally associated with the city center; it became an improvisational site for strange encounters with unforgettable characters. "Small as our street was," declared Ellen Chase, "there was always something going on." "There was always a spice about 'going into the street,' at Deptford, for you could never tell what you might hear or see." Flypaper men, circus performers, and animals would suddenly appear and interrupt the daily monotony, as well as the weddings, departures, and Saturday night marital rows that residents regarded as "highly diverting" and not as a "shame." "Our life was full of interest, change, and excitement," declared Margaret Nevinson, who went to Whitechapel as a young bride and pioneer settler attached to Toynbee Hall and worked as a rent collector in Katherine Buildings. "I never remember one dull moment during the two years we lived there."[52]

These women enjoyed the freedom of the streets, not because they were in fact invisible, but because they wielded considerable authority. Female charity workers who controlled an important resource like housing or who provided needed medical services enjoyed an immense power and prestige in poor neighborhoods (other female philanthropists who could offer only culture and refinement to entice working girls into classes often found themselves the object of ridicule and derision as "old maids"). As agents of the landlord, rent collectors were spared the "embarrassing sense of intrusion which sometimes accompanies other forms of visiting," explained Ellen Chase, who worked for Octavia Hill in South London. "We were able to govern our little domain as we liked and make of it what we could. It was for us to decide who amongst the applicants for rooms should be accepted, what families should live side by side." The responsibilities of rent collectors led them to develop sleuth-like abilities, to detect forged testimonials from legitimate ones and to explore the neighborhood in search of references. Beatrice Webb recorded in her diary "long trudges through Whitechapel after applicants and references."[53]

Some tenants clearly resented this "petticoat government." Women chafed at the audacity of mostly single, middle-class women telling married women how to raise their families. Men complained of interference in family disputes as an unwarranted collusion between the rent collector and female neighbors. Others were angry at being evicted for nonpayment, for moral transgressions, or for other infractions of the innumerable rules governing residences. At the same time, poor neighbors recognized female charity workers as influential and friendly mediators with the more anonymous state agencies. When a respectable widow was faced with separation from her children because she had applied for poor relief, she pleaded with Ellen Chase to intervene on her behalf: "You are a big tax-payer, Miss can't you write a strong letter to the Vestry?"[54]

The middle-class charity worker who enjoyed the greatest prestige in the slums was the district nurse.[55] The nurse's uniform offered middle-class women special protection in public, transporting them beyond gender. "As the nurse passes into some low court" in "her long coat and white apron, and simple bonnet," explained the *Woman's Penny Paper*, "she is greeted by sundry nods and salutations from children playing in the gutter." Novels and social commentaries of the period affirmed her privileged immunity from violence. Such was the authority of Marcella, the aristocratic eponymous heroine of Mrs. Humphry Ward's novel (1894), who spent a few penitential years as a district nurse in Soho slums. In one episode, while a frightened policeman ran off for reinforcements, Marcella stepped forward and fearlessly intervened in a marital dispute. Charles Booth, who relied heavily on the districts nurses' assessment of local neighborhoods in his great study of London poverty, also testified to their local prestige and authority. He recounted one nurse-informant's impression of Bethnal Green: "'Monday morning business of the pawn-shop, drink quarrels, and neglected children. . . . It would be difficult to find rougher streets anywhere in London,' but she adds that the people all respect the nurse's uniform."[56]

Male Reversals and Appropriations

Female charity workers often enjoyed less prestige among middle-class male philanthropists than among the working people they served and observed. Male settlement workers tried to emulate the personalism of female charity workers while at the same time keeping real women reformers at bay. Samuel Barnett, for instance, had worked under Octavia Hill as a curate and helped her to organize the first committee of the Charity Organization Society in Marylebone; thanks to Hills's patronage, Barnett was appointed vicar of St. Jude's, Whitechapel, an appointment that provided his income at Toynbee Hall, the university settlement he founded in 1884, until 1906. He borrowed the ethos of female philanthropy, its emphasis on service, "neighborliness," and "community," on being rather than doing.[57] Yet, with the exception of his formidable wife, Henrietta, who offered a "touch of womanly refinement" to the male society of Toynbee Hall, local maids to clean the rooms, female clients, and the occasional female lecturer, Barnett barred women from his settlement because he feared they would take over the movement.[58]

Barnett was intent on shaping settlement work as a male enterprise, an extension of elite male university life in the slums. To attract young intellectual men to philanthropy, a task previously left to women and men of "advanced age," Barnett had to reinvent it as a modern expression of the medieval chivalric ideal, a manly code for a new urban squirearchy.

Barnett hoped his new squirearchy of East London, imbued with Arnoldian conceptions of culture, would forge a brotherhood, however asymmetrical, with the men and boys of East London. To this end, Barnett initiated "Pal's Parties," consisting of men only, and other clubs and associations for "East London friends." The homosocial focus of settlement work attracted many Oxbridge graduates who took to the slums to escape the social and sexual oppressiveness of bourgeois culture, attracted by the prospect of forming a bond of comradeship with "rough lads." These young men included socialist homosexuals like C. R. Ashbee, who had been initiated by Edward Carpenter into the "mystery of comradeship." By giving lectures to working men, Ashbee believed himself to be "nearer to these men, and beginning to understand the Whitmanic position . . . the B.W.M. [British Working Man] is no longer a terror to me."[59]

On the whole, however, settlement and religious workers found men and boys of the slums less receptive to their cultural services than were girls to the efforts of their female counterparts. Girls' clubs, reported Booth, "constitute a far more social movement." Toynbee Hall's clubs and classes compensated by attracting a following among clerks, teachers (mostly female), and skilled artisans residing outside of Whitechapel. Partly because male settlement workers failed to bond with the casual laborers of Whitechapel, and partly because Christian socialists pressed them to use their legal and political influence for policy ends, male settlement workers at Toynbee Hall would turn away from feminized activities of neighborliness and from the sexually ambiguous bonds of comradeship with "rough lads" towards social investigation in the 1890s. Toynbee Hall's greatest achievement would be the "training of a new kind of elite" of "enlightened bureaucrats": the men "who went into service" to Canon Barnett, observed George Lansbury, the Poplar political leader, "could always be sure of government and municipal appointments."[60]

Like a number of other cultural projects of the 1880s, Barnett's settlement scheme revealed masculine self-doubt, gender and sexual ambiguity, and cultural crossovers among professional men, the self-constituted urban gentry engaged in constructing new patterns of hierarchy and deference. To renovate philanthropy for men, Barnett evoked a chivalrous feudal code that repudiated the aggressive materialism of modern commerce, the brute exercise of power, and the detached, elevated gaze of "science." But the individuals who most closely realized this "neighborly" ethos were female charity workers, who felt at home on the streets of East London and took pleasure in ruling a "wild, lawless, desolate little kingdom." Barnett's appropriation of feminine qualities to complete the masculine did not, as we have seen, entail including 'real' women in the social task. Nor did this new male androgyny allow for a female androgynous counterpart. As Carolyn Heilbrun observes, "Many men . . . have tried and sometimes succeeded in including aspects of the feminine in their art or philosophy or psyches, but they seldom return the compliment of allowing women to incorporate the masculine."[61]

Fictional accounts of philanthropy also highlighted the male tendency to emulate female philanthropy in pursuit of the spiritual. In Edward Berdoe's *St. Bernard's* (1887), Harrowby Ellsworth, a young doctor disillusioned with the sadistic practices of hospital doctors, draws inspiration for a new kind of medical charity from the self-sacrificing activities of female charity workers of the East End.[62]

Berdoe had clearly modelled his novel on Walter Besant's *All Sorts and Conditions of Men*, which had assimilated the story of philanthropy to the imperatives of heterosexual romance, a narrative task that involved weaning the heroine away from the lure of voluntary spinsterhood and a "career." The narrator of *All Sorts and Conditions of Men,* for example, introduced Angela Messenger, the heroine of the novel, as a Newnham girl, trained in political economy, and heiress to a great brewery fortune made in the East End. Proud of her independence, symbolized by the "latch key," Angela forswore marriage (it spoils "a woman's career") to go *incognita* among the East End poor as a "dressmaker." In the end, Angela, "the strongminded Newnham student," showed herself a "womanly woman" at heart and found her destiny in marriage and a joint philanthropic project (recommended by the male love interest) of bringing culture and rational entertainment to the people of the East End, in the form of a cultural center, the Palace of Delight.[63]

Barnett, Besant, and Berdoe were all deeply attracted to certain qualities that were culturally coded as feminine in Victorian society, but they refused women the same exploratory possibilities and greeted with some suspicion "manly women" who poached on male preserves. *St. Bernard's* contrasted the womanly philanthropists of the East End with the dangerous, unsexed New Women of West End salons, the young ladies of socialist and freethinking circles who quietly conversed with young men in drawing rooms about nihilism, "dynamite mission work," and the loosening of moral fetters. Although no dangerously emancipated females appeared in *All Sorts and Conditions of Men* (only an unattractive lady mathematician), Besant's dystopic novel of the same year, *The Revolt of Man,* vividly renders the disastrous consequences of a female revolution, the "Great Transition." For a hundred years after women took over the reigns of power, "everything fell to pieces": industry declined, the government was unstable, higher education deteriorated, men were unmanned, and women married younger men. At last the "Great Revolution," bloodless, without pillage, corrected this unnatural turn of events, returning men to their rightful place of dominance.[64]

The Glorified Spinster and the "Manly Woman"

To a great extent, middle-class women accepted the same division between masculine and feminine propensities, even though some tried to imagine a new female synthesis. Like male philanthropists, female reformers were attracted to social practices and personal styles that challenged gender and social boundaries. While working as a rent collector at Katherine Buildings, for example, Beatrice Webb wrote to her father of the women who found a "matrimonial career" shut to them and were bent upon finding a "masculine reward for masculine qualities." These women were not "inferior Men," but possessors of a "masculine faculty" combined with the "woman's temperament." "I only hope," she added, "that, instead of trying to ape men and take up men's pursuits, they will carve out their own careers, and not be satisfied until they have found the careers in which their particular form of power will achieve most." Following her own program, Webb self-consciously forsook female philanthropy for socialism and the masculine activity of scientific social investigation. In her search for a new "craft" and "creed," she rejected COS political economy and women's philanthropic culture to investigate the conditions of dock labor, female sweatshops, and working-class cooperatives. In the late 1880s, other women would try another strategy of cultural expansion: they returned Barnett's compliment by appropriating his settlement model to create a home for themselves in the East End and South London, a community of women also modeled on the homosocial community of Oxbridge women's colleges.[65]

Webb imagined the new social type of "working womanhood" as a female androgyne, thus invoking a popular iconography at least four hundred years old, carried on through print culture, song, oral tradition, and word of mouth. Adopting the clothes and/or the life-style, work, mental disposition, or manner of the opposite sex was generally associated with female proletarian behavior, but it gained some devotees among middle-class women bent on freeing themselves from the constraints of their own sex. In the culture at large, cross-dressing remained a common trope of female disorder and infringement of male prerogatives. Caricatures depicted nagging wives and aggressive women as masculine-featured viragos trying to wear the breeches; the pejorative noun "Georges Sandism" appeared in English (as well as French, German, and Russian) to denounce women who dared to emulate Sand's transgressive life and behavior. Doctors began to collect case histories of "mental and physical hermaphrodites" who eschewed feminine identity. But, in response, rebellious women often took up the cross-dressing role; of the "manly woman," the *Woman's Penny Paper* remarked, "Who has not met her? With her hair cut short or tightly braided so as to be hidden under her billycock hat; with her coat-like jacket, her gloveless hands and walking stick, and her loving dog companions," a critical and anxious appraisal that provoked one correspondent to pen a lively defense of the "manly woman" to dress as she pleased. Instead of reviling Sand, late-Victorian feminists in the 1880s embraced her as the embodiment of woman's genius and her dangerous side, even if they did not take to wearing trousers themselves. When, in 1888, the *PMG* asked prominent women of the day to identify the greatest "ladies" in history, Sand topped the list, followed by Joan of Arc, another French androgyne.[66]

In 1888, Webb and Ella Pycroft, her coworker at Katherine Buildings, read with amusement "a cleverish paper" in *Macmillan's Magazine* on "glorified spinsters," a "new species" of women not "looking forward to marriage as their ultimate destiny." Webb and her friend immediately recognized themselves in the portrait. The "Glorified Spinster," the article explained, was an evolutionary product of modern environmental forces: the contraction of means among the professional classes, precipitating a decline in marriage and increase in the marriage age; the "democratic spirit of the age," leaving women unwilling to acquiesce "in a position of dependence and subjection"; and the general spread of education, "which has enabled many women to find happiness in intellectual pleasures and to care comparatively little about social environment." One marked characteristic of this new specimen was employment in the feminized tertiary sector. Other telltale signs included "her agility in gaining the tops of omnibuses, her power of entering a tramcar without stopping the horses, her cool self-possession in a crowd, her utter indifference to weather, and, it must be added, an undoubted disposition to exact her rights to the uttermost farthing." In spite of the smallness of her resources (evident in her bare, modest lodgings and limited, drab wardrobe), the Glorified Spinster managed to satisfy a keen appetite for urban amusements, always "extracting the greatest possible amount of pleasure out of every shilling."[67]

Like the "Girl of the Period," the Glorified Spinster was a highly stylized cultural construction. She was a partial reflection of the experience of a small number of self-supporting or financially independent single middle-class women, who began to define a new urban female style of being at home in the city. "Taking her for all in all," observed *Macmillan's*, "the Glorified Spinster is a most curious product of our civilization." A liminal figure, she united "some of the characteristics of both sexes," but "differs from each in essential points." Like a meteor she wandered "free in inter-familiar space, obeying laws and conventions" of her own, and "entering other systems" only as a "strange and rare" visitant.[68]

The article that had so amused Webb and her friend had acutely identified a series of discursive and material developments that propelled this "new species" into existence in the last decades of the nineteenth century. These included gains in women's higher education, an ethos of voluntary spinsterhood, employment opportunities, new roles in public life and philanthropy, as well as emerging urban female "life-styles" and debates about marriage and women's sexual destiny.

Schooling, like shopping, was part of a new urban adventure for girls and women. Molly Hughes, who disliked North London Collegiate, nonetheless reveled in the freedom and status attached to using public transport to commute to school: she was as proud of her "season ticket from High-bury to Camden Town (where the school was located) as any girl of later years with her latch keys." Female memoirists, particularly those who had attended day schools in London and subsequently used their education to pursue a career, often remembered their school experience as transformative. Helena Swanwick, who suffered "acutely" from the efforts of her mother "to distract my attention which endured for the whole of my girlhood," felt liberated from the "vague and most sentimental exactions of home" when she entered Notting Hill High School. "'Oh mother, just think! I've got a number!' Mother thought it terrible to be reduced to a number." Sickert "couldn't explain" that "the taking of my place among schoolfellows in an ordered system," "having defined rights and duties" instead of the "irregular" personal services she was obliged to perform at home represented a complete emancipation.[69]

The unprecedented expansion of private female secondary schools, teacher training, and, to a lesser extent, women's education at university levels precipitated new expectations and social possibilities for women. Although historians have correctly noted the conservative ethos and curricula of the new schools,[70] these institutions also provided women with intellectual skills and an ethos of public service. They added two new roles to the repertoire of genteel femininity: the celibate career woman and the intellectual companionate wife. Although neither of these roles challenged the legal or economic subordination of women in marriage, they did expand middle-class women's options, by redefining both heterosocial and homosocial norms. "We should be ticketed Not in the marriage market," declared one independent woman to the narrator of the "Glorified Spinster," in order to mix "more freely with men on whose moral and intellectual level we more nearly are." Conversely, other spinsters adopted a more separatist strategy, deeming that "the best way to keep one's independence" was to "avoid the society of men" and "keep to one's sex."[71]

Even so, independent single women of the order of the Glorified Spinster were very much a minority. Marriage remained the approved female destiny for all classes, although the percentage of women who never married increased slightly in the late-Victorian period. Among the professional "educated" classes the proportion of spinsters could be striking: a study undertaken in 1887 by Eleanor Mildred Sidgwick into the marriage and fertility patterns of former students of Oxbridge women's colleges and their siblings estimated that only 30 percent of former students were likely to marry. This low number was consistent with more general patterns; whether they attended university or not, Sidgwick concluded, only a minority of females in the "educated" classes ever married.[72]

Sidgwick's study, published in 1892, went to great pains to vindicate educated women from any responsibility for remaining single: spinsterhood among former students was not a function of the inadequacy of educated women, she argued, but of the shortage of suitable men. Although sympathetic to the plight of spinsters, Sidgwick underplayed any choice or agency on women's part in eschewing marriage. Yet, as a number of historians have argued, a small group of women do seem to have chosen a life and career outside of heterosexual domesticity. Among the Glorified Spinsters of the fin de siècle, "female marriages" became more common than they had been earlier in the century. New occupations in the "helping" professions, new social spaces—the college and the settlement house, as well as the availability of flats and ladies' residences by the end of the 1880s—encouraged some women to choose the company of a long-time friend.[73]

The advent of the New Woman was also heralded by the entrance of middle-class women into new forms of waged work. The Glorified Spinster's list of genteel occupations in the tertiary sector—including teachers, nurses, clerks, librarians, heads of certain business departments—covered many of the gains and new directions of middle-class female employment.[74] However small, these gains acquired considerable significance, as contemporaries saw in them the beginnings of a significant trend. In her 1892 statistical appendix to the Royal Commission on Labor, Clara Collet noted only a slight increase in women's employment between 1881 and 1891. She ascribed the "prevalent" belief in women's "greater employment" during the 1880s to an awareness of "the entrance into the wages market of women in the middle class, counting numerically but a small section of the community, and in many cases taking up new employments."[75]

The last decades of the nineteenth century also inaugurated a new era of female participation in civic life. When Karl Pearson identified women and labor as the "two most important movements of our era,"[76] he was undoubtedly thinking of Josephine Butler's "Revolt of the Women" and even the decorous suffrage movement, both of which dramatically represented women's entry into the public domain to defend the rights of women and to protest their wrongs. But he was also responding to the recent success of individual women in gaining public office and the presence of "platform women" who commanded public attention at demonstrations, street corners, and meeting halls.

Despite the fact that the struggle for the national suffrage confronted serious impasses, women had made a number of important legal gains in the 1880s. The passage of the Married Women's Property Act of 1882, heralded by the *Women's Suffrage Journal* as the "Magna Carta" of women's liberties, gave a wife control over her separate property and recourse to the same civil and criminal remedies available to an unmarried woman. In addition, women with the appropriate property qualifications could vote in municipal elections after 1869; after 1888, they could vote for county councils. Within a few years of their municipal enfranchisement, women stood successfully for local offices, particularly those that fell within the "female caring sphere," such as school boards and poor-law guardianships. By 1885, 50 women had been elected to poor-law boards nationally; by 1879 there were seventy women on school boards. The London School Board (LSB) was the most significant of these bodies nationally; it set precedents and served as a "polestar and guide" for boards throughout the country.[77]

An extraordinary group of political women served on the LSB in the 1880s. Prominent among them were "advanced" women whose lives testified to the new opportunities available to heterodox London women and to their personal struggles for a new spiritual and public identity. They included Helen Taylor, the stepdaughter of John Stuart Mill, whose candidacy was endorsed by trade unions, workingmen's clubs, and the Irish interest; Florence Fenwick Miller, trained in medicine, suffragist, Neo-Malthusian, and prominent journalist; Henrietta Muller, Girton-trained, well-to-do, who "cast men aside" and lived among women dedicated to the "public service," later publisher of the first women's newspaper in London and theosophist; and the indomitable, charismatic Annie Besant, heroine of free thought and birth control, now a socialist, who just prior to her school-board campaign in 1888 had led the match girls' strike to a spectacular conclusion, and who would soon have another "life" as the leader of theosophy.[78]

Running for the school board, an unpaid elected position with a three-year term of office, required women to engage in active campaigning, to make spectacles of themselves. Fenwick Miller's considerable skill at debate served her well in her three campaigns. During each campaign, for three weeks, she made two or three public appearances an evening; like a music-hall star, she dashed from "turn" to "turn" in a hired carriage.[79]

Once elected, Fenwick Miller continued to give bravura performances of school-board meetings. In 1881, a reporter for the *Lady's Pictorial* observed the "young" Mrs. Miller, plainly though attractively dressed, seated at the horseshoe table, "her hands . . . frequently locked together behind her waist," to denote "earnestness of purpose." "Searching for weak points" in an opponent's argument, using a pen to gesticulate on a point, she was ever "forceful" and "logical." To convey Fenwick Miller's aggressive body language and verbal style, the reporter invoked the phallic image of the warrior-queen Boadicea, driving "a war chariot with scythes project-ing from the axles of the wheels."[80]

Outside board meetings, "warrior-queens" like Fenwick Miller and Besant were in constant demand as public speakers. Memoirists and auto-biographers recalled them as part of the spectacle of London life in the eighties, provocative signs of modernity and vibrant radicalism. Frederick Rogers remembered Fenwick Miller as "brilliant . . . very much a de-magogue," "daring enough to talk frankly on public platforms," lecturing on "human physiology" to halls packed "to suffocation." He also pro-nounced Besant the "triumph of feminine charm on the platform," exhibit-ing "the glamour of sex." Even George Bernard Shaw, who haunted all sorts of public meetings, from the West End Zetetical Society to East End workingmen's clubs, as part of a self-education program in public speak-ing, acknowledged Besant as the master orator of the decade. When she joined the Fabian Society in 1885, she was instrumental in committing the group to direct political action on behalf of striking miners, match girls, and dockworkers. While praising Besant's "out of doors" politicking, Shaw distanced her performances from the mode of rational debate that came to epitomize the Fabian style. Besant became "a sort of expeditionary force" for the Fabians,

> always to the front when there was trouble and danger, carrying away audiences for us when the dissensions in the [socialist] movement brought our policy into conflict with that of the other societies, founding branches for us throughout the country, . . . and generally leaving the routine to us [the inner male sanctum] and taking the fighting on herself.[81]

Prominent figures like Besant and Fenwick Miller epitomized the new phenomenon of "platform women," who demonstrated an "unmistakable 'gift of speech'" and desire to be a "visible" power in the world at large. Like "shopping ladies," platform women seemed to exhibit a penchant for "egotistical" self-display, that disquieted many observers, both female and male. Women "exhibiting themselves, their persons, talents, and opinions, upon platforms" transgressed the acceptable boundaries of gender and sexual decorum, argued a *Nineteenth Century* article on platform women; they lowered the "standard of womanhood." Beatrice Webb also responded to platform women with considerable ambivalence. She acknowledged Besant as "the only woman I have ever known who is a real orator." But to "*see*" her speaking made her "shudder." "It is not womanly to thrust your-self before the world. A woman in all her relations of life, should be sought." Yet Webb was surprised by the pleasure she herself experienced when she spoke publicly for the first time before a meeting of dock laborers at the Tabernacle, Canning Town. "I was the only woman present and as I made my way up to a platform I enjoyed the first experience of being 'cheered' as a public character."[82]

Platform speaking and political work forced women into a working relationship with men. This often proved to be a formidable challenge. "There is nothing at all new in women working together," observed Emily Davies. "The new and difficult thing is for men and women to work together on equal terms." Female political workers often found themselves better received and more at ease in the company of East End workingmen than among gentlemen or even ladies of their own class. "Fine ladies make me nervous," Florence Balgarnie, a suffrage speaker, declared. "I do not prefer speaking at drawing room meetings. I am more at home when addressing working people, especially working men. Above all I delight in debate."[83]

A social ease with workingmen encouraged women to experiment with unconventional social encounters. After a visit to Victoria Park to survey the Sunday speakers, Webb and her friend returned with their guide, Mr. Kerrigan, a board school visitor and "most amusing Irishman," to his lodgings. She tried to imagine what "the conventional West End acquaintance" would say to "two young women smoking and talking in the bed, sitting, working, smoking and bathroom of an East End visitor . . . . We have entertained freely and thoroughly enjoyed our life in working-class society."[84]

Heterosocial Spaces and the New Urban Style

An ability to get around and self-confidence in public places became the hallmarks of the modern woman. Not only could she be seen in the shopping districts of the West End and in the poor neighborhoods of the East, but she also made an appearance in other public spaces, alone or with a friend, at concerts, picture exhibitions, the galleries of Albert Hall and the pits of the playhouse. "Our social life has changed," proclaimed the *Woman's Penny Paper* at the end of the decade. "One could hardly walk a quarter of a mile in any street of London without seeing instances of it, particularly in [the] dress and manner of women, in the things they do, in the words they say."[85]

Unconventional in their intellectual and political interest, advanced women rigidly observed the standards of public decorum in dress, manner, and movement (motivated, at least in part, by a strong desire to avoid attracting "male pests"). A few independent women adopted a less "ladylike" public style to match their heterodox views. Annie Besant affronted the sensibility of many by her working-class dress, her heavy laced boots, short skirts and red neckerchief, and close-cut hair. Novelist Olive Schreiner, a "colonial comet" who talked with her hands and rode on the top of omnibuses, was only slightly less shocking to conventional sensibilities. Nevertheless, she utterly charmed the equally unorthodox Edward Carpenter, who recalled her as a "pretty woman apparently of lady-like origin who did not wear a veil and seldom wore gloves, and who talked and laughed in the street quite naturally" (a "free" public style that may partially explain why Schreiner was accosted by a policeman as a prostitute in 1887).[86]

Advanced women not only invaded governmental bodies and assumed a commanding presence in the streets, they encroached on other male preserves as well. One prime target was the British Museum Reading Room. The Reading Room became the stomping ground of the "bohemian set," a place where trysts were made between heterodox men and women. In the refreshment room or behind a pile of books one could find Olive Schreiner or Eleanor Marx, her "curly black hair flying about in all directions," known for her "'natural' relations with men," who complained "that the translation of the Kama Sutra was locked up in the library and refused to women." Some male habitués did not take well to this invasion of "scribbling women." Letters complaining of female "intrusions into men's places at the British Museum" appeared in the *Pall Mall Gazette* in 1883. "Two long tables" had been set apart in the Great Reading room for ladies only, one male correspondent complained. "But there ladies will not go!" There were too many "fair readers" than the tables could accommodate, explained a female correspondent, forcing women like herself to take a seat at a section "regarded as the property of men."[87]

Outside the museum, the same female readers moved between heterosocial and homosocial spaces: between the settlement houses, ladies' residences, and teashops available to them by the end of the decade, and the mixed discussion clubs held in drawing-room settings that proliferated in 1880s London: the Proudhon Club, the Browning Society, the Zetetical Society, and, for more radical souls, the Fellowship of New Life, Fabian Society, and Men and Women's Club.

Discussion clubs provided a safe, intermediate meeting place, between public and private, for heterosexual encounters outside of traditional middle-class institutions. The drawing-room settings of discussion clubs were refashioned as a new political space for women, but also for lower-middle-class men like Shaw or Sidney Webb, who could not penetrate elite political circles to test out ideas. These societies tried to embody the companionate ideal of free and open intellectual exchange between men and women as the most productive way to arrive at social truth and future programs for social change. As we shall see, however, power relations between male and female members in places like the Men and Women's Club were in fact less symmetrical than club rules mandated. Many advanced women, who were deeply preoccupied with aspects of the Woman Question, found their concerns unwelcome and their personal status marginal in these societies. Other women were reluctant to introduce topics specific to women's interests, fearful that these topics would jeopardize their equal standing in the group. Most of them, however, felt exhilarated, if frustrated, by the new social experiment.[88]

For men and women, discussion clubs were a way station in a personal quest for a new spiritual and social identity: political women, like Besant and Muller, might begin with the Browning, Fabian, or the Men and Women's Club and then gravitate to other heterosocial spaces such as theosophy, where women occupied a more privileged position as centers of spiritual power and knowledge, and where the boundaries of gender, sexual orientation, and the unitary, coherent self were tested. In the early 1880s, the leading female theosophist in London was the "divine" Anna Kingsford, tall, pale, and beautiful, an alluring and inspirational woman who thought she could destroy her enemies—the deadly materialist vivisecting scientists—with a single spiritual blast. Her friends liked to think of her as a reincarnation of the Goddess Isis herself. "[S]he seemed to me the living type of what a goddess should and does look like!," declared her friend Isabelle de Steiger.[89] In the mid-1880s, Kingsford's leadership and platform charisma were challenged by an even more exotic transgressor, Madame Helena Blavatsky, who was in London trying to launch a branch of her Theosophical Society. An elderly "foreign" lady with a shady personal past, a cigar-smoking bohemian with a flair for self-dramatization, dressed in "orientalist" attire, Blavatsky exerted a decidedly sexually ambiguous power over men and women. Annie Besant, who would soon convert to theosophy, remembered the erotic power of "H.P.B."'s "compelling eyes" and "yearning voice" that provoked in Besant "a well-nigh uncontrollable desire to bend down and kiss her."[90]

Female memoirists identified with the sense of adventure as well as the vulnerability associated with the new style of independent womanhood. The pleasures and dangers of being alone in the city excited the imagination of female contemporaries. Writing to her sister Eleanor from "exile" in a working-class suburb of Paris, Jenny Marx recollected with pleasure her trips by underground to "Farrington Street, where when I was not sti-fling with asthma I could at least indulge in my morning daily, and on alighting could run down the muddy Strand and stare at the advertise-ments." Among the most intrepid urban adventurers were secondary-school teachers whose salary allowed them to explore the commercial attractions of London. "I was very happy in London," remembered Margaret Nevinson; "I liked the freedom, especially when I got a latch-key, the symbol of bachelor independence." As a young teacher, Molly Hughes rebuffed the offer of a man to see her home after an evening entertainment. " 'Thank you,' said I, 'but I can get a bus all the way from Gower Street to Kensington and there are no real dangers on the route'."⁹¹

"Real dangers" presented themselves in other guises. Glorified Spin-sters who lacked an independent income or family support and who had to struggle with a life of genteel poverty recalled the difficulty of eking out a living and residing in inadequate, cramped lodgings. When W. T. Stead in-troduced a series on "Women who Work" in the *PMG*, he began with a preliminary conversation with Miss King at the office of the Society for the Promotion of the Employment of Women. "Whatever you do," she warned him, "don't make it out that it is an easy thing for women to gain a liveli-hood." Rachel McMillan's first venture into the "open market of woman's labour" was as a "helper" and junior superintendent in a working girl's home in Bloomsbury. Margaret McMillan, her sister and biographer, soon joined her in this "anxious, eager, perilous life." Their fellow residents, shopgirls, office workers, and students, held "ill paying jobs precariously," and were "in constant danger of losing them altogether." They all "won-dered at the new untried element and felt a thrill of hope . . . as they realised they were afloat . . . for the first time."⁹²

Margaret McMillan, an orphan raised in genteel surroundings, associ-ated urban adventure with a transgression of gendered class identity. "We lived the life of adventures," she recalled of her Bloomsbury days, prepared to "take our chance," in the "roaring boundless human sea" "strewn with wrecks." Identification with her fellow residents meant embracing an exis-tence outside the constraints of genteel femininity, taking one's "chance" in the "roaring boundless human sea." Like male novelists of the 1880s, she associated the anonymous freedom of the streets with the condition of the shopgirl, self-supporting and self-reliant, but ambiguously attached to the market. Her liminal consciousness resembled that of the female pro-tagonist of Gissing's *In the Year of the Jubilee*, Nancy Lord, who found herself in a similar déclassé state when she managed to escape her escort and merge with the "millions walking about the streets because it was Jubilee Day." "Nancy forgot her identity, lost sight of herself as an individual. She did not think, and her emotions differed little from those of any shop-girl let loose."[93]

The New Woman's Social Influence

The independent, "advanced" woman constituted a small percentage of the female population in London; yet her public vitality and the discourses surrounding her exerted a powerful, informing presence in contemporary discussions of gender. Knowledge of "the type," as we have seen, could be acquired by sightings across the public spaces of London, but also by reading countless newspaper and magazine accounts of her. They ranged from a cartoon in *Punch*, to an article in *Tit-Bits* on "The Lives that Girton Girls Lead," to ponderous disquisitions on the mental and physical capacities of women in the *Nineteenth Century*, to letter correspondence in the *Woman's Penny Paper* on the "manly woman." The late eighties also witnessed an extraordinary level of public debate and criticism of marriage in its relationship to both prostitution and voluntary spinsterhood.[94]

Fiction also played a central role in disseminating knowledge of the New Woman. Olive Schreiner claimed to have received hundreds of letters from readers of her New Woman novel, *The Story of an African Farm* (1883), "from all classes of people, from an Earl's son to a dressmaker in Bond Street, and from a coalheaver to a poet." When Mary Brown, Schreiner's friend, asked a Lancashire working woman what she thought of *The Story of an African Farm*, a "strange expression" came into her face as she said, "'I read parts of it over and over.' 'What parts?' I asked, and her reply was, 'About yon poor lass [Lyndall, the protagonist],' and with a far off look in her eyes added, 'I think there is hundreds of women what feels like that, but can't speak it, but *she* could speak what we feel'."[95]

The New Woman set a standard against which others felt compelled to measure themselves. This included "womanly women" of the middle classes, even those who deprecated female emancipation, but who nonetheless attended lectures on the "Progress of Women" or confronted friends who talked of "emancipation from the shackles of home and hearth." Lower-middle-class and working-class women also positioned themselves in relation to a new, assertive, self-confident urban style. Even the *Girl's Own Paper*, a great defender and interpreter of domestic femininity to lower-middle-class and working-class girls, began by the late 1880s to run articles on working women and demanded equal pay for equal work. Its pages testify to the contradictions experienced by girls in the last quarter of the century, between new personal aspirations for independence and conventional family expectations. In 1889, it ran a series on "How Working Girls Live in London," and insisted that "the girl who by steady industry makes a living for herself need be in no haste to change her condition." This independence, it argued, "is one of the present features of a working girl's life." In its "Answers to Correspondents," it rebuked an "Old Maid" for wanting to marry: "But why should you think it so desirable to marry?" In another issue, it instructed "An Ignorant One" that there "would be no difficulty getting a flat in London, and the best way for you to proceed would be to find a lady to share it with you."[96]

Cultural Crossovers to Working-Class Women

On the whole, historians have assumed an impenetrable class divide, beyond which the cultural example of the New Woman could not permeate. The middle-class independent woman might refuse to accept the place laid down for her by others, but, insists David Rubinstein, "The experience of the working-class girl . . . was another matter." With the exception of the northern-based Women's Cooperative Guild in the nineties, he observes little evidence of a stirring of consciousness or movement for personal change among working-class women. "Exploited by their husbands, by their employers, by society at large, most working-class women were in no position to rebel against social injustice."[97]

To be sure, the life-style of philanthropic spinsters often provoked incomprehension and hostility from their working-class charges. "Ye're losing yer chances, y'know," jam-girls and mill-girls taunted independent woman Margaret McMillan, who ran a class for Whitechapel factory girls in the late 1880s. The material conditions of working-class women were certainly less conducive to fantasies of female autonomy and self-creation. Yet signs of gender unrest may still be detected in the lives of individual working women and in the collective experience of women drawn into the vortex of political and religious activity in the 1880s.[98]

Prominent among the new entrants to the public sphere were the Hallelujah Lasses of the Salvation Army. Their presence signaled a new style of working-class woman, with a new relation to the family, to social destiny, to the city as a place of experience and adventure. The Salvation Army gave religious expression to women (and men's) dissatisfaction with the organization of gender within the working class, at the same time that it contained and channeled discontent into obedience to a highly authoritarian institution.

Like the Glorified Spinster, the Hallelujah Lass emerged as a "new species" of working womanhood who both challenged and accommodated herself to conventions of gender. Through her public activity, the female salvationist stretched the boundaries of a working woman's space and prerogatives within her community and impinged on the civic spaces of her class superiors. She resembled contemporary platform women in manifesting a gift of speech and a willingness to be a visible presence in the world. Unlike political orators such as Annie Besant and Eleanor Marx, who "thrust" themselves "before the world" on their own merits, Salvationist women relied on the traditional sanction of religious inspiration and the more innovative fact of institutional endorsement of the Army itself. In so doing, female salvationists followed the lead of Catherine Booth in legitimizing female ministry, but they rejected Booth's "genteel" mode of preaching in favor of a more popular "rough-and-ready" performance style appropriate to proletarian audiences.[99]

To many hostile critics, the presence of "Happy Elizas" in the streets epitomized the disruptive, "rowdy," circuslike character of the Army's street activities.[100] In contrast, Christian feminists like Josephine Butler and W. T. Stead praised the Army for providing working women with an "honourable livelihood" and new public dignity. "Whatever else General Booth and his wife have failed to do, they have at least accomplished one notable thing," the *Pall Mall Gazette* observed with more than a whiff of condescension in 1884: "they have created a new career for women." Out of servant girls and factory hands, the "inventors" of the "Hallelujah Lasses" had created nearly one thousand evangelists, capable of "addressing large audiences, performing heavy pastoral work and management of the affairs, financial and otherwise, of mission stations." Butler waxed even more enthusiastic: not only had the Army "absorbed" a portion of "surplus womanhood," it had disciplined and drilled a number of "our women of humbler ranks" for public work, elevating them above class limitations into the embodiment of a gracious national womanhood, "singularly free of affectation."[101]

The spectacle of women offering salvation in the streets helped the Army to expand beyond its initial base in Whitechapel to become a national institution. Female preachers, argued Catherine Booth, attracted more attention than brass bands, uniforms, music-hall songs, and mass advertising and leafletting. Women were more successful in "gaining the ear of the people" than men. "No doubt . . . generations of the suppression of woman, and the consequent prejudice and curiosity with respect to her public performances, conspire immensely towards her attracting the people." As a rule, she continued, "we have only to announce in any city, town or neighborhood that meetings will be conducted by women, and, no matter what the place or the hour, the building will be crowded to its ut-most."[102]

To attract sinners to its "penitent form," the Army manipulated a double image of the female salvationist as public woman: she was simultaneously a disorderly woman of the streets, renowned for her spontaneity, physical courage and pluck, and an embodiment of national womanhood, "free of affectation."[103] In a style pioneered in the late 1870s by "Happy Eliza" Haynes, who dashed up and down the back streets with "streamers falling from her unbraided hair," an army of "loud-voiced fearless preach-eresses" regularly opened fire on the "heathen masses" by rushing like a "whirlwind" through the "haunts" of vice, shouting invitations to the meetings.[104] Alternatively, the Salvationist woman cultivated a more re-spectable demeanor: dressed in "military" uniform, topped by a "Quaker-like bonnet," she presented herself as an androgynous figure, whose liminality allowed her to travel through a range of social spaces in London. The Army uniform enabled her to cross over to the West End; it also marked her off visually from the "dangerous" fallen women of Piccadilly and protected her from "male pests" while serving on midnight patrol.[105]

It did not render Army officers invisible: on the contrary, the red jersey with the Army's name emblazoned in yellow as well as the "boisterous high spirits" of "bonneted Amazons" contrasted sharply with the discrete body language and neutral tones adopted for street dress by middle-class women. Whereas ladies were intent on speeding through London without incident, Hallelujah Lasses were intent on creating *incidents,* exhibiting their "unselfish abandonment" to attract "great rough men" to the peni-tent form.[106]

Salvation Army women made public spectacles of themselves, but they also orchestrated public spectacles of men, who struggled for a new mas-culine identity. The lasses' main targets were the "worst characters" with whom they "grappled" in "deadly spiritual conflict." Navvies, boxers, fighting sweeps, converted guzzlers all testified to the power of "spiritual womanhood": "nobody ever [before] fetched tears to their eyes . . . not even within an hour and three quarters battering in the ring." By reducing laboring men to tears and transforming them into speaking subjects, female preachers attracted enormous audiences, who arrived in droves "to look at the Bills and Dicks, the prizefighters and bird and dog fanciers, who have been converted, and . . . they come still more to hear them speak." Salvationist women took special pride in converting wife-beaters and drunkards. Converted men, asserted Army leaders, produced "happy homes, happy wives, happy children, and money to spare." In demanding that men abjure their former leisure habits and live peacefully with their wives, the Army gave "expression to struggles over resources," argues historian Pamela Walker: "women objected to sons spending money on beer and betting and rebelled against a masculinity that affirmed men's prerogative to spend their wages on such leisure pursuits."[107]

To reach women, Army lasses had to engage in house-to-house visitation. Building on the tradition of Ranyard Bible women, female Salvationists in East London practiced rescue and slum work in their own neighborhoods well before it had become an important program of the Army in the mid-1880s. To be sure, there were significant differences between the Army "slum saviours" and middle-class female philanthropists—slum saviours lived among the poor, on approximately the same material level, they performed domestic chores for their poor neighbors, and they could speak in their idiom. Yet the women who underwent training in slum work could also articulate a distancing rhetoric and romance of philanthropy that approximated the speech of their middle-class counterparts. When respectable workingwomen from the north of England or from other parts of London were sent to slum stations in Whitechapel or Seven Dials they registered shock at the "buying and sellin, the drink, the sin, the bairns wi hardly any clothes,—oh its awful." Bessie Wilkins's account of her recruitment to slum work suggests the literary shaping of her encounter with "Outcast London": while working as a housemaid in Northamptonshire, she read about slum work in the *War Cry.* "When I read of the slum work it made me so miserable I used to say I'd never read any more. But as soon as the 'Cry' came, I'd have to."[108]

The match-girl strike of 1888 represented another strategic encounter between a new style of womanhood and Outcast London. Known for their "rough-and-ready manners," the "freedom" of their walk, the "numbers" of their friends, the "shrillness" of their laughter, and the flamboyance of their Sunday dress, the match girls of Bow were even more unlikely participants in the public sphere than the Hallelujah Lasses. Their brash street-style notwithstanding, matchmakers were vulnerable, unskilled workers in an unregulated labor market, who did not present themselves as likely heroines of labor militancy. Yet their demonstration of mass solidarity in 1888 set off a new pattern of unionization, whose effects, historians of labor have argued, extended well beyond the boundaries of the East End. The alliance between Outcast London and the new collectivist spirit of middle-class reform had a very strong gender component. If the match girl strike "sparked off" new unionism, the explosive tinder turned out to be the alliance between young women demanding their rights and their "pennies" and the charismatic New Woman, in the person of the indomitable Annie Besant.[109]

To contemporaries, the "notable" victory in 1888 of the match girls against the firm of Bryant and May demonstrated how, with the aid of a "sympathetic" press and public opinion, "the poorest and most helpless portion of the industrial community" could triumph over "the wealthiest and most powerful firms in the metropolis." Most chroniclers of the strike have credited Besant with masterminding the strike from start to finish, paying special tribute to her "indefatigable energy" and to the skill with which she "aroused public opinion in a manner never before witnessed." Through a brilliant orchestration of publicity, they argue, Besant and her collaborators transformed the match girls into a vivid spectacle of outcast and sweated London, underpaid, undernourished, subject to "Phossy Jaw," yet rising from the abyss to do battle with their oppressors.[110]

This interpretation derives from Besant's own account of the strike, in which she featured herself as the heroine of the story while casting doubt on the match girls' capacity to be effective social actors. Only a few contemporaries, notably the feminist leaders of the Women's Trade Union League, challenged Besant's star billing by emphasizing the solidarity and energy of the match girls themselves. Anxious to make the factory girls the agents and heroines of their own success, these feminists ascribed the "great success of the movement" to the "discipline, unity and steadiness of the girls themselves."[111]

Besant's narration of the events, first recounted in the *Link,* the left-wing journal inaugurated by Besant and Stead in response to Bloody Sunday and its repercussions, began with her attendance at a meeting of the Fabian Society at which Clementina Black of the Women's Trade Union League delivered a paper on female labor. In the discussion that followed, H. H. Champion drew attention to the working conditions at Bryant and May. When Besant and Herbert Burrows visited the factory and interviewed three girls, they heard complaints of bullying foremen, irregular lunch hours, penny fines for various minor infractions, including dirty feet. The girls were particularly indignant over the deduction of a shilling as a compulsory contribution to a statue of Gladstone. Besant published their complaints in the *Link* under the title, "White Slavery in London," in which she contrasted the girls' low wages to the high dividends of 23 percent enjoyed by the shareholders, many of them clergymen.[112]

Shortly after the publication of the article, Besant and Burrows stood at the gates of the match factory distributing the article to the girls as they came out. Yet Besant was skeptical of the ability of unskilled workers to sustain an organized resistance and criticized the Women's Trade Union League's call for organization and action among the unskilled female workers. As a consequence, when Besant received a letter thanking her for the "kind interest you have taken in us poor girls," she "little guessed" that it was "the signal of a coming storm." A week later, between one and two hundred match girls "flocked down" to Fleet Street to the office of the *Link*, provoking "considerable excitement"; they cheered vigorously as they saw the photograph of Annie Besant in the window. A delegation of "three sturdy respectable women" entered the *Link* offices "and told their story." The foreman had tried to pressure the girls to sign a paper repudiating Besant's assertions; the girls refused to sign—"You had spoke up for us and we weren't going back on you." When one girl identified as a ring-leader was fired, her workmates put down their tools, and the action spread to 1,400 more. An offer was made to take back the girl, "but the spirit of revolt against cruel oppression had been aroused, and they declared they would not go in 'without their pennies'."[113]

"'Can you help us?' This was the question asked of Annie Besant by look and gesture rather than by word." Besant, assisted by Burrows, quickly swung into action. She helped to organize them into a union, exposed the threats of their employers, called for donations for a strike fund, persuaded the London Trades Council to take up the cause (it successfully negotiated a settlement with Bryant and May), and announced meetings and demonstrations in four dailies—the *Pall Mall Gazette*, the *Star*, the *Daily News*, and the *Echo*—that agreed to publish her announcements. Some of her publicity stunts bore the marks of her "special touch," observes Asa Briggs: "she was said to have been greeted with delight when she carried a bunch of roses to the match girls in the Fairfield Works; they 'literally danced for joy'."[114]

Perhaps most striking, and politically ambiguous, was the manipulation of the spectacle of the girls themselves. A range of contemporaries—middle-class socialists, trade-union supporters of the strike, feminist reformers, the sympathetic daily press and its correspondents—interpreted the meaning of the match girls' actions through a number of conflicting discursive systems. Some, like Besant, struggled to credit the match girls with some agency as the "heroines of the hour," yet all incorporated them as figures of a degenerate urban landscape.

"They are just the girls that one reads about in a story of outcast London," declared the *Star*. "Clad in old, worn-out jaded jackets, or in ragged shawls and bedraggled skirts . . . they made indeed a strange gathering." "Bleer-eyed, with shiny skin, unnatural color, and misshapen features—their very physiognomy speaks of the hard life they live."[115] In an effort to soften the determinist analysis somewhat, the *Star* went on to attribute "this physical degeneration" "to their social environment rather than to the girls themselves." Besant and others presented the procession of match girls as a benign mockery of the danger fantasized by wealthy West Enders when demonstrations of "King Mob" passed through their part of town in 1886 and 1887. While the match girls presented no threat of revolution, to some they did epitomize the everpresent danger of female destitution descending into immorality. One commentator voiced a fear that, for these girls, "living amidst the most vicious and depraved surroundings,"[116] vice followed close on the heels of poverty and disease. "Although the girls bear good character for respectability," reported the *Echo*, "so large a number . . . out of employment, leading listless, idle lives, will . . . increase an already prominent social evil in the crowded districts bordering on Whitechapel."[117]

However much environmentally produced, the match girls constituted a curious "assembly" to be demanding national recognition and attention. It remained a challenge for their supporters to construct these "products of the slums" as "Heroines of the Hour." The *Pall Mall Gazette* declared itself unable to find a girl to interview, save one: "The girls are densely illiterate and quite unable to state their affairs." The *Link* took a more intermediate position. It deployed familiar tropes of bodily degeneration to describe a delegation of match girls who marched to Westminster to lay their grievances before sympathetic M. P.'s—"pale, thin, and underfed . . . their very appearance eloquent of hard labor unfit for childish frames," "representing the suffering of the East"; but it still tried to construct them as speaking subjects. When twelve matchmakers were admitted to the House of Commons, they "told their own story and answered a number of questions put to them by the hon. members which showed how much might be made of them under fair and wholesome life-conditions."[118]

Other feminists offered a more optimistic perspective. For radical women in the Women's Trade Union League, to construe these women as helpless was to admit they could not be organized. As a consequence, women like Clementina Black and Frances Hicks, who urged women to combine and to help themselves, tried to discern features of the match girls' own culture and values that would make them susceptible to "stirrings of consciousness" or desire for change. "There is very much that is robust, independent, and womanly in the honest factory girl," concluded Hicks, who observed that short, localized strikes "are by no means so uncommon among girls as some think." Hicks noted their "boldness in company," their "genuine good-heartedness," and their "strict adherence to their own code of honour." Yet eugenic concerns over race deterioration constantly intruded into the picture: "Fashionable 'slumming' only petrifies and repels the object of curiosity," Hicks continued, "but a careful examination of the causes of all that is deteriorating our present generation of mothers is most necessary." One hope lay in the entry of matchmakers into the public life of the nation, an experience in discipline and organization that Charles Booth and others believed would extricate the casually employed from the abyss of Outcast London and, from a feminist perspective, would incorporate working women into the social contract of civil society.[119]

In the pages of the daily and periodical press, protesting workers, platform women, girls in business, and Glorified Spinsters appeared as telling and disturbing signs of modernity. Their presence challenged the spatial boundaries—of East and West, of public and private—that Victorian writers on the metropolis had imaginatively constructed to fix gender and class difference in the city. However stylized, these figures signaled the forceful entry of diverse social constituencies, each with different claims to political and social authority, into a fractured, heterogeneous public sphere. As one marginal group after another endeavored to establish its place and viewpoint in the urban panorama, it often found its example emulated, incorporated, or contested by another constituency.

Sensational media stories of sexual danger that were produced in this decade both highlighted and managed the boundary disputes paradigmatic of metropolitan life. Spectacular narratives like the "Maiden Tribute," to be explored in the next two chapters, turned on the seeming paradox of the city as a place of danger and possibility for women. As cautionary tales, such narratives functioned as counterweights to the fantasies of access and movement that also compelled Londoners in this period. Yet the telling of these stories helped to consolidate a new public sphere and to publicize the presence of new social actors in a national political culture. Disciplining as well as inciting, fictions of sexual danger significantly shaped the way men and women of all classes made sense of themselves and their urban environment.

THREE

"*The Maiden Tribute of Modern Babylon*"

n 4 July 1885, W. T. Stead, the editor of the *Pall Mall Gazette*, issued a "frank warning" to readers. All those "who are squeamish, and all those who are prudish, and all those who prefer to live in a fool's paradise of imaginary innocence and purity, selfishly oblivious of the horrible realities which torment those whose lives are passed in the London inferno, *will do well not to read the Pall Mall Gazette of Monday and the following days.*"[1] As "Chief Director" of a "Secret Commission," he and others had spent the last four weeks painstakingly investigating the traffic in girls in London's vice emporiums. Stead published his "findings" in a four-part series, the "Maiden Tribute of Modern Babylon," one of the most successful pieces of scandal journalism of the nineteenth century.

The "Maiden Tribute" documented in lurid detail how poor "daughters of the people" were "snared, trapped, and outraged, either when under the influence of drugs or after a prolonged struggle in a locked room."[2] The series had an electrifying effect: by the third installment, mobs of "gaunt and hollow-faced men and women with trailing dress and ragged coats" were rioting at the *Pall Mall Gazette* offices, in an attempt to obtain copies of the paper. When W. H. Smith, the newsagent, refused to carry it, the *PMG* relied on newspaper boys and volunteers to sell copies on the streets. George Bernard Shaw, thrilled with its indictment of the vicious upper classes, offered his services to hawk "as many quires of the paper as I can carry" on any thoroughfare in London.[3] The *PMG*'s advertising placards

—"Five pounds for a virgin warranted pure"—were as sensational as Stead's subheadings. Two fifteen-year-old girls were reputedly accosted outside the Charing Cross Station by a hawker crying out, "Come on Miss 'ave a copy. This'll show you 'ow to earn five pounds."[4]

Telegraphic services rapidly transformed the "Maiden Tribute" into an international event. Stead proudly boasted that his "revelations" were printed in every capital of the Continent as well as by the "purest journals in the great American republic." Unauthorized reprints were said to have surpassed the one and a half million mark. Not surprisingly, the other London dailies were furious and jealous, at first stonily ignoring the crusade and then condemning it as "the vilest parcel of obscenity." Unsympathetic members of Parliament called for the paper's prosecution under the obscenity laws, and indignant fathers, concerned about the effect of the stories on innocent family members, canceled their subscriptions to the *PMG*.[5]

Nonetheless, Stead's campaign forced the passage of age-of-consent legislation that had been stalled in Parliament for years. An enormous public demonstration was held in Hyde Park (estimated at 250,000) to demand the enforcement of the new legislation. Meanwhile, plans were underway to prosecute Stead for committing precisely the same crime, the purchase of a young girl in the London "slave" market, that he had set out to expose. Throughout the autumn of 1885, the same newspapers that maintained a "conspiracy of silence" against the "Maiden Tribute" devoted considerable space to Stead's ensuing trial, during which they tried to transform Stead from a campaigning hero to a denigrated criminal faced with a prison sentence. This worked in the short run only, for Stead emerged after three months from Holloway Prison a martyr to the cause of social justice and social purity.

The political effects of the "Maiden Tribute" were as startling as its dramatic unfolding. The Criminal Law Amendment Act of 1885 not only raised the age of consent for girls from thirteen to sixteen, but it also gave police far greater power to prosecute streetwalkers and brothel-keepers. In addition, the act made indecent acts between consulting male audits illegal, thus forming the basis of legal proceedings against male homosexuals until 1967. The excitement generated by the "Maiden Tribute" also stimulated grass-roots political activity: throughout Britain, social purity groups and vigilance committees were organized to oversee the local enforcement of the act. This loose network of campaigning groups, populist, feminist, and nationalist in their political zeal, was dedicated to eradicating vice and imposing a single standard of chastity on men and women.[6] Vigilance committees attacked music halls, theaters, and pornography as manifestations of "male lust"; their signal triumph, however, was to force police crackdowns on solicitation and brothel-keeping in the metropolis and the major provincial cities. Hence a massive political initiative against non-marital, nonreproductive sexuality was mobilized, whose initial victims were working-class prostitutes, precisely those women who had been the original objects of concern for Stead and his feminist allies. Repercussions from the "Maiden Tribute" were felt throughout the Empire, in the form of age-of-consent (marriage) laws, efforts to abolish state-regulated prostitution, and, eventually, official prohibitions against liaisons with "native" women.[7]

Quite a story. Historians who have considered it have tended to focus on one of three issues: the reliability of Stead as a narrator (whether or not he told the "truth"), his sexual psychology (his status as a latter-day Puritan whose "repressed sexuality" was the "motive force" of his activities, according to Havelock Ellis); or the impact of the "Maiden Tribute" and the legislation it provoked on class politics, the idea of childhood, and the political economy of sex. These are all important questions, which I intend to address as well, both in relation to each other and in connection to another area of inquiry, surprisingly ignored by previous commentators: the narrative of the "Maiden Tribute" itself.[8]

In imposing a certain narrative logic on the story of prostitution, "Maiden Tribute" exaggerated the role of children in the social economy of prostitution[9] and misrepresented the way young girls were recruited for the streets. Even Stead's account of his own purchase of a young girl for five pounds remains an indeterminate and unreliable narrative. I am nonetheless interested in why the "Maiden Tribute"'s distorted representation of prostitution was compelling to a variety of social constituencies; how it ordered people's experience and helped to construct a sexual subjectivity for men and women.

By focusing on narrative, I hope to explore how cultural meanings around sexual danger were produced and disseminated in Victorian society, and what were their cultural and political effects. Narratives of the "real," such as history and news reporting, impose a formal coherence on events: they "narrativize" data into a coherent "well-made" tale, converting "chaotic experience into meaningful moral drama."[10] Yet different narrative forms construct different worlds of meanings marked by different levels of coherence, integrity, fullness, and closure. They address different audiences and accord varying degrees of agency to their main characters. In all such narrative forms, meanings are structured textually through a set of conventions that establish a flexible contract between a writer and her/his readers for making sense of experience. These conventions and their systematic deviations provide "clues," to quote Fredric Jameson, "which lead us back to the concrete historical situation of the individual text itself, and allows us to read its structure as ideology, as a socially symbolic act, as a prototypical response to a historical dilemma."[11] Despite this "flexible contract," narratives may also provoke an unexpected set of reader responses.

Stead intended the "Maiden Tribute" to "rouse the nation" by purifying "the heart with the emotion of pity and horror." To establish an "emotional bond" between himself and a new mixed-class public, he introduced the New Journalism: that "personal style, that trick of bright colloquial language, that wealth of intimate picturesque detail, and that determination to arrest, amuse or startle." By incorporating into his pages new topics and new voices (via the "universal interview"), Stead tried to democratize the newspaper and make it less estranged from ordinary "daily life." At a time when urban life seemed to segment the "public" from the "private" and to isolate the "classes" from the "masses," Stead introduced human interest stories that exposed the secrets of the rich and incited sympathy for the domestic plight of the poor.[12]

Through the New Journalism, Stead helped to mainstream a commercial formula already in practice since the 1840s among the half-penny Sunday newspapers, such as the *News of the World, Reynolds' Newspaper,* and *Lloyd's Weekly Newspaper.* The Sundays had already reshaped the staid format of news reporting of respectable dailies by incorporating narrative codes of popular literature, organized around themes of sex and crime, and by refashioning the prurient exposé style of the "crim. con." and "bon ton" journals of the early Victorian years.[13] In the process, these newspapers linked sexual concerns to national and class concerns, thus constructing sexual issues as news. By adapting these techniques to a gentleman's newspaper that sold for one penny, Stead extended this news presentation to a more elite readership. He elevated sexual narratives to the level of sexual scandal, to a social drama that exposed social divisions and forced people to take sides.[14]

Stead constructed sexual danger as a national issue for a national readership, building on the prior reform agitation against the state regulation of prostitution and the grass-roots organizing efforts of an emerging social purity movement. He tried to transform the newspaper into a public forum of critical opinion for an expanded public, one that would include working people and women traditionally excluded from what Habermas has described as the classical "bourgeois public sphere." This expanded public sphere would be the place, as critic Simon Watney put it, where "modern society and individuals made sense of themselves," where symbols, images and words circulated that provided "the basic raw materials from which human subjectivity is constructed." Stead hoped to harness those structures of feeling to fashion a new political formation under his own editorial direction, to construct a "Government by Journalism."[15]

Stead's project was both controlling and inciting, inclusive and restrictive, unifying and fragmenting. Contributing to these contradictory effects was the heterogeneous nature of the newspaper page: on contiguous pages and columns appeared numerous subgenres—weather reports, shipping news, foreign and domestic news, police columns, correspondence columns, and human interest interviews—all with different pretensions to factuality or opinion, as well as different relations between author and readers. One consequence of this mixed format was to represent a world in flux, fragmented and disconnected. Stead further encouraged a proliferation of meaning by shifting genres within his narrative account of the "Maiden Tribute," by reporting the multiple perspectives of readers to the "Maiden Tribute" through the "universal interview," and by reprinting both supportive and critical commentary of the "Maiden Tribute" from the contemporary press.

Stead also tried to impose a totalizing unity on this multiplicity. Although he opened his pages to new social constituencies, the editorial and reportorial tone of the *Pall Mall Gazette* addressed a "unified general public" that submerged class, age, ethnicity, and any particularity into a single moral entity. Like Henry Mayhew and Frederick Greenwood before him, Stead established a special personal relationship to this general readership. Through his own first-person narratives he spoke directly to his "mass" readership, vividly conveying the experiential quality of his own excursion into the urban unknown—in a way that demanded a response.

Melodramatic Tradition and the "Maiden Tribute"

To construct his narrative, Stead drew on older cultural forms—particularly melodrama and the literature of urban exploration—but grafted on newer forms—late-Victorian pornography and fantasy, the Gothic fairy tale—that were also not of his own construction. Through this mélange, he produced an unstable text and a contradictory, obsessive discourse around sexuality that remain a legacy for the modern era. His narrative was taken up, reworked by different constituencies and social forces. These multiple transformations gave rise to complex political effects, which were not exhausted in the nineteenth century.

In the "Maiden Tribute," Stead used the journalistic innovations of the New Journalism to tell an old story of the seduction of poor girls by vicious aristocrats. Traditionally, this story had been cast in political terms as a melodrama, a form that allowed the weak to speak out and gain agency in their own defense. Melodrama dramatically expressed a language of politics that had tremendous currency throughout most of the nineteenth century. As the "man who wrote the Maiden Tribute," Stead proudly positioned himself in relation to this political tradition as the champion of working people and women. Yet he wrote in a different direction from earlier feminist melodramas and more traditional working-class forms. When Stead grafted pornographic scenarios onto melodrama and refocused the drama from the perspective of the elite male villain, he significantly transformed the story and its meanings.

Melodrama was the most important theatrical and literary form of the nineteenth century. Peter Brooks has located its historical formation in working-class theater of the early nineteenth century—in the vital, illegitimate popular theater that flourished on the margins, in the "Boulevards Du Crime" of Paris or in the unlicensed minor theaters of working-class districts in London. During the first half of the century, melodrama expanded rapidly beyond popular theater to shape both popular fiction and popular political discourse. As a "system of meaning," "a certain fiction system for making sense of experience," melodrama came to serve as a primary imaginative structure for a wide array of social constituencies.[16]

In both form and content, melodrama was an appropriate genre for working-class audiences, evoking the instability and vulnerability of their life in the unstable market culture of the early nineteenth century, where traditional patterns of deference and paternalism had been eroded. Below the surface order of reality lurked a terrible secret that could erupt unexpectedly with violence and irrationality. The melodramatic narrative acted arbitrarily, in its very structure calling into question the operation of law and justice. Melodramatic plots overwhelmingly reinforced the sense of destiny out of control; for most of the time, the villain remained in total command, ultimately overthrown not by reason but by chance, which in effect was the desire of the audience.[17]

The social meanings of melodrama were also responsive to the patriarchal and democratic expectations of its popular audience. In domestic melodrama, melodrama's most popular form, class exploitation—that terrible secret—was imaginatively represented and personalized as sexual exploitation of the daughter, which was a threat to family hierarchy and an infringement of male working-class prerogatives. A familial drama was thereby entwined with a class drama, as represented in the erotic triangle of upper-class male villain, passive plebeian hero or grieving father, and passive, victimized heroine. Melodrama also celebrated the firm boundaries of the home, as a haven in a heartless world, a trope that tended to erase women's larger social connections and resources beyond the home as well as the intensity of female domestic labor within its walls. As historian Anna Clark suggests, melodrama could condense the diverse experiences of family economies found among working people into a nostalgic evocation of a patriarchal golden age which functioned as a rhetorical foil for the miseries of the present.[18]

Melodrama became a customary and familiar form of storytelling that was widely deployed in radical politics, in good part because the melodramatic representation of power and virtue was entirely compatible with the democratic, antiaristocratic, and antistatist traditions of popular radicalism.[19] The attack on aristocratic seducers, for example, became a rallying cry in the anti-Poor-Law campaign of the 1830s. According to nearly every radical newspaper of the period, the Bastardy Clauses were introduced to "screen a vile aristocracy, who seduce and ruin more young girls than all the male population put together."[20] However much this political melodrama entailed a displacement of sexual danger and oppression outside the working class, it nonetheless inserted gender into the discussion of class politics. It placed women on the political agenda and acknowledged them as members of a class community for whom men struggled.[21]

Feminist critics Martha Vicinus and E. Ann Kaplan have pointed out that melodrama particularly appealed to female audiences, writers, and performers, precisely because it foregrounded issues of gender and power and highlighted the role of the heroine, however passive and suffering she might be. When middle-class female writers such as Mrs. Gaskell and Mrs. Wood produced literary melodramas in the mid-Victorian period, they extended the heroine's repertoire and revised melodrama's social meanings. In the women's fiction of the 1840s and 1850s, the fallen woman remained an object of charity and pity who was clearly proletarian; by the 1860s her class identity had shifted, and she became a genteel projection of the reader's own identity and the emblem of women's power and agency. The fiction of the mid-Victorian period articulated a new constellation of feeling and identification with the fallen woman's plight that found expression in feminist politics in the decades to come.[22]

One dramatic example of the power of literary melodrama to crystallize female reformist consciousness may be found in Josephine Butler's reminiscences about her own entry into rescue work. Butler identified Mrs. Gaskell's *Ruth* and the controversy surrounding its publication as the immediate circumstances that propelled her into "scavenger" work among "ruined" women in the 1850s. While living in Oxford with her clergyman-husband George (who was then an examiner at the university), Butler listened in silent anger to the denunciation of *Ruth* by the masculine society of "celibates" who assembled at her home in the evenings. "A moral sin in a woman was spoken as immensely worse than in a man; there was no comparison to be found between them. A pure woman, it was reiterated, should be absolutely ignorant of a certain class of ills in the world, albeit those evils bore with murderous cruelty on other women." Inwardly furious at the audacity and arrogance of one young man who "seriously declared that he would not allow his own mother to read such a book," she "resolved to hold my peace," to speak "little with men, but much with God." "Quietly," with the support of her husband, she began to seek out "ruined" women and welcome them into her home.[23]

Butler's rescue work took on new public dimensions in Liverpool in the 1860s. After the accidental death of her young daughter Eva, she "was possessed of an irresistible desire to go forth and find some pain keener than my own, to meet some persons more unhappy than myself . . . to say . . . I understand. I too have suffered." "It was not difficult to find misery in Liverpool," she wrote of her early social work there. In 1866, she began to work among the women of the Liverpool workhouse in the oakum shed, which functioned as a women's vagrant ward and Bridewell, where she practiced her transformative skills on the "wretched, draggled, ignorant" outcasts of the casual ward, persuading them to fall down on their knees and pray to Jesus. Butler's portrait of the women combined sympathy and social distance: they were poor dumb creatures, tamed and brought to Christ through her ministrations. The collective sound they emitted, she recalled, was more reminiscent of sacrificial lambs brought to slaughter than intelligent beings: "It was a strange sound, that united wail—continuous, pitiful, strong—like a great sigh or murmur of vague desire and hope, issuing from the heart of despair, piercing the gloom and murky atmosphere of that vaulted room, and reaching to the heart of God."[24]

From the workhouse, jails, and streets of Liverpool, Butler brought poor "ruined" young women, friendless, all physically worn out from their hard lives, to be nursed by her in her own home. Her widowed sister helped her in this "work without a name that came upon us." Butler kept a diary of her experiences with these dying girls, excerpts of which were published in the 1870s as antiregulationist propaganda, "The Dark Side of English Life: Illustrated in a Series of True Stories," and later included in her biography of her husband.[25] Butler's sketches of "Marion" and "Katie," of "Margaret" and "Emma" were literary melodramas, evocative of *Ruth* and the fallen-women fiction of the 1850s and 1860s. The narratives dramatize the same apotheosis of the fallen woman into saintly madonna that characterized Gaskell's novel, and they indict privileged men as the enemy. They assert a unified identity for women, an ideal of womanhood as "solidaire," yet they nonetheless reveal a complicated identification with the fallen woman as both a version of the self and residual Other.

The protagonists in Butler's sketches were dying magdalens who had finally found maternal protection and personal salvation under Butler's care. They were victims and heroines, "poor wandering lambs" ennobled by their suffering and sad life. Compared to the "outcasts" of the workhouses, these women were dignified, speaking subjects. Whatever their original class identity, as in literary melodrama, they tended to display "natural" refinement and gentility. Butler was originally attracted to Marion, her first case, when she saw her face, "full of piercing intelligence," across a crowded room. Laura, with her "white hands, dainty feet, graceful attire," had a "Queen-like" air and monumental grandeur even on her deathbed. Like Gaskell's Ruth, Butler's magdalens all died in a state of grace, having acquired spiritual insight and potency from their fall. Like the original Magdalen, they were closer to Christ for having sinned and been redeemed.[26]

Butler assumed a number of roles in these narratives: omniscient narrator, stage manager, and supportive, grieving mother. As narrator, she allowed her magdalens to voice their own anger, to "curse" men for their treachery. As stage manager, Butler provided the props for an appropriate deathbed scene. "I had filled Marion's coffin with white camellias, banking them all round her. With her hands crossed on her breast, and dressed as a bride for her Lord, she looked lovely." Butler also played the supportive role of mother to the girls. When she first met Marion she asked her, "Will you come home with me? I had a daughter once." As mother confessor (preempting her clergyman-husband) she reassured her dying magdalens about their spiritual future: Emma's "love for me," wrote Butler, "was very great—extraordinarily great. She seemed to think that whatever I said must be absolutely true—poor thing—and to take the hope of salvation on my word."[27]

It was as avenging mother that Butler assumed star billing. "Some years ago," she recounted, "I found a poor starved infant" whose mother sewed "hard, night and day, pale and lean, singing as well as her broken heart would let her."

I took it in my arms to the hotel where its father was staying for the hunting season. I held it up. "Look at him," I said, "Ay. look at him well, he resembles you, he is your son. Look well at him, for you will not see him again till he faces you at the last dread day." The man was glad to pay a pound or two to get rid of the annoyance, and then, springing into his "drag," with cigar in mouth, he lashed his horses off to the "meet."[28]

In this vignette, Butler has assembled and consolidated a series of visual and literary conventions associated with the fallen woman in the mid-Victorian period: the garret scene, the plight of the starving seamstress (reminiscent of Mrs. Trollope's *Jessie Phillips* and Gaskell's *Ruth*) seduced by an upper-class libertine, the sadistic hunter who whipped his horse as he had tortured and brutalized the violated maid. By inserting herself as a figure in the story, Butler accomplishes a series of substitutions. She replaces the wronged father of popular melodrama with an avenging mother who presents the magdalen's case to the dastardly seducer. But this self-presentation is also built on an alternative textual version that allowed the victim to speak out against male perfidy: according to this second version, Butler moves beyond the motherly vindication of suffering womanhood to actual impersonation of the magdalen herself. She shares the magdalen's sorrows but also her benediction.[29]

Butler's melodramatic performances acquired more notoriety and political meaning when, in the 1870s and 1880s, she and other feminists allied with radical workingmen and middle-class nonconformists to oppose the regulation of prostitution, as established under the Contagious Diseases Acts, and secured the repeal of those acts in 1886.[30] A desire to liberate women from male sexual tyranny and brutality led to feminist demands for "no secrets" on sexual questions. By setting a "floodlight" on men's "doings,"[31] respectable women asserted themselves in the public discussion of sexuality. During the repeal campaign, feminists staged two version of political melodrama: one that endorsed the model of female heroism celebrated in women's fiction and another that invoked the democratic and paternalist message of traditional stage melodrama.

Center stage in these public melodramas was the beautiful and histrionic figure of Butler, who combined in herself the role of prophet and suffering magdalen. A charismatic leader and gifted speaker, she inspired a personal loyalty among her female coworkers that bordered on idolatry. She and her female coworkers produced hundreds of pamphlets, edited numerous repeal periodicals, and mounted public platforms across the country to denounce the Acts as a "sacrifice of female liberties" to the "slavery of men's lust" and to describe in minute detail the "instrumental rape" of the internal examination.[32]

Although she had rarely spoken in public before 1869, Butler had been secretly and "inwardly" prepared by God through "sorrow" for her political mission. She believed that she received direct visions from God and that her mystical experience validated her right, as a woman, to speak out in public. In her political narratives, Butler superimposed her version of Christian eschatology upon a melodramatic narrative, integrating biblical references and prophetic insights into a secular political language that was radical, constitutional, and feminist. It was the role of the magdalen and the female prophet alike to suffer, to set a spiritual example.[33]

Butler played a crucial double role in the popular side of the repeal campaign, as principal propagandist and heroine/victim. To capture popular support, she resorted to daring acts of heroism that showed her solidarity with her fallen sisters. When a woman's meeting was held at Pontefract during the by-election of 1872, hired bullies "led by two persons whose *dress* was that of gentlemen" set bundles of straw afire while the metropolitan police casually looked on. Fortunately, "two or three working women placed themselves in front" of Butler and Charlotte Wilson, so that they could make their escape by jumping down the hatch of a trap-door: "It was not so much personal violence that we feared as what would have been to any of us *worse than death;* for the indecencies of the men, their gestures and threats, were what I would not like to describe."[34]

In these memoirs, Butler has presented us with a transformed melodrama, complete with stereotyped characters, extreme states of being and danger, rapid action, and the vindication of virtue over vice. In her melodrama, Butler emerges as the pure but not defenseless victim, threatened by the same sexual danger as her fallen sisters. No female villains appear in this narrative; only complicitous policemen and male brothel-keepers who "knew that their craft was in danger."[35] Her male friends were unable to protect her—only workingwomen could guide her to the trap door. Resourceful heroism was reserved for women.

"I always expected when it came to an election contest on this question that men's passions would be greatly roused and that the poorest among women would gather to us." Butler's repeal narratives assigned working-women a dignified place in the action, a voice and physical agency that extended even to the fallen. In Pontefract, a young Yorkshire woman, "strong and stalwart," with "bare muscular arms and a shawl over her head," came to her aid. In Colchester, Butler was protected by a "poorly-clad" "forlorn woman of the town."[36]

Fallen women appear in a number of guises in Butler's political melodrama. As heroines and victims, they ranged from pathetic and grateful ghostly figures of the night to defiant spokespersons for female indignation against the male conspiracy embodied by the Contagious Diseases Acts. In a series of public "letters" on the "Garrison Towns of Kent" (1870), Butler allowed fallen women to speak for themselves, indeed apparently to exercise more freedom of public expression than she did. The most powerful denunciation of men and male power emanated from a Chatham prostitute—a denunciation that conveniently incorporated the entirety of Butler's brief against the Acts: "It is *men, only men,* from the first to the last that we have to do with! To please a man I did wrong at first, then I was flung about from man to man. Men police lay hands on us. By men we are examined, handled, doctored. In the hospital it is a man again who makes prayer and reads the Bible for us. We are had up before magistrates who are men, and we never get out of the hands of men till we die!"[37]

Butler gave radical meaning to the melodramatic narrative of sexual danger by vindicating female activism, by dignifying the figure of the suffering fallen woman, and by inserting herself as a heroine/victim. She also celebrated a deferential politics of motherhood that aimed at subverting patriarchal authority: it gave mothers, not fathers, the right to control sexual access to the daughters. Butler tried to deploy the melodramatic convention of suffering womanhood to invert the prevailing view of "fallen women" as pollutants of men; instead she defended them as victims of male pollution, as women who had been invaded by men's bodies, men's laws, and by that steel penis, the speculum.

In other respects, her propaganda against the Acts faithfully adhered to the gender and class expectations of traditional stage melodrama. Feminist propaganda was severely constrained by a melodramatic vocabulary of female victimization, which demanded that registered women be innocent victims falsely entrapped into a life of vice—involuntary actors in their own history, without sexual passion, not yet "dead to shame," and still possessed of womanly "modesty."[38]

Butler also continued to represent regulationists as sadistic aristocratic villains who conspired to control women through state sanction and monopoly. The instrumental rape of registered women not only epitomized the villainous conspiracy of men, but it rendered that conspiracy even more sinister and perverse. In the name of medical science, it legitimated a cruel and unnatural sexual violation, one that inflicted pain and sexual mutilation on women. Whereas the rape/seduction scene occurred offstage in melodramatic fictions like *Ruth* or *East Lynne,* repealers made instrumental rape a vivid and dominant icon of the campaign. Detailed accounts of the instrumental rape figured prominently in repeal propaganda: "It is awful work; the attitude they push us into first is so disgusting and so painful, and then these monstrous instruments and they pull them out and push them in, and they turn and twist them about; and if you cry out they stifle you."[39]

With great success, Butler actively encouraged workingmen to inscribe themselves within a traditional configuration of melodrama, to assume their prerogatives and responsibilities as the grieving fathers or popular heroes who rescued the passive female victims from upper-class libertines. Repeal literature specifically warned workingmen and women that the Acts would impose "the disgusting examination under the Contagious Diseases Acts" on virtuous wives and daughters of workingmen. For their own part, radical workingmen readily integrated this propaganda into the traditional political categories of popular radicalism. *Reynolds News*, a popular Sunday paper that catered to working-class readers, dwelt at length on the "horrors" of the medical examination, detailing how it subjected women to "torture" and "physical pain," outraging their feelings and causing an "agony of shame." In this case it was a "Woman" correspondent who put the workingman's case for civic virtue: "I have asked myself, was it possible that men could be found in the medical profession to undertake these offices?" "I am answered, and am satisfied that nothing is too filthy, nothing too low, for the hands of an English gentleman." The political lesson was clear: let the aristocrats "rotting with disease and sensuality" be "dragged from the seats of power" and replaced by "our honored working men" who would never "sanction these Acts."[40]

Melodramatic scripts shaped popular expectations for the roles that diverse constituencies would play in the political drama over state regulation. Melodrama was a remarkably malleable cultural form, containing a variety of potential meanings and scenarios. Butler herself staged two versions of political melodrama. The melodrama of female heroism and self-sacrifice celebrated an informal cross-class alliance between feminists and "strong and stalwart" workingwomen. A more traditional version of melodrama reinstated workingmen as the heroes of the piece—allied politically with "noble self-denying ladies" but acting as responsible patriarchs within the working class. Propaganda of this sort aroused popular indignation against regulation, but it also buttressed a patriarchal stance and a sexual hierarchy within the organized working class that feminists had vigorously challenged in other contexts. In this and other ways, recourse to melodrama was a contradictory political strategy for feminists. Melodrama offered a powerful cultural resource for female political expression, but it set limitations on what could be said, particularly in relation to female agency and desire.

Much the same kind of criticism could be made of the "Maiden Tribute of Modern Babylon." By the mid-eighties melodrama's role as a unifying cultural form was in decline. Melodrama had to compete with other genres of literary and theatrical representation, both popular and elite. West End audiences no longer thrilled to the old-fashioned melodramas—they sometimes laughed at them (although East End audiences still enjoyed them "straight"). In progressive circles, the older languages of radicalism, into which the melodrama of seduction so comfortably fit, had to contend with more scientific approaches to philanthropy and socialism. Whereas melodrama had personalized good and evil, had called into question the smooth operation of reason and justice, and had identified the state with corrupt power, these new scientific and realist discourses tracked the regular operation of laws of nature and society and looked to impersonal forces, including the state, as agents of change.

Scientific and realist discourses marked important intellectual developments of the 1880s, but they did not fully supplant the older language of popular radicalism. Far "from falling into decline, popular radical traditions continued to live on," declares Patrick Joyce, and to find expression in anti-aristocratic politics, in politically centered notions of oppression and justice, and in populist mobilizations that emphasized harmonic aspects of respectable class identity rather than class divisions.[42]

The "Maiden Tribute" exemplifies the attractions of the older language of popular radicalism. It amply demonstrates how a story that was increasingly discredited in the West End theater could still be compelling in the pages of the daily press, where Stead was able to mount a public show that captured the imagination of all but the most skeptical political avant-garde (and outraged a few "vicious aristocrats"). The "Maiden Tribute" resembled popular fiction and drama in that it contained a criticism of the "vicious upper classes," but, as in the case of stage melodrama, this class criticism was immediately undercut by sentimental moralism and a focus on passive, innocent female victims and individual evil men that diverted attention away from the economic and social issues relating to prostitution.

Stead may have positioned himself publicly in relation to the populist traditions of political melodrama, but in fact he kept shifting genres throughout the "Maiden Tribute," moving from costume drama to detective fiction, constituting himself corresponding as a modern-day Theseus or as a more up-to-date scientific investigator. The instability of his text is apparent from the beginning, where he introduces the "Maiden Tribute" in multiple frames: endowing it with the status of an official report of a special commission, complete with an exhaustive list of charity agencies and expert witnesses, but then introducing it again as a modern-day rendition of a classical myth of sexual violence. These different frames signaled different modes of address and levels of representation. They allowed Stead to impersonate a range of characters: from "Chief Director" of the "Secret Commission," he metamorphosed into a voyeuristic explorer and shadowy villain; and then, as he sensed the danger of this identification, he retreated once more into the impersonal persona of the "Chief Director." His ultimate defense against villainous self-identity was to shift the narrative to the feminized world of the fairy tale and to transfer the role of villain to proletarian women. Having used women as the guide to the dark center, he finally came to represent them *as* the dark center.

In the "Maiden Tribute" Stead combined the seemingly incompatible sensibilities of male feminist and voyeur: he endorsed female emancipation, yet his masquerade enacted the unequal power relations that underwrote Victorian heterosexuality. Like Butler, Stead was a larger-than-life crusader for democracy, morality, and women's rights, a provincial radical who detested the London elite.[43] The son of a Congregational minister, he believed that he had a personal pipeline to God, whom he referred to as the "Senior Partner."[44] As editor of the Darlington *Northern Echo* (1871–80), the *Pall Mall Gazette* (1883–90), and the monthly *Review of Reviews* (1890–1912), he promoted a collection of feminist, populist, and nationalist causes, including women's suffrage, the expansion of women's employment, world peace and universal military service (of both men and women), a stronger navy, the Salvation Army, anti-vivisection, spiritualism, and social purity. A self-proclaimed Puritan "barbarian" from the North, he had always regarded London life as "destructive of vigor and earnestness" and steeped in "cynicism and indifference."[45] Nonetheless, his sense of "effective calling" persuaded him to accept the position of assistant editor on the *Pall Mall Gazette* in 1880; when he assumed the editorship three years later, he set out to transform the *PMG* from a "gentlemen's magazine . . . redolent of Society and the clubs" into an engine of social reform and collective moral renewal.[46] Through a series of successful "escapades" in the 1880s, ranging from exposés of slum housing to a defense of General Gordon in the Sudan, Stead constructed the New Journalism as a compelling genre. His efforts culminated in the "Maiden Tribute of Modern Babylon" and established Stead as a "controlling force in English public life."[47]

Through the political movements he aided and inspired, and through his powerful influence on the mass media, Stead provoked contradictions that, according to Michael Foucault, are at the heart of bourgeois sexuality. Stead simultaneously helped to amplify the fear of sexual danger for women and to mobilize public outcries against it. He privileged sexuality as an important core identity and private experience, believing that "in sex lies the divinist element of our nature," and he encouraged movements that suppressed public expressions of the "sexual," in part because he construed such expressions as dangerously tied to commerce and the market.[48] Yet his exposé of the London slave market was itself a commercial triumph (although it did little to boost the circulation of the *PMG* in the long run): a milestone in the history of the mass media, the "Maiden Tribute" ushered in a new epoch of mass-market fantasies and desires.

In 1885, criminal vice represented a new journalistic venture for Stead, although he had long sensed its potential as good political copy. He had always been "mad on the C.D. Acts"—and as editor of the *Northern Echo* in Darlington had "intermittently . . . given such support as I could to the cause of Repeal." Then, in 1876, Stead was "stirred" by Butler's accounts of her mission to the Continent and of the horrors of the Paris brothels, published under the title of *The New Abolitionists*. He wrote to her offering editorial assistance. The only effective way of grappling with the subject, he assured her, was to deal with its "tragic and pathetic side." In short, prostitution "wanted its Uncle Tom's Cabin"; but "Who was to be its Mrs. Stowe?"[49]

Nine years later, Butler took up Stead's offer and, along with Catherine Booth of the Salvation Army, appealed to him to step into Mrs. Stowe's role. After the suspension of the Contagious Diseases Acts in 1883, Butler and other purity reformers turned their attention to publicizing the evils of child prostitution and white slavery, but they had been unsuccessful at lobbying Parliament for legislation to deal with the traffic in girls.[50] Even after an 1881 House of Lords committee report documented a small international traffic in British girls and a scandal erupted over the "police coverup" of a fashionable procuress, Mrs. Jeffries (who allegedly catered to the Prince of Wales), Parliament resisted at passing a bill to raise the age of consent and punish traffickers.

At first Stead balked at the "duty" thrust upon him: "Oh the agony of the thing. You know what a woman I am in these things." Then, with characteristic impetuosity, Stead seized the opportunity to show that "all that goes on in Brussels and Paris also goes on in London." A man of "excitable, impulsive, fiercely energetic temperament," he wrote the "Maiden Tribute" in a state of excitement and moral indignation: dictating to "relays of shorthand writers, marching up and down his office with an icepack on his head." Under these conditions, Stead's effort at literary cross-dressing went strangely awry: instead of Harriet Beecher Stowe he had metamorphosed into a compulsive voyeur and chronicler of sexual commerce. Instead of producing the New Abolitionist version of *Uncle Tom's Cabin*, he authored something in theme, language, and self-presentation closer to "Walter's" *My Secret Life*. However much his critics might decry the obscene lineage of the "Maiden Tribute," Stead consistently failed to acknowledge the transformation he had accomplished in this narrative.[51]

This metamorphosis demonstrates the affinity between the two literary genres of melodrama and pornography.[52] Both genres have a linked history in radical publishing: during the early Victorian period, both genres were produced and distributed by radical pressmen, after the market for radical literature contracted in the 1820s. As purveyors of irreverent, bawdy populism, French and Latin libertine literature, and popular melodrama, Grub Street publishers moved beyond an older restricted radical audience towards an emerging "mass" reading public which cut across middle- and working-class boundaries. In 1885, Stead adopted a similar publishing strategy: through the "Maiden Tribute," he endeavored to build a mass reading public by exposing the exotic culture of the metropolitan underworld.[53]

Given this publishing history, not surprisingly, melodrama and pornography contained the same sexual script, which focused on the transgression of class boundaries in the male pursuit of the female object of desire, the association of sex and violence, and the presumption of aggressive male sexuality bearing down on a passive asexual female. Both foregrounded power relations by emphasizing situation and underplaying character. Whereas melodrama permitted some power reversals and sympathy for the plight of the heroine/victim, late-Victorian pornography usually prohibited the female victim from mounting any resistance or telling her version of the story. Stead's own preoccupations with women and heterosexuality also precipitated his collapsing of narratives in the "Maiden Tribute." He had a penchant for "harmless flirtations" that were never consummated and openly bragged of his power of fascination over women: there were "five and twenty women" in London, he assured a reporter, who "would give their little finger for a kiss."[54]

In fact, Stead's story went further than Walter's sexual odyssey in its expression of extraordinary rage against women. To evoke that rage, Stead drew on an ancient fantasy of human blood-sacrifice, featuring a male protagonist engaged in a search-and-destroy mission against a powerful feminized monster at the dark center.[55] In his first installment of the "Maiden Tribute," he introduced the myth of the maidens and youths sent as tribute from ancient Athens to perish in the Labyrinth of Crete, victims of a devouring Minotaur, "a frightful monster, half man, half bull, the foul product of unnatural lust." In London's Labyrinth, thousands of "the daughters of the people" were "served up" nightly "as dainty morsels to minister to the passions of the rich"—horrors that should have raised hell, but, according to a high-ranking police officer, did not even "raise the neighbors."[56]

Stead selected the Minotaur myth from a number of ancient stories of monsters and maidens because of the specific typology of sexual danger it contained: it situated sexual crime in an urban setting, the Labyrinth, "as large as a town" with "countless courts and galleries" (as opposed to the lonely rock on which Andromeda was chained in the Perseus myth);[57] it referred to multiple sex crimes committed by a monster, himself the off-spring of unnatural female lust (thus underscoring the sexual nature of the crime and its origins in female depravity); and it made the state an accomplice to these crimes. Stead's revisions and deletions, moreover, were as telling as his initial selection of a story he attributed to Ovid. Two sets of characters drop out from the original story: the young men who served as tribute and Ariadne, Theseus' traditional guide, who let him a ball of yarn to find his way out of the Labyrinth.[58] The deliberate omission of the youth tribute was also a suppression of the homosexual theme (particularly homosexual prostitution) in his exposé of criminal vice—a suppression that nonetheless resurfaced in the margins of Stead's text, and more significantly in the legislative response it evoked. Ariadne's absence may well have been an attempt to protect Butler and her assistant from notoriety and exposure. Its effect was to erase the role of women's craft and craftiness in the drama (just as Stead would eliminate women's work from the discussion of prostitution) and to center the political fiction around a lonely male hero, Theseus, played by Stead as a democratic Christian knight and defender of social justice.[59]

The class address of this frame, with its mythological references and smattering of Latin quotes, was as ambiguous as the subsequent narrative episodes of the "Maiden Tribute." Although knightly/classical allusions were traditionally the province of an elite male culture, Stead tried to democratize their class meanings by invoking the "innate chivalry of our common people." Stead thus drew on Butler's second strategy for political melodrama, celebrating the popular heroism of those manly proletarians "now at last [thanks to the Reform Bill of 1884] enrolled among the governing classes." But immediately that democratic and collective impulse was recuperated into an elite construction: the person empowered to do and say what he wanted, to become a privileged spectator moving comfortably through all social spaces, was the omniscient narrator and urban explorer, W. T. Stead. Although Stead might introduce himself at times as a "North country lad, born in poor circumstances," without university education, "without wealth or position, or other material advantages in this world," he had in fact come a long way from his "humble" Tyneside origins. As the successful editor of a gentleman's newspaper, he had acquired the appropriate dress and gait to impersonate a privileged rake, to visit fashionable brothels and drink champagne and smoke cigars—thus enjoying a privileged mobility unavailable to workmen in their "work-a-day clothes" and "grimy faces." Stead thus reversed the masquerade of descent practiced by Greenwood and Charles Booth, to become instead a counterfeit swell and libertine.[60]

To carry out his investigation, Stead immersed himself in the picaresque nightmare world of London's inferno. "It seemed a strange inverted world, that in which I lived those terrible weeks—the world of the streets and of the brothel. It was the same, yet not the same as the world of business and the world of politics." Stead acted as tourist guide and social observer for the reader, outlining the moral and social landscape of the Labyrinth— the Leicester Square restaurants, the Aquarium, the roller-skating rink, the Hyde Park benches frequented by procuresses on the lookout for unsuspecting nursemaids, the private houses with underground rooms, the isolated villas with thick walls and double carpets on the floor. He also introduced his cast of characters: the violated maids, the evil procuresses, the doctors and midwives who certified the girls' virginity. Only one or two privileged villains made an appearance as individuals, most notably a retired doctor, called the London Minotaur, "who devotes his fortune to the 'ruin' of three maids a night."[61]

The "Maiden Tribute" not only mapped out the same social geography as late-Victorian pornography; it also replicated, in a moralizing frame, many of the sadistic scenarios that filled pornography's pages. Simultaneously, it established a continuity with some of the themes of sadistic hunting and instrumental rape raised in women's fiction and Butler's feminist propaganda.[62] In pornographic texts, sadistic practices appeared in three or four contemporary scenarios that reinforced each other: the hunt, evocative of upper-class male pastimes, sadistic violence, and passive, innocent victims; the discipline of the riding master, who broke the mare to the bit; school birching, administered by a governess in an aristocratic boarding school; and the gynecological exam, in which women are strapped down and "speculumed,"[63] both observed and violated by gynecological instruments. These scenarios were often conflated: the riding master was also a hunter; he could assume the scientific detachment of the medical examiner; the stirrups of his saddle evoked the paraphernalia of the gynecological chair.[64]

This pornographic repertoire finds a place in the "Maiden Tribute." Dispersed throughout the text were incidental references to innocent maids stalked as prey for the pleasure of the dissolute rich: no "subterfuges were too cunning or daring" for procuresses in the "pursuit of their game"; the "pathetic eyes" of a child prostitute still bore "the timid glance of a frightened fawn." In a "Close Time for Girls," Stead compared the age-of-consent legislation to the game laws, arguing that fish "out of season are not fit to be eaten. Girls who have not reached puberty are not fit even to be seduced."[65]

But Stead's Minotaurs had no interest whatsoever in good sportsmanship, for the "shriek of torture is the essence of their delight." In London's Labyrinth, flogging was one of the most popular pursuits of jaded old men "who by riot and excess had impaired [their] vitality."[66] In many of the brothels visited by Stead, flogging, "both of men and women, goes on regularly, but the cry of the bleeding subject never attracts attention from the outside world." To ensure submission, girls were sometimes strapped down "hand and foot so that all resistance save that of unavailing screams would be impossible."[67] Defloration was a second specialization of the London inferno. During his investigations, Stead encountered a highly businesslike firm of procuresses whose sole business, they assured him, was in "maidenheads, not in maids." The demand for "maidenheads" in turn stimulated a medical sideline in the certification of virgins by midwives and doctors. The medical motif in the "Maiden Tribute" was particularly striking in light of Stead's own opposition to the "instrumental rape" of the C.D. Acts. The medical exam revealed the steely scientific side of sexual torture in the Labyrinth; it was introduced to represent a ritualized degradation, an act of voyeurism and violation of female bodily integrity.[68]

Interspersed among these sensational accounts were "realist" "stories from life" of young girls drawn into the London Labyrinth. Some narratives, like that of "Annie, a London girl of singularly interesting countenance," were first-person confessionals, presented in the flattened tones of the charity case history. In other cases, Stead narrated his own interviews with girls "delivered for seduction." These interviews also presented the girls and their stories in a matter-of-fact-manner, that still reveals Stead's voyeuristic presence as well as his struggle to impose a meaning or moral on the story. When Stead tried to bargain with "one virgin," offering one pound in lieu of seduction instead of the promised two, she stood her ground, demanding to be "seduced." "We are very poor," explained the girl. "Mother does not know anything of this: she will think a friend of Miss Z's [the procuress] has given me the money; but she does need it so much." Could any "proof" be more "conclusive," Stead asked, of the "absolute inability of this girl of sixteen" to assess the value of the one "commodity" with which the law considers her amply fit to deal "the day after she is thirteen?" In most of these interviews, young girls appear as innocent informants, simpleminded in their storytelling. Yet every now and then Stead reversed the direction of erotic energy, presenting himself as unnerved by the presence of a little "brazen-faced harlot" masquerading as a *femme fatale.*

Disequilibrium and excess shaped Stead's account of the double life and took its toll on the investigator. For he seems to have gone over the edge in his attempt to authenticate and document criminal vice. Two eerie features of his narrative soon become apparent: the readers were shown London's inferno through Stead's elite gaze, and exploration led Stead into actual impersonation of a Minotaur. In order to prove to the public how easy it was to procure a young girl, Stead obtained one himself. In an episode entitled, "Why the Cries of the Victims are Not Heard," the brothel-keeper spoke confidentially to him (and therefore to the reader) as a potential customer for her services. " 'In my house,' said a most respectable lady who keeps a villa in the West of London, 'you can enjoy the screams of the girl with the certainty that no one hears them but yourself.' " Stead proudly documented his successful ventures into the black market for virgins. In "I Order Five Virgins" we have a fictionalized account of his transaction with a firm of procuresses. " 'Come,' said I, in a vein of bravado. 'What do you say to delivering me five on Saturday night [with the proviso that they had to be certified as *intacta* by a midwife]?' " " 'Five . . . is a large order,' she replied. ' . . . we will try, although I have never before dealt with more than two, or at the most three at one place. It will look like a boarding school going to the midwife'." In his fictionalized accounts, Stead openly engaged in the dialogue as a potential customer; but when he retold the story of his actual purchase of Eliza Armstrong, whom he called Lily in the press, he hid behind the third-person narrative and did not acknowledge his complicity. Yet this was the one story, he declared, that "I can personally vouch for the absolute accuracy of every fact in the narrative."[69]

The "Lily" story, Stead's pièce de résistance, appeared in the first installment of the "Maiden Tribute" under the subheading "A Child of Thirteen Bought for £5." It was told as a Gothic fairy tale, whose principal characters were evil women who preyed upon a passive, silent, female child. "At the beginning of this Derby week, a woman, an old hand in the work of procuration, entered a brothel in ——street, M——, kept by an old acquaintance, and opened negotiations for the purchase of a maid." While they were discussion the local candidates, a "drunken neighbour" came into the house and immediately offered her own daughter. "Don't you think she would take our Lily? I think she would suit." Lily, Stead tells us, was a "bright, fresh-looking child," "an industrious warm-hearted little thing" devoted to the "drunken mother" who wanted to sell her into "nameless infamy." She had never been outside her immediate neighborhood except for two school outings to Richmond and Epping Forest. She was just the kind of sturdy "cockney child" who "by the thousand annually develop into the servants of the poorer middle class."[70]

Unfortunately, "Lily's mother" had arrived too late. However, when a deal for another girl fell through, "Lily's mother" got her "chance." "The brothelkeeper sent for her, and offered her a sovereign for her daughter. The woman was poor, dissolute, and indifferent to everything but drink." The father, also a "drunken man," was told that his daughter was going to a situation; he received the news with "indifference." Financial arrangements with the brothel-keeper were finalized; she would receive £5—£3 paid down and the remaining £2 "after [the daughter's] virginity had been professionally certified."[71]

"The first step had thus been taken." The girl was taken to a midwife to be examined and then conducted to a house of ill-fame. Through the eyes of the omniscient narrator, we witness the defilement of the child, who was undressed, put to bed in the brothel, chloroformed, and who awoke to find a man in the room. "And then there rose a wild and piteous cry—not a loud shriek, but a helpless, startled scream like the bleat of a frightened lamb. And the child's voice was heard crying in accents of terror, 'There's a man in the room. Take me home; oh, take me home!' . . . And then all once more was still. * * * * * * * * * *"[72] The man was Stead, the actual rape was never attempted, but the young girl was terrified.

No fairy godmother appears in this inverted fairy tale to protect the young girl—only an evil procuress, an evil brothel-keeper, an evil midwife, and most shocking of all, an evil mother willing to sell her child into "nameless infamy." The entire "business" was conducted among working-class women, most of whom were friends and neighbors. The only innocent party was the "unsuspecting" girl child, whose sole protest was the bleat of a "frightened lamb." Men are curiously missing from the story, except for the omniscient narrator and the shadowy male figure at the end, the perpetrator of a crime so horrible that "Stead's delicate muse took refuge in a row of asterisks."[73]

Public Reaction

Stead's policy of "frank brutality" seemed to have stirred "London to its depths" and, in the view of his critics, set "class against class." Radical workingmen, trade unionists, and socialists responded warmly to Stead's

attack on upper-class profligates and readily integrated the "Maiden Tribute" into a traditional political analysis of "Old Corruption." Old-
fashioned conspiratorial fantasies reached their height when Charles
Spurgeon, the popular evangelist, publicly railed against the "princes of
the blood" and other royal patrons of London brotheldom. Both the Marxist *Justice* and the more traditionally radical *Reynolds News* (which called
for the passage of "Our Daughters' Protection Bill") endorsed the paternalist and democratic message of Stead's revelations, while feminists heralded
Stead as a "champion" of women whose campaign broke down a great barrier of silence surrounding the sexual crimes of men.[74]

As these responses suggest, "Maiden Tribute" provoked multiple and
contradictory readings on the part of a heterogeneous reading public.
Stead's journalistic conventions not only permitted evangelical reformers,
feminists, and socialists to speak out against male rakes, but allotted space
to the male libertine voice as well. Thanks to Stead's policy of the "universal interview," "Men of the World" were permitted to defend their own
sexual practices with adult workingwomen in the pages of the *PMG*. Perhaps the most striking feature of male libertine speech was its own negative
characterization of male sexuality—as compulsive and compulsory behavior. It was "no good railing against base appetite," warned the "Saunterer in the Labyrinth"; if you suppress prostitution, warned another
worldly correspondent in a private letter to Stead, "You have not reduced
the number of cases of illicit copulation on the part of men. They will take it
just the same—from maid servants, from ladies of position and from the
few skulking syphilised whores who survive the prosecution."[75]

Popular indignation forced the government to act. On 30 July, Sir
Richard Cross, the home secretary, opened debate on the third reading of
the age-of-consent legislation, as embodied in the Criminal Law Amendment Bill. In introducing the bill, Cross acknowledged, "this is a question
that has stirred England from one end to the other," because "there is nothing more sacred to the English people, and there is nothing which they are
so determined to maintain, as the purity of their own households." A
heated debate on the clauses ensued, and the bill finally passed through
Parliament on 10 August. The disreputable performance of parliamentary
members during these debates confirmed purity reformers' worst suspicions of the vicious upper classes. During parliamentary debates, old rakes
like Cavendish Bentinck treated prostitution as a necessary and inevitable
evil, while others objected to curtailing male sexual prerogatives to protect
girls who, they claimed, were already defiled by their sordid and vicious
environment. One member of the House of Lords acknowledged that "very

few of their Lordships . . . had not when young men, been guilty of immorality. He hoped they would pause before passing a clause within the range of which their sons might come."[76]

Even the sexual practices exposed in the "Maiden Tribute" received a curious endorsement when the Commons considered a clause to make flogging the punishment for violating young girls (since the 1870s, flogging was repeatedly proposed as part of legislation to punish assaults on women). Samuel Smith defended the flogging amendment as the "only kind of persuasion that brutal natures could understand." Others, including supporters of the age-of-consent bill like James Stansfeld and James Stuart, attacked the flogging clause as a "retrograde notion" that would not help to "humanize the man." At the time no one openly acknowledged the irony of proposing flogging, one of the featured vices of the London Labyrinth, as punishment for the crimes of the "Maiden Tribute" (although Josephine Butler recognized it as a male discourse and argued that if women had been present as members of Parliament, they would have "tempered" the discussions); but twenty-three years later, when flogging was again proposed for souteneurs (pimps), Bernard Shaw rose to the occasion and directed his pen against the "flagellomania" of legislators. Flogging was a "perfectly well known" form of "debauchery," he pointed out, a "mania which is based on the sensual instinct, though in some cases it takes a retaliatory form."[77]

Finally, on 22 August an enormous demonstration was held in Hyde Park to demand the rigorous enforcement of the new legislation. As one historian has observed, in calling this "monster" demonstration Stead "was looking beyond his original goals," "determined to keep alive the movement" which he had incited. Billed as "London's First Town Meeting," the Hyde Park demonstration would, Stead hoped, inaugurate a new political constituency that would transform the London Labyrinth from an "amorphous, anarchic, multitudinous mass of houses and streets" into a moral, known national community. Like most oppositional spectacles of the period, the Hyde Park demonstration was intended to display massive support for the cause as well as to present supporters to the public as respectable and reasonable citizens.[78]

With banners proclaiming "Protection of Young Girls," "Men, War on Vice," "Sir Pity Us," "Shame, Shame Horror," ten columns of people set out for the park. The East End and Pimlico contingents bravely marched through the "enemy" territory of the West End, observing the absence of "great ladies on the balconies of Belgravian mansions" and the virtual desertion of "clubland." Newspaper commentators were struck by the representation of women and workingmen in the crowd. Many acknowledged the "large muster of women" as "one of the unique features of the demonstration." Members of the Ladies National Association for the Repeal of the Contagious Diseases Acts, dressed in black, arrived in carriages, while "from another part of town" came the members of the Women Trade Unions and employees of the Army Clothing Establishments, led by Henrietta Muller, followed along by wagonloads of young virgins dressed in white, flying the banner "Innocents will they be slaughtered."[79]

The impressive spectacle of women in public was set against the overwhelmingly patriarchal sentiments expressed in the signs and iconography. The banners of working-class London enunciated a popular reading of the "Maiden Tribute" as traditional political melodrama, with workingmen as heroes of the piece. East London called on Englishmen to protect their daughters, while the South London delegation condemned "principalities and wickedness in high places." A similar representation of sexual difference and sexual hierarchy appeared on the surfaces of trade union and socialist banners that "waved to and fro in the wind": on their "crackled surfaces" appeared skilled workingmen with the tools of their craft, or as Herculean figures, endowed with classical bodies; while women only materialized either as bereft widows, deserving of fraternal protection, or as inspiring angels of justice and socialism.[80] Sympathetic observers also detected a sturdy proletarian manliness in the physiognomy of the crowd, as workingmen listened with "stern expressions" and "determined jaws" to reformers of all shades represented on the dozen demonstration platforms. For one brief moment, feminists and trade unionists joined with Anglican bishops, socialists, and nonconformist temperance advocates to protest the aristocratic corruption of young innocents.[81]

By assembling a range of news accounts, editorials, and opinions about the "Maiden Tribute," Stead promoted criminal vice as the "burning" question of the hour, endeavoring to incite through proliferation and cross-referencing a sense of the "Maiden Tribute" as hyperreal and world-encompassing. Despite his efforts to control the "moral" of his story, Stead had to contend with struggles over meaning partially activated by his own journalistic practices. The publication of the "Maiden Tribute" precipitated a chain of unexpected events that significantly transformed the original "plot," adding new installments and genre shifts. Outside of the newspaper, popular constituencies reinterpreted the meaning of Stead's actions; yet their own perspectives were rechanneled and reprocessed as they were reported in the columns of the daily press.

The Armstrong Case

As the carnival spirit excited by the "Maiden Tribute" reached its height, an ominous counterdrama began to unfold—first in the streets of a Marylebone slum, then in the local police court, to be amplified in the national press, and fully enacted in the Old Bailey. This counterdrama presented Stead's cast of characters in a new light and threatened to undermine completely the credibility of the "Secret Commission" and its "Chief Director."[82] Copies of the "Maiden Tribute" had found their way to Charles Street, Lisson Grove, Marylebone, where neighbors angrily confronted Mrs. Elizabeth Armstrong with "selling her child." Mrs. Armstrong recognized certain details of her own daughter's life in the Lily story and rushed to the local police court to demand her daughter back.[83] A reporter from *Lloyd's Weekly News* took an interest in the case and published an account of it on July 12, under the heading "A Mother Seeking Her Lost Child."[84] Eliza was not reunited with her family until the day following the Hyde Park demonstration. By then, plans to prosecute Stead and his confederates on abduction charges were already in the works; their criminal prosecution would occupy the attention of the national press throughout the fall.

This was an extraordinary chain of events. Most authors of political fictions did not expect to be pursued by their own characters into the law courts and confronted with opposing versions of the story.[85] However, Stead's own journalistic practice, particularly his policy of the "universal interview," seemed to call forth the retributive justice that followed. For, if privileged male villains, the "Men of the World," were allowed to present their case in the pages of the *PMG*, was it not fitting that other members of the cast—the silenced child and her evil mother—should find their own voices and establish their right to be heard in public? In so doing, they transformed Stead's role from that of a "campaigning hero" to that of a "denigrated villain" faced with a criminal charge.

Six defendants stood in the dock of Central Criminal Court on 23 October 1885: Stead; Rebecca Jarrett, the reformed "old procuress," now a member of the Salvation Army and matron of Hope Cottage, the rescue home for prostitutes established by Josephine Butler in Winchester; Bramwell Booth, son of General Booth of the Salvation Army; Samuel Jacques, an ex–war correspondent and agent of Stead; Elizabeth Combe, a Swiss lady and member of the Salvation Army; and Louise Mourez, the French "abortionist" and midwife. The main charge was abduction of a girl under sixteen from her parents' home; Stead, Jacques, Jarrett, and

Mourez were secondarily charged with indecent assault, on account of the midwife's examination of Eliza.

Beyond what was narrated in the "Maiden Tribute," few new facts emerged from the proceedings. The testimonies did reveal Eliza's subsequent history after the brothel scene: she was taken first to another house where she was again examined by a doctor, Heywood Smith, who again certified her virginity; and then she was spirited away to France to live with a Salvation Army family. None of Stead's own actions were disputed. Attention focused instead on his mental state: to a certain extent, on his motives for abducting Eliza; and more persistently, on what he knew of the conditions under which he had obtained Eliza. As a consequence, the spotlight fell on the female protagonists of Stead's fairy tale—on his informant, Rebecca Jarrett, and on Mrs. Armstrong and her female neighbors. At issue was their credibility as storytellers. Did Mrs. Armstrong knowingly sell her daughter into "nameless infamy," as Stead alleged? Or did she, with the help of her neighbor Mrs. Broughton, negotiate with Jarrett to send Eliza to service, as she stubbornly asserted? Did Jarrett misrepresent these negotiations to Stead as the prosecutor suggested, or did Stead misrepresent what she told him in the "Maiden Tribute"?

It is impossible to establish the absolute truth from the testimonies, even though three important witnesses, Eliza, Mrs. Armstrong, and Rebecca Jarrett, challenged the veracity of Stead's narrative. Much seems to have remained unsaid in the original transactions. As Jarrett herself acknowledged in her later memoir: "That Mother never asked me what I wanted her for or where I was going to take her [sic] never even asked when she would see her again [.] she had got the money there I could take her where I liked [.]" As interesting as the facts of the case are the attitudes and positions struck by the courtroom actors in their contests with each other, as they tried to reposition themselves (or were repositioned by the national press) within the fiction system of the "Maiden Tribute."[86]

The most unsensational and uncontroversial witness was the muted child victim of the "Maiden Tribute," Eliza Armstrong. Overall, Eliza showed remarkable self-possession in recounting her story, which largely paralleled the "Maiden Tribute," even to the point of casting the brothel scene in a matter-of-fact manner very different from Stead's voyeuristic perspective. Eliza also represented herself as an active agent in the negotiations about her "service." She had "worried" her mother to secure a position with Jarrett: "I was anxious to go out to work, our family, six or seven, lived in one room—my sister [who was at service] was not able to spare anything for my father and mother." She did not like the trip to the midwife, tried to get away from Mourez when she examined her, and later told Jarrett that Mourez was a "dirty woman." She was treated by the defense as a "truthful witness" and was not subjected to "severe cross-examination."[87]

In contrast, Mrs. Armstrong was subjected to a grueling cross-examination. When she first applied to Marylebone Police Court, *Lloyds* had depicted her as a "poor but apparently respectable woman" who "wept bitterly" and in a "faltering voice" "explained that her dear girl was only 13 years of age, and she feared some harm had happened to her." At the committal proceedings and then at the Old Bailey, she was obliged to defend herself and her family honor more forcefully. From bereaved mother, she became a saucy Cockney matriarch to the press, a "woman with a bold face," a "difficult witness" who talked back to "learned counsel." Although she not "infrequently contradicted herself" and "burst into tears" at the severe questioning of the defense counsel, on the "crucial point" of selling her daughter and receiving a "corrupt consideration" Mrs. Armstrong "never wavered." The defense could not discredit her testimony. "Rough in manners, far from refined in language the Armstrongs may be," acknowledged *The Times.* "But nothing which has come to light is inconsistent with motherly affection on the part of Mrs. Armstrong."[88]

Although press commentary generally treated social relations in the Charles Street slum as "incomprehensible" and comic, Mrs. Armstrong's own testimony presented the neighborhood norms as coherent and peremptory. Mrs. Armstrong could talk back to "learned counsel," but when she was stopped by neighbors who accused her of selling "my child," this woman "with a bold face" trembled in her boots. "I had got the scandal of the neighbors in the street," a scandal that jeopardized her standing in the community and threatened to isolate her from her safety net.[89] The wife of a casual laborer, she depended on the reciprocity and good will of her neighbors in times of trouble. Part and parcel of that mutual aid system was the collective supervision of children. Local matriarchs who might overlook the occasional drunken spree would take it upon themselves to administer a severe rebuke to a mother who violated the codes of acceptable mothering; for such a violation, like public fighting among women, threatened to "get" "the street a bad name."[90] "A good many people stopped me in the street" and "spoke to me rather angrily." To vindicate herself, as her female neighbors looked on, Mrs. Armstrong publicly confronted Mrs. Broughton, who was "standing at the street door," with conniving with Jarrett to buy Eliza.[91] Shortly thereafter, she proceeded to the Marylebone Police court to demand her daughter back.

The neighborhood, with its codes and rituals, marked the limits of

Mrs. Armstrong's social universe. She could apply to the police court when looking for her lost child because she regarded it, like the board school where she charred, as another resource of her neighborhood (even though she had been recently charged there with drunken disorderliness). But it did not occur to her to approach W. T. Stead and the *Pall Mall Gazette*. Stead clearly did not appreciate her intense localism when he asked Mrs. Armstrong why she did not contact him to find Eliza, to which she replied, "I did not know where you lived."[92]

The *Daily Telegraph* introduced Charles Armstrong to its readers as the epitome of Outcast London: a chimney sweep and former sergeant in the army, he was a man with "thinning" hair, a "florid" complexion, and "watery" eyes. At Stead's trial, Charles Armstrong's testimony was extremely important to the legal issues of the case; for the charge of abduction rested on the assumption that Eliza had been removed from her home without the consent of the legal guardian, the father. In his testimony, Mr. Armstrong defended his wife's respectability, but he nonchalantly recounted how he had beaten her twice in one day, first because she wanted to attend a local funeral and later because she had arranged with a neighbor to send Eliza off to service with a strange woman without asking his permission. He treated wife-beating as a natural male prerogative, a casual fact of daily life: when asked if he discussed their dispute with anyone, he replied, "Do you think I tell everybody that I knock my wife about?" The press, however, invested considerable significance in these beatings, interpreting them either as a sign of his callous depravity, or, contrastingly, as indicating his innocence in the negotiations over Eliza. Even *Reynolds*, formerly a supporter of Stead, but ever protective of slights against the working classes, took the latter line: as evidence that the parents were not "as bad" "as they seemed," it cited the facts that the mother was overjoyed when the daughter was returned and that the father hit his wife when he found out she had let Eliza got with a stranger.[93]

Through the "Maiden Tribute" and the ensuing prosecution of the "Chief Director," both Mr. and Mrs. Armstrong would be taken up by forces outside their locality, drawn into a national drama where they played enigmatic and caricatured parts before a bemused and distanced public. The reading public had to decide whether inhabitants of Charles Street were denizens of Outcast London, living in tainted surroundings, as Stead alleged; or whether the Armstrongs were a poor but respectable couple, who struggled to rear a modest, affectionate, industrious, "pure" child. Whether villains or innocent dupes, the Armstrongs articulated domestic values and relations that did not fit comfortably into the rigid gender and family boundaries of melodrama. Instead their public performances edged nervously into the conventions of the music hall, where the "struggle over the breeches" and the ineptitude of the male breadwinner regularly appeared as comic routines.

Mrs. Armstrong might have presented herself to the police court magistrate as a grieving mother searching for her lost child, but, within her own community, she knew her moral claim as mother and wife was based on her day-to-day labor as household manager, not on a higher spiritual and emotional nurturance, commonly sentimentalized in melodrama. Mrs. Armstrong's loyalties extended beyond the limits of the individual household, so centrally focused in melodrama, to the social world of the street. It was she who negotiated Eliza's "service" ("My husband leaves all those things to me"); it was she who took the initiative in defending the family honor, going to the police court, ultimately traveling up and down the country with a reporter in search of her daughter.[94]

All along, the father held the trump card. He took no responsibility for daily life, other than to pay out household money to his wife; but he had the final say, the right to discipline his familial subordinates if he was displeased. Like many other Cockney husbands, Mr. Armstrong tried to discourage his wife's social relationships outside the family and regarded female neighbors as competitors for her time and attention. However jealously he defended his domestic prerogatives, he remained passive in the face of the uproar over his daughter's disappearance until the state forced him to take an active role; Scotland Yard insisted that Mr. Armstrong, not Mrs. Armstrong, accompany one of their detectives to France in pursuit of Eliza. Eventually he began to realize the benefits of notoriety and entered into the spirit of the adventure, granting interviews to *Lloyds*.[95] Patriarchy functioned very differently in Charles Street than in the upper reaches of society, but there was enough of a family resemblance for the judge, newspaper correspondents, and commentators to translate Armstrong's actions into a version of respectable paternalism.

Two more witnesses from Charles Street substantiated Mrs. Armstrong's account of her transaction with Jarrett. Then, Rebecca Jarrett, the "old procuress," a tall woman, between thirty-five and forty, not "very prepossessing," took the stand. The *Daily Telegraph* introduced her as a "notorious" villainness, an abandoned woman whose cross-examination revealed the "repulsive features of the degraded life from which she is said to have been rescued." Alternatively, the defense counsel tried to salvage her reputation by recounting her story as a "sad one." She had gone into prostitution in her teens, Sir Charles Russell explained, having been taken "advantage of" by a "gentleman," and later kept gay houses in Bristol, Liverpool, and Manchester. Finally, in late 1884 she was converted and reformed by the Salvation Army and sent from the Army's shelter in Hanbury Street, Whitechapel, to work for Josephine Butler at her rescue home in Winchester. In May 1885, Russell continued, Butler sent Jarrett up to London to aid Stead in his investigations. Stead prevailed upon her to make reparation for her past life by resuming her old role as procuress to serve as his agent in the London inferno. To defend her status as a "changed woman," she reluctantly agreed to assist Stead, on condition that her old friends not be incriminated or punished for their activities.[96]

To supply Stead with young victims, Jarrett explained in her testimony, she visited a number of well-known haunts—including Lady Lake Grove in the East End where a ring of white slavers were to be prosecuted later that year—but failed to find a girl "in stock or in hand." She was forced to return to her old friends. When she arrived at the home of her friend Nancy Broughton, with whom she had worked in the laundry of the Savoy Hotel, she was running out of leads. As one commentator has observed, Broughton was clearly "in the nature of a last rather than a first resort."[97]

In her testimony, Jarrett firmly denied that she had ever called Broughton's home a brothel: "Mr. Stead did not write down what I told him." Her credibility was entirely demolished, however, when the prosecutor revealed that she had earlier lied about the addresses and names of the gay houses she had claimed to run. She was "not going to have her past looked into," she exclaimed. "You forced that lie out of me."[98]

This was the final blow for the defense. In his summing up speech, the prosecution dismissed Jarrett as a thoroughly discredited witness. She was "one of those women who are led to exaggerate their own guilt for the purpose of glorifying or exaggerating their degree of present merit."[99] Jarrett had mislead Stead about her former life, Mr. Webster assured the jury; and she then proceeded to mislead him about the deal she had cut with Mrs. Armstrong.

Even before Jarrett had left the dock, Stead knew he had lost the case. Unlike Jarrett and the Armstrongs, whose testimonies were first shaped by the courtroom interrogation and then reprocessed into newspaper accounts, Stead was able to present his own case directly to the public. *The Armstrong Case: Mr. Stead's Defense in Full* contained the full testimony Stead was not allowed to present in court (on the grounds that the discussion of motives was immaterial to the legal issues raised by the case). Stead defended his "work" on two grounds, first, as a necessary experiment to "verify the process," and second as "rescue and reclamation," an effort to "intercept" a girl intended for the London slave "market." He stuck to his previously stated summary of Eliza Armstrong's true history: she had been sold to Rebecca Jarrett for "immoral purposes and . . . the only hope of rescuing the child from a life of shame was to remove her to safety, far from the vicious surroundings of a drunken home in a Marylebone slum."[100]

Stead stressed his good intentions, but many questions remained nonetheless about exactly what he was trying to prove in buying Eliza and the manner in which he undertook to "save" her. Stead presented himself at the trial and elsewhere as a defender of women: "In the 'Maiden Tribute,' I do not say one hard word about [any] women, except those who made themselves agents to the men . . . , " he wrote to Elizabeth Cobb on 5 August. He took pride in leading a purity movement "in which fallen women were uniformly spoken of with real respect, admiration. Almost all previous movements have had a tendency to punish the erring woman. This at least is solely directed against the tempting man. It is a change for once to strike at the strong, instead of assailing the weak." In fact, Stead did say many hard words "against women" in the "Maiden Tribute." His behavior towards both Eliza Armstrong and Rebecca Jarrett, whom he acknowledged as innocent or well-meaning parties, was hardly one of "respect" or "admiration." He consistently glossed over his mistreatment of Eliza: the midwife's examination was necessary "to prove that a little harlot had not been palmed off on us." Besides the "momentary surprise" of the exam, he assured the jury, Eliza did not experience the "slightest inconvenience." Had she objected to the examination, they would have "discontinued that part of the project." But did Stead really expect a startled and vulnerable girl to voice her objections openly?[101]

Jarrett also suffered harsh treatment from Stead who used her, in her own words, as a "poor tool" to verify his experiment. After Jarrett had told him "details of a ghastly nature," Stead described how he exerted his "overbearing will" and considerable interviewing skills to coerce her to play a part for which she was "imperfectly fitted." He was "pressed for time"; she was "reluctant"; "I was inexorable." "I said that if she had procured girls for dissolute men she must procure girls for me, as if I was a dissolute man." He pressed her to buy "one, two, three girls merely to show that it could be done." Unfortunately, Jarrett was, according to Stead, "muddle-brained" and suffered from a "defective memory." Jarrett had insisted that "Mr. Stead did not write down what I said to him"; and Stead himself acknowledged that "three weeks had elapsed before I wrote the article." "Compelled to play a fictitious role she confused her parts, and involved everyone in a confused tangle of misconceptions."[102]

Despite his self-justifications, considerable evidence exists that Stead had confused his part as well, both by misrepresenting what Jarrett had told him and by identifying too closely and enthusiastically with the villain role. By his own admission, he was in an extreme state of excitement the weeks he was exploring the London inferno. "I had been visiting brothels and drinking champagne and smoking, which I was not used to, and was very excited and therefore I may have confused some of the statements Jarrett told me." "I wrote to the best of my recollection but I may have been confused in details."[103]

More than a confusion of details may have been involved. One cannot help feeling that Stead almost willed this sequel into being. Although he deliberately erased his presence from the Lily episode, he retained enough of Eliza Armstrong's history—reference to her outings at Epping Forest and Richmond, for instance—to make her recognizable. As with the staged rape itself, he seemed to be "playing with fire"—inventing scenarios that implicated him in illicit sexuality yet masked his involvement and permitted him to draw back at the last minute. His contemporaries began to suspect that he had entered too fully into the part of the rich debauchee: his "revelations," sneered the freethinking, republican *National Reformer,* "may be nothing more than the account of [his] own frenzied deeds and feverish sin-stained dreams." Stead seemed determined to keep up this role; throughout the autumn he continued to boast of his successful purchase of virgins, remarking that "if only I had violated Eliza Armstrong and taken the usual precautions . . . there would have been one more lost girl in London and I would have escaped scot-free."[104]

Stead continued to play with fire even after his conviction and prison sentence. His diary entries of 1886 reveal his continued deep absorption in the role of sexual libertine/explorer. He clearly did not want to give up his "night investigations." Night after night, following his release from jail, he prowled around Hyde Park and Waterloo Station, interviewing poor young streetwalkers and paid contacts of the underworld like the procuress "Carrotty Kate."[105]

If we treat these diary entries as representative of Stead's field notes we learn something of the kind of sources he may well have processed into the "Maiden Tribute" during the "Secret Commission's" four-week investigation in May and June of 1885. The difference in the narratives told to Stead by the streetwalkers and those presented by his paid informants was striking. Carrotty Kate told him stories reminiscent of the "Maiden Tribute" and of sensational pornography, of the adventures of the Earl of Nugent, known to her as the "gold stick," or the exploits of another titled villain, the "Master of the Black Rod." She urged him to buy "one or more of the children she had in stock" ("the girl Maggie, she thinks her mother would part with for £20"). In a similar vein, Mr. Cook, a private detective who had been dismissed "in disgrace" from the police force, assured him that "when the 'Maiden Tribute' appeared, four (I think) members of Parliament came down to his office, formed a Committee of Enquiry and desired him to investigate the whole thing." They said they knew these things went on; but they could not believe that it could be done so cheaply. Had I [Stead] said £25 or £30 instead of £5; they would have believed the story. I had got into the middle class, not into the swell, and as a consequence they did not believe it was true."[106]

Young girls on the street told a different story. Walking around Waterloo Station, Stead encountered "several girls about in clusters." "Two dressed in black said 'goodnight' and on my returning it came after me." "The older acted as a spokeswoman for her little friend Pat—a girl of 17." They were employed at Crosse and Blackwell's jam factory and lived together. Pat had been procured by the older girl, named Gunter, "on the order of Mr. M" who was "in the habit of going down to Crosse and Blackwell's factory gates at dinner time" and "watching the girls come out." "Mr. M. was an old gentleman—'much older than you; quite bald at the top of his head.' " "They did not like him, but he was a great swell, & had lots of money." Overall they liked "the work in the factory better than the work in the streets. But the difference in pay was very great. Times they said were hard; and beggars could not be choosers."[107]

The girls spoke the unsensational language of sexual bartering, not the melodramatic language of seduction. They consciously weighed the advantages of one form of work against another, the work of the jam factory against the work of the streets. These grim, exploitative alternatives indicated appalling economic choices, not an organized system of outrage or the collusion of villainous mothers, who delivered working girls up to Mr. M., the old swell. The matter-of-fact nature of sexual bartering only found partial expression in the "Maiden Tribute" in the interviews with juvenile prostitutes that resembled Stead's later diary entries. "They were poor, work was bad, every crust they ate at home was grudged, they stopped out all night with some 'gay' friend of the female sex and they went the way of the rest." But this alternative explanation for youthful prostitution remained submerged under an avalanche of horrifying tales of violated virgins, stories supplied by the likes of Carrotty Kate and other paid informants to feed Stead's own fantasies and facilitate his political project.[108]

Stead's own storytelling bore an uncanny resemblance to the literary difficulties encountered by his contemporary, Sigmund Freud, when he undertook to narrate the sexual history of a young girl, Dora. Both Stead and Freud were unreliable narrators who inserted themselves into the story as dramatic characters and callously enforced their versions of the stories. Both included an invasive gynecological theme in their narrative: Stead required Eliza to undergo two gynecological examinations, while Freud defended his discussion of sexual acts and positions with Dora by likening it to a conversation between a female patient and her gynecologist. Both composed their case histories considerably after the events had taken place and after the story was originally narrated to them. Although they privileged these cases by making them more finished narratives than most of their published investigations, they incorporated material from other cases into their "true" histories and omitted and "forgot" details from the original interviews. Neither provided information about how they reorganized the interviews into coherent narratives. From Stead's later field notes we have tried to reconstruct his process of inclusion and exclusion, and to hear the voices of his female subjects in a less mediated fashion than Freud allowed us to do in Dora's case.[109]

The Verdict

After twelve days of testimony, the jury reached its verdict. Booth and Mme Combe, who had taken charge of Eliza after the brothel visit, were acquitted, but Stead and Jacques were found guilty of the charge of abduction. The foreman expressed "the opinion at the same time that Stead had acted from pure motives and that he had been misled by Jarrett." Stead was sentenced to three months hard labor (Jacques to one month). He stayed in Coldbaths Field, "a gloomy bastille," for three days, then he was transferred "after strings were pulled" to Holloway Prison as a first-class misdemeanant, where he was allowed daily visits from friends. Altogether, he had rarely had a "happier lot" than the two months he spent in "Happy Holloway." Proud to be "the man who wrote the Maiden Tribute," he continued to wear his prison costume on the anniversary of his imprisonment until his death in 1912 (on the *Titanic*). As for the Armstrong family, they soon moved away from Charles Street; Stead later claimed to have received a letter for Eliza (who had been taken up by the Salvation Army) reporting that she had married a respectable man and had six children.[110]

"I have had a fair trial," wrote Stead, "a full hearing, and on the evidence before the court a just verdict." But, objected Josephine Butler, "what of the courtesy or even decent fairness shown in regard to Rebecca?" Jarrett and Mme Mourez (who was convicted of indecent assault and died in prison), were sentenced to prison terms twice as long as Stead's, and their hard labor was not commuted. Jarrett felt badly used by Stead and British justice: "The Salvation Army let Mr. Stead have me to be the poor tool to show it all up. I truly done it for God and for the poor child to show what some wretched Mother will do for money. When I found it was for a Public Show I felt it. It almost drove me back to drink."[111]

Jarrett was willing to assist Stead in part because the story of Eliza reso-
nated with her own history. Jarrett told her story in her memoir, dictated in
old age, "written by my own self not to boast of my disgusting life *no* but to
show how good *Jesus* is to a poor lost degraded woman." Jarrett mentioned no proper names in her text, with the exception of Stead and Butler
(a marker of their superior class), and she eliminated practically all the sub-
sidiary characters from the action. This exclusion extended to the men
who lived with her and off her earnings and who seem to have been
interchangeable— "I seemed to get one if one left me I soon got another to
take His place [.]"—as well as to Nancy Broughton, who had served as the
intermediary in the negotiations over Eliza.[112]

Overwhelmingly, Jarrett spotlighted the figure of the Mother—good
and bad—as the emotional focus, the archetypal presence, of her narrative.
Like the "Maiden Tribute," her personal memoir featured an exploiting
mother, but it evidenced considerably more empathy for the mother's own
plight, as a figure who was both oppressive and oppressed. Before Jarrett
was thirteen, her mother "got me in the way of looking for my share."
When her brothers returned from the sea, they threw Rebecca out. She
went away with a man who kept her for two years.[113] At this point, Jarrett
interrupted her narrative to defend the mother who led her into a "life of
infamy."

> Some of you will say as read this what a *bad Mother* she must have
> had [.] but Please don't she was a good Mother [.] it was my wretched
> Father's doing [.] He left her several times and lived with other
> women [.]my poor Mother was left with 8 children[.] I was the
> baby[.] that was his work[.] she took to drink [.] it was trouble that
> drove her to it [.] she had to work to keep us clean and respectable [.]

Jarrett's story continued to oscillate between mothers who saved and
mothers who betrayed. The mothers of the Salvation Army had rescued
Jarrett from drink and decline in late 1884, when at thirty-six she began to
"break up": "it was not the preaching that done the work in my poor soul it
was the care and trouble they all took of me." She was then placed in the
hands of Mrs. Josephine Butler where "I was watched over with the greatest
of care[.]"[114]

The drama of the Mother continued to dominate Jarrett's narrative of
her work for Stead. Stead had told her to prove "her words were truth" that
"the Mother thinks of the Money not her poor child," a task she first
avoided by seeking girls in the open market from brothels. Failing in her
search, she "changed my dress put on some very showey thing went into the
street [Charles Street]" where "I had seen these poor children running

about no one seemed to care for them I got my eye on a very pretty girl but dirty." Jarrett assessed the street's reputation according to a semiotics that interpreted "dirty children playing in the street" as a sign of a rough and "tainted" neighborhood, where mothers might well sell "their daughters," even though her own mother who had "ruined" her had kept her "very clean."[115]

Having assessed Charles Street as a street where mothers failed in their duty to their children, Jarrett proceeded to represent her purchase of Eliza as a dramatic confrontation between herself and one such mother. "I asked to see the Mother I told her I wanted to take her child away with me she did not ask me what for or how I was going to use her." Yet Jarrett's identification with her own mother made her "repent of the work" Stead had "thrust" upon her; she sent Eliza all dressed up to say good-bye to her mother "so that if the mother saw the child dressed up and looking smart her mother's heart might relent [.]she might say that she should not let her go."[116] Even after Eliza was sent off to France, she would dwell "night and day upon the thought" of rewriting the inverted fairy tale Stead had scripted, to make "the whole story 'end well.'" According to Josephine Butler,

> She built a sort of castle in the air, in which she continually dwelt. Her plan—her dream—was as follows: To get the child from Paris; to have her with us here to train and teach her; then a little later to take her herself to Charles Street, London, to present her to her mother and father, and to Mrs. Broughton . . . to convince these poor people that she (Rebecca) was indeed a changed character.[117]

Butler, who felt protective towards and responsible for Jarrett, tried in 1886 to make amends by writing Jarrett's biography. In recounting Jarrett's life, Butler returned to female literary melodrama: she blamed an upper-class seducer for Jarrett's fall and virtually eliminated the "evil mother" from the action, while retaining the figure of the grieving mother in the person of Jarrett herself. According to Butler, at fifteen Jarrett went to service, where "she came in contact with one of the gentleman visitors" who led her "away from the path of virtue." Jarrett lived with him for two years, and she bore two children. Deserted by her lover, deprived of her children—whose "voices would have woke up her mother's heart within her"—she returned to London and "drowned her sorrow in drink." She became a landlady who "encouraged young girls in sin." Then came her conversion and rescue work.[118]

Butler presented Jarrett as a sympathetic figure, a social heroine and magdalen mother; nonetheless Butler's relationship to Jarrett was just as complicated and manipulative as Stead's. As Amanda Sebastyn has observed, Butler's pamphlet shows the "steely side of the professional organiser when she described her star rescue worker as 'clumsy in all her ways' and called her 'the first instrument which came to hand' in the fight to save children."[119]

This condescension was complemented by an identification with the saintly Mary Magdalen as the ultimate female victim, a sign of the approaching apocalypse. Butler even refashioned Jarrett's "clumsy" performance in the dock into a staged martyrdom that ratified her own prophetic power. "I had a strange inward feeling of prophetic joy, let them abuse her and let the men sitting all round me whisper amen as they did to all the judge said against her," she wrote to Stead. "Don't you see that in this crisis of the world's moral history, the situation would have been incomplete . . . unless there had been prominently among us—even in the Dock that sad, pitiful typical figure—the fallen woman . . . in all her moral rags and tatters."[120]

Both Stead and Butler constructed the fallen woman "in all her moral rags and tatters" as a dramatic character in an intensely charged scenario.[121] Both set out to expose a conspiracy of privileged men in which the state functioned as an accomplice. Both represented sexual perversion as an expression of corrupt male power. There was not much difference between Butler's vicious officialdom as featured in her repeal propaganda and Stead's debauched statesmen or sadistic judges. Both Stead and Butler foregrounded heterosexual violence, literal rape and its medical variation. Both produced political fictions that disseminated images and narratives of scientific and sexual violence more widely than other literary voices at the time, including those heard in pornography. Their representation of perverse sexuality contained a homosexual and homophobic subtext, usually expressed in the margins of their texts: in a *private* letter to the permanent home secretary in 1870, Butler had charged the Admiralty with using prostitutes to cover up homosexual practices in the Royal Navy;[122] while Stead, as we have seen, deliberately suppressed the "youth tribute" from his story of the "Maiden Tribute," even though he incidentally mentioned establishments where flogging of both "men and women" occurred.[123]

Although Butler and Stead graphically recounted tales of sexual violation, Butler's repeal stories and her life of Jarrett sharply diverged from the class and gender imagination of the "Maiden Tribute." In each case, Butler told the story of sexual violence from the perspective of the female victim and her avenging mother, even allowing her fallen magdalens to "curse" men for their iniquity. Stead, by contrast, recorded no towering voices of female indignation in the "Maiden Tribute," only the frightened "bleat" of the muted child victim. Because of their extreme youthfulness and inexperience, Stead's violated maids lacked the practical resources of Butler's prostitutes; as prepubescents, they were devoid of the sexual agency that might threaten the ascendancy of male desire, a threat that increasingly preoccupied a wide range of fin-de-siècle male intellectuals and artists.[124]

There was also a marked shift in the class meanings of Butler and Stead's fiction. In her repeal propaganda, Butler had fashioned two melodramas, one that celebrated an informal cross-class alliance, based on a deferential code of reciprocity, between feminists and "strong and stalwart" workingwomen; another, more traditional version, that reinstated workingmen as the heroes of the piece. In both versions, she assigned working people a dignified place in the action, a voice and physical agency. No female villains appeared in her story, only incidental references to male brothel-keepers who "knew their craft was in danger."[125] Overall, Butler represented working people as more virtuous and devoted to justice than their social superiors. Readers of the "Maiden Tribute," by contrast, were shown London's inferno through Stead's elite "male gaze." Heroic workingmen were completely obliterated from the text (further diminishing the presence of men in the story, aside from anonymous "minotaurs" and the omniscient male narrator), and slum mothers were transformed into the principal villains.

Butler's representations of working people were shaped by her perception of them as political allies (more reliable, in fact, than middle-class men), while Stead, despite his Radical politics and his subsequent support for the socialist demonstrators, represented the London poor as outcast denizens of the slums. He incorporated into the "Maiden Tribute" certain themes and motifs derivative of his earlier journalistic coup, "The Bitter Cry of Outcast London," excerpts of which he had published in the *Pall Mall Gazette* in 1883.[126] Overtones of "Outcast London" had found expression in the Lily episode, where, Lily, the sturdy cockney girl, living in "vicious surroundings," was sold into "nameless infamy" by her dissolute, drunken mother.[127] By representing the unrespectable poor in the figure of the slum mother (rather than her "shiftless" husband) Stead anticipated a tendency to imagine the urban poor as 'actively' (and perniciously) female. To a certain extent, his representation of the slum mother accorded with the actual sexual division of labor in poor families: as household managers, mothers like Mrs. Armstrong *were* responsible for the moral and physical welfare of their families. In subsequent decades, female social investigators and settlement workers, who studied the distribution of resources within the household, would champion the cause of the mother and use their expertise to lobby for a family policy, an "endowment for motherhood," that would support and empower poor mothers at home.[128] But recognition of the "power" of the mother provoked other middle-class observers, female and male, to blame "bad mothers" for the degenerate conditions of the slums and the physical degeneracy of slum-dwellers, while ignoring the actual constraints on women who appeared powerful but who suffered from male domination and the inequities of class.[129] This paradox of the powerful but oppressed (and oppressing) mother was at the heart of Rebecca Jarrett's narrative of her own mother. As her biographer, Butler attempted to pull back, to bring Jarrett's story in line with traditional female literary melodrama. She desired to project a more respectful image of the working class and of working-class women in particular, but she also resisted confronting the dangers and deprivations that proletarian women faced within the family. For Butler, sexual danger came from without—outside of the family context, from another class.

Butler and Stead were both masters of imposture and disguise, crossing over the stable boundaries of class through their respective identification with working-class victims and upper-class villains. Their impersonations constitute, from a twentieth-century perspective, unsettling forms of identification, but they set up different political potentialities for action for men and women. Whereas Butler extended the boundaries of female heroism through an identification with "suffering womanhood," Stead's impersonation of the sexual libertine allowed him considerably more license to do and say what he pleased, while building a defense against guilt and moral judgment. Yet these performative roles by no means exhausted the political and cultural repercussions of the "Maiden Tribute," whose contradictory effects on cultural production, politics, and subjectivities will be explored in the next chapter.

FOUR

"The Maiden Tribute": Cultural Consequences

o a considerable degree, the "Maiden Tribute" and its aftermath manifested all the symptoms of a classic moral panic: the definition of a "threat"; the stereotyping of main characters in the mass media as particular species of monsters; a spiraling escalation of the perceived threat, the taking up of absolutist positions, including the mounting of "barricades"; and finally the emergence of an "imaginary" solution, in terms of tougher laws, moral isolation, and symbolic court action. Yet, argues Simon Watney, this kind of structural analysis fails to acknowledge the special role of representation and mass media in energizing and shaping moral panics, particularly the media's intrinsic involvement with *excess,* "with a voracious appetite and capacity for substitutions, displacements, repetitions, and signifying absences." Moral panics are not, Watney contends, bounded phenomena, but repetitive, "fundamentally *serial*"; they assume an "infinite variety of tone and posture." Finally, Watney observes, "moral panics do not speak to a 'silent majority' which is simply 'out there' waiting to listen. Rather they provide the raw materials, in the form of words and images, of those moral constituencies with which individual subjects are encouraged to identify their deepest interest and their very core of being."[1]

The proliferation of meanings and escapades surrounding the "Maiden Tribute" certainly bears out Watney's generalizations about media excess, repetitions, shifting targets, and subjectivities. As the author of prostitution's *Uncle Tom's Cabin,* Stead ostensibly tried to contain the meanings of the "Maiden Tribute" within the populist traditions of melodrama, but he failed. Through a series of resonating and overlapping sexual exposés, Stead initiated an era of media scandals around sexual violence, with varied political effects.[2]

Like the "Maiden Tribute," these later causes célèbres empowered a host of social actors to speak their minds about sexuality, employing a wide "variety of tone and posture." Some followed Stead's imaginative lead and located sexual danger in the dark corners and subterranean spaces of the London Labyrinth, while others mapped the site of sexual danger on to the illuminated landscape of commercialized culture. Select members of the reading public used the occasion of Stead's media scandals to imagine new sexual possibilities as well as sexual dangers in the city. Sometimes they shifted genres, transforming Stead's melodramatic scenarios into farce; alternatively, they situated the melodrama in a new landscape of daydream and individual reverie, in the inner recesses of the divided self.

Pornography

The "Maiden Tribute" set into motion a movement to repress the obscene, yet it incorporated the entire repertoire of late-nineteenth-century pornography. This irony was not lost on Stead's opponents, who blamed him for unleashing destructive energies of the street by encouraging and disseminating pornography. Stead's publication, they declared, had created an "appetite for obscene literature," while his "allies," the "howling dervishes of the street," had made the major thoroughfares of London virtually impassable.[3]

Immediately after the Hyde Park demonstration, the *Daily Telegraph* ran an extensive correspondence on the "State of the Strand," the traditional center of the pornography trade. "Ashamed" complained of the "terrible crowd scenes" composed of "the sellers of obscene literature, the beggars, the thieves, the idlers, swearers and blasphemers [who] mixed with the respectable passers-by at will," all hawking "prints which I do not think ought to be sold in secret." Ragged and dirty urchins "pushed a picture . . . into my face" about "Satan in his character of professed Lothario." Another "evil fellow" tried to sell him a packet of "French transparencies," pictures which he "had heard about years earlier in college," but was shocked to see vended in public "under the eye of the police."[4]

Strand merchants held an "indignation meeting" to demand the "purification" and "disinfection" of their thoroughfare. They were soon joined by "representatives of the working classes" led by the trade unionist George Potter, who was concerned that the sale of obscene literature would undo "all the good work that had been done" to "educate and elevate" the children of the poor.[5]

When other London dailies attacked the "Maiden Tribute" as a great incentive to the "unchecked sale" of obscene literature, they were certainly motivated by economic jealousy, but they had some basis for complaint, although they exaggerated Stead's innovative role. The "Maiden Tribute" appeared during a brief hiatus in the prosecution of obscene texts and photographs. In 1880, the Vice Society, which between 1868 and 1880 had confiscated a quarter of a million photographs and, according to Edward Bristow, "forced, through legislation and pressure on the police, Holywell Street purveyors of 'erotica' to decamp to the Continent," finally ran out of money. No more was heard of the Vice Society in court after that date. In the five years prior to the "Maiden Tribute," vendors in cheap wares had returned in force and made their presence known in a most public way during the time of the "Maiden Tribute."[6]

The publication to capitalize most successfully on the sensation of the "Maiden Tribute" was *Town Talk*, an inexpensive penny weekly that specialized in flagellant correspondence. Featuring a series of cover illustrations entitled the "Maiden Tribute Illustrated," *Town Talk* claimed a family connection to the exposés of the "Maiden Tribute." Its editor quoted one fictitious letter from a "popular East End clergyman" who wished "your work success": "There is no doubt at all that you have inspired the *PMG*, and in several of your contemporary's articles I have read things which I well remember to have seen in *Town Talk*."[7]

As upsetting as the pornographic content of "objectionable street literature" was the fact that it was being hawked by young boys and girls. Numerous complaints were registered about boys in the street "quoting pungent sentences" from the "Maiden Tribute" or trying to pick their way through Stead's classical allusions. Even more distressing were the "shoeless, impudent, little girls" who pushed vile pictures into the faces of passersby. Even Stead's own supporters were concerned with the demoralizing influence of the *PMG*'s "disgusting placards" on London girls: Ellice Hopkins warned him against encouraging the "love of excitement that makes our little girls find the only respectable life open to them simply intolerable, and that loathsome 'five pounds' irresistible."[8]

Stead's opponents interpreted the aggressive sale of the "Maiden Tribute" and other "obscene literature" as an act of class antagonism by the "howling dervishes" who used the occasion to harass their betters and to jostle "innocent" women. Observers complained of ruffians thrusting objectionable literature under the "eyes of two, quiet, respectable young ladies," or into the "faces of delicate mothers and wives, and fair young maidens, huddling close to their male consorts like frightened sheep."[9] In one instance, elite male paternalism was doubly affronted when another gentleman walking with his daughter in the Strand was accosted as a potential Minotaur. According to the gentleman's own account, a detective had been ordered to follow him by a barrister, "who thought he [the gentleman] was suspicious" and his daughter "was not my property." "What a pretty fool he must have felt, when, for all his trouble, he found the supposed wicked nobleman luring his prey to his ancestral abode to be none other than your obedient servant."[10]

The class provenance of Stead's narrative also became a subject of heated debate. Exactly whose language was it, this "Romance of the Brothel"? Was it a version of a Gothic pennydreadful or a knockoff of expensive libertine literature? Whereas Stead's opponents bracketed the *PMG* with "gutter publications," written in the terms of the "ignorant and uneducated," Charles Bradlaugh's *National Reformer,* equally dubious of Stead's motives, criticized his "callous adhesion to the verbiage of the upper classes." Bradlaugh and Besant could not help resenting the apparent tolerance of Stead's "highly coloured adaptations" of expensive "works printed abroad" when they had previously suffered prosecution (and in Besant's case been deprived of legal custody of her daughter) for distributing Knowlton's "dry physiological tract" on birth control.[11]

The "Maiden Tribute" and its imitations, Stead's critics argued, actually encouraged the crimes it had set out to expose. At the Middlesex sessions, on August 24, the judge linked cases of indecent assault to the "flood of obscene literature" brought "within the reach of the poorest class of the population." "A Saunterer in the Labyrinth," writing into the *PMG,* believed that the "Maiden Tribute" had "put the notion of buying a virgin into the heads of a great many men who never entertained it before," and even "told them how much it would cost." The *PMG* actually reported two cases of sexual assault of "virgins" where monetary reparations were offered at the valuation set by the "Maiden Tribute": in Manchester, a father whose daughter had been assaulted, "having read the *Pall Mall Gazette* and the *War Cry*" (Salvation Army paper) demanded "no less than £5" as consolation for "wounded honour"; while a farmer, charged with assaulting a domestic servant in his employ, offered £5 to "square the matter."[12]

One of Stead's most irritating crimes, his critics asserted, was inadvertently to have "democratized" pornography: for a mere one penny he had put into circulation lurid images and narratives that were usually restricted to readers of three-guinea volumes. As the Middlesex judge complained, he had brought explicit obscene literature "within the reach of the poorest class in the population." He had brought out into the open what should at least have remained secret, and made the "lingua franca of the brothel" available to constituencies for whom it was never meant: women, children, and the working class in general.[13]

Whatever his intentions, Stead seemed to have encouraged an explosion in the dissemination of "sexual knowledge," much of it fiercely misogynist, but some of which was on the order of *Aristotle's Masterpiece,* a popular self-help medical text principally directed at a female readership.[14] His publication simultaneously incited an interest in the sexual and helped to mobilize a new offensive against the obscene. The newly organized National Vigilance Association readily entered the fray, taking up where the Vice Society had left off. It received the full cooperation of Sir Charles Warren, the new chief commissioner of police, who issued new instructions for 1886 that required the strictest possible enforcement of the law against the sale of indecent literature and photographs. Vigilance groups also condemned the works of Balzac, Zola, Boccaccio, and Rabelais as obscene and successfully prosecuted their British distributors; they attacked birth-control literature and advertisements for "female pills" (abortifacient drugs) on the same grounds. To these moral crusaders, pornographic literature, thus broadly defined, was a vile expression of the same undifferentiated male lust that ultimately led to prostitution and homosexuality. As we have seen in relation to the outcry over the "Maiden Tribute," the fact that pornography, and even the *Decameron* and *Germinal,* were now available in cheap editions undoubtedly heightened middle-class concern over the emergence of a degenerate and unsupervised urban popular culture.[15]

Sex-Crime Reporting

The index of the *PMG* for the late 1880s strikingly reveals both the proliferation of discourses around sexual danger and new definitions and categories of that danger. After the "Maiden Tribute," the amount of reporting of sexual crimes in the *PMG* increased dramatically, mirroring in part the actual increase in charges against men for sexual assault and in part Stead's new concern over sexual crime.[16] Stead's crime reporting carried mixed messages. Wherever possible, Stead tried to highlight sex exploitation as class exploitation, to expose the iniquity of wicked baronets who preyed on schoolgirls or affluent Minotaurs who drugged innocent country girls, or to deplore judicial bias towards female plaintiffs. However, most incidents reported in the *PMG* (including assault as well as disorderly-house cases) involved working-class "villains" and were accompanied by few editorial comments; in their objectifying and sensational character, they were indistinguishable from contemporary news items in *News of the World* or *Illustrated Police News*.[17]

Sexually Dangerous Men

After his trial and imprisonment, Stead promised Mr. Thompson, his publisher, that there would be "no more Maiden Tributing" to shock respectable readers of the *PMG*. Yet, between 1885 and 1889, he continued to manufacture "thunderbolts" and "escapades" that politicized sexual danger, turning his attention first to privileged men who "ruined" women and ultimately condemning the police for their "attacks" on women.[18]

Stead's first target was the prominent Radical politician, Sir Charles Dilke, who had the misfortune of being named a correspondent in a divorce case soon after the "Maiden Tribute" had appeared.[19] In Crawford v. Crawford, Dilke was accused of seducing Virginia Crawford, the girl-bride of his M.P. colleague, who was herself the daughter of one of his old mistresses. Mrs. Crawford had confessed to her husband that Dilke had initiated her into all the mysteries of "French vice," including a three-in-a-bed episode with Dilke's servant, "Fanny." "He taught me every French vice," she confessed. "He used to say that I knew more than most women of thirty."[20] Although other newspapers seized the opportunity of transforming a scandal in high life into good copy (they could choose between the Crawford case and another sensational divorce case, Campbell v. Campbell), Stead's relentless prosecution of Dilke in the *PMG* was probably decisive in alienating Dilke from the Nonconformists in his party and ruining his political career.[21]

Stead's motives for pursuing Dilke were undoubtedly complex (Lady Dilke believed he was using Dilke to get back at Joseph Chamberlain, another prominent Radical and close political associate of Dilke).[22] What seems to have excited Stead's particular hostility and what he highlighted in his pamphlets against Dilke were the perverse sexual practices he had allegedly forced on Mrs. Crawford. Dilke's crime, Stead emphasized, involved "not only adultery" but "French vice": Dilke had subjected a young woman "to the last outrages of depraved and unnatural vice."[23] Stead continued to expose the sexual sadism of privileged men in his next campaign to protect womanhood, the Langworthy case of 1887. In the pages of the *PMG*, Stead demanded that justice be "done" "to a woman cruelly deceived": he recounted the story of Mrs. Langworthy, the unfortunate victim of a fraudulent marriage to a millionaire named Edwin Langworthy, who fathered her child, filed for bankruptcy, and fled the country, leaving her destitute. "Strange True Stories of Today: the Langworthy Marriage," appearing on April 18, 1887, opened with a "bizarre tale" of an "immensely rich" Englishman on his honeymoon at Lisbon amusing himself by torturing and killing cats who frequented the hotel garden, foreshadowing the "cruel sport" he was to have with his bride, "a refined and cultured lady."[24]

The Langworthy campaign was a popular success for Stead, significantly boosting the *PMG*'s sales and encouraging him in his grandiose schemes for a "government" and "justice" by journalism. However, when Stead tried to intervene in judicial proceedings in a real crime of sexual sadism, involving a Jewish immigrant, Israel Lipski, he suffered his first mortifying failure. The Lipski case involved a murder and sexual assault on a Jewish woman in Whitechapel by her lodger, and established one immediate precedent for racist and anti-Semitic theories of Jack the Ripper as a Jew. It also illustrates Stead's continued interest in cases of sexual sadism even in the different milieu of the East End, where the male protagonists were initially identified as black proletarian villains rather than as the Sadeian rakes of the "Maiden Tribute."[25]

Police Attacks on Women

Stead did not stop with exposés of sexually "dangerous" men. He soon turned his critical gaze on the police, towards whom he had developed a particular animus ever since the Armstrong trial[26]—a hostility exacerbated by their inept and brutal suppression of socialist-led unemployment demonstrations in 1886.[27] By the end of 1885 Stead had begun to criticize the police for making the streets unsafe for women.[28]

In January 1886, Stead reprinted a letter from a "lady" published earlier in the *Standard* and the *Daily News,* under the heading "Police Outrage on a Lady." The anonymous writer complained of being accosted by a policeman when a friend, "a well-known physician," had escorted her home one night. The policeman told her friend " 'I've nothing to do with you, Sir; I don't want to interfere with you. It's her I want'." He also made it clear that he "wanted some money." The letter writer was Olive Schreiner, whose spiritual identification with fallen women, thanks to the police constable, had found poignant expression: she had "merely experienced for once a very little of what her forlorn sisters have to put up with always."[29]

By 1887, the *PMG*'s index had appended "police assaults on women" to its listing for "assaults on women" (followed by "police assaults" more generally).[30] In June that year, press complaints over false arrests and police blackmail exploded over a sensational case involving Miss Elizabeth Cass, a respectable milliner, who was falsely arrested for streetwalking on Regent Street.[31] Accompanied by her stalwart and protective employer, Miss Cass protested her innocence in police court and insisted that she was on her way to purchase gloves. The magistrate, Mr. Newton, dismissed the charge against her, but also noted that no respectable woman would be found walking on Regent Street at 9:00 in the evening.[32] Indignant M.P.s from the North raised questions about the magistrate's handling of the Cass case in Parliament and achieved the virtual censure of the government and the home secretary (who had defended Newton) by successfully moving a motion to adjourn. In the end, Sir Charles Warren, the police commissioner, issued new orders, prohibiting arrests of streetwalkers without a citizen complaint. After the Cass case, police repression of street prostitution declined precipitously between 1887 and 1889 (although the police assault on brothels was sustained).[33]

Meanwhile, a large section of the daily press took up Miss Cass's cause, using the pretext of wounded female honor to defend the "liberty of the subject" and to demand the public suppression of "foreign" vice. One correspondent in the *Daily Telegraph* expressed patriotic outrage that "foreign women" and their bullies were allowed to "infest" the area at will, while "an innocent and most respectable young English girl is pounced on." In a private letter to Stead, Butler, who always loved a good female martyr, welcomed the "case of Miss Cass" as "providential": "One of the humblest and weakest girls in the metropolis has all but upset the Home Secretary and has completely upset the Supercilious Contempt of the Government. . . . I have been waiting for such an event for many years." Through the Cass case, Stead tried to vindicate the right of respectable working women to be on the street alone at night, but his defense of them largely rested on their virtue and chastity. And, of course, his "New Crusade" had intensified pressure on the police to crack down on streetwalkers in the first instance.[34]

A telling and controversial feature of this cause célèbre was the occupational identity of the victimized heroine: she was a milliner, newly arrived from the North of England, employed to assist the large numbers of shopping ladies attracted to the feminized world of shopping that had been created for them in the city center. The Cass case provoked a renewed discussion of the West End as contested terrain, as not only the heart of Stead's dark labyrinth but also as an illuminated commercial landscape, where women and men of different classes mixed. The false arrest of Miss Cass for streetwalking, turning as it did on the theme of mistaken identity, epitomized the charged and ambiguous nature of gender encounters in London's West End, an urban setting that was traditionally male territory, an eroticized zone of commercialized sex, yet also a fashionable shopping area for ladies.

In the pages of the *PMG*, middle-class female correspondents shifted the discussion away from the "police outrage in Regent street" to a consideration of respectable women's vulnerability to well-dressed civilian "male pests." Most of these female correspondents remained anonymous, simply designating themselves "Indignation," or a "Lady of Forty," but they did include the self-identified feminist and social-purity advocate Laura Ormiston Chant. These "ladies" used the correspondence columns to vent their anger against sexual harassment which, during their quotidian travels through the city, they had to endure in silence. Some offered remedies for the problem. In "Going to the Root of the Matter," a female correspondent insisted that the "remedy for the state of things in Regent street and other streets is for respectable women to make a point of walking there and anywhere else they like, and at any hour they like." She deplored the "unnatural [restrictive] training" women received as a consequence of the evil of "vicious men." Male annoyance, stated another correspondent, was "not sufficient" to make it impossible for a young married woman to walk out alone, "yet it is quite sufficient to be a constant source of anxiety and discomfort." To women who complained that they had been accosted in the middle of the day even when "wearing sober black or blue dresses," one female correspondent recommended "an infallible specific"—"a Salvation Army bonnet!"[35]

Stead, characteristically, allowed "vicious men" to respond in "What the Male Pests have to Say for Themselves." These male correspondents defended their own practice of "following after and speaking to respectable women," insisting that a woman who goes about the "haunts of men" in a "tailor-made dress" (whose tight fit, according to one private letter circulated at the time, simply accentuated the "false bottoms and stays—and other erotic adornments," that women wore to "excite the male sex") should not feel "insulted" if approached by a stranger. Male correspondents also attacked the ignorance, class prejudice, and misguided assumptions of "outraged females." "Like most people who know nothing about the matter," "outraged females" seem to "divide women into two classes—the strictly virtuous and the strictly the other way," declared "Le Monsieur qui a suivi les dames." "There are hundreds of girls, without being vicious, who *will* enter into conversation"; these included not only "girls" or "silly," "half-educated middle-class women" but "ladies who ought to and do know better." Another "Man of the World" focused on the habits of girls in business. "There is nothing which tens, hundreds of thousands of girls more desire than to be addressed by unknown men in the streets," declared a "Socialist." "At work all day, . . . with no parties in the evening" they held their "evening parties in the street."[36]

"Men of the World" invoked the "middle ground" of open yet licit sexuality that, according to Peter Bailey, had been constructed by the consumer culture of the nineteenth century, as an ensemble of sites, practices, and occasions that "mediate across the frontiers of the putative public/private divide." In this "middle ground," the objects of desire were mostly women of liminal status, neither ladies nor prostitutes, but girls "who are not vicious, but *will* enter into conversation." Male correspondents endowed these women with a sexual "knowingness," in sharp contrast to the sexual "prudery" of middle-class feminists, who would deprive the people of their pleasures and gentlemen of access to girls who "have their evening parties on the street." When a "Woman's Rights advocate" came to the "rescue" of a "victim," "Socialist" reported, "speechless was her astonishment when the 'victim' rounded upon her, in very strong language for her officious interference in other people's affairs." "The girls who really feel insulted by strangers addressing them in the street are, in general, only ladies, and the 'insult' oftenist consists, not so much in what is said, as in being taken to belong to a lower class of girls, who welcome such self-introduction."[37]

As with other media scandals, Stead tried to use the Cass case to create a single moral majority out of an expanded, heterogeneous public. To a certain extent, he succeeded. Stead and the entire daily press embraced the cause of the pure and innocent working girl from the North, as a nationalist defense of the "liberty of the subject" against the threat of "foreign vice" and a "Continental-style" police. Yet, the *PMG*'s correspondence between "male pests" and "outraged females" also extended the meanings of the Cass case well beyond the "police outrage in Regent street" to elaborate many subject positions and to delineate new forms of heterosexuality. In the midst of media scandals of sexual danger in the London Labyrinth, Stead allowed shopping ladies to voice their anger against ordinary "Male Pests," while enabling the "Men of the World" to extol a new kind of diffuse, healthy sexuality—the middle ground—associated with the new spaces of consumer culture and with girls who were neither "strictly virtuous" nor "strictly the other way."

In their correspondence, "Male Pests" documented and acclaimed a distinctive street style—of verbal chaffing, of carefully managed eroticism—that working women may well have carried with them into the city center. This endorsement was in no ways innocent; on the contrary, the male fantasy of "parasexuality" also operated strategically and politically to counter a feminist melodrama of sexual danger, that would deprive the people of their pleasures and gentlemen of access to female companions who "hold their evening parties in the street."

Stead and Late-Victorian Fictional Forms

If the correspondence of "Male Pests" articulated one form of mass market fantasy—of a normalized, carefully channeled sexuality of everyday life— other male genres of the period still represented men as enmeshed in the sexual dangers associated with the dark side of London life. According to the new male fictional forms of the period, this "dark world" respected no geographical or class boundary, because the predatory Other made its home in the inner recesses of the Self.[38] Like the "Maiden Tribute" itself, fictional writings such as the detective novel and the male Gothic both ratified sexual difference and contained scenarios of considerable sexual ambiguity. Through fantasy, elite men were able to project their sexual fears and anxieties on to a "male killing force," but in the person of the detective hero they quickly invoked a superrational superego to hunt down those same repressed desires and to restore order. *The Strange Case of Dr. Jekyll and Mr. Hyde,* written by R. L. Stevenson in the autumn of 1885 (after his friend, W. E. Henley, had excitedly forwarded to him the install- ments of the "Maiden Tribute"),[39] was the first of the late-Victorian Gothic works to take up these themes, anticipating *Dracula, The Picture of Dorian Gray,* and *The Island of Dr. Moreau.* With Conan Doyle's Sherlock Holmes, whose first story appeared in 1887, the amateur detective hero also attained "mythic stature."[40] The social response to the Ripper mur- ders of 1888 also stimulated widespread male fascination with and emula- tion of both those roles—of the Ripper as a "hero of crime" and of the scientific investigators on his trail.[41]

Within three years, Stead's radical formula for scandal journalism would be taken up by the tabloid and conservative press, denatured of whatever populist critique and political idealism it possessed, and deployed to defend the dominant order of both class and gender relations. Yet there were striking similarities between the two media events. In particular, the form of sexual violence which the Ripper murders came to represent bore an uncanny resemblance to the typology of sexual crime foregrounded in the "Maiden Tribute" (a family resemblance later specified by at least one sexologist in his psychiatric assessment of the unknown murderer). Both the Ripper and Stead's Minotaur committed anonymous, multiple sexual crimes in urban settings. Both were products or purveyors of unnatural lust. Like the Minotaur, the Ripper's sexual appetite was considered to be perverse and unbounded; instead of defloration and flogging, the Whitechapel killer preferred "lust murder" as an "unnatural" alternative to heterosexual copulation. Both had a taste for clinical, sadistic practices. Both committed crimes against poor women, but their activities implicitly placed all women who traversed the social spaces of the city at risk. The terror of their acts was amplified by the New Journalism of the 1880s, particularly the "universal interview," which encouraged anonymous male villains like the Ripper or the rakish "Saunterer" to communicate with a mass public through the newspaper.

The Legacy for Feminism

These villainous roles were not available to women, however compelled they might have been by multiple and conflicted fantasies of sexual danger. Feminists who tried to salvage the "Maiden Tribute" for emancipationist purposes, as an opening for women to discuss sexual matters in public, had to recast Stead's drama considerably to make it an imaginative vehicle for themselves. They treated the "Maiden Tribute" as if it had addressed women and called them into action. Their reading of Stead's text was dynamically creative; they resisted his innovations and read the story back into the traditions of female literary melodrama. Ignoring the fact that Stead had obliterated any positive female voice from his narrative, feminists returned to Butler's political melodrama for their model of female heroism. Elizabeth Cobb was overwhelmed by the "new possibilities of thought" opened up by the "Maiden Tribute." Stead's revelations, wrote Maria Sharpe, another London feminist, broke down "a great barrier for women." "After them no one was of necessity to be in ignorance."[42]

Feminist supporters of Stead used the new "license" to speak publicly on sexual matters to voice their own fears about sexual danger and to attack institutions of male power that encouraged violence against women. Exclusion from the social contract, liberal feminists insisted, made women vulnerable in public places. They identified the "outlawed political condition of women" as the root cause of the crimes exposed in the "Maiden Tribute"; legal indifference and female economic dependence, they charged, placed all women, regardless of class, at risk.[43]

In a culture where women were often the victims of sexual coercion yet blamed for crimes committed against them,[44] and where it was difficult even to conceive of female sexual agency and choice as long as women lacked agency in other vital areas, defenders of women's rights could and did regard the social purity doctrine of female passionlessness and male sexual self-control as a significant advance over traditional assumptions of a dangerous and active female sexuality.[45] Whatever its drawbacks (particularly in relation to the advocacy of birth control), this sexual strategy resulted in some permanent gains for women: it made it possible for women to name incest and rape as crimes against their persons (rather than against the property of men).[46] In feminist hands, desexualization could empower women to attack the customary prerogatives of men; it could also validate a new social role for women outside the heterosexual family. "The new possibilities" opened up by the "Maiden Tribute" helped the New Women of the late-nineteenth century to mark out a "passionless" sexual identity independent of men.[47]

The "Maiden Tribute" also stimulated middle-class women to express their solidarity with their poor sisters. Stead's revelations propelled a number of women, including Rachel McMillan and Olive Schreiner, into socialism. Olive Schreiner organized an emotional women's protest to the *PMG:* the revelations, wrote Schreiner, "have shown us what lay behind our smooth lives. They have filled us with remorse. Have we cried out 'All women are one'. . . . Have we been content to be ignorant." The letter was never published because some feminists judged it "too emotional," but Schreiner's friend, Elizabeth Cobb, praised its social identification with poor women. "I like Olive's 'all women are one'."[48]

Like the work of Butler and female writers of literary melodrama, this call to female unity based on the example of suffering, fallen womanhood was fraught with contradictions and difficulties. While championing the cause of the fallen woman and the "endangered" girl, feminists established a hierarchical and custodial relation to the "daughters" they had set out to protect. As members of the propertied classes, feminists felt obliged to redress the sexual wrongs done to poor girls by privileged men, and they often registered the same repugnance and ambivalence toward "incorrigible" girls as they had towards unrepentant prostitutes. For them, as for more repressive moralists, the desire to protect young girls entailed imposing on them a social code that stressed female adolescent dependence. This code was more in keeping with middle-class notions of girlhood than with the lived reality of the exposed and unsupervised daughters of the laboring poor who were on the streets. Yet this unitary model of an appropriately protected "girlhood" coexisted with unexamined assumptions about the fate of sturdy "young cockney[s]" like Eliza Armstrong who had to be saved from a life of vice and outrage to become a servant "of the poorer middle classes."[49]

Social purity generated practices and narratives that empowered and disabled women of different classes in complicated ways: although it imposed a disciplinary regime on working-class women, it simultaneously stimulated new "possibilities of thought" among middle-class women, inciting them to explore their own sexual subjectivity. Driven by "fear" into "speech,"[50] progressive New Women ultimately transgressed the boundaries of social purity to contemplate free monogamous unions based on intellectual sympathy and mutual heterosexual passion. In this exploration, they were even prompted to reconsider their view of "preventive checks" (birth control), which they previously condemned as one further means of "making the woman into an instrument for the use of the man."[51] Their explorations, however pioneering, continued to be marked by a sense of sexual vulnerability and by reservations about men. The next chapter, featuring Karl Pearson's Men and Women's Club, highlights the determined efforts of freethinking women and men to imagine new heterosexual possibilities as well as the sexual dangers marked out by Stead. In an urban setting considerably removed from Stead's labyrinthine cityscape, these intrepid explorers set out to examine the "complex thought and feeling" unleashed by Stead's revelations.

1. "The Vile Traffic." From *Town Talk*, 18 July 1885 (British Newspaper Library. By permission of the British Library).

2. "Sexual Danger in the East End and West End: the Cass Case and the Lipski Case." From *Police Illustrated News*, 16 July 1887 (British Newspaper Library. By permission of the British Library).

3. Karl Pearson, The Man of the Study (University College, London).

4. Maria Sharpe, member of the Men and Women's Club (University College, London).

5. Members of the Men and Women's Club at play: a picnic, 1887 (University College, London).

6. Mrs. Weldon as the "Portia of the Law Courts." From *Vanity Fair*, 3 May 1884, 243 (New York Public Library. General Research Division. Astor, Lenox and Tilden Foundations).

7. Mrs. Weldon, a Disorderly Woman. From "Days with Celebrities: A Woman's-Rightess." *Moonshine*, 10 May 1884, 217.

8. Pears Soap advertisement. From *Illustrated London News*,
11 February 1888, 152 (New York Public Library. General
Research Division. Astor, Lenox and Tilden Foundations).

THE NEMESIS OF NEGLECT.

"THERE FLOATS A PHANTOM ON THE SLUM'S FOUL AIR,
    SHAPING, TO EYES WHICH HAVE THE GIFT OF SEEING,
INTO THE SPECTRE OF THAT LOATHLY LAIR.
    FACE IT—FOR VAIN IS FLEEING!
RED-HANDED, RUTHLESS, FURTIVE, UNERECT,
'TIS MURDEROUS CRIME—THE NEMESIS OF NEGLECT!"

9. "The Nemesis of Neglect." From *Punch*, 29 September 1888 (New York Public Library. General Research Division. Astor, Lenox and Tilden Foundations).

10. "Ready for the Whitechapel Fiend." From *Police Illustrated News*,
22 September 1888 (British Newspaper Library. By permission of the British
Library).

1. Polly Nicholls's Last Words. From *Police Illustrated News*, 12 October 888 (British Newspaper Library. By permission of the British Library).

No. 1424.—Vol. 55

SEPTEMBER 15, 1888

THE·PENNY
ILLUSTRATED·PAPER
AND·ILLUSTRATED TIMES

REGISTERED AT THE GENERAL POST-OFFICE AS A NEWSPAPER.

London : Printed and Published at the Office, 10, Milford-lane, Strand, in the Parish of St. Clement Danes, in the County of Middlesex, by Thomas Fox, 10, Milford-lane, Strand, aforesaid.

REAR OF Nº 29, HANBURY ST

Nº 29, HANBURY ST

⊕ WHERE BODY WAS FOUND

We depict the site of the barbarous murder at 29, Hanbury-street, Whitechapel, and the scene in front of the house last Saturday. Succeeding, as it did, several terrible outrages of a similar nature in the same district, this foul assassination of the unfortunate woman, Annie Chapman, alias Sievey, has naturally aroused East London to take sensible precautions to prevent the recurrence of these deplorable murders. A few days after the discovery of the mutilated body of a woman in George-yard last month, a Committee of Safety was formed to assist the Police. Once let every citizen be on the alert to aid the ends of Justice, and such outrages should be stamped out. London needs to be more neighbourly in order to checkmate the criminals in our midst.

SCENE OF THE TERRIBLE MURDER IN HANBURY-STREET, WHITECHAPEL.

12. "Scene of the Terrible Murder in Hanbury-Street, Whitechapel." From *Penny Illustrated Paper*, 15 September 1888 (British Newspaper Library. By permission of the British Library).

13. "The Miller-Court Murder, Whitechapel: Site of Mary Kelly's Lodgings."
From *Penny Illustrated Paper*, 17 November 1888 (British Newspaper Library.
By permission of the British Library).

A LOST WOMAN
MARY KELLY
IN MILLER'S COURT

14. "A Lost Woman: Mary Kelly in Miller's Court." From *Penny Illustrated Paper*, 17 November 1888 (British Newspaper Library. By permission of the British Library).

15. "The Seventh Victim." From *Police Illustrated News*, 17 November 1888 (British Newspaper Library. By permission of the British Library).

FIVE

The Men and Women's Club

n the summer of 1885, as the "Maiden Tribute" rolled off the press, Karl Pearson, socialist and future eugenicist, founded the Men and Women's Club to talk about sex. Pearson assembled a group of middle-class radical-liberals, socialists, and feminists who shared his high seriousness and sense of intellectual adventure. Over four years, club discussions ranged from sexual relations in Periclean Athens to the position of Buddhist nuns, to more contemporary discussions of the organization and regulation of sexuality, particularly in relation to marriage, prostitution, and friendship.[1] Members drew on biography, novels, anthropological writings, Darwin, and personal experience to interpret the changing features of sex and gender. Heterosexual fantasy and ideology set the boundaries of club discussions: some individuals may have analyzed the changing social organization of female sexuality, but all participants treated sexual feeling and identity as unquestionably heterosexual, variable only in its intensity between male and female.[2]

Middle-class participants imagined their club as a genteel, restricted, semiprivate space set off from the vulgarized arenas of popular culture. However, this self-conscious separation from the popular arena was illusory. Although the members of the Men and Women's Club tried to separate their scientific work from the vulgarity and crass sensationalism of the surrounding market culture, they drew upon a repertoire of themes and narratives that circulated widely in 'high' and 'low' places. Moreover, through the newspaper page, the commercialized, sensation-seeking world outside directly impinged on the protected environment of the Men and Women's Club: media scandal, in particular Stead's exposé of white slavery and child prostitution in London, had helped to call the club into being and a media extravaganza over marriage and its discontents served to publicize its ideas.[3]

Stead's New Journalism and Pearson's discussion club constituted new forms of social communication that expanded the boundaries of the public sphere in the 1880s. Both were part of the proliferating discourses over sexuality that also marked the 1880s, when utopian projects for a "new sexuality" flourished alongside new repressive legislation against prostitution, homosexuality, and pornography. Like Stead, club members were key participants in an effort to specify a new heterosexual (nonprocreative) marital norm for the middle class, while simultaneously marking off a range of sexual practices as dangerous. Like Stead, they too were implicated in and imaginatively engaged with the same dangerous sexualities they had banished from club practices and discussions; and they too enacted their own melodramas as a series of interlocking human plots.[4]

The Men and Women's Club was remarkable for its ambitions but also for its members' sense of their historical importance. The latter is registered in the archives the club left to posterity, now available in the Pearson collection at University College, London. To prove their earnestness and to immortalize their experiment, club officers kept careful records of session meetings, including minutes and copies of the formal papers. To this has been added Pearson's private correspondence with a multitude of members and nonmembers about the club, as well as a separate correspondence conducted by Maria Sharpe, the club's secretary, whose autobiographical memoir of her experience most closely approximates a "comprehensive" history of the club. In their correspondence with Pearson and Sharpe, club members wrote about what they thought of the club and about each other. The documents permit this historian, who has attempted a narratorial voice-over, to present the club discussions stereophonically, in multiple voices, to offer an interpretation of the silences as well as the interventions at club meetings.[5]

However pioneering, club discussions were nonetheless fraught with male-female tensions and antagonisms. The sessions, which extended over four years, became increasingly stalemated and deadlocked, while frustrations at the sessions generated their own smaller dramas offstage. These exchanges reveal, first of all, a discourse of power, where men dominated and intimidated women, who resisted with impressive tenacity. Battle lines were sharply drawn, but also transgressed. Women were implicated in the discourse of power: female members often disparaged each other and only reluctantly upheld the solidarity of their "sex" against the "dominant tone" of the men. Although the men assumed an authoritative voice in club discussions, they often found themselves frustrated by the limits of their own rationalist formulations to express desire.

Club discourses were also dialectical. Onstage and off, club members explored the dialectic of sex in the 1880s: the dialectic was between sexual possibility and sexual danger, and it reveals radically different attitudes towards masculinity and femininity, and especially heterosexuality on the part of men and women. Besides provoking female defiance, the discursive struggle also served to elaborate an erotic script by generating resistance and deferral, those indispensable components of a Victorian sexual narrative. There existed within the club, then, a symbiotic relationship between censorship, secrets, and sexual incitement.[6]

Two Beginnings

The club had two beginnings and, as we shall see, multiple endings. It had its first origins in the personal and political agenda of its founder, Karl Pearson, whose motives for establishing the club were complex: a response to his own unhappy family history, a scientific interest in fieldwork, his own courtship ambition.

At the time of the club's founding, Pearson was a young barrister beginning a career in mathematics at University College, London: a young man of "immense, humorless, and self-important rectitude." A convinced Darwinist and socialist, Pearson's beliefs accorded with the two marked tendencies of intellectual life in the 1880s, as described by Beatrice Webb: a preoccupation with science and a transferal of the ideal of "service" from God to man. As a an undergraduate, he had lost his Christian faith, refused to attend divinity lectures, and turned to Spinoza and free thought for spiritual enlightenment. He was above all a rationalist, intent on subjecting all social conventions to the cold eye of reason. And he saw himself as an intellectual adventurer, prepared to dedicate his life to "destroying old idols" and hewing "new paths" through the "jungle."[7]

As rationalist and explorer, he was a fitting founder of the Men and Women's Club; but his cold personality was strikingly ill-suited to the delicate task of drawing women out on the subject of sexual relations. Friends and enemies alike described him as hot and cold: physically attractive with "burning eyes" and a "beautiful face" ("I can't understand any woman seeing him without loving him, and wanting to fall down at his feet," one woman told Olive Schreiner); but remote and intolerant in conversation— a "lump of ice," "more impersonal than any one I know."[8]

Pearson's impersonal, cold rationalist side structured his public stance toward and theoretical interest in sexuality. Pearson was sympathetic to a positivist variant of Darwinism; he was eugenic in his sympathies before he had espoused eugenics as his grand project. Biology had absolute determining power for him; but he was searching for new ways to guide it, to shift the theater of evolution from nature to society, to snatch the threads of life out of nature's hand to be pulled by human experts.[9] This involved the institutional regulation of human—i.e., female—reproduction by male "brain workers" like himself. The state management of human reproduction was at the heart of his interest in socialism, which he interpreted as support for a strong state. His socialism was fueled by a hostility to an aristocracy of wealth, whether landed or industrial, as well as by an antipathy to the values of an expanding consumer culture. His political platform furthered the interests of a professional middle class, whose status derived from specific mental skills and accredited knowledge rather than ownership of capital or land. Pearson's project, moreover, was inextricably bound up with racial and imperial politics, with devising an appropriate reproductive strategy for a class of imperial administrators fit to oversee a world empire inhabited by "inferior races."[10]

Pearson's Woman Question

Pearson's response to the Woman Question was marked by the same proto-eugenic interests. He identified bourgeois women—those "shopping dolls"—as offensive symbols of the conspicuous consumption of the wasteful propertied classes; while the causes closest to his heart, social evolution and race survival, depended on the proper ordering of sex relations and management of women's reproductive lives.[11]

But Pearson had a personal agenda that partially conflicted with his well-managed and abstract social program. His interest in women was intensely personal, motivated in part by a desire to reach out to them, as he watched his Cambridge bachelor friends, one by one, fall "below the ballast" and marry. In 1886, the death of Henry Bradshaw, Pearson's friend and mentor at Cambridge, created an emotional hole in his life and definitively tipped the scales in favor of heterosocial attachments. Within the first year of the club's existence, Pearson had entered his heterosexual phase.[12]

Pearson's interest in the organization of sex and gender also derived from his firsthand experience of the unhappiness of his own parents' marriage. His father, William Pearson, was a successful barrister who dominated his family "to the point of tyranny."[13] Too delicate to be sent away to public school, Karl remained at home and sided with his ineffectual, emotionally distracted mother. His family's history gave him some insight into the material foundations of male domination: "There is always a demoralizing influence in the power of one individual over another . . . and this to a great extent must accompany the power of the purse."[14] From his mother he also learned how a woman's love for her children can be "a great unlimited social force" if "only directed into the right channels."[15] However, close identification with a weak mother may have bred contempt as well as sympathy for women.[16] Pearson's ambivalence was reflected in his hostility to conventional middle-class women and in his condescending relations with the women of the club. However much he championed the sexual choices of the advanced New Woman in the abstract, he was terrified and disoriented by any signs of female sexual agency in the flesh.[17] He was one of those "New Men" of the 1880s—like George Gissing—who criticized and heralded the end of the patriarchal era but looked with fear towards the new feminist order.[18]

The Selection of Members

Pearson began his exploration by attaching himself to a safe, older married woman, Elizabeth Cobb, herself a "restless spirit," dissatisfied with domesticity and with her marriage to an "intensely practical," unimaginative solicitor M.P. husband.[19] Cobb provided Pearson with crucial assistance in recruiting female members for his "young people's club." Her recruits included her two sisters, Loetitia and Maria Sharpe, and other women of her acquaintance whom she could "trust." Throughout 1885, Cobb's letters to Pearson contain tantalizing sketches of possible candidates for the club. She judged Mrs. Parker, the new wife of one of Pearson's close friends, too conventional—"not much depth in her" (she became a member in any case); while Kate Mitchell, a female doctor, was ruled out as "unrefined." Cobb predicted that Pearson would like a Miss Shedlock (a mathematics teacher in a girl's high school), because he seemed to respect those women most "who hate men" and regard "sympathy a mark of women's slavish nature." Alternatively, Cobb hoped Miss Muller, another prominent "man-hater," would not "set the tone of the club."[20]

Cobb's most impressive recruit was Olive Schreiner, who had just published her widely acclaimed novel, *The Story of an African Farm*, and who was in London under a doctor's care. She was the toast of London: *African Farm* was second only to Mill's *Subjection of Women* in communicating the wrongs of womanhood to late-Victorians, particularly the thwarting of female individuality; it was preeminent in representing female sexual desire, however hapless and ill-fated. Schreiner herself was a cultural phenomenon: a "new style of womanhood" who adopted an unguarded manner in public and privately exhausted male admirers with hours-long discussions in her bare lodgings, much to the disgust of her landladies. She was part of the bohemian, radical circle of the British Museum Reading Room, a great friend of Eleanor Marx Aveling, the revolutionary "platform speaker." But she also found time for her more "commonplace friends" like the maternal Mrs. Cobb.[21]

Schreiner was interested in the club's topic but she mainly had her eye on Karl Pearson, for whom she developed an intense but unrequited passion (she left the club at the end of 1886, after Pearson had rebuffed her). Like Pearson, she claimed to be at work on a "woman book" that would look at women from a historical, biological, and sexological perspective. She proved to be a most unreliable club member, "too emotional" to treat the discussion of sex "dispassionately." Her dramatic interventions appear out of place in the staid club minutes, and she herself felt uneasy in the presence of more conventional middle-class Londoners: a South African who talked with her hands, a lonely bohemian, who was, according to Cobb, "excitable," wanting in "earnestness," taking "honey where she finds it."[22]

Schreiner was an unusual bohemian presence in the club. On the whole, club members were not sexually adventurous and showed little enthusiasm for free-love doctrines. When Pearson wanted to name the club after Mary Wollstonecraft, the great founding feminist who, in her own life if not in her writings, had broken with the sexual conventions of her day, the women objected: Wollstonecraft's name would personally embarrass them and call into question their own respectability. Maria Sharpe raised similar objections to the membership of Eleanor Marx Aveling (who had contracted a common-law marriage with Edward Aveling). Pearson disagreed; he believed Aveling's example was "the direction marriage ought to go." On the other hand, Pearson drew the line at sexual experiments outside monogamy. He was horrified at the sexual scandal unfolding around the followers of the late James Hinton, a prophet of polygamous free unions; fearful lest the club be tainted by association with "Hintonianism," he carefully monitored the club membership to exclude any individual with a Hintonian past.[23]

The effect of these exclusions was to ensure that female club members were not only sexually unadventurous but also sexually inexperienced. Pearson was left, in the words of Olive Schreiner, with a "lot of old maids and man-haters" to feed his curiosity about female sexuality—often forcing him to inquire circumspectly about the habits of their domestic servants.[24]

Pearson had an easier time collecting men, most of whom were his old Cambridge friends, radical-liberals or socialists like himself, and mostly single. Kinship, friendship, and political alliances linked men and women in the club, but male institutional ties and loyalties were more powerful than those of their female counterparts. On the whole, the men were barristers and doctors, products of public schools, Oxbridge, and the great European universities, who extended and consolidated their old-boy networks in London at the Saville, Atheneum, and National Liberal clubs, and in their professional lives. They moved comfortably between the world of radical London and the institutions of the male ruling class.[25]

The women's associations testify to the widening public and professional life of "new women" in the 1880s. All but two of the female members of the club were single, and many fulfilled the image of the "Glorified Spinster" who possessed an independent income or who earned her own living in the tertiary sector of the economy and chose not to marry. With one exception, the women were active philanthropists and reformers devoted to the cause of women's emancipation, serving on the London School Board, Charity Organization Society, Fabian Society, and women's suffrage societies. These women had benefited from the expansion of women's secondary-school education in the second half of the nineteenth century. Compared to the men, however, the women lacked advanced training and professional expertise. Of the female members, only Henrietta Muller, an "advanced woman" who "cast men aside" and lived among women dedicated to the "public service," had been educated at university. As an experienced publicist and former member of the London School Board, Muller was a fearless defender of a feminist agenda within the club: "Miss Muller," wrote Maria Sharpe, "helped us much with her power of speaking consecutively and argumentatively—which most of us women sadly wanted." Most of the other female members were, in the words of Sharpe, "middle-aged" women of "character" but wholly "untrained," not part of the new university student generation. They were a transitional generation, straddling two worlds and, as we shall see, two sets of languages.[26]

A group of even more formidable and activist socialist women, including Annie Besant, Eleanor Marx Aveling, Charlotte Wilson, and Emma Brooke, was associated with the club through correspondence and papers, and as visitors. Some of these women, particularly Aveling, had been deliberately excluded from the club as unrespectable, while others proclaimed themselves too timorous to join even if they were asked. A friend asked Emma Brooke if she belonged to the club and approved of it; "I answered that I did approve of it in a *measure,* that even if I were asked to belong I could not do so because I had not the nerve." Besant and Aveling looked upon female club members as timid and apolitical, living in a "cosy nest of their own" and only hearing "of the rough side of the outer world." Nonetheless, these women's shadowy presence was crucial to the club: their views on sexual desire, birth control, free unions, and state support for motherhood shaped Pearson's evolving position on these topics. As women of the "market," public orators and publicists, they helped to disseminate club research and thought. They also participated in the secretive ethos of the club; desperately concerned with maintaining her anonymity, Emma Brooke asked Pearson on more than one occasion to burn her letters, or not to circulate her private note (whose very writing "was . . . an act of sacrifice made at your own request").[27]

Male and female members of the club shared Pearson's elitist, reformist, and evolutionary predilections. Darwinism, in its social and biological formulations, was the official language of the club. The books most frequently cited and circulated among club members included the works of Bebel, Bachofen, McLennan, and Morgan as well as Wollstonecraft's *Vindication of the Rights of Woman* and Meredith's *Diana of the Crossways*. Yet, not all members had advanced as far as Pearson in the transition from radical-liberal individualism to a more collectivist and Darwinian scientific socialism. Both gender and political location shaped members' commitment to and understanding of the Woman Question. Pearson's Darwinian program appealed to feminists; it placed women, at least in their reproductive capacity, at the center of history. It seemed to offer a vital new channel for that "influence" which women were supposed to exercise over public events. Yet, even those female members who identified themselves as Darwinians and socialists remained committed to a middle-class feminism of individual rights and political solidarity with other women, emotionally fueled by a sense of sexual grievance against men. As they grappled with the "needs" of the race and with new socialist feminist goals of economic independence through social labor and state support for the welfare of mothers and children, these feminists still upheld the liberal feminist ideal of autonomy, the notion, to quote Frances Power Cobbe, that woman was not created for the "service she can render to man" but "for some end proper to herself."[28]

In contrast, male members tended to subordinate discussions of sex equality and women's rights to the imperatives of racial progress. They often delivered abstract pronouncements on this latter subject, but their relationship to feminism could also be deeply personal. Ralph Thicknesse was typical of his generation of male feminists, in being recruited to feminism through the writings of John Stuart Mill. After reading Mill on the subjection of women, he became so distressed that he seriously questioned whether he could marry under existing legal and social conditions, or find a wife who would share his "mental outlook."[29] Ever since Mary Wollstonecraft, feminism has held out the promise to men of providing them with worthy mates, and this was an assemblage of persons in their thirties on the lookout for "worthy mates."

The women's motivations for joining the club could also be intensely personal. Most were flattered at being asked to join men in an intellectual adventure, and were appreciative of contact with male "minds immensely cleverer than their own." Some women clearly harbored courtship ambitions. They too were exploring sexual possibilities, at least in the abstract, and searching for a new language of desire in which to encompass "complex thought and feeling." But they came to this revolutionary undertaking with a vision of sexuality at least as dangerous as it was pleasurable and with certain reservations about men.[30]

"Clear-headed" and self-contained, Maria Sharpe upheld the "puritanical" traditions of her distinguished Unitarian family in club discussions. Photographs of the period show her austerely dressed and coiffed, a "Nonconformist, blood and bone." Although the Sharpe family was well known for its high-minded commitment to culture and to an ethic of "moral action, duty, and unselfishness," the question remained how to translate duty and culture into a female vocation. The Sharpe sisters had to depart from the traditional family repertoire to carve out a public role for themselves—much to the regret of their widowed mother, who looked on sadly as "one daughter thought it desirable to go to Newnham, . . . another took up a line of reading or of work that did not approve itself to her and . . . all would go out in all weather for work and undertakings and come home late at night by omnibus from meetings."[31]

At the time of the club's founding, Maria Sharpe was thirty-three years old, single and living at home, subject to bouts of depression, anxiously searching for intellectual, spiritual, and political direction.[32] She was drawn to the subject of "sex" through the public discussions of prostitution, which she believed lay at the back of "every branch of the woman's question." At the age of twenty she read Mrs. Linton's novel, *Joshua Davidson,* and then "a certain amount" of pamphlet literature concerning the feminist agitation against the Contagious Diseases Acts. She did not herself join the repeal agitation, deeming it more appropriate for "married people." "Still the figure of the prostitute continued always to be a spectre in my mind."[33]

Before she joined the club, Sharpe had always thought the "best way to keep one's independence was to avoid the society of men and keep to one's sex." She had resigned herself to playing "maiden aunt" within her family (living for others, "standing and waiting so that other people may not be overdone") and to the companionship of Lina Eckenstein, an old child-hood friend and future member of the Men and Women's Club. Eckenstein and Sharpe vacationed together, shared family occasions; Eckenstein wrote Sharpe ornate, sentimental letters, in which she pledged undying love. They were a female couple, enjoying what Americans at the time termed a "Boston marriage."[34]

Then came Pearson's invitation: it seemed "ungenerous" not to "take up this offer to discuss, after complaining that men preach too much." Sharpe was also eager to find a "channel" for "feelings" let loose by recent "revelations."[35]

Revelations

These recent "revelations" were the second origin of the club. Pearson's in-vitation coincided with W. T. Stead's "Maiden Tribute of Modern Babylon." The series had an electrifying effect on public opinion and on female members. Writing to Pearson, Elizabeth Cobb was overwhelmed by the "new possibilities of thought and action" opened up by the *Pall Mall Gazette*. In practical terms, what the "revelations" had done was to facili-tate her task of recruiting women to the club. Previously she had encoun-tered some difficulty in filling the female quota for the club: "We talk of women not knowing men's thoughts on these subjects, why we don't even know other women's and it seems so difficult to find women one is quite sure have thoughts." The "Maiden Tribute" had changed all that. "I be-lieve I [could] now find women for the club to match any man."[36]

"Maiden Tribute" set the scene for the club's inauguration and gave women in particular the courage and incentive to undertake such a daring venture. "Maiden Tribute" and the feminist politics of prostitution had made public discussion of sexual danger possible for women, and brought into the open the ominous "shadows," "spectres," and "haunting fears" that darkened their views of heterosexual relations. In the club and else-where, melodrama provided women with a cultural resource, a language of emotion, in stark contrast to the disembodied voice of reason and science that presumably set the tone of the club. Melodrama was also a politicized language that drove women "by fear into [public] speech." The women of the club brought to their discussions and debates a pervasive sense of sex-ual vulnerability, organized around a specific melodramatic script of sex-ual danger.[37]

By and large, the men were not caught up in the melodrama of the

"Maiden Tribute." On the contrary, they were anxious to distance their activities from the feminine emotionalism of the purity crusaders who had engineered the "Maiden Tribute" and who had checked the expansion of state medicine in the area of sexual regulation. Compared to the women, the men assumed a detached position towards the subject of prostitution. Karl Pearson's only personal foray into the study of prostitution was to assemble statistical impressions of the age and number of young street-walkers in the Strand, as he made his way from his law chambers to his Pall Mall club. Despite his aloofness, he was more compelled by the subject than he was willing to acknowledge. However much Pearson tried to interpret prostitution as a question for science, he too had something personal at stake in the discussion: his letters and published work were punctuated by periodic outbursts against female temptresses, in the form of female servants and prostitutes, who seduced young men. Nor did Pearson's science ensure emotional distance: on the contrary, his reliance on Darwinism implicated him in a set of metaphors and a narrative plot organized around "love intrigues" and nature's own erotic script.[38]

Club Rules

At the first meeting of the club on July 9, 1885, club members ratified seventeen rules that stressed the "difficulty of the undertaking," their "earnestness of purpose," and the need for the careful selection of members and guests. Membership was to be limited to twenty, with equal numbers of men and women; meetings were to be held once a month and members were expected to rotate responsibility for presenting papers.[39]

Formal equality was structured into the rules of the club; in reality, the distribution of power and prestige between male and female was anything but equal. Among the women, only Olive Schreiner could rival Karl Pearson as an intellectual of public standing. Moreover, despite the insistence that a disinterested tone dominate conversation, this abstract ideal was profoundly subverted by personal animosities and romantic entanglements. Men in the club were not only more socially and politically powerful than the women; as rejected suitors, dominant romantic interests, tutors, and, in one case, consulting physician, they exercised a supervisory role over the women at the most personal level. The debilitating nature of these personal intrigues surfaced in private letters, where many of the women, who defended an opposing position in public, assumed a deferential, placating tone towards Karl Pearson, who was the center of at least three romantic entanglements—with Olive Schreiner, Elizabeth Cobb, and

Maria Sharpe. Homoerotic relations between women, particularly Cobb and Schreiner, and Sharpe and Eckenstein, further complicated the multiple, overlapping erotic triangles with Pearson at the center.[40]

There was another impediment to free and equal conversation: the tendency of the men to treat the women as objects of study rather than as equal participants in a joint inquiry. As time passed, female club members regularly complained that Pearson had quoted from their private correspondence to demonstrate the idiosyncrasies of the female perspective;[41] that the men expected the women to "defend conventional morality" and put forward views which women "held no more than the man in the moon";[42] that men's curiosity only extended to the female sex, and tended to treat male sexuality as unproblematic and given.

Finally there was the rule of science itself. According to club rule no. 17, discussions were to be conducted "from the historical and scientific as distinguished from the theological standpoint." Science, Pearson would later assert in his *Grammar of Science,* trained the mind to "an exact and impartial analysis of facts." It provided a method of analysis that was at once antimetaphysical and universally applicable to all areas of knowledge. The "sceptical inquiring spirit" of the club opened up discussions of sex relations by assuming that nothing was given, that everything had to be proven. "Everything that helps us to understand physical nature better is really a stage in human freedom and in the higher stage which regards the mind without differentiation of sex," Pearson would later assert. Yet this scientific standpoint also presupposed a master intelligence, a stable, privileged subject, whose identity was coherent and autonomous; who was capable of reason and its "science" of establishing a reliable and universal knowledge of "man" and his world, however changing that human and physical landscape might be.[43]

This alone placed women in a defensive position. Women were expected to work within a scientific ideology that denied the validity of female subjective experience, and over which the largely "untrained" female members had only an uncertain command. Awed by the "masculine minds of the club," the "possessors of the keys of . . . knowledge," women like Maria Sharpe felt themselves obliged to undergo a wrenching conversion. First they had to divest themselves of "sex prejudices, partizanship and general self-consciousness." Second, they had to "learn a partially new language before they could make themselves intelligible." But this conversion was not entirely successful. However anxious women were to use the "scientific method," Sharpe wrote to R. J. Parker, they found the language of science inadequate for "complex thought and feeling." It also failed them when discussions became "too connected" with the difficulties of their "own life" for them to write of it in the "Darwinian spirit" they might desire. "Very few people's emotions will stand the test of being held out at arms length and looked in the face for scientific purposes," Maria Sharpe wrote to her sister Letty. "They shrink and shrivel."[44] Only rarely did men acknowledge the same dilemma, partially because they masked their subjective responses and relied less on "self-analysis" than women. At certain points, as we shall see, even masters of nature and the scientific method like Karl Pearson openly faced the contradiction between the dispassionate language of science and their own transgressive desires.[45]

By "science," club members meant specifically Darwinism. a scientific ideology that in its dominant representations justified female inferiority and identified women with less-evolved nature. In *The Descent of Man* (1871), Darwin delineated a polarity between males and females, based on men's active role in sexual selection. Quoting Schopenhauer. Darwin placed "love intrigues" at the heart of social evolution, identifying them as the dynamic engine that determined not only the "weal or woe of one individual, but that of the human race."[46] Since men were more actively engaged in the struggle for sexual selection, they were more evolved than women.[47] Elizabeth Cobb found it depressing to read that male animals had superiority over females "all before men and women [evolved]." However, evolutionary science, including Darwin's own writings, permitted multiple political interpretations. Feminists within the club could find some support in the Lamarckian theory of inherited characteristics (present in Darwin's own formulations), which argued that socially learned traits could be passed on to future generations, thus softening the blow of Darwinian determinism that forever handicapped women in "life's race."[48] Some feminists extended the Lamarckian interpretation further: because women had learned moral restraint from centuries of self-suppression, they could claim moral and spiritual superiority over men. As we shall see, from another direction, Pearson himself would extend Darwin's dynamic and indeterminate system of change to reconsider women's place in history.[49]

The challenge facing the club, according to Pearson, was to determine the natural capacities of women and their proper social role for the improvement of the race. He addressed this question in his first paper for the club, entitled "The Woman's Question." "With rare insight and foresight," wrote Maria Sharpe in her autobiographical memoir, "Mr. Pearson laid the most pressing of our problems before us." Whether club members agreed or not, or whether they followed all of it or not, the performance was an "education in itself" and "set the tone of the club."[50]

Pearson intended the paper to be an "agnostic" presentation that posed questions rather than offered solutions.[51] He began by acknowledging the fact of female emancipation as a sign of the times, but cautioned that the movement needed to be "channeled" to ensure gradual change and social stability at home and abroad. A "want of preliminary sexualogical investigation" rendered much of J. S. Mill's writings "nugatory" as it did to a "lesser degree" the "more powerful work of Mary Wollstonecraft." The platform of women's rights was unscientific, because it was based solely on individual rights rather than on an appreciation of women's social duties: "We must first . . . settle what is the physical capacity of woman, what would be the effect of her emancipation on her function of race reproduction before we can talk of her 'rights'," argued the professor. The debates and categories of sexual science, not rights theory, framed Pearson's discussion of female destiny.[52]

Pearson accepted physical distinctions between men and women, based on childbearing, as given: "Race-evolution has implanted in women a desire for children, as it has implanted in man a desire for woman." But do these differences, he asked, "make a fundamental distinction in the social and political position between men and women? Do they connote a physical and mental inferiority on her side?" To address these thorny questions, he proceeded to divide women into two classes, childbearing and nonchildbearing, according to their reproductive responsibilities. How do "we" treat the 20 percent of women who are nonchildbearing? They most probably are less, not more, "influenced" by the sexual instinct than the average man. How do we account for the low remuneration they receive for their work? Is it because they stand in competition with women in other sexual spheres, notably childbearing women and prostitutes? Although not physically inferior, is the nonchildbearing woman intellectually deficient? Is this inferiority due to "centuries of suppression" or lack of intellectual training in the present? Are the current social restrictions on women "necessary to society or a hindrance to the race"?

Childbearing women, on the other hand, suffered from the difficulty of maintaining their individuality in marriage. Was the intellectual development of childbearing women compatible with the reproductive needs of the (English) race? "If childbearing women must be intellectually handicapped," he declared, then "the penalty to be paid for race-predominance" was female self-sacrifice, the "subjection of women."

Pearson moved from a reproductive classification of women to a consideration of them in relation to three areas of heterosexual activity: friendship, marriage, and prostitution. Once again, he posed his questions problematically, in the "sceptical inquiring spirit" of the club. Was marriage a real "hindrance to progress"? Under existing conditions, how necessary or evil was prostitution? Could men and women be friends? Was it possible for the sexes to mix freely in all relations of life?

For all his "sceptical inquiring spirit," Pearson contemplated the inevitability of female emancipation with some dread. Female enfranchisement, he speculated, might result in a majority party of women who could demand "a vast economic reorganization" of society as "the only means of preserving . . . self-respect and the independence of their sex." This political program might end in "social stability," but, he warned, it could equally result in "another subjection of sex."

By the end of the essay, Pearson could not resist telling women what he thought of them. Throwing down the gauntlet, he challenged women as a future electorate to familiarize themselves with the sex problems of the day, particularly prostitution, and to change their ways. He compared the conventional "shopping dolls" who "gaze intently at bits of gauzed ribbon" in shop windows in fashionable London thoroughfares to the "mob" of women who frequented those same streets "between twelve and one at night"—thereby linking the image of respectable and fallen women, joining marriage and prostitution, but omitting any discussion of male responsibility for these debased female states.

Opposition

Pearson's paper did indeed set the "tone of the club" and raised most of the questions the club would address for the rest of its sessions. But it also incited a spirit of "opposition" among the women, who were variously offended by his radical proposals about marriage and prostitution and by his patronizing, "elevated" tone. Two female correspondents, friends of Mrs. Cobb, were shocked at the essay. Mrs. Brown found the paper a "deep humiliation to the sex," with no "reverence for the mother of the race." "I did not realize that women were so looked down upon." Miss Mills was sorry for "poor Letty and Maria" that "they should think it their duty to take up such questions like these." It was different "for Miss Schreiner": judging from her book "she had been forced to live in contact with coarse and brutal natures."[53]

Schreiner herself complained that it "left out one whole field": "Man." "Your whole paper reads as though the object of the club were to discuss woman, her objects, her needs, her mental and physical nature, and man only in as far as he throws light upon her question. This is entirely wrong." Perhaps the most thoroughgoing critique came from Emma Brooke, a novelist and member of the Fabian Society, who accused Pearson of being "unsocialistic" in his attitude. "You underrate women . . . you are hard because you have so little knowledge of that very woman nature you cannot help from despising." His scorn and hardness towards "shopping dolls" gave her pain, while his attitude towards "superior women" was distinctly "dominant."[54]

Brooke's private note to Pearson, written as an essay and entitled "Thoughts on the Man's View of the Woman's Question," repudiated Pearson's assumptions of female inferiority and the necessity of female renunciation in the interest of race survival. It also tried to disentangle the categories of sexuality and reproduction that Pearson had confused in his classification schemes. Pearson, she asserted, underestimated the strength of female sexual passion and exaggerated the maternal instinct. "The Madonna and Child" figured conspicuously in his discussion of childbearing women, simultaneously exposing a tendency to credit women with "occult feelings" about childbearing and his own mystified attachment to maternal self-sacrifice. Far from there being the "Desire for Children," personal testimonies of married and unmarried women documented the opposite, a "heavy dread" of "having a child." Preventive checks (birth control), she insisted, were the "only moral basis of marriage." Women "would prefer self-control and long seasons of abstinence" but they "must help themselves as best they can."

In "touching" on the subject of nonchildbearing women, Brooke insisted, Pearson was "still hampered by the same tendency to credit woman with mystic qualities." By assuming a sexual polarity of desire, "it is implied that [a woman] is not only different from a man, but is mysteriously delivered over to the tyranny of the natural function which has no corresponding side in himself." Although she herself believed that "men and women always would be different all through," this did not signify the substitution in women's case of maternal instinct for sexual desire. "Chastity," she assured him, was a "hard battle," resolutely "fought through life." While asserting the reality of female sexual passion, Brooke was nonetheless alert to women's deep sense of vulnerability about sexual relations, in good part due to unwanted pregnancy. "The truth is, you men have murdered love. . . . You have killed the inspirations in the woman's heart by abuses of all kind." The woman question, she warned him, would not be solved by male prescriptions about female self-sacrifice, but through female initiatives and male self-reform: "this woman question . . . cannot be solved until women were allowed to work out their own ideas about duty and ideals" and men left off being a "beast of prey towards both the working class and women."

Only one female correspondent did not seem offended by "The

Woman's Question." She was Charlotte Wilson, another nonmember and Fabian, who chose to ignore Pearson's condescension and to concentrate positively on his critique of marriage. Children apart, "it is an intolerable impertinence that Church or State or Society" should interfere with lovers. Marriage should be a free contract, not a "woman's profession," but the culmination of friendship between a man and a woman; this would safeguard against, rather than encourage, "loose living." Unlike other correspondents, Wilson made no reference to Pearson's "dominant tone," but her closing remarks implicitly challenged his assumption of male superiority. In general, she thought, "women initiate and supply the active principle" for most innovations, which men then "work and shape out." Certainly this was true of her own formulations: Pearson was sufficiently impressed by her letter to publish long excerpts as part of his text in his next published foray on the subject, "Sex and Socialism" (1887). This was one of the many "secrets" of the Men and Women's Club: the intellectual debt men owed to their female colleagues.[55]

As these interventions demonstrate, there was a wide range of heterodox female opinion on questions of sexuality and sexual morality. Most female correspondents were indignant at Pearson's tone: they all insisted that *men* must change; and that social institutions, not just sexual morality, must be reformed before utopian sexual possibilities could be realized. All agreed on the existence of some fundamental difference between the sexes that resided in the body. But how this "marked distinction of sex" manifested itself remained highly contested. On the intensity of female sexual passion or even maternal instinct, female correspondents were very much at odds with each other.

The Other Side

This was all "behind the scenes" correspondence. At club sessions themselves, the "women's response" was delivered by the journalist Henrietta Muller, who read "The Other Side of the Question," a Lamarckian interpretation of female spiritual evolution. Muller accepted Pearson's conventional proposition of greater male sexual passion, and used it to support her indictment of male hypersexuality. "Self control," she argued, was the moral basis of life; and it was precisely this absence of sexual passion, gained over centuries of self-restraint on the part of women and transmitted to subsequent female generations, that made women free. Male sexual license was also transmitted over generations to make men a prey upon women and their moral inferiors. As far as Muller was concerned, women did not need men. As long as society had depended on physical strength, men had wielded power. But times had changed. Now that "moral strength" was the new criterion of social power, the dominion of man had ended, to be replaced by that of woman.[56]

A "desultory" conversation followed Muller's paper, as members struggled with their own embarrassment to establish a basic vocabulary of sexual desire. At one point, the migratory habits of the birds were invoked to illustrate the meaning of "instinct." Olive Schreiner and her friend Dr. Donkin took issue with Muller's argument about female passionlessness; for "something sexual" lay at the "root of all intellectual and artistic achievement." R. J. Parker laid out the alternative evolutionary interpretation about female passionlessness: if indeed women were less sexual, they were also less evolved.[57]

Although one member later told Maria Sharpe that he had found Muller's paper "great fun,"[58] Karl Pearson was not amused. He wrote another paper, circulated and not read to the club, that tried to clarify the question of sex attraction and sex impulse. The paper reveals a marked conflict between his own personal desires and the sexual science he espoused as truth, an intellectual system notable for its limited representation of male eroticism as well as female desire.

A good scientific naturalist, Pearson rooted his understanding of sexual dynamics in the laws of conservation: "Physicists have long held as a fundamental principle of this science that all natural processes are due to a transference of energy and laid it down as a general rule that the amount of energy in any isolated system might change its forms, but cannot change its total." So it was with sexual energy, which was interchangeable with the intellectual and physical energy systems of the body. According to this model, sexuality was compulsive and compulsory; it belonged to a spermatic economy harnessed to a Darwinian racial imperative. The sexual norm in this system was essentially "plotless." That is, it acted without impediment to reach expression; it contained no complicated script of resistance or deferral of gratification. Only perversions, displacements in sexual aims or objects, offered variations in this version of nature's sexual economy. Although this was implicitly a male model, Pearson drew upon male and female examples in his case studies of sexual types. He cited "J, K, and L," sailors on leave with "stored sexual energy," who resorted to prostitutes for sexual outlets; "C," an unmarried woman, deprived of intellectual work, whose sexual impulse was manifested in hysteria; "D," an intellectual human at work, whose "physical impulse and sexual impulse hardly make themselves felt."[59]

By its very aggressive and disruptive nature, the sex impulse seemed to preclude male-female friendships untainted by erotic attraction—precisely those relationships that Pearson wanted to ease into with women in the club. "Surely the happiest state of the individual is to disregard sex and not to be conscious in . . . friendship . . . of the likeness or difference of sex at all," Pearson wrote Sharpe in 1887. In order to secure a "safe" basis for male-female friendships, he formulated the theory of sex attraction. He looked to male friendships as a precedent—"No one can say that the friendship between man and man is based on any 'conception of sex'," he wrote to Maria Sharpe, a point privately disputed by his friend R. J. Parker, who reminded him of the vices in "our public schools," vices that remained one of the sexual secrets between men in the club. This kind of friendship could extend to men and women, with the advantage that men and women were so "intellectually and physically different" that they would see problems differently. Sex attraction, Pearson argued, was based on this principle of complementarity; but in a singular note of humility, he admitted his "complete incapacity for describing what sex attraction might be." He had not read the paper at the club because, he explained to Maria Sharpe, "friends" had told him "he was engaging in personal prejudice" and that he should stick to "marked distinctions of sex."[60]

Sharpe liked Pearson's essay and responded with unusual warmth and support. It must have been a "man who dissuaded you" from reading the paper, she wrote to Pearson. Men "did not realize that women married men for their minds," that they entered marriage with "no desire for children and repulsion toward the exercise of the sex function." Men's failure to see this shows either "their contempt for women's minds or because their bodily need is so strong." Pearson's letter had tapped a deep-seated anger and sexual resentment in women—indeed a revulsion towards sex.[61]

Sharpe was wrong in assuming that "some man" had advised Pearson to keep his theory of sex attraction to himself. That advice had come from Olive Schreiner, who liked the first part on the sexual case histories, but sensed a hidden agenda at the end of Pearson's paper. "The last bit [on sex attraction] doesn't seem worthy of you. I have a feeling you are trying to prove a foregone conclusion for some purpose or other."[62] Schreiner was on the mark here. Pearson was trying to resolve a personal dilemma at the theoretical level; how to reach out to women, in particular Sharpe, without violating sexual decorum and exposing his vulnerability. He had already experienced the danger of overstepping social proprieties in his friendship with Schreiner, who responded to his friendly attentions with what he interpreted as explicit sexual overtures.

History

Discussions around sex, then, were fraught with personal meanings, gender antagonisms, and erotic incitements. It was with great relief, wrote Sharpe, that the club turned its attention to historical questions. Sharpe welcomed Mr. Parker's paper on Periclean Athens as a "good substitution for general attacks on men"; but she was shocked at his eloquent defense of "boy love" among the Athenians, the one overt reference to homosexuality in club discussions. History was not quite as safe as she thought. However, she was truly inspired by the lessons of history that Pearson was able to extract from his "Sketch of Sex Relations in Primitive and Medieval Germany." This study, Pearson later wrote, represented his "passage" from "agnostic questioning" through "historical inquiry". to a more definite "social theory."[63]

Like many other Victorians, Pearson used the history and anthropology of "early societies" to work out sexual politics and dilemmas that were all too contemporary. Like Bachofen and Morgan, he engaged in a massive exercise in circular reasoning: he read back contemporary social struggles into history and then used the weight of the past to justify or dictate the direction social relations should take.[64] But he drew a somewhat different moral lesson than did Bachofen and Morgan: in locating the Mother-age civilization as a predecessor of the patriarchal society, Pearson did not interpret its decline as the world historic defeat of women in the face of a more potent and superior patriarchy, but as a sign of the plasticity of all social relations and of women's role as sexual force and agent in history.

Before the heroic age, Pearson explained, a different type of civilization arose that owed its "impetus" and "its victories over nature" to the "genius" of women rather than to that of men. This was the Mother-age, when lineage was derived through the mother, and when women invented agriculture, traditional religion, and culture. The age had its "dark" side: human sacrifice, periodic sexual license, and the absence of "strong incentives to individual energy." A slow transition to patriarchy occurred, precipitated not by male intellectual superiority or by lack of female self-sufficiency, but by women's physical need for male protection from roving bands of male hunters. Medieval witchcraft, peasant customs, and even prostitution, he hypothesized, were all strange survivals of Mother-age promiscuity, all signs of a potent female sexuality. The lesson he drew from his historical research was positive and feminist: there was no "rigid law" of female inferiority, "woman" was not "hopelessly handicapped," intellectually or socially, by the function of childbearing, and she was capable of sexual desire. With the patriarchal age drawing to a close, women could well assume an entirely different role in the new social order.[65]

Friendship, Marriage, and Prostitution

In 1886, the group decided to devote the entire year to a study of the "relation of the State to sex questions, particularly marriage and prostitution." As the group turned its attention to contemporary heterosexual issues, R. J. Parker cautioned members not to lose their "historical sense." During the marriage discussions, the male members were more adventurous than their female counterparts in their critique of legal marriage; yet they were more tied to seeing women as natural and to viewing women's sexuality as the problem. The women members were fearful of dispensing with the legal institution of marriage, yet they were more assertive about the social construction of their own sexuality. As earlier, the women divided on the intensity of female sexual passion and the impact of sexual restraint on female mental health (there was even some discussion as to whether female hysteria was a result of enforced chastity). But what is striking, even among those women who asserted the right of women to sexual pleasure, was the intensity of their sense of sexual vulnerability.[66]

During the marriage sessions, two emotionally laden themes surfaced in discussion: the potential conflict of interest among childbearing and nonchildbearing women; and sexual abuse in marriage. In her paper, "The State and Sexual Relations," guest speaker Annie Besant insisted that the state should not interfere in questions of sex relations unless children resulted. The same libertarian position on nonprocreative heterosexuality was reiterated in the next paper on the agenda, "Women's Sphere in Modern Society," whose author, nonclub member Emma Brooke, principally focused on the policy implications for reproductive sexuality.[67]

The first part of "Women's Sphere in Modern Society" (written for the Fabian Society and presented anonymously to the Men and Women's Club) considered women in relation to their "sexual sphere," as legal wives, prostitutes, or celibates.[68] Brooke devoted the second part of her essay to a defense of the state support of motherhood. As a good Darwinian, she began with a story of origins. In early society, due to the "exigencies of motherhood," women were brought under the "subjection of men." The function of motherhood constituted "the real difference between the sexes," creating a "natural" division, but the subsequent status and degradation attached to male and female labor, respectively, was "artificial." Men's labors gained a certain "prestige," while women's work was held in "contempt." The same "broad division" and valuation, she argued, "follows us still in all our complicated civilisation." The nearer any industry partakes of "femininity," of "life-nourishing quality," the less it is remunerated. Motherhood itself "remains still unrecognized and still unpaid."[69]

Motherhood, Brooke insisted, needed to be recognized as "State work," "national work," abidingly "useful work," and supported by the state. She held up the example of the heroic and unselfish "mother of a poor household," who labored to bring a contribution to the household, yet who suffered as a sexual martyr to her shiftless husband, and was subject to the "ill-consequences" of his "unreflecting sexual license." Following Bebel, Brooke predicted that the "population problem" would solve itself once women were emancipated: "it is in the last degree unlikely," Brooke declared, "that a freed and intelligent woman would voluntarily incapacitate herself . . . by becoming a mere machine for the production of superfluous children." Failing this, she advocated, in a "Socialistic regime," the state's right to regulate the population, including legal punishment of the "unrestrained license of the producers of superfluous and diseased children."[70]

Brooke's paper departed significantly from her earlier private note on Pearson's "Woman's Question," both in maintaining a silence on sexual desire and in implicitly collapsing, rather than distinguishing, women's sexuality and reproduction. According to Polly Beals, the omission of any discussion of female sexual desire and the concentration on women's connection to productive relations may have represented a deliberate political strategy. With the Fabians in mind, Brooke may have tried to legitimize "women's reproduction as work, a form of social production that must be backed by a program for endowed motherhood."[71] The same legitimizing strategy may also account for her effort to represent the policy of endowing motherhood in relation to working-class women, rather than to economically dependent married women of the middle class, who were the prime focus of the Men and Women's Club discussions. The result was not only to bring the "rough . . . outer world" into the discussions of the club but also to distance and suppress Brooke's own identification with the issues at hand.

Brooke's paper engendered a discussion marked "by occasional warmth."[72] Karl Pearson stood alone in his enthusiasm for the state support of motherhood. In a note, later developed into his essay, "Sex and Socialism" (1887), he endorsed many of the positions set out by Brooke, Besant, and Charlotte Wilson (without specifying his sources): equality of opportunity for nonchildbearing women; opposition to state involvement in sex relations, "children apart"; state support of "sanctioned births" (three being the recommended eugenic number).[73]

Pearson also attacked the "home duties" of women outside of child care as "useless" labor. "There is an independence of spirit about the woman earning her own livelihood by contributing to the social labour stock, which I never find in the woman whose claim to independence consists in fulfillment of the 'home duties' for a woman."[74] Like Brooke, he interpreted such "home duties" as a form of degraded sexual service,[75] what Schreiner would later term "sex parasitism."[76] In club discussions, he accused the single women in the club who opposed state assistance to mothers of being indifferent to the plight of married women: single women, he commented, seem to be "satisfied with things as they are for married women." They failed to see that the "woman question" was "more pressing for married women."[77] It was "curious" to observe, seconded Thicknesse, how the "single women threw the married women over. . . . All they cared for was freedom for single women, education and making money."[78] "I think it quite possible," Pearson wrote Sharpe, "there may be a real divergence of interest between single and married women, just as I feel sure that, apart from personal bonds, in the long course of evolution there has been and will be a struggle between men and women."[79]

Female members bitterly denied these charges. Spinster daughters like Maria Sharpe were particularly affronted at Pearson's disparagement of their home obligations and angry at the continuing tendency of men to lecture women on their "spheres and duties." They denied an antagonism or jealousy between married and single women; there was a simple "division of labour," not "antagonist relations," insisted Sharpe. All in all, the women suspected the men of inventing an antagonism between women to displace the more "seething question" of the agonized "relations of the sexes."[80]

This "seething question" and the sexual fears underlying it erupted during the discussion of "preventive checks" (birth control), a topic first addressed by Annie Besant in her paper. Club members emphatically disagreed on the "morality" of preventive checks. Pearson came to Besant's support, and so did Muller, who defended preventive checks as women's protection against "unwelcome motherhood." Sharpe and her sisters disagreed; besides encouraging "immorality" and "vulgarizing the emotions," birth control was one further means of "making the woman into an instrument for the use of the man."[81]

During the subsequent sessions devoted to the "Limitation of the Family," coercive marital sex emerged as a powerful, emotional subtext of club discussions. Pearson took exception to two "notes" written by women, one opposing preventive checks and characterizing "coition on the part of the man" as "a violent action, bordering on convulsions and causing great exhaustion," the other by Muller defending their use by women as self-protection against the "dominion" of man. Both papers, Pearson complained, assumed something that was not proved, "that the sexual passion of women is less than men." Both put forward two erroneous theses: (1) that the "sexual act" was "unnecessary" and "unhealthy" for the male and tended to "destroy the finer emotions between men and women"; (2) that the "majority of men are either wanting in morality or positively vicious." Anything "unnatural" was probably "unhealthy," he conceded, but "there is nothing to show that there is anything 'abnormal' in the sexual life or impulses of the *average* man or woman." He defended the "sex act" as a "harmless physical pleasure," one that enhanced rather than coarsened the "finer feelings": "sexual intercourse, if exercised in healthy moderation and accompanied by a due regard to the bodily freedom of both man and woman, tends to increase the intellectual sympathy, (just as the intellectual sympathy heightens the physical pleasure), not to destroy it."[82]

Pearson posed an ideal of nonreproductive, noncoercive sexuality, based on intellectual sympathy and mutual sexual passion. This represented an important evolution in his thinking. Unfortunately, his imagination could not match his desire; and the coldness of his language—particularly when he likened sexual intercourse to mountain climbing with a friend—gave offense. "My chief objection to Mr. Pearson's way of treating the subject was that he appeared to treat sexual intercourse on a footing with other pleasures," wrote Maria Sharpe. Expressions such as "harmless physical pleasure," a "mere transient pleasure," "purely physical pleasure," were "misleading," "as suggesting that there is no classification of physical pleasures, and that the taste of a strawberry and the kiss of a friend are fairly on a level, both very nice." Sexual intercourse could not be represented as a "harmless physical pleasure," precisely because it carried "grave personal consequences" for women.[83]

Such "grave personal consequences" are poignantly illustrated by Elizabeth Cobb's story. From 1881 to 1887, she remained Pearson's touchstone on the "married woman's question" and she helped him through his "troubles" with "Olive" in 1886. But she had clearly lost ground, first to Olive Schreiner and then to Maria, as Pearson's favorite female correspondent and confidant. In 1887, she underwent a marital crisis of her own. Writing to Pearson in May, she explained that she could no longer help him on the "married woman's question"; a "great change" in her life has occurred. In her mid-forties, she was about to have her fourth child (she was stepmother to six others). She felt deeply depressed and out of control: "I often feel face to face now with nature's independent force, one is so helpless before it, it sweeps according to its law, thru one's fragile form." Under these conditions, the "talk of the Club" has been "too painfully personal." "I daresay I shall not be there again."[84]

Prostitution

For the women of the club, nothing more vividly symbolized the drama of female victimization and male sexual abuse than prostitution, the next subject on the group's agenda. Prostitution and its melodrama undermined their efforts to imagine a utopian sexual alternative or to engage in a rationalist discourse on sex. It was the essential paradigm of heterosexual relations, a social fact that darkened all other relations between the sexes, and an emblematic state of being that symbolized sexual danger in and outside of marriage.[85]

The discussion of prostitution, coming on the heels of the marriage sessions, presented women with an opportunity to vent some of their anger and anxiety over coercive sex. They could do this more easily with prostitution than with marital sex, because the feminist discourse around prostitution had already been constituted as a politicized language, a civic discourse, in which one could discuss sexual danger. By contrast, the issue of marital rape was a new formulation and did not come into its own as an independent political cause until one hundred years later.[86]

In 1887, club members proceeded to reenact the battle of the sexes over the Contagious Diseases Acts, recently waged in public between regulationists and their feminist opponents. The men defended the Acts as simple sanitary measures to control the spread of venereal disease; the women attacked them on moral grounds and as an insult to women. To Pearson the Acts were an effective illustration of the state management of sexual hygiene and reproduction that was at the heart of his theoretical interest in sexuality. Pearson and his male friends belittled the efforts of Josephine Butler, the feminist leader of the repeal movement, and disparaged her as a religious fanatic and sexual puritan. They interpreted repealers' insistence that morality should take precedence over science as an ominous sign of the philistinism and irrationality to be expected from a "women's party."

To the women, the Acts also constituted a powerful drama of sexual politics, entailing the male "medical rape" of working-class women and an inspiring example of female heroism in the figure of Josephine Butler, who rallied middle-class women to the defense of their "fallen sisters." Although they did not speak in a religious idiom, they defended Butler's prophetic vision and their own emotional response to her "war cry."[87]

Open warfare erupted when Ralph Thicknesse declared that "few of us have made up our minds as to what we thought of prostitution." He later asserted that, while the "Maiden Tribute" showed that prostitution produced "grave social evils," he did not admit that the "sexual part of it" was "evil in itself." This was a remarkably modern-sounding view, partially based on the perception that prostitution could be and often *was* a voluntary activity. But his speculation was imprecise and ideologically loaded: it was also based on a social Darwinist and hierarchical view of the division of labor and social utility: if the prostitute fulfilled a "useful" calling for society, then her activities were not "immoral." This, however, did not place prostitution in the same category as mental work, nor did Thicknesse imagine that such an occupation would be suitable to a brain worker like himself. Prostitution was a lowly female occupation that served male needs. It was precisely his elision of social needs and male needs that infuriated the women.[88]

Thicknesse's remarks were met with total silence on the women's part, and they precipitated a crisis in women's participation in the group. Henrietta Muller, one of the more outspoken female members, interpreted this silence as a sign of their intimidation within the group—"women do not know how to use their own voice"—and angrily resigned, promising to form her own discussion group of women only.[89] Sharpe took a different view of women's reticence on this occasion: it wasn't that women were afraid to speak, it was that they were "too stunned" by Thicknesse's cavalier attitude toward prostitution to say anything. Under pressure from Pearson, the women mobilized to present their case and to defend the solidarity of their "sex."[90]

Unlike Ralph Thicknesse they had no doubt about what they thought of prostitution: it was the "spectre" in their minds, the polluting fact of social existence that tainted all intercourse between the sexes. They took a more rigid and unspeculative position than the men, because more was personally at stake for them: their own identities were organized around the figure of the prostitute; they could not consider sexual relations abstractly or disinterestedly, for it was precisely "the region where women are possibly bodies only to men that casts a dark shadow across their own relations to the other sex."[91]

Sharpe vs. Pearson

In these discussions, men self-confidently assumed the position of innovators and explorers, while women were forced into a defense of traditional values and customs. There were episodes, however, in which a role reversal transpired between the male innovator and the female traditionalist—when a woman adopted a more avant-garde position on sex than Pearson and placed *him* on the defensive.

One such episode involves Maria Sharpe, perhaps the most transformed female member of the club, who slowly evolved into a much more self-confident and independent intellectual during the four years of the club's history. An important impetus to Sharpe's personal transformation was research undertaken by her on the history of prostitution. We have already seen how prostitution occupied a deeply symbolic position for women in the club. Middle-class women organized their own identity around the figure of the "fallen woman," a figure which inspired fantasies about male sexual danger and women's own dangerous side that respectable women reshaped and manipulated to explore their own subjectivity. Maria Sharpe's representation of her encounter with the wild, licentious women of the medieval "stews" is a case in point.

In 1886, Sharpe offered to write two papers on the "laws and regulations" dealing with prostitution from 800 to 1800 A.D. "I had . . . a strong feeling that I must go into it, that I would not leave it in the hands of the men to interpret as they liked." She was nonetheless overwhelmed by the immensity of the undertaking. Mr. Pearson said dryly, "Well the books are there, it only remains to read them." Under Pearson's tutelage, she learned how to do historical research, even summoning up the courage to submit order slips for books on prostitution at the circulation desk of the British Museum. Reading the books was a trial. "Not a book did I come across by a woman in all my readings. . . . [T]he way in which all the men accepted prostitution as an institution which always had been and always would be" appalled her. It was "so very terrible" as well to be "so long" among the "degraded of one's sex," to realize "in part the misery and the way in which men looked at them." Sharpe tried to build intellectual defenses against the intrusion of "personal feeling" into this impartial undertaking. She studied Anglo-Saxon and German dialects—the dry discipline of philology always serving as a good way of creating distance. By the second half of her study "I had gotten into the habit of expressing myself. . . . the simple pleasure of finding myself capable of arranging facts intelligibly was new to me." At home, she was even able to claim space, a study room of her own, and time for her work. "Lately . . . I have taken to improving my mind instead of looking after people's affairs so much." She even went off on a field trip to Germany with Lina Eckenstein, to find out about the regulation system there.[92]

After completing her papers, however, Sharpe fell into a depression—not only because the men passed over her papers in silence, but also because she could come to no new resolution on the social evil. She refused to have the paper typed up and circulated outside the club because the lessons "the facts would teach" might be used against "the truth." What were those lessons?

Sharpe had relied heavily on Pearson's "Sex Relations in Germany" for intellectual guidance on the folk history of medieval sexuality as well as on other histories of "early societies."[93] Like Pearson, she tried to emphasize the plasticity of social relationships and refuted the operation of any absolute code of morality. She too identified prostitutes as disorderly, licentious women, sexual survivals of the matriarchate age. "[My] study brought women before me in a new light, not as always the seduced but often the seducers." Medieval prostitution, she further discovered, had expanded precisely when church reforms narrowed the boundaries of legal, sanctified marriage. Pearson's study of the matriarchate impressed on her the need to study the past in order to gain a "right understanding of present and future." But an appreciation of "earlier matriarchal stages" would, she feared, arouse in "women a consciousness of a side of their nature which they had been tempted to think of as nonexistent, or if existent, to be condemned." "To feel that strength of sexual passion might possibly go along with strengths of other kinds, that faithfulness to marriage had also come with greater subjection. . . . [This] and other thoughts . . . necessarily work disturbingly on women who grasped them at all."[94]

Originally a social purity feminist, Sharpe amended her opinions on sexual questions and became persuaded of the morality of "preventive checks" and free monogamous unions. This occurred as part of a crisis in religious faith, a conversion to socialism, immersion in her own historical studies, and growing emotional involvement with Pearson. Despite the indifferent reception of her papers in the club, she began to realize her intellectual ambitions and desire for a vocation; it was a source of great satisfaction that her club paper on Ibsen's men and women was published in the *Westminster Review.* But this was all heady stuff for a woman who had trained herself to live "philanthropically" for others. Struggling against conventional social expectations and her own traditional beliefs often left Sharpe emotionally and physically exhausted: she sometimes "sat down on the floor . . . and cried" when she thought of the forces aligned against women in their struggle for individuality. To represent her intellectual and emotional odyssey, Sharpe drew upon the textual strategies of psychological realism championed by Meredith, Ibsen, Pearson, and Shaw. Her explorations provoked personal turmoil and generated tensions in her relationship with Pearson, who was clearly playing Henry Higgins to her Eliza Doolittle (and who, like Higgins, would come to regret the success of his pedagogical experiment).[95]

Complicating this courtship was a tangled set of emotional relationships: between Sharpe and Eckenstein, who over many years had regarded Sharpe as her inamorata, her "all in all," and was deeply resentful of having to share Sharpe with another, and who in turn satisfied some deep "emotional need" of Sharpe's.[96] Also overshadowing the courtship was Pearson's relationship to Cobb and to Schreiner. Compared to her other two competitors, Sharpe played her hand shrewdly. Unlike Cobb or Schreiner, she never catered or deferred to Pearson: she never entreated him to come visit her; and she never inquired into his health.[97] She never overstepped decorum, either in her personal confessions or in her "field work"; whereas Schreiner regaled Pearson with tales of personal encounters with prostitutes[98] to entice him into conversation, Sharpe proved her intellectual mettle by discreetly plugging along at the British Museum. She maintained a cool and controlled distance and stood her ground against Pearson's bullying and condescension (a typical Pearson intellectual exchange would begin combatively, "I agree with what you have to say [and *yet disagree*]").[99] More than any other female correspondent she talked back to Karl Pearson, especially when he was insulting.

In the early autumn of 1888, club members took up the question of female emancipation. "You are all individualists," complained R. J. Parker to female club members, too absorbed in the struggle for women's rights to consider women's duties to the race. Nor could he see how the emancipation of women was possible without interfering with the racial demands of motherhood, a point supported by Pearson. Sharpe sensed "a spirit of reaction" among the men, who initially were willing to treat a "subject theoretically," but who "shrank back" when they began to see the "practical outcome." Club discussions reached an impasse, with angry outbursts by Pearson, who once again dismissed middle-class women as inert and lazy, using "home duties" as an excuse to avoid socially useful work.[100]

Sharpe was stung by Pearson's remark. To provoke him, she wrote and asked his advice about a suitable occupation she might take up. Pearson sensed she was taunting him: "I should feel that your letter was evidence of some faith in my friendly judgement," he wrote, "if I had not a half suspicion you were poking fun at my theories." He then went on to propose that she undertake a massive investigation of the peasants' revolts of the later Middle Ages, probably realizing this was too awesome a task for her. She was not "joking," she wrote back in return, but the "ridicule" came "back" to her, for she could not possibly undertake that study. "I suppose there was in my letter something . . . which you felt as a challenge, namely a desire to remind a theorist that the masses whom he lashes, to *him* impersonal, are composed of [individual] units."[101]

Six months later, Sharpe wrote to Pearson that she had now decided that legal marriage was indeed an "impediment" to female emancipation. Pearson was vaguely alarmed: "Your letter," he wrote, was of "much interest, although a little perplexing." "If you feel the strength" to mount "a political campaign"—which required ten thousand pounds a year, he assured her—or have "saleable beauty" or can pen a novel like Miss Schreiner, then "nail the flag o' your creed to the mast." But if not, he advised her to keep it in "your innermost pocket," away from public view. "You do indeed write to me as a grandfather," Sharpe wrote back furiously, "but every woman is used to that from men younger than herself." She did not deceive herself that she had talent or saleable beauty or great wealth, but that did not mean she should conceal her opinions. "I will take no one's advice to keep my opinions secret so [long] as my reason has worked them into a conviction."[102]

First Ending

The Men and Women's Club disbanded in 1889, mainly because men were dissatisfied with women's performance. In the eyes of Pearson and his friends, the women had proved incapable of the level of scientific work the men demanded. They were serious but did not go "very deep"; they were unformidable adversaries, prone to defer on most questions but unwilling to relinquish their commitment to "individualism." One also suspects that after Schreiner left the club in 1886, the erotic and intellectual charm of sexual discourse in a mixed group waned for men. Over a period of four years, club sessions became increasingly deadlocked and stalemated: the group was unable to define prostitution or to agree on the issue of female sexual passion. The women mounted occasional protests, only to lapse again into resisting silence. Still, they were much sadder about the breakup than were the men; despite their sense of being dominated and forced into a "performing role," the women had learned something and gained more confidence in their ability to take command of the tools of Darwinian, evolutionary social science.[103]

A definitive study of sex and society awaited future developments in sexology, Pearson concluded. Nonetheless, the evolutionary perspectives of the club and its historical findings continued to be disseminated in feminist culture into the early twentieth century and forcefully contributed to an emerging feminist sexual science. Feminists would claim Pearson as an authority on women's heroic prehistory in the Mother age,[104] while Fabian feminists repeatedly cited Pearson to validate women's labor and their own proposals for an endowment of motherhood.[105] Olive Schreiner upheld the banner of social labor and inveighed against sex parasitism in that "Bible of the Woman's Movement,"[106] *Women and Labour;* while Lina Eckenstein used her training in historical research gained from the club to write her historical defense of celibacy and women's community, *Woman under Monasticism.*[107]

Second Ending: The Marriage Resolution

After the club disbanded, Pearson immediately proposed marriage to Sharpe; she initially accepted him, but then her "nervous system failed her," and she broke off the engagement. Both Pearson and her own family were stunned and heartbroken. Writing to Pearson, Elizabeth Cobb tried to explain the causes of Maria's "hysteria": she was "overwhelmed with sexual feeling"—afraid of sexual relations and of losing her independence, feeling too old for Pearson (she was four years his senior), and afraid of failing to live up to Pearson's "requirements." Sharpe had earlier expressed her fears of sex and dependency to Pearson: "In struggling for individuality," she wrote, women often had to sacrifice physical desire—"since that is so closely connected with the desire for self-surrender." Sharpe finally recovered, and their marriage took place in 1890. From outward appearances, it was a most successful Victorian marriage. It was not, however, the intellectual partnership Pearson had promised during courtship. During the honeymoon, Maria and Pearson collaborated on translating Ibsen's "Brand" together, but Maria experienced considerable difficulty in keeping up with Karl—she was daunted by the "muscular strength of a man's mind. He can work longer and more continuously than I." By 1896, her three eugenically-fit children had become her "field of work." Apart from a few letters to the newspapers, Maria Sharpe Pearson never published anything after her marriage.

This domestic arrangement clearly suited Pearson's professional ambitions, but it occasionally weighed on his conscience. Some of the old doubts lingered on after 1890. Out of "duty," Maria had fulfilled her role as wife, mother, and hostess at Pearson's academic soirees, Pearson wrote

Cobb in 1927 at the time of Maria's death; but he doubted if he ever "won her."[108]

Third Ending: Ibsen and Galton

The Men and Women's Club was not a self-contained intellectual exercise. Its discussions, as we have seen, were very much a part of the "spirit of the times" and they in turn contributed to other debates circulating in "high" and "low" places. The last two topics on the club's agenda, the writings of Henrik Ibsen, who served as the standard-bearer of advanced thought on the Woman Question, and Francis Galton, the father of eugenics, point to intellectual and political closure as well as avant-garde exploration. At the same time that Maria Sharpe's article on "Henrik Ibsen: His Men and Women" appeared in the *Westminster Review* (one of the earliest essays on Ibsen in the periodical press), the first unbowdlerized production of *A Doll's House* was privately staged at the Novelty Theatre. Bohemian London packed the theater, including members of the Men and Women's Club, as well as Emma Brooke, Olive Schreiner, and Eleanor Marx. Ibsen, declared Olive Schreiner, "shows some sides of . . . a woman's nature that are not spoken of, and that some people do not believe exist—but they do." Edith Lees, who later married Havelock Ellis, recalled the first night when "a few of us collected outside the theater breathless with excitement. . . . We were restive and almost savage in our arguments. What did it mean? . . . Was it life or death for women? . . . Was it joy or sorrow for men? That a woman should demand her emancipation and leave her husband and children in order to get it, savoured less of sacrifice than sorrow!"[109]

The last reading for the club was Francis Galton's *Natural Inheritance*. Pearson initially expressed skepticism about making heredity an exact science, but *Natural Inheritance* eventually became Pearson's bible and converted him to eugenics, the statistical study and manipulation of human heredity (in 1911, he was appointed Galton Professor of Eugenics at University College, London). Pearson had begun an emotional and intellectual odyssey away from the heterodoxy of his youth. August Weismann's work, that refuted the Lamarckian assumption that inherited characteristics could be modified by environmental factors, opened the way for a sustained attack on environmentalism, a campaign in which Pearson was to play a leading role. In the 1890s, Pearson, in collaboration with biologist W. F. R. Weldon, would develop a battery of new statistical methods that, he claimed, would enable man to master his organic environment, to regulate life itself.

Pearson's collaboration with Weldon in 1892 in creating "biometrics" marked a final absorption into scientific professionalism, a reentry into the homosocial world of male intellectual companionship. Thereafter, Maria would take second place to Weldon. Although Pearson supported single women professionally as his assistants, and still called himself a socialist, his "woman book" which had preoccupied him into the early nineties was indefinitely postponed. After 1893, "there seem to have been no more poems nor songs, contributed to the Socialist Song Book or otherwise; after . . . the *Chances of Death* (1897), no more miscellaneous studies, but only the overwhelming mass of scientific work." As one former colleague speculated, bitter controversies and feuds with Mendelian geneticists seem to have become Pearson's sole public outlet for emotion.[110]

Fourth Ending: The Marriage Debate and Sexual Danger in the Popular Press

In the other endings, we have seen how Karl Pearson, like a protagonist in a classic Victorian novel, found his destiny through marriage and a life's work (while consigning Maria Sharpe to the domestic sphere). But, this story had *two* beginnings, one private and one public. Media scandals like the "Maiden Tribute" had called the Men and Women's Club into being, and the club itself stimulated a media extravaganza on marriage and its discontents. Let us return to the pages of the daily press.

In early August 1888, the great marriage debate commenced in the pages of the *Daily Telegraph*, triggered by an article on marriage by Mona Caird, a freethinker and feminist who had been rejected for membership in the club but who brought her views before the wider public in the *Westminster Review*. Caird relied heavily on Pearson's historical and evolutionary approach to marriage. Conventional marriage, she wrote, was a failure. A true spiritual union was possible only if marriage constituted a free contract between men and women, if men and women could enter into a spirit of comradeship before marriage, and if women could gain economic independence so that they did not feel compelled to enter into mercenary marriages.[111]

There was nothing particularly remarkable about these sentiments; they had been voiced before, by John Stuart Mill and by other feminists as well as by members of the Men and Women's Club. What *was* remarkable was the public response it evoked and the positioning of that correspondence on the newspaper page. Twenty-seven thousand letters poured into the *Daily Telegraph* on the question "Is Marriage a Failure?" in August and September 1888. From lower middle-class suburbs, "the draper's victim" complained about his wife's clothing bills; a "matrimonial failure" detailed the horrors of enforced companionship with a man "brutalized by drink"; and "Anti-Club" indicted men's clubs as "the greatest curse of our enlightened country."[112]

Club members discussed the correspondence among themselves, attributing it to their own efforts, yet disconcerted by its "philistinism" (intensifying Maria Sharpe's disillusionment with conventional views on marriage). They noted, along with the *Pall Mall Gazette,* that the correspondence must have been expurgated, because all that touched on "delicate and unexplored territory" (precisely what they were trying to get at in *their* discussion) had been suppressed. But slowly, those subterranean topics started to creep out onto the other side of the newspaper page. On the left-hand side of one page, men and women squabbled about the amount of time men spent at their club or the heavy bills husbands had to pay to dressmakers; on the right-hand side of an adjoining page came headlines of the "Whitechapel murders" of Jack the Ripper, "Extraordinary Revelations," descriptions of terrible mutilations and of the "man monster who stalks the streets in search of fallen women."[113]

These two media events, the marriage debate and the Whitechapel horrors, tensely coexisted for four weeks, but the balance of interest and fascination began to shift from West to East, from left to right. Finally, after 29 September the marriage correspondence ceased publication, and the Ripper murders took over the whole newspaper.

The newspaper columns thus reveal a schizophrenic division of the sexual drama—the apparently petty disputes and squabbles of middle-class marriage were juxtaposed in apparent contrast to the degradation of East End prostitution. Except for their proximity, the sanitized domestic drama/music-hall routine of the marriage correspondence and the Gothic horror story of death and sexual mutilation would seem to have been enacted in two distinct social universes. Yet the imaginative fantasies woven around the story of the Ripper murders implicitly connect the two scenarios, and explicitly link the world of West End gender relations with the carnage of the East End. This is particularly seen in two assumptions: that the murders were committed by an upper-class male pervert, possessing rare cunning, intelligence, and genius; and that the perpetrator was most likely a mad syphilitic doctor, a savage/savant, skilled in scientific butchery who took pleasure in the sexual mutilation of the prostitutes he murdered. The theme of "science gone mad" dominated public speculations even as sexologists and "mad doctor" alienists emerged as the official experts in the case. Most of the terrible secrets of marital life and gender antagonism suppressed in the marriage debate and raised by the Men and Women's Club—sexual abuse, medical rape and outrage, prostitution and venereal disease—appear in the newspaper columns devoted to the Whitechapel murders. Science and melodrama met again, this time locked in a deadly embrace.[114]

SIX

Science and the Séance: Transgressions of Gender and Genre

he *Daily Telegraph*'s marriage correspondence was only one of many media extravaganzas exposing the plight of wives in the last decades of the nineteenth century. Another cause célèbre was Georgina Weldon's highly advertised campaign against her husband, Henry, and a mad-doctor alienist, L. Forbes Winslow, for conspiring to intern her in an insane asylum because she was a spiritualist. At the height of her fame, when headlines of the half-penny newspapers constantly broadcasted "Mrs. Weldon again," the indomitable Georgina Weldon was reputed by one newsclipping service to have commanded as many newspaper columns as a cabinet minister. Mrs. Weldon was a great favorite of W. T. Stead, who admired her pluck, her canny manipulation of publicity, her populist defense of the "liberty of the subject," and her struggle against materialist science in the name of female spirituality. On all these counts, she would have provoked a very different response from Stead's contemporary, Karl Pearson, who had little sympathy for a "woman of the market" such as Mrs. Weldon who used the commercial spaces of the city to parody and campaign against male professionalism.[1]

Mrs. Weldon's "woman in the city" story celebrates the possibilities of metropolitan life in the 1880s for enterprising middle-class women like herself. Moving comfortably and speedily across the social spaces of London, refashioning different versions of herself, Georgina Weldon was able to publicize her situation and expose the private male plot that failed. Between 1878 and 1885, Mrs. Weldon played out her story in the newspapers and the medical journals, amplified it in street advertisements and processions, extended it to the lecture circuit, the law courts, and ultimately, that premier commercial space of the 1880s, the music halls. Combining courage, virtuosity, and slapstick comedy, Mrs. Weldon's campaign of revenge vastly amused the educated reading public, yet it pressed an open nerve about fears of madness and of wrongful confinement, thereby continuing a melodramatic narrative of family-medical conspiracy that Wilkie Collins and Charles Reade had popularized in their sensational novels of the 1860s.[2]

Spiritualism and the Mad Doctors

Mrs. Weldon was a target of lunacy confinement because her husband tried to use a public controversy between doctors and spiritualists to further his private designs—that is, to rid himself of a nuisance wife. Medical men, alarmed by the growing popularity of spiritualism among the educated classes, had themselves instigated this larger conflict.[3] They caricatured spiritualists as crazy women and feminized men engaged in superstitious, popular, and fraudulent practices. Spiritualists responded by elaborating an iconography of male medical evil, imagining the doctor as a trader in lunacy and as a sexually dangerous man, a divided personality, whose science made him cruel, bloodthirsty, and hypermasculine, because it suppressed his feminine, spiritual part. Both sides engaged in a symbolic struggle, in a dialectical battle of words and images, often inverting the same metaphoric language as their opponents. In so doing, spiritualists and their adversaries took up positions already marked out by feminists and doctors in the campaign against the state regulation of prostitution and echoed contemporaneously in the antivaccination and antivivisection movements.[4]

The men who organized the attack on spiritualism were mostly specialists in neurophysiology and psychiatry. They entered the fray after some of their most eminent colleagues, such as Sir William Crookes and Alfred Russel Wallace, had lent their name and reputation to spiritualism.[5] Adversaries of spiritualists believed their own materialist scientific culture was under attack and, as experts in "morbid" and "abnormal" states of the brain, they wanted to assert an "epistemological sovereignty" over the discussion.[6] The brain, insisted William Clifford, the noted physiologist, "is made of atoms and ether, and there is no room in it for ghosts."[7]

Throughout the late 1870s, William Carpenter, a professor of zoology, and E. Ray Lankester, a young biologist, waged an unremitting campaign against the "Epidemic of Delusions." The extraordinary claims of spiritualists, Carpenter insisted, required extraordinary tests; they must be subjected to the clinical eye of dispassionate observers, not casually verified by their loyal adherents.[8] Lankester intensified the campaign in 1876 by exposing the writing medium, Henry Slade, as a fraud, and, with Horatio Donkin, a Harley Street doctor and later member of the Men and Women's Club, filed suit against Slade under the Vagrancy Acts for being a trickster.[9]

Hostile scientists further repudiated spiritualists as maniacs.[10] Medical critics denounced the trance as a form of hysteria, an "anomalous state of the brain," to which women, given their inherently unstable reproductive physiology, were peculiarly liable: wherever there were "strange manifestations," asserted Dr. George Savage, the director of Bethlehem Hospital, there was "sure to be found a girl with hysterical symptoms." Spiritualism, declared Henry Maudsley, ought to have a place among the causes of mental malady. Following the lead of medical scientists, psychiatrists translated spiritualist communications into the esoteric language of materialist science, representing them as local lesions of the brain or unconscious cerebration.[11]

One alienist who enthusiastically joined in the public attack was Dr. L. Forbes Winslow, the operator of two private asylums in Hammersmith. Winslow's own family history was intimately linked to the history of British psychiatry. His father, Forbes Winslow, the great pioneer of psychological medicine, was personally responsible for the legal acceptance of the insanity plea in the 1840s. The son, L. Forbes, was educated at Rugby and Cambridge and groomed to follow in his father's footsteps and take over the family business. Throughout his professional career, the younger Winslow continue to live in his father's shadow: he "lacked the original powers of his father" and made no "noteworthy contribution" to his specialty. The medical establishment tended to regard him with some condescension, at best as an undistinguished asylum keeper unconnected to the higher-status specialty of neurology, at worst as a "trader" in lunacy, soiled by his connection to the market.[12]

Part of Winslow's difficulty lay in the declining status of asylum psychiatry since his father's time, and of private asylum-keeping in particular. Asylum treatment manifested little connection to the new organic theories expounded to professionalize and modernize psychiatry. Alienists still based their diagnosis on behavioral symptoms and other social indicators, which were unconnected to demonstrable lesions of the brain. Somatic theories offered little in the way of cure, and alienists failed to reverse the tendency towards the "silting up" of institutions with chronic patients in the late nineteenth century. As long as alienists were connected with asylums, they were tainted by association with low-status patients, enjoyed very limited access to research and hospital appointments, and were essentially trapped in a dead-end specialty.[13]

An enterprising man nonetheless, L. Forbes Winslow seems to have compensated for unimpressive professional credentials by pursuing a career as expert witness and medical publicist. By his own account, he testified at "practically every major murder trial of criminal insanity"; and he further enhanced his reputation in lay circles by producing a number of popular texts on forensic psychiatry.[14]

Following the lead of E. Ray Lankester, Winslow became an enthusiastic "ghost grabber," who exposed a public medium as a fraud in 1877 by squirting red ink at his "spirit face."[15] In *Spiritualist Madness* (1877) he identified spiritualism as the principal cause of the increase of insanity in England, particularly among "weak-minded hysterical women" (psychiatrists like Maudsley had merely listed it among significant causes), and he claimed that upwards of forty thousand spiritualists were interned in American asylums.[16] Winslow's pamphlet generated a wave of anxiety among spiritualists;[17] it also brought him to the attention of Henry Weldon, who asked him to interview his wife and then find an asylum for her. Winslow clearly regarded Weldon's request as routine.[18] As lunacy certification required the signature of two doctors (independent of the asylum operator) who had conducted separate examinations of the prospective patient, Winslow concocted a scheme to interview Mrs. Weldon: he and his medical colleagues would visit her, under the guise of interested philanthropists inquiring about her orphanage. After these interviews were completed, he suggested a companion for Mrs. Weldon; when told by Mr. Weldon that would not be "practical," he readily accepted her as a patient for an annual fee of £400.[19] Unfortunately, both Weldon and Winslow had underestimated the ingenuity, determination, and performing skill of their adversary, Georgina Weldon.

The talented and beautiful daughter of a Welsh landed gentleman, Georgina Treherne had married the impecunious Henry Weldon against the wishes of her family in 1860.[20] Their 1860 marriage was a "love match," but also a way for Georgina to escape the control of her authoritarian father and gratify her desire for a theatrical career. Since Harry had only a small private income, she insisted that, as a condition of their marriage, he agree that she be permitted to "go on the stage and make a fortune."[21]

Georgina soon learned that a marriage contract—even with an inadequate breadwinner—was no ticket to the stage. Once married, Henry reneged on his promise and Georgina had to settle for amateur theatrics and charity musical-benefits. She kept the household afloat by observing the "strictest economy" and by "singing for her supper" at Society events.[22] However, by the late 1860s, Georgina's popularity began to wane, and she herself found the role of performing amateur increasingly distasteful. Disillusioned with her childless marriage and fed up with "singing for her supper," she returned to teaching as a new avenue for fulfillment. In the ninth year of her marriage, she developed the idea of a National Training School to teach music to poor children in a "naturalistic" mode.[23] She persisted in this plan, over the objections of her husband, who disliked her proposal to recruit "dirty, diseased orphans" from the streets and place them "beneath his roof to be fed, clothed and educated."[24] As a result, Harry Weldon (who in the meantime had come into a comfortable inheritance) separated from his wife in 1875, giving over to her the lease to Tavistock House, their Bloomsbury townhouse, and a thousand pounds a year.

Mrs. Weldon's philanthropic scheme, coupled with her marital troubles, estranged her from genteel society and her own family.[25] Society was further shocked by the unconventional regime at Tavistock House. Mrs. Weldon's progressive methods thoroughly violated social and class decorum.[26] The children "were taught to sing and recite from the earliest age, they were sent to the opera"; they were brought up as vegetarians; they were not allowed to cry; they were permitted to go barefoot and yell for a quarter of an hour; they were not subjected to rigid rules nor were they trained up in a manner that would fit them for a menial station in life.[27]

Equally unconventional and indecorous were her advertising techniques on behalf of the orphanage. The children were carted around from one event to another in an advertising van, a retired horse van with "Mrs. Weldon's Sociable Evenings" emblazoned on it in enormous letters—an object so "outlandish" that her brother begged her to "keep it from his door." The sociable evenings themselves were only slightly less outlandish; frequently Mrs. Weldon combined musical entertainment with a reading of the history of her orphanage, and the entire evening culminated with a dramatic recitation of the "Spider of the Period," performed by Sapho-Katie, aged three.[28]

Meanwhile, Mrs. Weldon plunged deeper and deeper into heterodox activities. She became an enthusiast for rational dress: "I had simple tastes. . . . I did not take to crinolines when they were in fashion. . . . I wore my hair short. . . ." She embraced a number of other "eccentric" causes associated with radical politics and popular health: vegetarianism, mesmerism, the occult.[29]

Spiritualism was a natural extension of her countercultural interests. Her progressive views on child-rearing were compatible with the innovative pedagogies of the spiritualist Progressive Lyceums, that featured, according to one historian, "variety, learning-by-doing and dancing, no harshness."[30] Mrs. Weldon also participated in the larger community of spiritualists: she won the praise of the spiritualist press as a "keen and true friend" for her defense of the notorious Mr. Slade and for her gratuitous singing at spiritualist meetings.[31] She even experimented in "social levelling" within her own household by enlisting her maid and her orphans in spirit communication.[32] Given her own marital difficulties, Mrs. Weldon may have also sympathized with the spiritualist critique of patriarchal sexual power within marriage and its insistence that women be the "monarch of the marriage bed."[33] Humble female mediums with marital problems frequently looked to the spiritualist lecture and séance circuit as a source of employment and refuge from unhappy homes. Before very long, Mrs. Weldon would herself appeal to spiritualists for collective protection and support against patriarchal plotting.

As a spiritual practice, spiritualism had particular appeal to women, who significantly outnumbered men as adherents and mediums. The private, homelike atmosphere of the séance, reinforced by the familial content of spirit communication with dead relatives, was a comfortable setting for women. The séance reversed the usual sexual hierarchy of knowledge and power: it shifted attention away from men and focused it on the female medium, the center of spiritual knowledge and insight. As the scene of popular "hands on" female healing, the séance also constituted a female consumer challenge to orthodox allopathic medicine.[34]

Equally important was the fact that spiritualism provided spectacular entertainment directed at all the senses. Most private séances featured trance or inspirational speaking, but a wide assortment of "physical phenomena" was included in the repertoire of professional or "test" mediums: table-tilting, floating furniture, musical instruments playing by themselves, the wafting of mysterious incense in the air.[35] Even more dramatic sexual displays and inversions were accomplished at materializations: a medium, usually an attractive young girl, would be placed in a cabinet, bound and gagged, while a fanciful spirit would issue forth, sometimes a red Indian, sometimes a swearing buccaneer, sometimes a lovely young female spirit in a diaphanous white gown who sat on the laps of her favorite gentlemen.[36]

As other historians have noted, trance conditions legitimized a wide range of "bad behavior" on the part of women by allowing them to engage in a subtle subversion—but not repudiation—of the "separate sphere" construction of "true womanhood." Spiritualists deemed women particularly apt for mediumship because they were weak in the masculine attributes of will and intelligence, yet strong in the feminine qualities of passivity, chastity, and impressionability.[37] Female mediums were receptive vessels for other spirits—usually male spirits—who acted as the medium's control or "guide" in the spirit world.[38] This form of male impersonation reflected the contradictory dynamic operating around gender in spiritualist circles: women could authoritatively "speak spirit" if they were controlled by others, notably men; their access to male authority was accomplished through the fragmentation of their own personality.[39] There was a further irony and danger: these special female powers also rendered female mediums vulnerable to special forms of female punishment, in particular, to medical labeling as hysterics and to lunacy confinement.

Mrs. Weldon undoubtedly found spiritualism's penchant for theatricality very appealing.[40] What most attracted her were the opportunities it offered women for vocal performance. As we have seen, ever since she was a young woman, Mrs. Weldon had tried to devise ways to perform in public, from amateur theatrics to charity benefits, to her sociable evenings. Not surprisingly, she was attracted to the séance, a home-based entertainment that featured women *speaking* rather than *being*.[41]

Mrs. Weldon first attended séances in France, but soon found that she was temperamentally unsuited for mediumship. Although she continued to experiment with other forms of spirit communication, her taste tended to run to the mystical (hence, her attraction to French spiritualism and to a heterodox Catholicism) and she herself had little interest in the physical phenomena of spiritualism. During her first séance in France, for example, when she "desired ardently" to communicate with dead friends, "scarcely any phenomena occurred." When at the advice of the medium, "she remained perfectly passive, marked manifestations of the table began." But clearly Georgina Weldon was not the type to remain "perfectly passive" for long, or to allow herself to become a transparent vessel for other spirits. She was insufficiently passive and impressionable. Her energy and determination would serve her well in her impending struggles against the "plot that failed."[42]

The Plot That Failed

In 1878, Mrs. Weldon and her orphans were visiting a convent in France, when she had a premonition that she must return home. Perhaps she had heard rumors that her husband, grown dissatisfied with the terms of their separation, wanted to retrench and sell the lease of their Bloomsbury townhouse, Tavistock House. Leaving her orphans in the care of the convent nuns, she immediately crossed the Channel and returned to London. She soon became embroiled in a criminal charge against a servant who, she claimed, stole possessions from the house. During her cross-examination, the defense counsel tried to cast doubt on her testimony by claiming that she was suffering from delusions. Within a few days of this public accusation, Mrs. Weldon found herself visited by a series of mysterious strangers.[43]

As she recounted her story—and what follows is a summary of her own account—Mrs. Weldon was dusting the music books in her library on 14 April 1878, when a servant announced that two visitors, Mr. Shell and Mr. Stewart, were in the hall. Thinking they were her music publishers, she had them admitted. Instead, they turned out to be two strangers, an older gentleman who sat "on the middle of his spine" with his hands clasped on his stomach, and a younger one resembling a "Christy minstrel," "all blinks, winks, and grins." They introduced themselves as fellow spiritualists interested in her work on musical reform and children. She told them she was a "firm believer in spiritualism." After a half-hour conversation, they went away.[44]

At eight o'clock her servant announced that the visitors had returned. They rushed into the room, and to her surprise, they were another set of complete strangers, this time, a "Tubby One" and a "Taciturn One" with the aspect of a "seedy dentist's assistant." They too asked her about her spiritual communications; whether any of her children were mediums and whether she believed her animals possessed souls.[45]

During these initial encounters, Mrs. Weldon answered their questions positively and directly. "I did not think it strange; I suspected that it was all about some rich and mysterious orphans." After they left, she gradually came to realize that the mystery pertained ominously to herself. Mrs. Weldon began to feel "dreadful" and sensed "some horrible trap." She remembered there were rumors afoot about her suffering from delusions and began to suspect that this masquerade might be part of an attempt to confine her for lunacy. She told the servant to "lock and bolt up the house." Within twenty minutes a carriage arrived and the bell rang. "Who's there?" "A gentleman and two ladies to see Mrs. Weldon!" Bell, the caretaker spoke to them outside. Finally he shut the door in their faces. "They knocked and they rang three times, but we turned out the gas; they got tired of waiting, and at last we heard the carriage drive off."[46]

"For the first time in my life I felt nervous." "[S]omething I call my guardian angels, had given me a sign warning me I was in very immediate and grave danger."[47] "[P]ale and trembling," Mrs. Weldon posted letters to several friends to warn them of her predicament.[48] She sent one letter to W. H. Harrison, editor of the *Spiritualist,* who had published a series of letters from Mrs. Louisa Lowe. In her letters, Mrs. Lowe, a former inmate

of a private asylum, had warned spiritualists of the dangers of wrongful confinement in lunatic asylums. Nothing in England, wrote Mrs. Lowe, "was easier than to get a sane person into a lunatic asylum."[49] None were more likely to be "put away" without due cause than "women in general" and "wives in particular."[50] "All the morning I was thinking," wrote Mrs. Weldon, " 'Oh that I dared to go out to Mrs. Lowe.' "[51]

At 2 P.M. the following day, the "bell rang again." "A note from Mrs. Harrison introducing who—but Mrs. Lowe!!! The very woman I was longing and praying for." Mrs. Weldon had begun to tell her story when the bell rang again. The caretaker appeared much agitated: "Those three have come have pushed their way in and say they will wait till they come to see you."[52]

Mrs. Lowe took command of the situation and went off to fetch the police; when she arrived with "two stalwart policemen," a newly emboldened Mrs. Weldon confronted the "trio" at door. The two women "darted upon me and seized me." Mrs. Weldon felt inclined to fetch a poker and break their heads, but Mrs. Lowe advised a more discreet course. "Give them in charge for assaulting you," said Mrs. Lowe. "Policeman," said I, "take them in charge, they are assaulting me." "I might have spoken Hebrew or Chinese; they never moved, and I feel convinced they would have let me be carried off bodily." On the advice of Mrs. Lowe, she barricaded herself in her room.[53]

At last, a friendly policeman (who had been warned the evening before) arrived and forced the trio to produce the lunacy order, signed by her husband and a family friend, General de Bathe, who had briefly visited Mrs. Weldon the previous afternoon. "They then left, I telegraphed to my husband to come and save me." Mrs. Weldon insisted her husband's signature must be a forgery, but the cynical Mrs. Lowe responded, "[You] don't know how bad husbands [are]." Both her servant and the kindly policeman supported Mrs. Lowe's advice to "go" rather than to than to trust to her husband's benevolent intervention. "[S]o in greatest haste, I threw my cloak over my shoulders, my bonnet, without waiting to put on my boots, in a pair of wonderful old slippers ran down the square, the policeman stopped a cab ('I am not looking at the number!' he said) jumped into it, Mrs. Lowe took me to her house and I was . . . SAVED!!!!" When the "madhouse-keeper" Winslow returned that night, he was furious to learn that his quarry had escaped. "Mrs. Weldon is a dangerous lunatic! Where has she gone? A thousand pounds for any one who can find her."[54]

Mrs. Weldon first accompanied Mrs. Lowe to her home and then went underground for the seven days that the lunacy order remained in effect. When she surfaced, she was determined to avenge herself on the parties responsible for the assault. Acting on her own behalf, she appeared before Mr. Flowers of the Bow Street Police Court. Mr. Flowers sympathized with her ordeal and condemned the action of Dr. Winslow as "an unjustifiable design upon her liberty"; but he could offer no legal redress against the assault. Legal authorities were powerless to take up her case, he explained, unless she had been confined in a lunatic asylum; nor could she, a married woman, institute a civil suit against them.[55]

Georgina had nonetheless won a moral victory. Mr. Flowers's statement of sympathy legitimated her case and quickly established her sanity, even to the medical press, who acknowledged her to be a "lady abundantly capable of enjoying her liberty without harm to herself or others."[56] Even though she had been debarred from pursuing her case in court, Mrs. Weldon proceeded to assail her enemies on all other fronts. Following the advice of Charles Reade, the novelist, she adopted an "American" style of publicity.[57] She published her story in the spiritualist press, offered interviews to the daily newspapers, tried to provoke libel suits from the participants, stood on public platforms and embraced the cause of lunacy reform, hired sandwichmen to parade in front of Winslow's home with signs denouncing him as a "bodysnatcher,"[58] and launched a public concert career, as well as continuing her social events at home, where between musical performances she read her lecture "How I Escaped the Mad Doctors."[59]

Mrs. Weldon's Narration: A Story Retold

Mrs. Weldon survived her husband's conspiracy and proved herself a forceful antagonist to psychiatric medicine. She was able to elicit support and sympathy, even from unusual quarters like *The Times* and the medical press, for a number of reasons. Mrs. Weldon was a female rebel who retained the "aura" of "true womanhood." Although the turmoil and drama of her life were the direct result of her determined resistance to the conventions of gender, she presented herself as a sweet, gracious lady with a feminine voice who led a "quiet, domestic life." In stretching but not repudiating the boundaries of "separate spheres," she adopted a strategy similar to other female spiritualists.

But in other ways, she manipulated her femininity very differently than did spiritualist performers. As Regenia Gagnier notes, she tended to parody those same female domestic virtues—from maternal feelings to musical soirées—that she claimed to uphold.[60] Moreover, the same "unfeminine" qualities that made her temperamentally unsuited for mediumship—her strong personality and her active, restless temperament—enabled her to fight back in public, to break out of the controlling dynamics that rendered other female spiritualists, particularly mediums, more vulnerable to medical supervision. Even her spirit communications were of an intensely practical sort, counseling self-protection and decisive action.

Class and age also set Mrs. Weldon apart from the nubile, young women of artisanal and lower-middle-class background who performed materializations and became "test mediums" under the patronage of some wealthy gentleman.[61] With more resources at her disposal, Mrs. Weldon could choose a more independent means of public presentation. To be sure, there was some affinity between Mrs. Weldon and materializing mediums; in her search for employment, she would eventually turn her hand to commercial performances, and she too had a penchant for a certain linguistic cross-dressing. Instead of hypermasculine lower-class sailors or soldiers, her impersonations extended to authoritative, elite men of the law. Having experienced considerable difficulty with musical impressarios, Mrs. Weldon would dispense with male patronage altogether when she went public as a "lunatic lawyer in petticoats."

Differences of class, age, and temperament could not protect her from lunacy certification—they only enabled her to escape incarceration once threatened. When Mrs. Weldon finally read her lunacy order, she learned "for the first time" that "because I was a spiritualist they wished to examine the state of my brain." More precisely, because she was a spiritualist *and* the estranged wife of a man who wanted to "retrench," her liberty was endangered. But her social position was also her defense: well-connected and self-possessed, she was able to turn the tables on her enemies, the psychiatric "bodysnatchers," and to seriously undermine their public credibility.[62]

Mrs. Weldon was also a very good storyteller. As a campaigner and "lunacy lawyer" she triumphed over her enemies because she was able to explain her plight in ways comprehensible to a reading public. As soon as she sensed her "danger," she recognized the outlines of a familiar plot. She immediately thought of Mrs. Lowe's letters in the spiritualist press, themselves derivative of Reade and Collins's sensational narratives of family intrigue and betrayal.[63] Like other sensational novelists of the 1860s, Collins and Reade had revised the representation of sexual danger enacted in traditional stage melodrama, to focus on middle-class marriage. For them, female powerlessness and vulnerability began at home; women were less endangered by illicit sexual encounters outside the family than by male sexual abuse within its circle. Marriage no longer resolved the female dilemma; it compounded it. The insane asylum simply amplified the danger of the domestic asylum; it was a supplementary patriarchal structure, a place of madness and sexuality where doctors substituted for tyrannical husbands as the keepers and tormenters of women.[64]

In her public pamphlets, Mrs. Lowe had characterized her experience of the asylum in much the same way: as a place to stash away unwanted wives (or relatives) and as a place of sexual danger. She accused her husband of arranging for her incarceration after her spirit writing had exposed his adulterous activities. She described the lunatic asylums where she was confined as places of institutionalized irrationality, where the doctors were crazier than their patients and the whole atmosphere was suffused with an unrestrained sexuality and indiscipline designed to drive any rational person mad.[65]

By drawing on the tradition of the sensational novel filtered through Mrs. Lowe's own "history," Mrs. Weldon retold an older narrative of entrapment. In this story of male villainy and female victimization, Mrs. Weldon cast herself as an endangered heroine, who was assisted in the nick of time by Mrs. Lowe, another sister "lunacy lawyer in petticoats."[66] Together they were able to foil a patriarchal plot to deprive her of her liberty. Her first installment of this story, summarized above, included a full repertoire of melodramatic motifs and tropes: rapid action, the profusion of secrets, stereotyped, interchangeable villains who possessed no psychological depth, extreme states of being and danger, multiple disguises and impersonations, the operation of sinister forces directed by some unknown mastermind.[67] As in stage melodrama, servants and policemen embodied comic relief—they were sympathetic but impotent figures, powerless to repel the advances of menacing invaders. Only the courage and determination of Mrs. Weldon and Mrs. Lowe saved the day and turned the "bloodhounds from the door."[68] To escape incarceration, Mrs. Weldon had to flee her own domestic asylum, the safe and comfortable scene of daily life, and go disguised as an anonymous denizen of the city. Later she would resurface as a "public" woman bent on vindicating her honor and sanity.

"Truth is stranger than fiction," declared the *Medium and Daybreak,* commenting on the Weldon case. "[S]omething is radically wrong when a virtuous and highly-talented woman can with impunity be torn from her home and doomed to worse than penal servitude."[69] But who was the ominous force behind these machinations?[70] Mr. Weldon's involvement remained obscure until the climax of the first scene, when the lunacy bill was finally read and his signature disclosed.[71] Only then were the actions of the mad doctors unveiled as part of a "little family conspiracy" and only then did Mrs. Weldon come to realize, in Mrs. Lowe's words, "how bad husbands [are]."[72]

Mrs. Weldon's melodramatic story of her "escape" remained the same throughout its many recitations, with one important elaboration: the progressive sexualization of her story as her husband's involvement became clarified. Shortly after her escape, in an interview in the *London Figaro*, Mrs. Weldon accused her husband of conspiring with General de Bathe to get rid of her in order to marry de Bathe's young daughter; she further claimed that de Bathe had nurtured a long-standing grievance against her for having spurned his sexual advances when she was a girl.[73] Mrs. Weldon interpreted the male conspiracy of doctor-family friend-husband as a "traffic in women,"[74] in which doctors colluded in the private sexual designs of men by defining female resistance as madness.[75] Contemporary observers, commenting on her story, further amplified and extended the theme of sexual danger. The spiritualists likened the actions of the "mad doctors" to the sadistic pleasures of the hunt; while even the *British Medical Journal,* not commonly given to Gothic allusions, invoked the example of Rochester and Jane Eyre to illustrate how men might use lunacy confinement to further their sexual self-interest.[76]

Subverting Melodrama

Sensational melodrama, however, was only Mrs. Weldon's starting point. She would show herself infinitely more resourceful than Laura Fairlie, the victimized wife of *Woman in White,* or even her ingenious "detective" sister, Marian Halcombe. Both of these characters had to rely on men to do the legwork and could not draw upon public resources to assist them in their private travail.[77] Mrs. Weldon, in contrast, countered the private conspiracy against her by going *public* and entering male domains. She successfully renovated the older melodramatic script by providing different endings, thanks to the new commercial spaces and legal opportunities available in the 1880s to "new women" like herself. Mrs. Weldon's triumph thus illustrates how external conditions can shape narrative structures, at least for social texts.

Mrs. Weldon's first subversive act was to satirize the melodrama of sexual danger itself. Reversing the usual sexual script, she sued her husband in 1882 for the restoration of conjugal rights (her agent having managed to subpoena him in his London club, that ultimate enclave of male privilege); she won her case, although Harry defied the court order and would not return to the matrimonial bed. Then, after the passage of the Married Women's Property Act later that year, a whole new world of legal action opened up to her. "I am no longer an outlaw," she jubilantly informed her mother. Not only could she now sue in her own name, but she also chose to appear in person, without counsel. Before long she would be dubbed the

"Portia of the Law Courts" and praised as the "universal genius—the advocate, actress, songster, and orator."[78]

Mrs. Weldon conducted her own legal case partially out of financial necessity, but partially because, as she realized her forensic powers, she came to take great pleasure in providing legal entertainment of a high order. Her first legal success as "plaintiff in person" came in July 1884 when she won her suit against Dr. Semple, one of the doctors who had signed her lunacy certification, and was awarded five hundred pounds in damages. Judge Hawkins, the presiding magistrate, actively took her part and posed some hostile questions of his own to the defendant. Summing up, he found it "incredible" and "astonishing" that Winslow, the asylum operator, "should select the medical men" and let them read a "statement of facts [indicating insanity] made by her husband who had not seen her for three years." Judge Hawkins's indignation was shared by the law journals, who denounced the apparent collusion between the asylum operator and his medical colleagues, and further criticized the "perfunctory" way the examinations were performed. Slipshod and lax procedures endangered the "liberty of the subject," a cause close to the heart of male jurors, judges, and barristers, whatever their sentiments about the plight of victimized wives.[79]

Mrs. Weldon failed in her first suit against Winslow in March 1884, but she gained her revenge six months later, in her second legal engagement against the madhouse-keeper. By that time, Winslow had lost his asylum and his lucrative patients, and had to appear in person, without benefit of counsel.[80] With humor and intelligence, Mrs. Weldon sustained her case. She openly acknowledged her efforts to provoke him into a libel suit: asked whether she had harassed Winslow with sandwichmen, she couldn't "recall" at first, although she declared "That is, by the bye, a good idea." "Yes," she remembered, "I did everything I could to get a rise out of him."[81]

Mrs. Weldon's chief objective was to vindicate her own sanity and to prove that a belief in spirits was less dangerous than a belief in "mad doctors." She pitted the authority of the law against the authority of medicine and forced the medical witnesses into exposing the absurdity of their own expertise. She was greatly assisted in this endeavor by the ridiculous performance of her own doctors, not to speak of her medical opponent's pathetic defense. Doctor Edmunds, appearing as her witness in both the Semple and Winslow cases, denied that she was insane, and claimed that she was only eccentric, because of her peculiar ideas of children's education and the "simplification of women's dress." When asked about the insanity of eminent men, he acknowledged the temporary insanity of notables from St.

Paul to John Wesley (Isaac Newton, he recalled, had once fancied himself a "teapot") and concluded that "all persons were in a sense of unsound mind"—"all persons except your lordship"—a comment that elicited wild peals of laughter.[82]

Winslow fared no better in his own defense. Contradicting Dr. Edwards, he insisted that eccentricity was indeed insanity; it was "born into the subject." He presented himself as an expert who patrolled the borderland; only those who have dealt extensively with lunatics could tell whether they were harmless or dangerous lunatics. He made a futile effort to appeal to the jury on the basis of masculine solidarity: "The jury ought to consider what idea they would form of their wives if they should fill their houses with children picked up in the street, and drive around with large placards advertising 'social evenings'." Judging from the trial's outcome, the jury and the judge did not place much confidence in his scientific expertise or his professional probity; the jury found for the plaintiff, and the judge condemned Winslow for being "motivated by other motives than the interest of justice," and ordered him to pay Mrs. Weldon a thousand pounds in damages.[83]

In his testimony Winslow had complained that the proprietors of private asylums did not have the support of the medical press. Since the beginning of Mrs. Weldon's crusade, the *Lancet* and the *British Medical Journal* had tended to regard Winslow personally as an "adventurer" and they expressed concern that lunacy cases such as Mrs. Weldon's would give the false impression that "medical men will do anything for a fee."[84] Nonetheless, medical spokesmen were clearly nervous about the 1884 decision against Winslow: for it not only repudiated Winslow as venal and inept, but implicitly cast doubt on the professional competence of all doctors to certify lunatics. What the *British Medical Journal* termed the "unfortunate plight of Dr. Forbes Winslow"[85] generated a new wave of anxiety among medical practitioners. Since all doctors had the power to sign lunacy certificates, all doctors were "endangered" by the verdict against him. "Ever since Mrs. Weldon began her campaign," certifying doctors "have good cause to tremble," summed up *The Times*.[86]

Meanwhile Mrs. Weldon continued her campaign. Between 1883 and 1888 she successfully sued all the participants in the "plot that failed." In 1884, she had seventeen cases proceeding at once—"my children," she explained to an amused reporter.[87] Dressed in a simple black gown and Florentine-looking cap, she became a favorite of the press.

Reporters loved to interview her in her office, off Red Lion Court, where they could juxtapose her "sweet voice," her "sweet smile," and "sympathetic manners" to the masculine clutter of the law, the "chaos of ink bottles, stumps of pen, papers and memoranda."[88] Her cross-examinations were praised as "works of art," and her long speeches were noted for their oratorical eloquence—no "hemming and hawing" for Mrs. Weldon.[89] Immensely proud of her legal performances, Mrs. Weldon presented herself as a defiant, talented amateur, scornful of the "paraphernalia of the law, jaw, and justice,"[90] but determined to use the machinery of the law to undermine the authority of medicine. On the whole, barristers and judges tended to regard her legal impersonations and breaches of legal etiquette with amused toleration.[91] They could afford to be more tolerant than medical men: their professional conduct was not on trial, and they did not feel threatened by an "army" of aspiring Portias waiting in the wings. Whereas women had already penetrated the ranks of the medical profession, barristers were more securely ensconced in a tightly restricted and exclusively male professional world, that seemed impermeable to female invasion.[92]

Mrs. Weldon won her actions against the "mad doctors" but fared less well in other disputes related to her musical career, which had been ongoing during this whole time. Yet even here she turned defeat into publicity for herself and a political cause. A dispute with one business associate had landed her in Newgate Jail for libel in 1880, where she occupied her time mending the laundry of the establishment.[93] Another libel suit in 1885 sent her to Holloway Jail for six months; as she exited, she was cheered by a huge crowd, organized by the Mrs. Weldon's Legal Defense Committee, whose officers were Dr. L. Forbes Winslow and Dr. Semple (!), now mysteriously her staunch allies and friends.[94] They were accompanied by a delegation from the plebian radical Nottingham Magna Carta Association, a support group for the Tichborne Claimant.[95] With bands and banners, they all marched in procession from Islington to Hyde Park Corner, where she called for the creation of a Court of Criminal Appeal. As a result, Mrs. Weldon added prison reform and judicial reform to her list of causes, and, like her friend W. T. Stead, she took to wearing her prison garb when lecturing on these subjects. Plebian radicals remained her most loyal supporters, and she responded in kind by embracing—with characteristic eclecticism—a potpourri of populist causes of the late 1870s and 1880s: the Tichborne Claimant, the secularists Charles Bradlaugh and Annie Besant, as well as the Salvation Army (despite a professional distaste for their music).[96] To support her legal habit, she went on the music-hall stage, turning her "voice to account to pay bills."[97] In 1884, she sang two songs nightly at the London Pavilion, for seventy pounds a week. In 1886, she briefly appeared in *Not Alone,* a melodrama featuring a crusading heroine who lambasted husbands and lunacy doctors; unfortunately it was neither

a critical nor a commercial success. The public preferred her legal entertainment or her personal appearances as a songster on the boards, where
she performed her own compositions and those of her new friend, Forbes
Winslow.[98]

The originality of Mrs. Weldon's story derived from her active transgression of gender and genre, the variety of public spaces she occupied to
state her case, and her versatility in deploying a multitude of forms for self-
expression, from melodrama and music-hall comedy, to the esoteric discourse of the law. With her van of orphans and Florentine gown, she managed to parody, as Regenia Gagnier notes, both female domesticity and
male professionalism. As a "lunacy lawyer in petticoats," as a lady who
performed at the halls (but did not sing "music hall songs" or wear "music
hall dress"),[99] she was a liminal figure, a cross between Joan of Arc and P. T.
Barnum. Absolutely self-possessed, always ready with "dates, facts, figures," Mrs. Weldon "behaved like a woman but . . . thought and expressed herself as a man."[100]

Three visual images of the time suggest the contrasting way in which
Mrs. Weldon's transgressions were interpreted and contained. The first
two represented her as versions of the extraordinary. In 1884, she graced a
"Spy" cartoon in the May issue of the toney publication *Vanity Fair*,
dressed in a costume that strongly resembled the uniforms of Salvation
Army lasses: a simple black dress, complete with black military cape, a
black hat with wimple, and a brief marked "Weldon v. Winslow" in her
hand.[101] *Vanity Fair* praised her "indomitable courage," her "marvellous
energy," and "incredible activity" all of which made her unique—"not as
other women."[102] A less flattering cartoon in the more downscale *Moonshine*, however, transformed her into an updated version of the termagant
wife and manly woman of popular tradition who challenged men in "the
struggle for the breeches."[103] In *Moonshine*'s illustration, Mrs. Weldon
appeared as a monumental "women's rightess," tyrannizing over a midget
Forbes Winslow, and bragging, "Anyone Else Like to Say I am Mad." She
was surrounded by other sexual "inverts" who also liked to play the "trou-
ser role": homely bluestockings, marching in procession with men's trousers emblazoned on their banners, and a henpecking wife who rebuked her
husband, "Now can't you keep those children *quiet?*"[104] Popular
iconography of this sort undoubtedly framed Mrs. Weldon's appeal as a
music-hall performer. The transformation of the "Modern Portia" into a
genteel serio-comic for the halls appears less incongruous in the context of
the sexual inversions and gender antagonisms that were staple fare of
music-hall entertainment: we need to imagine her in the company of other
male impersonators like Vesta Tilley who emulated the dress and privileges

of men, and alongside feisty female stars like Marie Lloyd who merrily enacted the battle of the sexes waged there nightly.[105] Like Mrs. Weldon's
own parody of male authority, these entertainments always possessed a certain "edge," a level of gender consciousness that partially echoed the more
politicized struggles among men and women of the propertied classes.[106]

A third image represented Mrs. Weldon as a version of the ordinary. As
the centerpiece of a Pears Soap advertisement (honoring her jubilee birth-
day), Mrs. Weldon achieved the highest rung of commercial fame.[107] Her
image was placarded on every omnibus in London, placing her in total circulation, yet returning her to the private space of the home where people
washed themselves. For a few years, Mrs. Weldon enjoyed the ephemeral
status of the female celebrity, whose "face" was her fortune, but also a vehicle for the selling of other commodities.[108] She became a facet of everyday life in commercialized culture, a curious blend of the extraordinary and
the ordinary, very much like spiritualism itself.

By the end of the 1880s, however, Mrs. Weldon's star was in decline.[109]
She had, of course, aged, but so had her cultural transgressions, which had
lost their novelty and failed to evolve; they remained at the level of popular
symbolic behavior and serio-comic inversion. They were not consciously
theorized; they did not lead to new narrative forms or speculations about
female consciousness and identity. For there were contemporaries who began to take up these cultural tasks. Theosophists like Anna Kingsford and
the followers of Madame Blavatsky would pursue more seriously the implications of female consciousness and identity implicit in Mrs. Weldon's
public performances. On the whole, they would restrict their activities to
the interior of the self, in accord with good taste and sexual decorum—and
not extend their appeal to the popular constituency enjoyed by Mrs.
Weldon.[110] From another direction, the learned men of the Society for Psychical Research would undertake to recuperate female spiritualism for
male science, translating spiritualist communions with the "Other World"
into manifestations of the multiple personality.[111]

According to Alex Owen the moral panic and threat of lunacy confinement itself had abated by the end of the 1880s: Mrs. Weldon's campaign
had finally put the mad doctors on the defensive.[112] Nonetheless the
iconography of medical evil that Georgina Weldon helped to publicize continued to be elaborated by others, particularly by the opponents of vivisection, who concentrated on the nefarious activities of experimental
scientists.[113] They shared Mrs. Weldon's enthusiasm for publicity, but they
lacked her light touch; they dramatized medical sexual danger as pure melodramas unrelieved by Georgina's skillful comic reversals.

Even as Mrs. Weldon's star was in decline, Dr. L. Forbes Winslow managed to regain the limelight in 1888—enjoying his second "fifteen minutes" of fame as the principal newspaper expert and possible police suspect in the Jack the Ripper case. It was Winslow, writing once again to the newspaper, who first proposed the theory that the murderer was a homicidal maniac of the upper classes of society. The evidence Winslow offered was the perverted cunning with which the killer had performed the mutilations and evaded justice. Winslow was also one of the most persistent amateur detectives to descend upon Whitechapel to hunt out the Ripper, using his scientific intelligence to process into clues the fragmentary details that the "poor creatures of the streets" had brought him. He was so omnipresent that Scotland Yard detectives, on the lookout for a "mad doctor," began to suspect that he *was* Jack the Ripper.[114]

Mrs. Weldon did not set out to discover Jack the Ripper, although female mediums throughout London tried their hand at armchair detection—and when they communed with the spirits of the murdered women they were informed that the Ripper *was* a mad doctor.[115] Still, she may be credited with some impressive accomplishments of her own. Into the 1880s, she helped to sustain the story of lunacy confinement as a "little family conspiracy" between doctors and husbands at a point when gender struggle in marriage had become immensely more politicized than it had been in the 1860s. Unlike her literary predecessors, Mrs. Weldon showed how women could take matters into their own hands and act publicly in their own defense. The range of her activities was breathtaking, a testimony to the possibilities of metropolitan culture for women. In her various campaigns, Mrs. Weldon bridged the domains of politics and culture, high and low forms. Not content with simply authoring her story, Mrs. Weldon presented herself bodily to the machinery of justice and to an expanded public. By parodying lawyers and unmasking medical men as traders in lunacy, she implicated male professionals in the operations of the market, while simultaneously claiming the commercial spaces of the city as an appropriate setting for respectable women.

Mrs. Weldon's successful negotiation of urban spaces and cultural styles depended on her willingness to make a spectacle of herself and to allow her image to be refashioned, circulated, and ultimately discarded by a fickle marketplace. In 1888, not only did her star go into decline, but the same engines of daily journalism began to tax themselves to the limit in projecting a new metropolitan star, also emblematic of transgression and mobility, but who evoked the darker and erotic elements of the fantastic: Jack the Ripper.

SEVEN

Jack the Ripper

here is only one topic throughout all England," wrote W. T. Stead in the *Pall Mall Gazette* on 1 October 1888, and that topic was the Whitechapel murders of "Jack the Ripper."[1] Stead himself took the lead in extracting copy from the Ripper murders: acting in collusion with the entire London daily press, he compiled and summarized news accounts from the morning papers in his evening publication, offering some characteristic twists of his own.

Thanks to Stead and his newspaper contemporaries, the Ripper story became national news. It was constructed piecemeal over a period of several weeks, as observers struggled to discern patterns from a murder sequence that they regarded as unique in the annals of crime. Throughout the autumn of terror, the daily press, catering to many different reading publics, was hard at work distilling meaning from the news breaks of the day, while also backtracking and retrospectively establishing a pattern of significance for preceding murders. Drawing on cultural fantasies—about the grotesque female body, about the labyrinthine city, about the mad doctor—that had long circulated among different strata of Victorian culture, media coverage also highlighted new elements of late-Victorian conceptions of the self and London's imaginary landscape.

Media organization of the Ripper narrative helped to contextualize the events of autumn 1888 and to manage anxieties unleashed by the murders. Contemporary observers, keenly aware of the Ripper episode as a media event, periodically took the press to task for provoking hysteria and interfering with the police investigation; but they, along with the experts and the general public, gained their understanding of the Ripper murders through the newspapers. However much diverse constituencies intervened to shape the media's interpretation of the Ripper crisis according to their own political agendas, they were also compelled by the overall *gestalt* produced by the media.

As the property of the entire daily press, the Ripper story represented a different kind of media production, with a decidedly more ambiguous political message, than Stead's "Maiden Tribute" or Mrs. Weldon's populist campaign in defense of the "liberty of the subject." In contrast to these two causes célèbres, media organization of the Ripper story had no defined political center, and women were significantly marginalized from the public telling of the story. This is not to say that all public interventions carried the same weight or that women were completely outside the cultural production of the Ripper narrative. At the local level, working-class women participated in informal storytelling, providing information that others used to process into clues. A similar reprocessing occurred in relation to feminist and antivivisectionist representations of prostitution and of the sexual danger of medicine. Media coverage of the murders took up the themes and narratives of female reformers and reworked them into a male-directed fantasy, closer in tone and perspective to the literature of urban exploration and the male Gothic than to female political melodrama.

This chapter examines the media scandal of Jack the Ripper in two parts. "Making the Case" lays out the barebone elements that were culturally stressed in press coverage, elements that found expression in the cries of newspaper boys hawking the latest particulars of "Murder, Murder, Mutilation, Whitechapel," and the "Mystery of Jack the Ripper." The second section, "Playing out the Story," details how and when these elements entered the Ripper narrative; it outlines the additional stories woven around and superimposed upon the prevailing media coverage of Jack the Ripper by diverse social actors, eager to articulate their version of the "truths" and "fictions" of the Ripper episode.

Making the Case

Over the course of ten weeks, the newspapers were able to consolidate a small number of "facts" about the cases. Between 31 August and 9 November 1888, five brutal murders of prostitutes took place, all but one within an "evil quarter of a mile" of Whitechapel, East London (the exception occurring just within the boundary of the City of London).[2] The murdered victims were Polly Nicholls, 31 August; Annie Chapman, 8 September;

Catherine Eddowes and Elizabeth Stride (the "double event"), 30 September; Mary Jane Kelly, 9 November. The murders were performed at night, four in the open, with great daring and speed. All five took place in a densely populated area where local residents kept close watch on each other's movements. Still, there were no witnesses to the crimes; the police could uncover no clues or "rational" motives for the murders.[3]

The first element underscored by press coverage of the Ripper murders was their setting: Whitechapel, a notorious, poor locale, adjacent to the financial district (the City) and easily accessible from the West End by public transportation and private carriage. Part of London's declining inner industrial rim, Whitechapel stood at the edge of the vast East End, London's proletarian center, a "city" of nine hundred thousand. To middle-class observers, Whitechapel was an alien place, a center of cosmopolitan culture and entrepôt for foreign immigrants and refugees, whose latest wave consisted of poor Jews escaping the pogroms of Eastern Europe in the 1880s. Whitechapel was also notorious for its transient and homeless poor, living out-of-doors or in those "thief preserves," the common lodging houses.[4]

By the 1880s, Whitechapel had come to epitomize the social ills of "Outcast London." Casual and seasonal employment, starvation wages, overcrowding at exploitative rents, an inhumane system of poor relief, declining traditional industries, and an increase in "sweated" labor were all marked features of living and working conditions there. Worsening conditions, recent historians have argued, precipitated a mounting political crisis in 1888, driving the East End destitute and unemployed towards defiance, and unleashing anti-alien and anti-Semitic protests. But, as Jerry White has observed, the middle classes of London were far less concerned with the material problems of Whitechapel than with the pathological symptoms they spawned, such as street crime, prostitution, and epidemic disease—"the whole panoply of shame of this 'boldest blotch on the face' of the capital of the civilized world."[5]

For the respectable reading public, Whitechapel provided a stark and sensational backdrop for the Ripper murders: an immoral landscape of light and darkness, a nether region of illicit sex and crime, both exciting and dangerous. Like the deserted wasteland of Stevenson's "city in a nightmare," Whitechapel's empty spaces could rapidly fill with a menacing crowd. "All sorts and conditions of men" could be met with on Whitechapel Road, the district's main thoroughfare, with its "flaunting shops," piles of fruit, and "streaming naphtha lamps." A principal entertainment center for working-class London, Whitechapel Road also proved a magnet for rich young bloods from the West End who would tour the "toughest, roughest streets, taverns and music halls in search of new excitements."

This was Charles Booth's "Tom Tiddler's Ground"—imagined as a place of Darwinian drama and excitement—as compelling to the respectable observer as it was frightening.[6]

At night, commentators warned, the glittering brilliance of Whitechapel Road contrasted sharply with the dark mean streets just off the main thoroughfare. Turning into a side street, one was "plunged" into the "Cimmerian" darkness of "lower London." Here in the Flower and Dean Street area, with its twenty-seven courts, alleys, and lanes, stood one of the last remaining rookeries of late-Victorian London. "In these squalid parts of the metropolis," reported the *Daily Telegraph*, "aggravated assaults, attended by flesh wounds from knives, are frequently met with, and men and women become accustomed to scenes of violence." In streets with nicknames like "Blood Alley," "Frying Pan Alley," and "Shovel Alley" lay the "warrens of the poor," "all packed by a species that multiples with astounding swiftness and with miserable results." Here "it may be well to tuck out of view any bit of jewelry that may be glittering about." Even the police hesitated to enter the notorious Wentworth and Dorset streets alone. In the Flower and Dean Street area it was useless for "them to follow when they happen to appear on the scene, as the houses communicate with one another, and a man pursued can run in and out." In the same back slums and alleys, poor prostitutes, "fourpenny knee tremblers," lived and worked, often bringing their customers into dark corners to avoid the price of a room. And here, in Buck's Row, Hanbury Street, Berner Street, and Dorset Street (better known in the locale as "Do as You Please Street"), during the "autumn of terror" of 1888, the bodies of four of the victims of Jack the Ripper were found.[7]

In the pages of the daily press, this sensational landscape was juxtaposed to descriptions of the more mundane features of daily life among the poor. Inquest testimonies revealed that most of the bodies, for example, were found by people going to and from work: Robert Paul, a cabman on his way to Covent Garden market at 3:30 in the morning, found the crumpled body of Polly Nicholls in a doorway in Buck's Row and made a "mental note" to tell the police; Louis Diemschutz, an "unlicensed hawker" and steward of the International Working Men's Educational Club on Berner Street, was returning home from work at 1:00 A.M. when he found Elizabeth Stride's body in a courtyard adjacent to the club, where he resided. The same mean street that provided the setting for a murder also served as workplace and residence for poor inhabitants engaged in casual and sweated trades. In 39 Hanbury Street, "whose back premises" became the "scene" of Annie Chapman's murder, "no fewer than six separate families reside[d]." Its inhabitants included a packing-case maker, two cabmen and their families, a proprietor of a cat-meat shop (run on the premises), an old man and his "weak-minded" son, and an old lady kept "for charity" by the woman who "tenanted" the house. Political and social institutions—the settlement house at Toynbee Hall, the Jewish socialist club at Berner Street, the Salvation Army mission, the London Hospital, the bastillelike board schools, the pubs and cheap music halls—all figured as part of the physical setting for the murders and the investigations. To evoke a sense of place, the kitchens of the dosshouses, the shed on Dorset Street where homeless women congregated, and the interior of the room where Mary Jane Kelly was killed appeared in great detail in the daily press.[8]

This physical evocation was not intended to elicit human sympathy for the "people" of Whitechapel as much as to promote an "argument from geography" about the territorially based nature of the crime. Newspaper reports applied Lamarckian theories of urban degeneration to the Whitechapel horrors, diagnosing them as a product of a diseased environment whose "neglected human refuse" bred crime. "We have long ago learned that organic refuse breeds pestilence," declared *The Times*. "Can we doubt that neglected human refuse as inevitably breeds crime, that crime reproduces itself like germs in an infected atmosphere, and becomes at each successive cultivation more deadly, more bestial, and more absolutely unrestrained." This perspective extended well beyond elite circles. Representations of urban degeneration also appeared at the lower end of the spectrum of print culture. *The Curse on Mitre Square,* a Gothic penny dreadful rendering of the Eddowes murder that was hawked on Whitechapel streets, depicted Whitechapel Road as a "portal to the filth and squalor of the East," where several strata of humanity passed along, from "half-starved clerks," to factory hands "limping to the badly-ventilated rooms to work," each more physically dilapidated than the other.[9]

As a sign of racial and class otherness, Whitechapel became a dreaded name, the East End Murderland, infamous throughout the world. Contradicting this totalizing hyperreality were news accounts of Whitechapel's actual diversity, particularly the tense polarity between the Anglo-Irish casual laboring poor and the immigrant Jewish community, and between the rough elements and the respectable citizens of Whitechapel who wanted more police protection. Whitechapel's physical proximity and social connection to respectable parts of London proved even more unsettling: "Unhappily for all of us," declared *The Times,* "the Whitechapel murderers and their victims are neighbours of every Londoner." Although the press tried to stigmatize Whitechapel as a place apart, it also depicted it as a place where many parts of London met: a magnet not only for a "vast floating population—the waifs and strays of our thoroughfares"—but also for young West End bloods and for scores of respectable "slummers" who visited and even settled in the area.[10]

Another compelling aspect of the Whitechapel murders, as the media covered them, was their mystery, the secrecy and impunity with which the murders were committed in public spaces, and the "mystery" as to "motives, clues, and methods." Unable to find historical precedents for the Whitechapel "horrors," commentators resorted to horrifying fictional analogues: "to the shadowy and willful figures in Poe's and Stevenson's novels" or the "stealthy and cunning assassins in Gaboriau and du Boiscobey." Indeed the events of autumn 1888 bore an "uncanny resemblance" to the literature of the fantastic: they incorporated the narrative themes and motifs of modern fantasy—social inversion, morbid psychological states, acts of violation and transgression, and descent into a social underworld—and gave utterance to "all that is not said, all that is unsayable through realism."[11]

Whereas Mrs. Weldon's spiritualist adventures combined themes of sexual danger and fantasies of urban access for women, the Ripper murders exclusively evoked the darker social and erotic meanings of the fantastic. Commentators came to believe that the murders, which seemed so senseless and motiveless, possessed a deep meaning. The analytic method for uncovering this occulted truth was twofold. First, it involved an obsessive scrutiny of petty details as signs and codes that would allow the observer to uncover the system of meaning which the fragmented surface masked. Newspaper headlines advertised "New Particulars of the Whitechapel Horrors," while subheadings seized upon a "piece of an apron," a "black bag," "mysterious pawntickets," an "extraordinary parcel," "strange communications," "the writing on the wall," as potential clues to the murders. But the search for meaning was not simply fixed at the level of extreme nominalism; it also led to theories woven "from the merest figments of fancy." At the height of the crisis, cultural fantasies ran rampant in speculations about the murderer's identity and the social and political significance of the crimes.[12]

These speculations also resembled the literature of the fantastic in their symptomatic expression and management of anxieties over social and political disorder. The murders had caused a social breach and crisis that could only be healed by penetrating the "dark cloud of mystery" which "conceals the guiltiest wretch in London from the sight of innumerable eyes peering in every direction, night and day." Commentators likened the Ripper story to a "dark labyrinth" where every corner revealed a new "depth of social blackness"; they also superimposed this labyrinthine image on the besieged city itself, represented as incoherent, fragmented, ungovernable. In the absence of reliable official statements on the progress of the investigation, rumors flew.[13]

Expressions of social and epistemological disorientation were coupled with repeated denunciations of the representatives of law and order, already under fire for their mishandling of street prostitution and demonstrations of the unemployed. Inept bureaucracy, the faulty leadership of the police commissioner, Sir Charles Warren, who was trying to "militarize" the police, futile competition between two police forces (the City and the Metropolitan) aggravated a situation already experienced as chaotic. "The triumphant success with which the Metropolitan Police have suppressed all political meetings in Trafalgar Square contrasts strangely with their absolute failure to prevent the most brutal kind of murder in Whitechapel," sneered the *Pall Mall Gazette*. The "East Enders have lost faith in the capacity of the Executive to exorcise the grim spectre by which they are haunted," declared the *Daily Telegraph*. In the absence of clues or motives, declared the *Star*, the "only practical moral to be drawn from the wholesale massacre . . . is the inadequacy of the police force from top to bottom." The Conservative press would join issue with the Liberals in denouncing the Ripper murders as one of the most "ignominious police failures of all time," when, to quote the *Daily Chronicle*, the Metropolitan Police "simply" let "the first city of the world . . . lapse into primeval savagery."[14]

A final element signified by the "mystery" of the murders was sexual. Faced with a "senseless crime," press commentary invoked the figure of the Gothic sex beast, a "man monster" motivated by "bloodthirsty lust" who "goes forth stealthily and takes his victims when and where he already pleases," akin to the "were wolf" of "Gothic fiction." Declared the *Daily Telegraph*, "we are left . . . to form unpleasant visions of roving lunatics distraught by homicidal mania or bloodthirsty lust . . . or finally we may dream of monstres, or ogres." In the East End, monstrous metaphors assumed a literal status: "People allowed their imagination to run riot. There was talk of black magic and vampires."[15]

When contemporaries invoked fictional analogues of the monstrous, argue cultural critics Deborah Cameron and Kathleen Fraser, they drew on a "transitional language" to represent "sex crime," just at the historic moment when scientific discourse was transforming the figure of the sex beast into a "sexual deviant" and his sinful crime into a "disease." In the long run, they argue, the Ripper murders would emerge as the most publicly advertised in an emerging series of case histories of sex crime, thus serving as a media vehicle for concealing yet suggesting the "truth" of "sex." At the time of the Ripper murders, however, the medicalizing effort to diagnose the "monstrous" motives of the murders as "sexual" (and as encapsulated within the figure of the sex pervert) was incomplete; the meanings of the murders, like the figure of Jack the Ripper himself, remained ambiguous and polymorphous, encompassing social and geographic, as well as individual, associations of the monstrous.[16]

The fact that most of the murders were accompanied by acts of sexual mutilation also contributed to the grisly notoriety of the crimes and provided the most sensational stories the newspapers were to present. At the time, contemporaries disputed whether the murders evidenced anatomical skill and knowledge of the female body. Some believed that the principal objective of the murderer was evisceration of the body after the woman had been strangled and had her throat cut. When the murderer had enough time, observers committed to the "medical theory" believed, the uterus and other internal organs were deliberately removed, while the woman's insides were often strewn about. Conversely, when some murders did not "extend so far," when no "portion" was "missing," this same school of thought assumed that "the miscreant had not time to complete his design."[17]

The "mangled remains" of the Ripper victims triggered off a set of psychosexual and political fears that resounded, in different ways, across the social spectrum. Body fragments testified to the monstrous nature of the crime, of the criminal, and of the social environment. If, traditionally, the "classical" body has signified the "health" of the larger social body—of a closed, homogeneous, regulated social order—then the mounting array of "grotesque," mutilated corpses in this case represented the exact inverse: a visceral analogue to the epistemological incoherence and political disorientation threatening the body politic during the "autumn of terror."[18]

Because they were committed on female bodies, particularly on the bodies of prostitutes, the mutilations carried especially transgressive associations. These were not the elegant, dignified female bodies of civic statuary that graced the public squares of the West End, embodying the abstract virtues of race and nation; nor were they the "salon body" of elite females that lined the walls of art galleries and lay on "tea tables in open photo albums" or "animated advertisements for household products." They were instead "women of the people" "cut to pieces," grotesque body fragments, replete with gaps, orifices, missing body portions, emblematic of female vice and the teeming multitudes of the East End and their "symbolic filth."[19]

The mutilated bodies of the Ripper victims evoked the "ensemble of representations" that had authorized regulatory policy and official disposition towards prostitutes throughout the nineteenth century. According to

Alain Corbin, these negative body images included the prostitute as putrid body, as sewer, as syphilitic carrier, as corpse, and as link in a chain of re-signed female bodies "at the beck and call of the bourgeois body." Media representations at the time of the Ripper murders called all these images into play, accompanied by renewed demands for the reintroduction of state-regulated prostitution to restore order, but they placed particular stress on the cultural fantasies and associations of the prostitute body as corpse. Not only did the Ripper murders seem to literalize the moral truth that the wages of sin was death—that the "awful being who haunts White-chapel" presented himself as "an embodied judgment to the women of evil life"—but the murders themselves occurred in the shadow of two death houses: the Aldergate slaughterhouse and the great London Hospital. As experts debated whether the murder exhibited the skill of a butcher or a "scientific anatomist," commentators on the crime scenes described the victims variously as slaughtered animals, "ripped open just as you see a dead calf at a butcher shop," or as dissected cadavers, reminiscent of "those horrible wax anatomical specimens" on display in medical museums and in the windows of anatomical shops.[20]

As Elaine Showalter observes, the Ripper murders "eerily evoked" themes of medical violence against women that pervaded fin-de-siècle literature—of opening up, dissecting, or mutilating women: indeed, they may well have helped to consolidate and disseminate those themes publicly to a wider readership. They also played on—and seemed to play out—popular fears of surgeons, gynecologists, vaccinators, vivisectors, and dis-sectors as violators of, in this context, the innocent bodies of women, chil-dren, and animals, that had found considerable expression in a range of popular health and antimedical campaigns of the 1870s and 1880s.[21]

The grisly mutilations, provoking a full range of social and political anxieties, and apparently establishing the signature of the killer, intensified public fascination with the mutilator, who acquired the sobriquet "Jack the Ripper" in the course of events in fall 1888. At the time of the "double event" of September 30, an anonymous letter forecasting the murders and signed by "Jack the Ripper" had been sent to the Central News Agency. A facsimile of the letter, and a postcard that followed from "Jack the Ripper," were republished in all the newspapers and posted at street corners. A fort-night later, a third letter addressed to the chairman of the local vigilance committee in Whitechapel and accompanied by half of a human kidney reinforced suspicion that the murderer was a necrophiliac. These letters set the tone for the rest (of which 350 have been collected in the files of Scot-land Yard). The first two were addressed "Dear Boss," all three were jocu-lar and teasing. They bragged of past and future exploits, and of how much the writer enjoyed his "work." "I am down on whores," declared the Ripper, "and I shan't quit ripping them up until I am buckled." Police authorities believed that these letters were a "creation of an enterprising journalist"; whether authentic or not, the letters helped to establish the murders as a media event by focusing social anxieties and fantasies on a single, elusive, alienated figure, a figure who craved "sensation" and who communicated to a "mass" public through the newspaper. Written in an informal, "Cockney style," the letters also consolidated the murderer's reputation for irony and wit. Anonymous yet polymorphous, the murderer was presumed to be, at various points in the discussion and by different constituencies, a Russian Jewish anarchist, a policeman, a local denizen of Whitechapel, an erotic maniac of the "upper classes" of society, a religious fanatic, a mad doctor, a scientific sociologist (George Bernard Shaw's facetious suggestion, which was taken up by the press), and a woman.[22]

In the telling of the Ripper story, the stigmatized identity of the victims was another striking feature. The social profile of his victims emerging from the local interviews and testimonies of the inquests seemed to be remarkably detailed and precise. "Painfully familiar have become the proceedings of the inquests on the victims of the Whitechapel assassin," commented the *East London Advertiser*. All the inquests seemed to tell the "same old story of want, immorality, and inhuman crime." In the case of the first four victims, all were, according to the *Daily Telegraph*, "women of middle age, all were married and had lived apart from their husbands in consequence of intemperate habits, and were at the time of their death leading an irregular life, and eking out a miserable and precarious existence in common lodging houses." These "drunken, vicious, miserable wretches whom it was almost a charity to relieve of the penalty of existence" were "not very particular about how they earned a living." When they could, they worked as charwomen, street sellers, or picked hops during the summer months in Kent. If they had to, they resorted to the streets as casual prostitutes.[23]

Economic need forced them to take to the streets on the nights they met their deaths. Newspaper headings and woodcut illustrations persistently fixed on the final dialogues of Polly Nicholls and Annie Chapman before they met their death, as if these statements encapsulated a deep moral meaning. A short time before she was murdered, Polly Nicholls was seen staggering along Whitechapel Road by Emily Holland, her friend and neighbor. Holland offered to take her home, but Nicholls explained that she had no money for her lodging. "But I'll get my 'doss' money," she declared. "See what a jolly bonnet I've got now." Annie Chapman voiced a similar intention, after she had been denied admission to her lodging house on Dorset Street because she did not have the fee of eight pence. "I haven't enough now, but keep my bed for me, I shan't be long."[24]

To middle-class readers of *The Times* and the *Morning Post*, as well as socialist readers of *Commonweal*, the murders constituted a morality tale of stark proportions. These were economically desperate women, who violated their "womanhood" for the price of a night's lodging, and for whom the wages of sin was death. Outside of Whitechapel, the victims became unsympathetic objects of pity—for radicals and conservatives alike. Whatever guilt middle-class readers may have experienced over the "mangled remains" of Annie Chapman, their compunction was soon overwhelmed by feelings of fear and loathing towards the spectacle of the victims themselves. This paradoxical response to the "great social evil" was not unique; it was embedded in the literature of prostitution and in earlier reformist campaigns such as the "Maiden Tribute" and the feminist opposition to state regulation. But reformers such as Butler and Stead had sympathized with the history of young prostitutes, if not with their present reality; and they adopted a protective and custodial attitude toward fallen women as "errant daughters." Both the older age of the Whitechapel victims and their apparent culpability in departing from the patriarchal home rendered this parent-child paradigm inapplicable. This negative feature of reformist propaganda set limits to the kind of sympathy which could be extended to the fallen women of Whitechapel (and may partially explain feminist reticence to enter into the public discussion).[25]

In sum, the degraded social setting, the mysterious circumstances, the grisly mutilations, the ominous figure of Jack the Ripper, and the "deviant" lives of his victims combined to produce a dark media fantasy of the Ripper murders. Media coverage transformed the unsolved murders of five poor women into a national scandal; and it incited a wide range of social actors to immerse themselves in the details of the cases, compelled by sexual titillation but also by the desire to extract meaning out of apparent disorder.

Playing Out the Story

The Ripper case, never solved, offers no closure or resolution to the problem of sexual violence and the social order that produced it. Because it achieved no closure, it remains, well into the later-twentieth century, an enigmatic thriller that continually reverberates and reconstructs itself over time. In this section, we shall examine some of the parties to the initial "creation" of the Ripper stories. Following the Nicholls murder, the story gained momentum, direction, and focus, but it never emerged as a unified,

stable narrative. Complicating the process of interpretation was the "introduction" of new narrative elements in successive cases, such as a coroner's
revelation, mysterious "writing on the wall," the "Jack the Ripper" letters,
as well as apparent contradictions within and between the explanatory systems invoked to make sense of the crimes. At strategic moments, different
social actors—from Whitechapel residents and friends of the victims testifying at the inquest, to medical correspondents writing to the daily press—
played a key role in providing clues or redirecting the interpretation of the
crimes.[26] Both on the streets of London and in the pages of the national
press, diverse constituencies offered competing social perspectives, revising
and reprocessing the available media fantasies about the Whitechapel horrors.

The first to intervene and organize opinion on the subject were the police themselves, who followed up clues provided by local residents. Initially,
the police treated the murder of Polly Nicholls as one of many cases of unsolved assault; only later at the morgue was it discovered that the body had
been severely mutilated. Acting on suggestions of local prostitutes, they first
investigated street gangs who preyed on prostitutes and who extorted money
from them. However, they soon came to imagine that they were in the presence of a serial killer who had concentrated his activities on a particular
locale and who preyed on women of "evil life." The murders, accordingly,
took on a new status, and police authorities shifted the supervision of the
Nicholls murder away from the local police to Scotland Yard. Simultaneously, news accounts enlarged the significance of the murder, transforming it
into national news. Linking the event to two recent cases of unsolved homicides involving poor prostitutes in Whitechapel (despite the fact that these
earlier homicides revealed totally different murder patterns), headlines announced "Another Murder in Whitechapel" and the "Whitechapel Horror:
Third Crime of a Man who must be a Maniac." Following the lead of local
police, the press now declared that the murders were the work of "one individual."[27]

Police continued their manhunt by investigating men in the local
neighborhood who might have the tools or skills to perform the bloody
mutilations—butchers and shoemakers. They eventually turned their attention to other occupational groups, such as sailors on board cattle boats,
whose presence in and out of London would explain the timing of the crisis
and the mysterious disappearance of the murderer. The growing list of candidates reflected the local social economy of Whitechapel; it also mirrored
the prejudices of the police and local residents.[28] Whitechapel had a large,
mobile, and rootless population of men who looked and acted in ways

police found suspicious. They were obvious targets of police and popular suspicion.

Jews were targets of both. An endemic form of anti-Semitism existed in the East End, in part an expression of traditional xenophobia and in part a response to the unstable economy and shrinking material resources of the area. Whitechapel was experiencing a severe housing crisis due to the influx of Eastern European Jews and the conversion of housing stock into warehouses and commercial properties. Jews and gentiles, constituting, to a certain extent, two separate classes, had to coexist in the same small area and compete for resources.[29]

Anti-Semitism in 1888 was one articulation of a rising tide of nationalism and racism orchestrated by the popular media. As early as the Nicholls case, Radical dailies helped to stir up local sentiment against Jews by identifying one "Leather Apron" as the "only name linked [locally] with the Whitechapel murders." Leather Apron was, according to the *Star*, a Jewish slippermaker by trade, a "Strange Character who Prowls about Whitechapel after midnight," inspiring "universal fear" among women. Leather Apron's candidacy also gained support from the *Pall Mall Gazette*, which republished a description of "Leather Apron" compiled by a *Star* reporter after he had made inquiries among a number of "polyandrous" women in the East End: a man of "sinister" expression, with "small" and "glittering" eyes, "repellent" grin, his business was "blackmailing women late at night. . . . His name nobody knows, but all are united in the belief that he is a Jew or of Jewish parentage, his face being of a marked Hebrew type." While other dailies republished this new "theory," they were also quick to point out the "fictional" nature of the description: "He is a character so much like the intention of a storywriter that the accounts of him given by all the streetwalkers of Whitechapel district seem like romances," declared *Lloyd's Weekly News*.[30]

John Pizer, who had been "fingered" by the *Star* man as Leather Apron, finally turned himself into the police, in order to vindicate himself publicly and to escape the fury of the crowd.[31] The "Jacob the Ripper" theory[32] led to two local developments: denunciation of Jews at the inquests as ritual murderers and widespread intimidation of Jews throughout the East End. On the streets, popular anger precipitated anti-Jewish riots—one of three such outbreaks in late-nineteenth-century London. After the Chapman murder, crowds of roughs assumed a "threatening attitude" toward the "Hebrew" population of the district. "It was repeatedly asserted that no Englishman could have perpetrated such a horrible crime."[33] Speculations about "Leather Apron" also provoked false accusations against individual Jews, which in turn gave local youths license to rob and beat them. Along with "Lipski," a Polish Jew executed for violating and murdering his landlady in 1887,[34] the sobriquet "Leather Apron" became a common term of abuse applied to Jews.[35] Well after the police had discredited the "Leather Apron" theory and declared "Leather Apron" to be a "mythical personage,"[36] the man with a knife and leather apron remained an enduring popular image of the murderer. Thanks to continuous verbal and visual representations of the "mysterious" killer in the press as a "foreigner of dark complexion," the Ripper continued to be imagined, both by the police and local cockneys, as a "marked Hebrew type."[37]

West End dailies made their own contribution to the excitement by lending credence to the worst kind of anti-Semitic fantasies emanating out of Eastern Europe. On 2 October, *The Times* published a suggestion from its Vienna correspondent that the Whitechapel killer might be following the Talmudic injunction requiring a Jew who has been intimate with a Christian to atone for this pollution by slaying and mutilating her. As evidence for this practice, the correspondent cited a recent Galician case involving a Jew named Ritter who had been charged with outraging and murdering a Christian girl. Alarmed by what seemed to be a widespread media effort to connect the Jews with the Whitechapel murders and to revive the "legend of blood," the leaders of Anglo Jewry roundly condemned these speculations as "baseless and without foundation."[38]

In apprehending Jews as religious fanatics, police followed the lead of the local gentile population. But in suspecting Jewish socialists and revolutionaries, they acted on their own suspicions and on instructions from above. However, police soon found that anti-Jewish feeling, which they had helped to foster, was getting out of hand. After Chapman's murder, hundreds of police were drafted into the East End to forestall a possible pogrom. The double murders of Eddowes and Stride on 30 September cast further suspicion on East End Jews and intensified police concern. Stride's body had been discovered in front of the Working Men's International Club, a political club mostly frequented by Jewish socialists, whose members had just finished hearing a lecture on "Judaism and Socialism." Later that night, a bloodstained portion of Catherine Eddowes's apron was found in front of a building on Goulston Street inhabited by Jews. Above it on the wall was written in chalk, "The Juwes are not the men that will be blamed for nothing." Believing that the message was written "with the intention of inflaming the public mind against the Jews," Police Commissioner Warren wiped out the "writing at once" when he arrived on the scene. His actions provoked severe press criticism for destroying a valuable clue, but they won grateful thanks from the Chief Rabbi of London.[39]

By mid-September local police had their hands full. After Chapman's murder, a diabolical pattern of crime seemed to have been confirmed, and the impotence of the police to track down the culprit inspired a rising tide of public indignation. Popular rumors of extensive mutilations committed on Chapman's body added to the sensation. Press coverage vastly expanded, as the murder story spread over numerous pages and columns, encompassing leaders, correspondence columns, human-interest stories, official announcements, and police-court anecdotes. Woodcut illustrations of Hanbury Street, maps of the murder sites (showing escape routes to the West End), and clinical drawings of the victims surrounded by cameo portraits of expert witnesses testifying at the inquests, augmented the printed reports. Retrospectives of the life stories of the victims were juxtaposed to future projections of "more" murders to "follow." Sensational language of "bloodthirsty" monsters and fiends in "human shape" intensified, as did reports of copycat activities on the part of men who menaced women. To amplify the news further, papers included ancillary activities within Whitechapel, including local petitions, demands for an official reward and more police patrols, as well as the organization of citizen action groups.

Annie Chapman, declared the *Daily Telegraph,* did "more by her death than many long speeches in Parliament and countless columns of letters to the newspapers could have brought about." Her "mangled remains" provoked a "crisis of conscience" over the failure of Christian charity and the "social organization" to address what *Punch* labeled the "nemesis" of poverty and social neglect in Whitechapel. As police searched two hundred common lodging houses for the murderer, news investigations appeared on "Crime in Whitechapel," and the "Insecurity of Our Streets." Wherever you "inquire," declared the *Star,* there were "fresh stories of robberies and outrage, committed with impunity." Simultaneously letters on the "Moral of the Murders" appeared in the proprietary press, with conventional proposals to cure the social ills of Whitechapel: philanthropic plans for model dwellings, better lighting, improved paving, more Bible women, more night refuges where poor women could sleep, and more laundries where they could work. The letters focused not on the pathology of the murderer but on the degraded lives of the victims. The "Whitechapel horrors will not be in vain," declared "S.G.O." in *The Times,* "if 'at last' the public conscience awakes to consider the life which these horrors reveal. The murders, it may almost be said, were bound to come."[40]

Amidst this extensive soul-searching and philanthropic appeal, an alternative inquiry into the self and the social order materialized in the press. Suspicion shifted from the East End to the West End, as representations of the Ripper oscillated from an externalized version of the Other to a variation of the multiple, divided Self.

In "Murder and More to Follow," W. T. Stead, that great crusader against libertine debauchery, was the first journalist to draw attention to the "sexual origins" of the crime and to invoke Dr. Jekyll and Mr. Hyde as a psychological model of the murderer. *The Strange Case of Doctor Jekyll and Mr. Hyde,* Stevenson's enormously popular "shilling shocker" of 1886, had featured a murderer with a divided personality, who encompassed within himself the two social extremes of London: the urbane Dr. Jekyll, who used his scientific knowledge to create another self, the stunted, troglodyte, proletarian Mr. Hyde, as a cover for "secret pleasures" and "nocturnal adventures." Influenced by French writings on the multiple personality as well as Lombrosian theories of criminal anthropology, Stevenson's story represented the "thorough and primitive duality of [urban] man." Despite the author's repeated denials, contemporary readers and reviewers immediately interpreted the undisclosed nocturnal adventures and pleasures of Jekyll/Hyde as illicitly and violently erotic. When the theater version starring Richard Mansfield opened in the West End in August 1888, it adhered to the interpretation of Jekyll/Hyde as sadistic sex criminal. Mansfield played Hyde as a manifestation of Jekyll's "lust," a creature of infinite sexual drive who, unable to fulfill his desires in conventional heterosexual sex because of his "hideous imagination," "proceeds to satisfy his cravings in violence." To stabilize and fix Hyde's sexual obsession within the boundaries of heterosexuality (the original story remained obscure about the object and aim of Jekyll/Hyde's libidinal desire), the theater version added a new female character, Jekyll's fiancée, murdered by a jealous Hyde, thus injecting heterosexual love and sadism into the closeted professional bachelor world of Jekyll and his friends.[41]

With repeated allusions to Stevenson's story and to evolutionary anthropology, Stead characterized the "real-life" murderer in Whitechapel as an evolutionary throwback and sadist. The crime was a "renewed reminder of the potentialities of revolting barbarity which lie latent in man"; it was committed by a "Mr. Hyde of Humanity," a "Savage of Civilization" from "our slums," as capable of "bathing his hands in blood as any Sioux who ever scalped a foe." Animated by a "mania of bloodthirsty cruelty which sometimes springs from the unbridled indulgence of the worst passions" this midnight murderer might well be a "plebeian Marquis de Sade at large in Whitechapel," who, Stead warned, may not confine his activities to the East End.[42]

"Murder and More to Follow" located the urban savage in London's "teeming" slums. A few days later, however, Stead suggested a more respectable identity and address for the murderer, more akin to Jekyll's urbane appearance and stately West End mansion. In an "Occasional Note," Stead "hoped" that authorities were not confining their attention to those who looked like "horrid ruffians." "Many of the occupants of the Chamber of Horrors look like local preachers, Members of Parliament, or monthly nurses." Even the Marquis de Sade was an "amiable-looking gentleman." In keeping with the case-study approach of Stevenson's *Strange Case*, Stead diagnosed the murderer as a sadistic "victim of erotic mania which often takes the awful shape of an uncontrollable taste for blood."[43]

Thanks to Stead, speculations about the Ripper as a "dual personality," an "amiable-looking gentleman" who was also a "hard ruffian," who "did his bloody work with the lust . . . of a savage, but with the skill of the savant," began to percolate throughout the press. Other dailies took up the "Jekyll and Hyde" theory and fantasized about a "crazed biologist" who took scientific delight in the "details of butchery" or a "mad physiologist looking for living tissue." Indignant correspondents accused Richard Mansfield of being the Ripper because he played his part so convincingly; alternatively, they complained that he provided a role model for some unstable personality. In deference to the public uproar, the play shut down; fittingly the last performance was held as a benefit for night refuges for homeless women.[44]

As Christopher Frayling has observed, the Jekyll and Hyde model represented the most accessible "explanation" of psychopathology for English newspapers to exploit.[45] Nonetheless, Stead's reference to "sadism," as a "mania" from which the murderer was "suffering," invoked the concepts of sexual sadism and lust murder, recently introduced into the medical lexicon by Dr. Richard Krafft-Ebing, professor of psychiatry at the University of Vienna, and a pioneer of sexology, the scientific study of human sexuality.[46] Krafft-Ebing's professional duties included assessing proof of morbidity or "degeneracy" for sexual offenders brought before the court to determine whether they should be held responsible for their actions. Krafft-Ebing collected his case histories and published them in *Psychopathia Sexualis* (1886), a "medico-forensic study" of the "abnormal." Although the most explicit portions were printed in Latin, the book provoked an enormous popular as well as professional response. Krafft-Ebing found himself deluged with confessional letters from sufferers of sexual misery, which he added to his own body of case histories.[47] The appearance of *Psychopathia Sexualis*, observes Jeffrey Weeks, marked the "eruption into print of the speaking pervert, the individual marked or marred by his (or her) sexual impulse."[48]

A series of anxieties about the gendered self and the social order underwrote Krafft-Ebing's assessment of sexual pathology. In *Psychopathia Sexualis,* he produced an elaborate classification scheme, intended to mark off the perverted Other from the normative Self. Nonetheless, the distinctions he drew between natural/unnatural, normal/abnormal, and progressive/regressive, remained ambiguous.[49] Sexuality, declared Krafft-Ebing, "is the most powerful factor in individual and social existence"; yet all "acts" that deviated from the "purpose of nature"—i.e. propagation of the species—were "perverse."[50] Unfortunately these perversions were "progressively increasing" in advanced societies; they were component parts of progress, telling expressions of the "nervousness of modern society."[51] Both "unnatural habits" and physical degeneracy accounted for their prevalence: they could be a product of acquired vice as well as congenital defect. Only the case-history approach that investigated the "whole personality of the individual and the original impulse leading to the perverse act," could differentiate disease (perversion) from vice (perversity).[52]

Krafft-Ebing's taxonomy highlighted two general categories of sexual degeneracy: perversions committed with members of the opposite sex and those practiced between members of the same sex. In this schema, sexual sadism, rape, and lust murder were heterosexual analogues to homosexuality. Like homosexuality, sadistic sexual crimes were "progressively increasing in modern sexual life"; even more so than homosexuality, they were the acts of men. "Man," Krafft-Ebing explained, has a "more intense sexual appetite than woman"; sadism was nothing else than "an excessive and monstrous pathological intensification of phenomena—possible, too, in normal conditions in rudimentary forms—which accompany the psychical *vita sexualis* particularly in males."[53]

At the time of Chapman's murder, other publicists lent support to the upper-class-maniac theory; they too debated whether the murderer in the Ripper case was mad or vicious, a victim of a disease or a practitioner of "mere debauchery," a "homicidal maniac" bent on violence or an "erotomaniac" bent on sexual satisfaction. In a letter to *The Times* on 12 September Dr. Forbes Winslow hazarded the opinion that the murderer was not of the class of "Leather Apron," but was instead a "homicidal maniac" of the "upper class of society, as evidenced by the perverted cunning with which the killer had performed the mutilations and evaded justice." Apparently sane on the surface, the murderer was following the "inclination of his morbid imagination" by "wholesale homicide." Winslow based his "method of madness" theory on the assumption that only a cultivated intellect run amok could have committed an act of such enormity. His reference to "morbid imagination" notwithstanding, Winslow proposed that the criminal suffered from "homicidal mania of a religious description," and that he had chosen "the immoral class of society to vent his vengeance upon."[54]

These discussions paved the way for the coroner's "bombshell" at the Chapman inquest on 26 September. Earlier at the inquest, Dr. Phillips, the division surgeon, had described the body as "terribly mutilated," noting "absent portions from the abdomen" (the uterus and appendages had been removed) and "indications of anatomical knowledge." Phillips was reluctant to give the details of the mutilations in open court, and he only agreed to do so after the room had been cleared of women and children. *The Times* pronounced the autopsy report on Annie Chapman "unfit for publication," but the *Lancet* published it in full: "The abdomen had been laid open, the intestines, severed from their mesenteric attachments, had been lifted out of the body and placed on the shoulder of the corpse; whilst from the pelvis, the uterus and its appendages with the upper portion of the vagina and the posterior two-thirds of the bladder had been entirely removed." In the midst of a saturnalia of destruction, Phillips observed, the murderer had stopped to place Chapman's belongings in "order" at her feet, demonstrating what coroner Baxter later termed "reckless daring" and "cool impudence."[55]

In his summary to the jury, Baxter challenged the suggestion circulating in the press "that the criminal was a lunatic with morbid feelings." Resisting the maniac theory, Baxter proposed instead a "rational" pecuniary basis for the crime. "But it is not necessary to assume lunacy. There was a market for that missing organ." A possible motive for the murder, he suggested, was the sale of the organ to American medical schools—recalling the body-snatching crimes of the early nineteenth century.[56]

Baxter's "Burke and Hare theory" alarmed medical authorities who worried that Baxter's "dramatic . . . revelation" might undermine confidence in medical research: "The public mind—ever too ready to cast mud at legitimate research—will hardly fail to be excited to a pitch of animosity against anatomists and curators, which may take a long time to subside." This animosity was already manifested in newspaper correspondence on the "medical question": in a letter appearing in the *Evening News,* for example, "Ex-Medico's Daughter" proposed that the murder may have been committed "in the cause of science" by a "medical maniac," investigating "the mysterious changes that take place in the female sex at about the age of these poor women." Pasteur, she reminded readers, was also a "human vivisectionist."[57]

Speculations about a "medical maniac" researching into the "mysteries" of the "female sex" built on antimedical propaganda produced by feminists, libertarians, and antivivisectionists throughout the 1870s and

1880s. This propaganda had imaginatively connected the fate of animals and women as victims of medical violence, and it widely circulated visual images and narratives of medical sadism and bodily mutilation.[58] Antivivisectionists like Frances Power Cobbe revived the figure of the scientist as a demonic genius: vivisection, Cobbe insisted, fostered "heteropathy," a "new vice of scientific cruelty," which "does not seize the ignorant or hunger-driven or brutalized classes; but the cultivated, the well-fed, the well-dressed, the civilized and (it is said) the otherwise kindly disposed and genial men of science."[59] Cobbe linked vivisection imaginatively to traditional fears of medical men as "bodysnatchers," thus calling into play older popular antagonisms toward anatomists as homicidal maniacs and desecrators of pauper graves. She equipped the "modern" bodysnatcher with the same antisocial associations as his predecessors: libertinism, atheistic materialism, contamination with dark, occult practices and revolutionary ideas gained from study on the Continent. All of these themes figured in *St. Bernard's*, an antivivisection novel published in 1887 and set in the East End, a text that seemed to offer an ominous premonition of the 1888 exploits of Jack the Ripper.[60] Anxiety over the medical "spaying" of women also peaked in 1886, when professional colleagues accused a Liverpool surgeon of performing ovariectomy and oöphorectomy at an excessive rate. By the late 1880s, then, medical spokesmen had good cause to be anxious over Baxter's "dramatic . . . revelation," for recent propaganda, fictional writings, and medical scandals had already cast a dark shadow over medical research into the "mysteries" of the female sex.[61]

The Mad Doctor theory enlarged on all these negative associations. To these, the Ripper formulation added syphilitic madness, introduced into the discussion in early October by Archibald Forbes, the foreign correspondent of the *Daily News*, who suggested that the murderer was a "victim" of a "specific contagion" and was avenging himself. From the "knowledge of anatomy displayed in the murders," Forbes speculated that he was quite possibly a medical student.[62] To be sure, madness had already been identified as a consequence of sexual impurity, and mid-Victorian doctors understood that the tertiary stage of syphilis could attack the brain, among other vital organs; but the specific connection between tertiary syphilis and general paralysis of the insane, or paresis, was only firmly established in the years immediately preceding the Ripper murders.

Scientific progress only partially accounts for the rise of venereal anxiety: as important, argues Corbin, were the propagandist "efforts of the medical profession to develop and exert its authority, first through social hygiene, then through the prevention of disease." Thanks to medical publicity, syphilis assumed a greater cultural significance in this period of biological anxiety, as fears of racial degeneration increasingly obsessed the dominant classes of society.[63] The theory of the Mad Syphilitic Doctor completed the cycle of venereal anxiety: it focused suspicion back on the "anxiety makers"[64] themselves, as deadly materialists soiled by contact with impure bodies.

At the time of the Ripper murders, medical spokesmen were clearly uneasy about the Mad Doctor theory even though they were deeply implicated in its production. It was, after all, Dr. Phillips who had first insisted publicly that the mutilations showed "indications" of "anatomical knowledge." At Chapman's inquest, Dr. Phillips drew a direct comparison between his own skill as a medical man and that of the "miscreant": "I myself could not have performed all the injuries I saw on that woman and effect, even without a struggle, under a quarter of an hour."[65] Claiming specialized knowledge of the "details of butchery" himself, Phillips remained extremely reluctant to share that knowledge with the public at large. By trying to restrict knowledge of the mutilations, yet allowing the full publication of the autopsy report in the *Lancet,* medical authorities enacted a well-established strategy designed to maintain a monopoly of expert knowledge over the body.

Yet this elitist and restrictive strategy clearly backfired: it made doctors publicly suspect as possessors of esoteric and occult knowledge. Moreover, by suppressing information about the mutilations, the medical establishment contributed to an explosion of popular rumors, speculation, and fascination with them. "There was no doubt this time," recalled Dr. Halsted of the London Hospital, that the murderer "had removed certain parts of the body not normally mentioned in polite society and *this perversion* almost *more than the murder itself* excited the frenzy of the large crowd which gathered round the spot during the following day" (emphasis mine).[66] The "frenzy" of the crowd at the prospect of a "woman cut to pieces" stood in stark contrast to the medical language of Chapman's autopsy report, whose Latinate terms ("mesenteric attachments") and detached clinical picture of a body dispossessed of any personal identity (including sexual identity) were rhetorical efforts to sanitize medical engagement with a "grotesque" female body. Taken together, elite and popular responses to the mutilations operated as a twin strategy in a single regime of knowledge, one that simultaneously incited and repressed the "truth" of "sex."[67] The "high" and "low" responses to the mutilations replicated the split "Jekyll and Hyde" personality of the miscreant, the "savage/savant" who also combined behavior of astonishing ferocity with a capacity for rational thought and skill.[68]

Although the mutilations committed on the last Ripper victims seemed to lack any indication of "anatomical knowledge," the Mad Doctor, as the possessor of privileged knowledge and technical skill, would remain the most enduring and publicly compelling member of a cast of privileged villains proposed by the press and by the experts.[69] Others included: the Sadeian Aristocratic Libertine; the Religious Fanatic; and the Scientific Sociologist (first proposed facetiously by George Bernard Shaw, who imagined him to be a social reformer trying to expose the conditions of the East End).[70] Fantasies ran wild in the correspondence pages of the national dailies, but the fantasies were never totally removed from social reality and contemporary political disputes. All these candidates were familiar protagonists in earlier sexual scandals such as "Maiden Tribute" and the campaign against the state regulation of prostitution. They were also representative of the urban male spectators who were in fact stalking the streets of London in search of fallen women. Just as striking, they were also representative of many men writing into the correspondence columns of the newspapers putting forth their own theories of the Ripper's identity. Sometimes these correspondents proposed versions of the self, sometimes a cultural/political competitor: the Ripper could be a mad syphilitic doctor or a "purity man" gone "mad on religion."[71]

Overwhelmingly, these speculations oscillated between two expert discourses: the language of the law, emphasizing free will, responsibility, and reason; and the language of medicine, which focused on nature, determination, and irresponsibility. Commentators tried to determine if the criminal was mad or bad, a "monomaniac" or a "hardened criminal"; whether his crimes were "the freaks of a madman" or the "deliberate acts of a sane man who takes delight in murder on its own account, and who selects his victims by preference from the opposite sex . . . as giving him the means of gratifying some horrid instinct of cruelty and perverted lust." With their emphasis on the cunning and "cool impudence" of the murderer, these speculations not only enhanced the standing of the murderer; like *Psychopathia Sexualis,* they also evidenced a good deal of self-incrimination, especially as they often articulated a very unclear boundary between normative male sexuality and its abnormal, violent expression.

Despite the theories about upper-class perverts and maniacal reformers, police still arrested the same motley collection of East End down-and-outers, including wandering lunatics, mad medical students, American cowboys, and Greek gypsies. They conducted a house-to-house search of Whitechapel, but not of the areas of London where the Ripper, if he were a "toff" (that is, a gentleman) would be lodging. Long-standing patterns of deference and assumption of bourgeois respectability ultimately prevailed over speculations about bourgeois criminality circulating in the press. Even when they apprehended respectable suspects in the act of harassing women, police did not follow through on the arrest—this despite the fact that the East End became a sideshow for West Enders fascinated by the murders, bent not only on observing but on hunting the Ripper and, in some cases, emulating his role as well. "No less a personage than a director of the Bank of England," reported the *Echo,* "is so possessed by personal conviction that he has disguised himself as a day laborer, and is exploring the public houses, the common lodging houses, and other likely places to find the murderer." Dr. Forbes Winslow became a common figure on the scene, interviewing the "women of the streets," processing their raw information into "clues," so omnipresent that police suspected him of being Jack the Ripper.[72]

Amateur detectives like Winslow supplemented "hundreds of police in uniform, in plain clothes and in all manner of disguise—some even dressed as women—who patrolled every end of every street in the 'danger zone' every few minutes." There were plenty of eccentric and disoriented men in Whitechapel to begin with, but the presence of amateur and professional sleuths, voyeurs, and cranks must have exacerbated the fears and anxieties of the local population.[73]

Respectable citizens of Whitechapel responded to the invasion of West Enders by organizing their own night patrols. The men of Toynbee Hall settlement house and of the Jewish community set up committees, and the socialist and radical workingmen's clubs formed the East London Trades and Labourer's Society Vigilance Committee.[74]

These activities were evidence of self-protection, but they also constituted surveillance of the unrespectable poor, and of low-life women in particular. Social reformers at Toynbee Hall used the evidence collected by the night patrols to document the vicious state of the Flower and Dean Street rookery and to agitate, as they had for years, for the closing down of those "nurseries of crimes," the common lodging houses. "The stories which they have to tell are of saddening uniformity," declared the *British Medical Journal:* "uncontrollable brutality; women turned into the streets . . . and shivering on the stones at night fleeing from the execrations and the violence of drunken men. . . . tragedies and horrors of public obscenity treated by the police as the ordinary incidents of dark alleys, unlighted courts, and low neighborhoods."[75]

By designating themselves "vigilance committees," the male patrols in Whitechapel explicitly modeled themselves on similarly named social purity organizations already active in the area. Purity groups had closed down two hundred brothels in the East End in the year prior to the Ripper murders, rendering hundreds of women homeless, hence vulnerable to attack, and certainly making the lower stratum of prostitution—where the victims of the Ripper were situated—even more precarious. The message of social purity was mixed: it demanded that men control their own sexuality; but it effectively gave them more control over the sexuality of women, since it called upon them to protect their women and to repress brothels and street-walkers. As Josephine Butler astutely observed, male purity reformers always found it more convenient to "let the pressure fall almost exclusively on women" as it "is more difficult, they say, to get at men." In Whitechapel, middle-class men, backed up by female moral reformers, spearheaded these efforts. Respectable workingmen, anxious to distance themselves from the "bestiality" of the residuum and to reinforce their male preroga-tives inside and outside the family, were also recruited into the assault on vice.[76]

Excluded from the mobilization and press debate were the rough ele-ments of Whitechapel, female or male. The poor expressed their engage-ment with the Ripper murders by rioting. The West End press tended to depict crowd activity in the East End as both ominous and irrational. But the victims of mob riot were not selected at random. The Whitechapel poor rioted against the Jews, against the police (for not solving the murders), and against doctors (they believed the Mad Doctor theory and popular an-tagonism toward regular doctors was intensified by the recent antivaccina-tion movement. Anyone walking around with a little black bag was in trouble). As press coverage of the murders increased, the poor began to act on information provided by the newspapers—particularly stories that the murders were committed by doctors and by "toffs"—and to describe pos-sible suspects who were "respectable in appearance" or who had the "ap-pearance of a "clerk." The assumption that the Ripper was a "toff" also gave young working men license to accuse and intimidate their betters. During the Ripper manhunt, more than one amateur detective touring the Whitechapel area was accosted and had his gold watch nabbed. Another gentleman making his way along High Holborn in the City was pounced upon by a man of the "laboring class" yelling "Jack the Ripper."[77]

The poor also gained access to the public sphere through the inquests, the central judicial dramas of the Ripper murders. At the inquests, a narra-tive was generated out of "brute facts," while meaning was "apprehended by looking back over the temporal process."[78] Inquests were also the cen-terpiece of newspaper coverage. Extending over a few weeks, they sus-tained the momentum of interest between fresh installments of new atrocities.

Although coroners and expert witnesses established an interpretive authority over inquest proceedings, the poor also took the occasion to produce their own truths and fictions about the murdered women. Neighbors and friends gave detailed accounts of the victims' lives and of the circumstances surrounding the crimes. Their reaction to the murders sharply diverged from those of the organized working class and middle-class philanthropists. To the Whitechapel poor, Annie Chapman and Mary Jane Kelly were not degraded outcasts but members of their own community. Mary Jane Kelly seems to have remained on good terms with a number of her regular customers. On the night of her death, she encountered George Hutchinson, who deposed that he had occasionally given her a few shillings in the past. Kelly had asked him if he had any money to give her. Most of the other murdered women had lovers with whom they lived and pooled their resources. These were practical relationships, but they often entailed strong emotional bonds. John Kelly explained how he and Catherine Eddowes paired off in the following way: "We got throwed together a good bit here in the lodging house," recounted Kelly, "and the result was we made a regular bargain."[79]

The murdered women were also part of an intense female network. Prostitutes as well as nonprostitutes inhabited a distinct female world where they gossiped, entertained each other, and participated in an intricate system of borrowing and lending. This female network supplemented women's heterosexual ties, but it occasionally challenged those male-female allegiances. When Catherine Picket, a flower seller and neighbor of Mary Jane Kelly, was attracted to Kelly's singing on the night of her murder, she arose from bed to go out and join her; at which point she was reprimanded by her husband, "You just leave the woman alone," and crawled back to bed. Kelly herself was not as deferential to male authority; according to Joseph Barnett, her lover, she had just separated from Barnett after the two had quarreled over her taking in another "unfortunate" named Harvey "out of compassion."[80]

Clearly the murdered women were well known in the neighborhood and many were well liked. Most popular of all was the last victim, Mary Jane Kelly. When local men were asked if they knew Kelly, they responded, "Did anyone not know her?" Kelly was respected in the neighborhood for being generous and gay-hearted, and "frequent in street brawls, sudden and quick in quarrels and—for a woman—handy with her fists." During Kelly's funeral procession, the coffin was covered with wreaths from friends "using certain public houses in common with the murdered woman." As the coffin passed, "ragged caps were doffed and slatternly looking women shed tears." Dense crowds also lined the streets for the funeral cortege of

Catherine Eddowes: "Manifestations of sympathy were everywhere visible," reported the *East London Observer,* "many among the crowd uncovering their heads as the hearse passed."[81]

In general, press commentary emphasized the "ghastly sameness" of the naturalistic stories emerging from the inquests and stressed that the "element of romance" was "altogether lacking in [the victim's] history."[82] The matter-of-fact manner in which poor neighbors seemed to recount the dead women's stories, with no moral gloss or condemnation, shocked respectable commentators, as did the tendency of the Whitechapel poor to treat screams of murder or the spectacle of bodies crumpled in a heap on a Whitechapel street as unremarkable and commonplace.

Yet the "element of romance" was not missing in the histories produced by the poor. Many of the witnesses consciously dissimulated, refusing to acknowledge that the victims drank or were streetwalkers. Sometimes they struck melodramatic poses and even resorted to exaggerated gestures to reenact their part "when called to the scene of the crime." Legal decorum did not inhibit one witness at Annie Chapman's inquest from performing an elaborate pantomime about his discovery of the body: "When he had arrived [in his performance] at the discovery of the body, . . . the hands of the witness were kept in constant motion—describing alternatively, in pantomime show, how the intestines of the woman were thrown slightly over the left shoulder, and what position the body precisely occupied in the yard."[83]

The murdered women were objects of fantasy for residents of Whitechapel as well as for the educated reading public. Fictions of kinship surfaced at the inquest of Elizabeth Stride, the "Berner street victim," who was "strangely identified as two persons." At Stride's inquest, Mary Malcolm came forward and insisted that "the woman who had been murdered was her sister because when she was in bed, the poor creature came and kissed her hand." Malcolm's testimony excited considerable attention, inspiring many newspaper readers to call for the "aid of spiritualism and other more or less occult agencies"; it was entirely discredited when her sister turned up alive and well and full of outrage. Michael Kidney also positively identified the body as that of Elizabeth Stride, whom he had known for nearly three years. Stride had told Kidney that her husband and children had died on the *Princess Alice* (a shipping disaster), but even this proved to be a fiction on Stride's part to conceal marital estrangement. After Stride's nephew recognized her photograph, he came forward to identify her as the widow of John Thomas Stride, a carpenter, who had died in a workhouse in 1884.[84]

The thickest layer of fantasy settled around the life and death of Mary

Kelly, the last and youngest Ripper victim, who had been brutally disembowelled and mutilated in her room in Dorset Street. Newspapers and memoirs from the period set Kelly apart as the least "impoverished," most attractive Ripper victim—"an aristocrat among street women" with "well-to-do" friends.[85] The principal identificatory witness at the inquest was Joseph Barnett, a fish porter, who "appeared to be in full possession of the facts of the unhappy woman's life." At the inquest, Barnett identified Kelly by "the ears and eyes." His narrative of her life history, based on Kelly's version of her own story, reads like a penny-dreadful rendition of the harlot's progress and the "Maiden Tribute." With the vaguest of story line and detail, Barnett outlined Kelly's career in West End vice. Widowed at twenty, she arrived from Wales and settled in a "gay house in the West End." "There a gentleman came to her and asked her if she would like to go to France, so she described to me." "She went to France," he continued, "as she told me, but did not stop there long, as she did not like the part." Reporting on the inquest, the *Star* immediately seized the opportunity to elaborate the melodrama of high and low life further: "It would appear that on her arrival in London she made the acquaintance of a French lady residing in the neighborhood of Knightsbridge who . . . led her into the degraded life which has brought about her untimely end . . . . while she was with this lady she drove about in a carriage . . . and led the life of a lady."[86]

After Kelly's return to England, Barnett continued, she went to the "Ratcliffe Highway." At this point in the narrative, "hard facts" creep into Barnett's "disclosures": she lived opposite the gasworks with a man named Morganstone, then went to Pennington Street and lived with James Flemming, a mason's plasterer. Barnett "picked up with her in Commercial street, one night when we had drunk together."[87]

This East/West romance set the scene for George Hutchinson's detailed description of the "gentleman" accompanying Kelly on the night of her death. One day after the inquest, Hutchinson, a laborer, deposed to the police that his "suspicions were aroused by seeing the man so well-dressed." He gave a remarkably precise description of the mysterious stranger: "age about 34 or 35, height 5 ft.6, complexion pale. Dark eyes and eye lashes. Slight moustache curled up each end and hair dark. Very surly looking. Dress, long dark coat, collar and cuffs trimmed astrakhan and a dark jacket under, light waistcoat, dark trousers, and gaiters with white buttons, wore a very thick gold chain, white linen collar, black tie with horseshoe pin, respectable appearance, walked very sharp, Jewish appearance." As a number of commentators have noted, this description carefully replicates the costume and stance of the classic stage villain, sinister, black-mustached, bejewelled, and arrogant, who manipulated his privilege and wealth to despoil the vulnerable daughters of the people. With Hutchinson's evidence, the "image of the toff, a man of education, influence, and money was consolidated." Inquest stories and depositions around Kelly's death provided fodder for the next one hundred years of conspiratorial theories, focused on Kelly as the intended object of the Ripper's revenge, and as the center of a set of interwoven relationships, linking high and low, East and West in class-divided London.[88]

Response to the Ripper murders, then, reveals significant class divisions and class-based fantasies. It also exposes deep-seated sexual antagonism, most frequently expressed by men towards women. This antagonism was aided and abetted by sensational newspaper coverage that blamed "women of evil life" for bringing the murders on themselves, though it warned elsewhere that "no woman is safe while this ghoul's abroad."[89] The popular press seemed to glory in intensifying terror among "pure" and "impure" women by juxtaposing reports on less serious "attacks on women" with an account of the Whitechapel "horror"; by featuring an illustration of a "lady frightened to death" by a Ripper impersonator on the cover of the *Police Illustrated News;* and by proposing that the Ripper might change his venue to more respectable parts as Whitechapel became too dangerous for him. Although the most popular theories and fantasies about the Ripper contained a coded discussions of the dangers of unrestrained male sexuality, misogynist fears of female sexuality and female autonomy also surfaced in speculations about a female Ripper. Most of these hostilities focused on prostitutes, who, in the words of one influential commentator, were so "unsexed" and depraved that they were capable of the most heinous crimes; but suspicion also extended to midwives and medical women inasmuch as the "knowledge of surgery . . . has now been placed within female reach." However different their social class and occupational mobility, prostitutes, midwives, and medical women shared two common characteristics: they possessed dangerous sexual knowledge and they asserted themselves in the public male domain.[90]

Copycat activities mirrored these misogynist attitudes and took a variety of forms, including a conscious imitation and impersonation of the Ripper as well as a more latent identification with the criminal and subtle exploitation of female terror.[91] In Whitechapel, it seems, gentlemen of all sorts were walking about in the evenings looking for women to frighten. Here is a case in point:

On November 11, a woman named Humphries was passing George Yard and she met a man in the darkness. Trembling with agitation she asked him what he wanted. The man made no answer but laughed. He then made a hasty retreat. The woman yelled "murder."[92]

She attracted the police, who caught up with him, but "he referred the police to a well-known gentleman at the London Hospital and as a result he was set at liberty." Similar incidents occurred in the West End, involving respectable women; as soon as the assaulting gentleman could produce his business card and show a respectable address, both the lady and the police dropped the case. Laboring men were not immune from acting out the Ripper role themselves. In pubs across London, drunks bragged of their exploits as Jack the Ripper. Some Ripper impersonators harassed prostitutes and tried to extort money from them. James Henderson, a tailor, was brought before the Dalston magistrates for threatening Rosa Goldstein, an "unfortunate," with "ripping" her up if she did not go with him and for striking her several hard blows with his cane. Henderson was let off with a fine of forty shillings, on the grounds that he had been drunk—this, despite the fact that the severely injured Goldstein appeared in court "with surgical bandages about her head" and "weak from loss of blood."[93]

Besides these public acts of intimidation, there was also a domestic reenactment of the Ripper drama between husbands and wives in various working-class districts. (I have no evidence of middle-class cases.)[94] In Lambeth, for example, right after the "double event," magistrates received many applications "with regard to threats used by husbands against their wives, such as 'I'll Whitechapel You' and 'Look out for Leather Apron'." The *Daily News* reported the case of a man who actually offered ten shillings for anyone who would rid him of his wife by the "Whitechapel process."[95]

One case that reached the Old Bailey may provide some insight into the circumstances that led up to the threat.[96] Sarah Brett of Peckham was living out of wedlock with Thomas Onley. On 3 October 1888, three days after the "double event," her son arrived home from sea with a friend. Brett permitted the friend, Frank Hall, to board with them. On 15 October, the common-law husband and the visitor went out and got drunk; when they returned, both abused and swore at her. Brett told the visitor not to interfere; he smacked her and she returned the blow, knocking him off his chair and ordering him to leave. This angered her man, who then declared they were not even married and threatened to do "a Whitechapel murder upon you." He was clearly too drunk to carry out this undertaking and so retired upstairs to bed, leaving her with the visitor, who then stabbed her, wounding her severely.

What sense can we make out of this event? Typically, alcohol consumption helped to precipitate the conflict. Sarah Brett's role was defensive but firm; she did not challenge the boundaries of her "sphere," but she did exercise her prerogatives as manager of household resources and amply demonstrated her own capacity to defend herself. Although her common-law husband abused her first, she only reprimanded the visitor. "It is quite sufficient for Mr. Onley to commence upon me without you interfering." By ordering the visitor out of the house, she nonetheless shamed Onley. She threatened his masculinity; he responded by denying the legitimacy of their relations—in sum, calling her a whore. He then invoked the example of that most masterly of men, the Whitechapel killer, leaving her with the young visitor, who had the strength to carry out the husband's threat.

I am not trying to argue that the Ripper episode directly increased sexual violence; rather it established a common vocabulary and iconography for the forms of male violence that permeated the whole society, obscuring the different material conditions that provoked sexual antagonism in different classes.[97] The Ripper drama invested male domination with a powerful mystique; it encouraged little boys in working-class Poplar and suburban Tunbridge Wells to intimidate and torment girls by playing at Jack the Ripper. "There's a man in a leather apron coming soon, to kill all the little girls in Tunbridge Wells. It's in the paper." "Look out, here comes Jack the Ripper," was enough to send girls running from the street or from their own backyards into the safety of their homes.[98] Whatever their conscious ethos, male night-patrols in Whitechapel had the same structural effect of enforcing the segregation of social space: women were relegated to the interior of a prayer meeting or their homes, behind locked doors; men were left to patrol the public spaces and the street. Male vigilantes also terrified women of the locale, who could not easily distinguish their molesters from their disguised protectors: "If the murderer be possessed . . . with the usual cunning of lunacy," one correspondent suggested in the *Saint James Gazette,* "I should think it probable that he was one of the first to enroll himself among the amateur detectives."[99]

Although the Ripper murders reinforced the spatial polarities of gender and class, they also stimulated male fantasies of vulnerability and identification with the female victims. Men fantasized about the female experience of terror; amateur detectives donned female garb to attract the murderer's attention. Although some boys played at being "Leather Apron," others found the Ripper episode to be personally threatening and terrifying. At three and a half, Leonard Ellisden believed the Ripper to be a particular "evil-looking man with a beard who used to eat fire at Margate sands." When this "worthy gentleman" entered his parent's tobacconist shop, Ellisden "drove the ladies of the family nearly round the bend by rushing in shrieking in terror 'Jack the Ripper's in the shop'." Middle-class boys as well as girls identified the Ripper with the dangers of the street—dangers that seemed to penetrate the sanctity of the home, thanks to the cries of the newspaper boys hawking news of the latest Whitechapel horror and the avid interest of maidservants and nannies, who spread copies of illustrated Sunday papers across the nursery table. The nightly "fears and fantasies" of Jack the Ripper made the prospect of "going to bed almost unendurable," Compton Mackenzie recalled:

> Whitechapel became a word of dread, and I can recall the horror of reading "Whitechapel" at the bottom of the list of fares at the far end inside an omnibus. Suppose the omnibus should refuse to stop at Kensington High Street and go on with its passengers to Whitechapel? What could that Eminent Q.C. in his wig . . . do to save everybody inside that omnibus from being cut up by the knife of Jack the Ripper?[100]

Women's reaction to the events surrounding the Ripper murders were as diverse as men's, yet even more heavily overlaid by feelings of personal vulnerability. Women in Whitechapel were both fascinated and terrified by the murders: like their male counterparts, they brought up the latest editions of the half-penny evening newspapers; they gossiped about the gruesome details of the murders; and they crowded into the waxwork exhibits and peep shows where representations of the murdered victims were on display. As we have seen, many also sympathized with the victims and came to the aid of prostitutes in their time of crisis. As one clergyman from Spitalfields remarked of the "fallen sisterhood": "these women are very good natured to each other. They are drawn together by a common danger and they will help each other all they can." Because the woman clubbed together, and because keepers of common lodging houses were generally "lenient" to regular customers, distress among prostitutes during the month of October was "not as great as one might expect," reported the *Daily News*.[101]

On the whole, respectable working women offered little collective resistance to public male intimidation. I found accounts of two exceptions among match girls and marketwomen who were part of an autonomous female work culture. On their own territory, marketwomen could organize en masse: a number of women "calling out 'Leather Apron'," for instance, chased Henry Taylor when he threatened Mary Ann Perry with "ripping her up" in Clare market; and similar incidents occurred in Spitalfields market, nearby the Ripper murders. Marketwomen enjoyed an esprit de corps akin to that of the feisty, street-fighting matchmakers, who had just won a successful strike from the Bryant and May Match Factory, and who, according to one anonymous letter purporting to come from Jack the Ripper, openly bragged about catching him.[102]

Those women who could, stayed inside at night behind locked doors, but women who earned a living on the streets at night—prostitutes—did not have that luxury. Some left Whitechapel, even the East End, for good. Others applied to the casual wards of the workhouse. Some slowly went back to the streets, first in groups of two or three, then occasionally alone. They armed themselves, and although they "joked" about encountering Jack—"I am the next for Jack," quipped one woman—they were obviously terrified at the prospect. Some even went to prayer meetings to avoid remaining home alone at night. "Of course we are taking advantage of the terror," explained one Salvation Army lass.[103]

Another woman who took advantage of the terror was Henrietta Barnett, wife of Samuel Barnett of Toynbee Hall. Distressed at hearing women gossiping about the murders, she got up a petition to the Queen and, with the aid of board (state) schoolteachers and mission workers, obtained four thousand signatures from the "Women of Whitechapel." The petition begged the Queen to call upon "your servants in authority" to close down the lodging houses where the murdered victims resided.[104] Although not entirely absent from the Ripper mobilization, female moral reformers like Barnett occupied a subordinate role within it; they remained physically constrained within the female sphere and bent on keeping neighborhood women there as well, moving them inside into prayer meetings, out of earshot of salacious discussions of sex and violence, relinquishing public spaces and sexual knowledge to men.

It is difficult to determine how much Barnett's petition truly represented the opinion of Whitechapel women. Jewish artisan wives regarded the women of the lodging houses as "nogoodnicks, prostitutes, old bags and drunks," but they still employed Catherine Eddowes and others like her to char and wash for them, to light their sabbath fires, sometimes even to mind their children.[105] There was a tense and fragile social ecology between rough and respectable elements in Whitechapel, one that could be easily upset by outside intervention. The murders threatened the safety of respectable women; they undoubtedly strained class relations in the neighborhood and intensified gender divisions. They temporarily placed respectable women under "house arrest" and made them dependent on male protection.

Local folklore, however, tested the spatial boundaries of gender erected by the Ripper danger. Family stories, passed down among Jewish and Irish cockney residents in the Whitechapel area over three generations, accorded working-class women a more active role in the Ripper episode than did the night patrols of Whitechapel. These tales recount how "mother," forced to go out late one "wintery" night either to obtain medicine for a sick child or to visit an ailing husband in the London Hospital, was accosted by a "stranger" in the darkness. After interrogating her about the nature of the medical emergency propelling her out of her home (or examining the visitor's card to the hospital), the mystery man realized she was "poor" but "honest" and let her go. The next morning, two hundred yards down the road the "mutilated" body of a prostitute was found.[106]

"Mother Meets Jack the Ripper" vividly illustrates how working-class women organized their own identity around the figure of the prostitute, who served as a central spectacle in a set of urban encounters and fantasies. In public, a poor woman continually risked the danger of being mistaken for a prostitute; she had to demonstrate unceasingly in her dress, gestures, and movements that she was not a "low" woman. Like her middle-class counterpart, a working-class woman established her respectability through visual self-presentation and through her status as wife and mother.[107]

As a wife and mother, the female protagonist in "Mother's" story claims immunity from the Ripper's knife. Although the tale vindicates female virtue over female vice, it also establishes a certain identification with the plight of fallen women. Unlike the men in their civic tales of hunting down Jack the Ripper, "Mother" could insert herself into the drama only by impersonating a potential victim, who is resourceful enough to talk her way out of a difficult situation.[108] "Mother's" story also draws on media fantasies of the Ripper as a dark representation of conflicted masculinity: the "midnight murderer" appears as a compelling but dangerous stranger, a savage/savant, knowledgeable about medical matters, able to interrogate and discern female virtue, yet capable of maniacal violence towards women of "evil life."

Women outside of Whitechapel also took a keen interest in the murders. Queen Victoria repeatedly wrote into the Home Office and Scotland Yard with her pet theories, and actually forced Lord Salisbury to hold a cabinet meeting on a Saturday to consider the question of a reward. All across London, female mediums tried their hands at armchair detection by calling up the spirits of the murdered women: at a private séance held in West Kilburn on October 16, the spirit of Annie Chapman directed the group to look to the "military medicals" who "want our bodies for a particular reason," "they want to find something." Female spiritualists restricted their sleuthing to the séance circle, unlike the clairvoyant R. J. Lees, who claimed to have used his powers to track down the "mad doctor" at his West End mansion.[109]

At least one woman emulated the copycat activities of men and gained some notoriety from the case: at Bradford Police Court on 10 October 1888, a "respectable young woman, named Maria Coroner, aged twenty-one, was charged with having certain letters tending to cause a breach of the peace; they were signed 'Jack the Ripper'." Like the Whitechapel mothers who encountered Jack the Ripper in the dead of night, one female correspondent believed that "respectable women like herself had nothing to fear from the Whitechapel murderer," as she thought it was true that he "respects and protects respectable females." This was, of course, the line taken by police officials, who expressed amazement at what they regarded as the widespread female hysteria over the murders, since they were perpetrated only on prostitutes.[110]

For many women, this was small comfort. While many middle-class women were determined to resist the panic and to assert their right to traverse public places, female vulnerability extended well beyond the boundaries of Whitechapel. Mary Hughes, a secondary-school teacher who lived in the West End in 1888, recalled "how terrified and unbalanced we all were by the murders. It seemed to be round the corner, although it all happened in the East End, and we were in the West; but even so, I was afraid to go out after dark, if only to post a letter. Just as dusk came on we used to hear down our quiet and ultra-respectable Edith road the cries of newspaper boys in tones made as alarming as they could: 'Another 'orrible murder . . . Whitechapel! Disgustin' details. . . . Murder!'"[111]

What about the politicized edge of middle-class womanhood, the feminists? Did they mount any counterattack? Josephine Butler and others expressed concern that the uproar over the murders would lead to the repression of brothels and subsequent homelessness of women. In so doing, they broke with more repressive purity advocates who were totally indifferent to the fate of the victims and to the rights of prostitutes. In the end, only the strict libertarians, female and male, came forward to defend prostitutes as human beings, with personal rights and liberties. "Not till the personal rights of the poor pariahs are counted as worthy of recognition and defense as, let us say, those of their patrons, will mankind [be on] the road towards the extinction of this evil," declared the *Personal Rights Journal*.[112]

Some female publicists also used the occasion to air feminist critiques of male violence in regard to medical sadism and wife-beating. Frances Power Cobbe enthusiastically entered into the fray; speculating that the murderer was a "physiologist delirious with cruelty," she called for the use of female detectives whose "mother wit" would guide them to the murderer. The only piece of feminist anger against male violence to receive extensive coverage appeared in the pages of the Liberal *Daily News*. The Whitechapel murders were not just homicides but "womenkilling," declared Florence Fenwick Miller, London journalist and "platform woman," in her letter to the editor. Researching the police columns, she concluded that attacks on prostitutes were not different from other violent assaults on women by men. They were not isolated events but a part of a "constant but ever increasing series of cruelties" perpetrated against women and treated leniently by judges.[113]

Miller's letter generated a small flurry of responses supportive of her position and calling for women's economic and political emancipation. Kate Mitchell, a physician and feminist, applauded Miller's letter and cited the case, mentioned above, of James Henderson, who was let off with a fine of forty shillings after severely beating a prostitute. Unless women were publicly emancipated, argued Mitchell, they would remain "ciphers" in the land and subject to male physical abuse. The letters made an important association between public and domestic violence against women, but it would be a mistake to exaggerate their political impact. They remained isolated interventions in an overwhelmingly male-dominated debate; they were discounted or ignored by other dailies and failed to mobilize women over the issues.[114]

The Radical *Star*, whose pages were open to socialists, disagreed with Miller. "It is the class question rather than the sex question that is the issue in this matter." The *Star*'s opposition of class and sex signaled a tendency among Victorians to conceptualize social problems and identities as stark dichotomies, rather than as multiple and intersecting determinants. Commenting on the Whitechapel murders in their own journals, prominent socialists like William Morris and H. M. Hyndman also refused to address the issue of sex antagonism; they tended to see gender oppression as a result of capitalist productive relations alone. For all their contempt for the proprietary press, the socialists' assessment of the murdered prostitutes as "unsexed," dehumanized "creatures" who had "violated their womanhood for the price of a night's lodging" was remarkably similar to that of the conservative and misogynist *Morning Post* and *The Times*. To distinguish themselves from the bourgeois press, socialists would have had to overcome their ambivalence towards prostitutes and the unrespectable poor of Whitechapel and address the subject of male dominance.[115]

The Whitechapel horrors provoked multiple and contradictory responses, expressive of important cultural and social divisions within Victorian society. Nonetheless, the alternative perspectives—of feminists and libertarians, of the Whitechapel poor themselves—were ultimately subordinated to a dominant discussion in the media, one that was shaped and articulated by those people in positions of power, namely, male professional experts. Within this dominant discourse, the discussion of class, particularly of a dangerous class marked off from respectable citizens and the "people" of London, was more explicit and self-conscious than that of gender. In part, this fact relates to the precise moment of class anxiety when Jack the Ripper stalked the streets of London. The events in Whitechapel could be easily slotted into the "Outcast London" theme. They reinforced prevailing prejudices about the East End as a strange territory of savages, a social abyss, an inferno. *The Times* might well wring its hands about the responsibility of "our social organization" for spawning the crimes, but this momentary soul-searching was readily domesticated into an attack on the symptoms, rather than on the causes, of urban poverty.[116]

Throughout the "autumn of terror," one theme overshadowed all the other proposals to cure the social ills of Whitechapel: the necessity of slum clearance and the need to purge the lawless population of the common lodging houses from the neighborhood.[117] "Those of us who know Whitechapel know that the impulse that makes for murder is abroad in our streets every night," declared two Toynbee Hall residents.[118] The "disorderly and depraved lives of the women," observed Canon Barnett, were more "appalling" than the actual murders.[119] Men like Barnett finally dominated public opinion and consolidated it behind razing the common lodging houses of the Flower and Dean Street area. The notoriety of the street impelled the respectable owners—the Henderson family— to sell their property as soon as the leases were up. The Rothschild Buildings (1892), for respectable Jewish artisans and their families, appeared over the site of the lodging houses where Catherine Eddowes and Elizabeth Stride once lived. Prostitutes and their fellow lodgers were thus rendered homeless and forced to migrate to the few remaining rough streets in the neighborhood. Through the surveillance of the vigilance committees and through this "urban renewal," the murders helped to intensify repressive activity already under way in the Whitechapel area.[120]

Such reform-minded responses coincided with a general dissipation of middle-class fears of "Outcast London." The disciplined and orderly 1889 dock strike persuaded many respectable observers that the East End poor were indeed salvageable because they could be organized into unions. Meanwhile, Charles Booth's massive survey of East London, also published in 1889, graphically demonstrated how small and unrepresentative the "criminal" population of the Flower and Dean Street rookery actually was. When another Ripper-like murder occurred in July 1889 in Whitechapel, newspaper coverage was far less sensational and relentless. In class terms, the immediate crisis had passed.[121]

The Ripper Legacy

Sexual fears and hostilities, on the other hand, were less satisfactorily allayed. After Mary Kelly's death, the police, finding themselves completely at sea, dropped the whole matter in the lap of Dr. Thomas Bond, syphilologist and expert in forensic medicine, asking him to provide them with a psychological profile of the murderer. In his letter to Scotland Yard, Bond pronounced the series of "five murders," beginning with Polly Nicholls and ending with Mary Kelly, to be the "work of one hand." Bond discounted the possibility that the culprit was a revengeful religious fanatic or that the mutilations demonstrated "scientific or anatomical knowledge." The murderer, Bond explained, was suffering from "satyriasis" (i.e. he was oversexed and resorted to violence to satisfy his excessive sexual cravings). In external appearance, he might well be a "quiet, inoffensive man probably middle-aged, and neatly and respectably dressed." ". . . he would be solitary and eccentric in his habits, since he is most likely to be a man without regular occupation, but with some small income or pension."[122]

To construct this profile, Bond relied on newspaper theories of an erotic maniac leading a "Jekyll and Hyde" double life, as well as on emerging typologies of sex crime formulated by Continental sexologists like Krafft-Ebing. Newspaper coverage of the Ripper murders not only helped to popularize expert medical opinion on sexual pathology; it also provided narrative materials that sexologists would process into the most notorious case history of sex crime to date. Contemporaneous with Bond's report there began a public recycling of Jack the Ripper as a medical specimen. In November and December 1888, two articles appeared in American medical journals, "Sexual Perversion and the Whitechapel Murders," by Dr. James Kiernan, and "The Whitechapel Murders: Their Medico-Legal and Historical Aspects," by Dr. E. C. Spitzka. Both articles catalogued prior case histories of "lust murder" to counter the impression that the murders were unprecedented in the annals of crime; and both located the Ripper along a spectrum of contemporary perverts, from female masturbators and "urnings" of both sexes, to the exclusively male perpetrators of "lust murder" and sexual sadism (including reference to the "Minotaur" of the "Maiden Tribute"). Both relied on newspaper accounts of postmortem reports of the mutilations and murders to diagnose the criminal; both remained undecided as to "his" legal responsibility, whether his actions were the result of congenital disease or acquired vice. In the published Jack the

Ripper letters that forecast more murders to follow, Spitzka found "the genuine expression of intention" to be at variance with any diagnosis of "impulsive," "periodical," or "epileptic insanity." Spitzka was quite taken with the discursive propensities of the murderer, a 'speaking pervert' who communicated his 'truth' to the reading public: "It would not be the first time that a subject of sexual perversion had entered the lists as a writer," he insisted, "no artifice . . . would be too cunning for one of this class." Drawing on the writings of Spitzka and Kiernan, Krafft-Ebing included the Ripper in his next edition of *Psychopathia Sexualis,* as a clinical specimen—the most famous clinical specimen—of lust murder. From newspaper accounts that linked a monstrous crime and a monstrous individual to a monstrous social environment, the Ripper story was reduced to a notorious case history of an individual erotic maniac, whose activities were seemingly unconnected to normal interactions of men and women.[123]

The social context of the Ripper's exploits, however, have not disappeared from twentieth-century representation, although they too have undergone a mythic revision. The Whitechapel murders have continued to provide a common vocabulary of male violence against women, a vocabulary now more than one hundred years old. Its persistence owes much to the mass media's exploitation of Ripper iconography. Depictions of female mutilation in mainstream cinema, celebrations of the Ripper as a "hero" of crime intensify fears of male violence and convince women that they are helpless victims. Changing historical circumstances, however, can provoke and enable a different response to these media productions. The case of the Yorkshire Ripper, to be considered in the epilogue, constitutes a late-twentieth-century 'replay' of the Ripper episode that engendered a different political reaction from contemporary British feminists, who took to the streets to protest the crimes and the media amplification of the terror.

EPILOGUE

The Yorkshire Ripper

adame Tussaud's Ripper street, installed in 1980, capitalized on a "real life" horror show that inflicted "years of stomach-churning fear" on women in the North of England.[1] Between October 1975 and January 1981, residents in Leeds and Bradford were terrorized by a mass murderer, dubbed the "Yorkshire Ripper" by the newspapers, who was believed—erroneously—to be the author of taped messages to the authorities and who was thought—also erroneously—to be a prostitute killer who left his signature on the bodies of his victims. By the end of 1980, he had already claimed thirteen murder victims, including six "innocent" women.

The Yorkshire Ripper murders and the response they provoked appeared to take their cues from the legendary events of 1888.[2] As in 1888, the same elements seemed to be present: a single mythic killer, "a series of similar murders, ritual slayings, stereotyped victims, intense publicity, and a specific, systematically terrorized region."[3] Newspaper discussion of these new "Ripper" murders reproduced the same categories that had informed press accounts of the Whitechapel "horrors" one hundred years earlier. Was the murderer mad or bad? Did prostitutes bring the murders on themselves? Were all women at risk? Did the setting of "mean streets" explain or generate the crimes? As in 1888, the murders precipitated an acute outbreak of "checkbook journalism" and a crisis in police credibility, as the police inquiry faltered in the face of bureaucratic rivalries and drowned in the chaos of information it had collected. By the end of the trial, the credibility of the media, the law, and the medical profession was severely tested. As in the case of the Whitechapel murders, this series of murders also gave rise to complex political effects: they provoked misogynist assaults on women's freedom, in the form of widespread copycat activities and police use of prostitutes as "live bait." They also provoked and reinforced purity campaigns to clean up red-light districts and to outlaw smut.

Some of these historical parallels were the deliberate result of media manipulation: the press consistently invoked the example of the legendary Ripper to enhance the contemporary power and prestige of this contemporary killer.[4] It not only gave the murderer his name, but it proceeded to cast "him" as a classic Victorian sex beast and to transform the North of England into the foggy gaslight "mean streets" of the Victorian East End.[5] "Bradford on a Saturday Night is pure Victorian Gothic . . . dank slate roofs gleaming, the blackened brick . . . even the quarter moon obliges, fitfully disappearing behind windswept clouds," declared the *Evening News Magazine*.[6] Other newspapers offered their readers a tour of "Vice Spots" of Chapeltown and maps of "Mean Streets of the Circuit." Both the British and international press represented Leeds and Bradford as the symbol of British industrial decline. *Esquire*'s description was typical: "A good deal of the British Empire was made in this part of Yorkshire, but these dark steep cobbled towns have been used up."[7]

Mythmaking of this sort had its material consequences.[8] The murder hunt was hampered by the investment of police themselves in the Ripper fantasy. Because they imagined the Yorkshire Ripper to be a "publicity hound" like his predecessor, police chose to accept as authentic what were in fact hoax communications, including three letters and a three-minute cassette tape, that mimicked the original (and equally bogus) Ripper letters "with their taunting of investigating officers and condemnations of 'whores.'" "Predisposed to believe the letters and tape, the police charged up a blind alley," asserted Joan Smith in the *New Socialist*. Police miscalculation culminated in the obsession that the Ripper was a "Geordie" (a working-class resident of Northeast England) and partially explains why Peter Sutcliffe, who was eventually convicted of the murders and who had a soft Yorkshire accent, was interviewed nine times by the police but never detained as a serious suspect (he was picked up for driving with false license plates).[9]

As in 1888, women were harassed on the streets by would-be Rippers, at the same time that they were told to look to other men for protection. One researcher uncovered three cases of men who raped women, terrorizing their victims by claiming to be the Yorkshire Ripper. Other men who offered to protect women from the Ripper turned out to be harassers or worse: Peter Sutcliffe, the man finally apprehended and convicted of the crimes, accompanied his employer's secretary home from work to protect her from the villain and participated in a citizen action group to "assist in the Ripper's Capture."[10] The murders, the widespread intimidation of women on the streets, and the media coverage terrified women living in Yorkshire, just as similar activities had provoked fear in Whitechapel and in the West End one hundred years earlier. "I have lived five years of utter fear," declared a female correspondent residing in Yorkshire in a letter to the feminist journal *Spare Rib*, "having to think twice before taking a trip to the corner shop. . . . I've had five years of looking hard at every man I know and fearing that *he* could be the one. I've had five years of impotent fury at being chained in [at night] when I'd rather be out."[11]

Yet there were differences. Because the "Yorkshire Ripper" was apprehended and brought to trial, his story achieved a closure absent in the original Ripper story. Indeed, the trial of the Yorkshire Ripper seemed to offer a retrospective "Final Last Act" to the Whitechapel horrors of 1888. Yet, this closure was simultaneously disrupted and undermined at the trial by the inability of legal and medical experts to unite in a single interpretation of Sutcliffe as "mad" or "bad," as a "religious maniac" or a "sadistic, calculated, cold-blooded murderer who loved his job," as a "prostitute killer" or a "woman hater," as a man prone to violence or motivated by "abnormal" sexual drives.[12]

Like many previous insanity trials, the Sutcliffe trial exposed the incompatibility of legal and medical discourses on insanity, organized as they were according to opposing categories of sanity/insanity, mind/body, will/passion, nature/reason, free will/determination, responsibility/irresponsibility. Although in the end, the prosecution's legal case triumphed and Sutcliffe was found guilty of multiple murders, both law and medicine found their discourses "severely tested" by Sutcliffe's example. Both sets of experts were bewildered by Sutcliffe's capacity, in true Jekyll-and-Hyde fashion, to lead two "hermetically sealed lives," to combine behavior of "startling enormity" with a capacity for rational thought.[13]

As in the nineteenth century, Sutcliffe's doctors found themselves articulating a fundamental contradiction: they claimed a scientific expertise by defining medical disease on a somatic basis, as "some organic impairment," but they based their diagnosis largely on behavioral symptoms and disturbances, rather than on the "general disinhibition of cerebral control mechanisms." The doctors and the prosecution agreed that the psychotic delusion in question was Sutcliffe's claim, that, while working as a grave-digger, he had received "messages from God" to kill prostitutes and that what he did was part of a "divine mission." The prosecution dismissed Sutcliffe's religious mania as a "convenient basis for an insanity plea," as a role that Sutcliffe adopted to deceive the doctors. The Crown tried to show that Sutcliffe had "duped" the doctors and was a "sadistic killer"; unless the defense could satisfy the jury that Sutcliffe genuinely believed that he had heard the "Voice of God," Attorney General Havers and later the judge insisted, the jury must find Sutcliffe guilty of murder on thirteen counts.[14]

The prosecution offered the jury two means to test Sutcliffe's veracity. If Sutcliffe were a true religious maniac, he could not have been sexually motivated; and he would have had to believe his victim was a prostitute at the time of each killing. If, on the other hand, it could be shown that he had derived "sexual satisfaction" from the murders or that he had not always cared if the woman was a prostitute, Sutcliffe stood condemned as "bad" rather than "mad." To prove that Sutcliffe was a "sadistic, calculated, cold-blooded murderer who loved his job," the prosecution introduced grisly evidence of his "sexually motivated" mutilations. It also challenged Sutcliffe's record as prostitute killer, citing evidence of Sutcliffe's more generalized hostility to women: "I realised Josephine was not a prostitute but at the time I wasn't bothered. I just wanted to kill a woman."[15]

Trial testimonies, psychiatric interviews, and investigative reporting of Sutcliffe's family life also forced a genre shift in this rendition of the Ripper story. While he was at large, the anonymous Yorkshire Ripper seemed to epitomize the "nonspecific male killing force" of the new brand of horror films, at the same time taking his "cues" from the Ripper of legend and popular culture.[16] However, this "male directed" fantasy was utterly shattered when Sutcliffe, a lorry driver and "shy" family man "who led an ordinary life before he became a killer of women," was apprehended as the culprit.[17] At Sutcliffe's trial, the press adjusted itself to the new facts by revising the narrative form of the Ripper story: a family melodrama superseded the Ripper "horror show," and Sutcliffe was transformed from an undomesticated monster into a troubled son and henpecked husband. In the process, his crimes became the result of "female precipitation."[18]

If doctors and their diagnoses were on trial at the Old Bailey, so were the women in Sutcliffe's life. Not only were the murder victims vilified by the prosecution and the press, but Sutcliffe's own female relatives also came in for harsh treatment. Both defense and prosecution introduced Sutcliffe's family history to document his psychoses and sexual history, but newspaper reports quickly sensationalized these family vignettes into steamy soap opera. Newspaper readers were told that Sutcliffe had a doting mother and macho sportsman father, an "inveterate liberty taker with the opposite sex," who regarded his son as a "mother's boy" and "introverted weakling." Press coverage focused on Sutcliffe's double life with good and bad women. In 1967, he began a long, serious courtship with Sonia Szurma, a woman obsessed about cleanliness and subject to nervous breakdowns, who "nagged" him. Press accounts documented how their long court-ship and stormy marriage was punctuated by Sutcliffe's clandestine attacks on prostitutes. During the trial, "Sonia's breakdown" was the front page headline of the *Daily Mirror;* " 'Nagging' may be link in tragic chain" was another trial report heading. The second woman spotlighted as a possible cause of Sutcliffe's bizarre behavior was his mother, Kathleen, whose affair with a policeman outraged "his youthful sense of propriety."[19]

The level of women's public and organized response to the murders and to the press coverage also marked an important departure from tradi-tion. This time around, the contemporary women's movement organized female patrols against the threat and a prostitutes' rights group protested at the murder trial. Women not only claimed public space as their right; they also tried to regain the terms of the debate. Feminists of all persuasions united in refusing to accept women's status of passive victim and in explod-ing the gender bias in police procedures, expert testimonies, and press coverage of the murders and the trial. Feminist interventions in the daily press generated a lively, passionate, and substantive discussion of sexual violence in the national press. Thanks to the Yorkshire Ripper controversy and to an emerging feminist antiviolence campaign, the new batch of Ripper books, appearing at the end of the decade on the occasion of the "Ripper Centenary," received a far more hostile reception than their earlier counterparts.[20]

"The Ripper has acted as a catalyst" for women's anger against male violence, explained a feminist attending a Conference on Sexual Violence against Women held in Leeds in November 1980. The conference had been organized to move beyond specific issues of male violence—such as rape, wife battering, sexual harassment, prostitution, and incest—to develop a unified national movement that would initiate "direct action" or "political propagandist work." Spearheading the national campaign were feminists from Bradford and Leeds, angered at the five years of "stomach-churning fear" they had undergone since 1975. Inspired by the writings and strat-egies of the American antipornography movement, they tried to link in-stitutional efforts against diverse forms of male violence to a struggle against violent media representations that degraded women. The York-shire Ripper murders, they believed, offered a ready opportunity to expose media encouragement to violence against women as well as to exploit me-dia coverage to beam their own message nationwide.[21]

When five hundred women arrived in Leeds for the Sexual Violence against Women conference, they found the press extraordinarily attentive and ready to treat "violence against women as a serious issue." To account for this new press interest, Ruth Wallsgrove, writing in *Spare Rib,* cited the "particular coincidence of four events, backed up by some excellent feminist organising." First, a "rash of look-alike sex-and-violence films" had made their appearance in Leicester Square, London; "their nastiness was obvious even to those who've never thought about the issue." Second, on 17 November, in Leeds, the Maw sisters were sentenced to three years for killing their father, who had battered them and their mother all their lives, and had tortured and killed family pets. "The same week, the Yorkshire Ripper killed again (another 'innocent' victim [Jacqueline Hill, a university student])"; and two day later, women met for the national Sexual Violence against Women conference. These last three all took place in Leeds."[22]

Even before the conference, the antiviolence movement in Leeds and Bradford had encouraged women to resist intimidation and to organise themselves in their own defense. "Self-defense classes are packed out," reported the *Yorkshire Evening Post.* In a letter to *The Times,* three university lecturers from Bradford University complained that "the media does not report" a series of collective efforts by women to protect themselves. Far from seeing women give into intimidation, they saw a "tremendous number of support networks spring up, of shared cars, telephone links, shared journeys on foot," reminiscent of the "sense of community that was shown in the 'blitz.'"[23]

In the weeks following the conference, feminists associated with "WAVAW" and "Angry Women" also engaged in a wide range of direct actions against "men" and the "media." "Slap a Curfew on Men" demanded hundreds of women during a march through Leeds city center. Some women started "'chatting up' passing men, pinching their bottoms (hard) and tweak[ing] their cheeks, whilst telling them they were 'asking for trouble' by being out at night."[24] Their actions were reminiscent of Zap actions—the "ogle-ins," the "sticker campaigns," and the protests at the Miss World contests—that British and American feminists had engaged in during the heady days of the early women's liberation movement. Then, as ten years earlier, these actions were intended to make men experience the forms of sexual objectification and public intimidation that confront women daily.

The activities in 1980 were a good deal fiercer than the street theater of the previous decade. Throughout Britain, "Angry Women" assaulted sex shops and cinemas showing what feminists termed the new exploitation films. In Leeds women challenged men in the street, asking them where they were at the time the "Ripper" killed Jacqueline Hill. They stormed the Odeon theater showing *Dressed to Kill.* "The film is sexist and exploits the sexual aspect of killing," explained a spokeswoman. "That's bad enough." But "how dare they show a film like that in Leeds at this time . . . a film which depicts Ripper style killings." The screening terminated when several dozen women started throwing "rotten eggs and paint bombs at the screens." A sex shop in Chapeltown, "close to where Josephine Whittacker had been murdered, had its windows smashed and the slogans 'Women are Angry' and 'No men after dark' daubed on the walls, and was later burned to the ground." A week-long campaign continued in other parts of Britain, leading to the arrest of over fifty women nationwide. Their actions included:

> Glueing up sex-shop door locks.
> Disrupting films by throwing paint and oil at the screens.
> Removing about 400£ worth of porn from an ordinary book-
> shop, and
> Sending the ashes [of the burned reading matter] out with press
> releases locally and nationally.[25]

Appalled and fascinated, the tabloid press tended to treat these activities as colorful sidelines to the Ripper story—a way to extend the coverage and sell more papers. They slotted the feminist spectacles into the centuries-old iconography of "disorderly women," evocative of the bloodthirsty and irrational female revolutionary crowd. "Girls in Ripper Riot Fury" headlined the *Sunday Mirror* on November 23: "The frenzied mob attacked several men and stormed cinemas showing sex films. . . . One reporter who tried to talk to the march organisers was left bruised and bleeding."[26]

From another direction, the political right also tried to co-opt feminist protests, as part of its own "law and order" campaign against obscenity and sexual permissiveness. "It has taken the 'Ripper' murders and the attacks by women on the sex cinemas in Leeds to bring into the headlines again what is surely one of the political and social scandals of our day," declared Mrs. Mary Whitehouse, the leader of the social purity campaign against media smut. Whitehouse's remarks carried a double meaning: she not only interpreted the feminist protests as supportive of her call for censorship, but by explicitly linking them to the murders, she made them symptomatic of the "sexual anarchy" of the contemporary period, which "is the forerunner of political anarchy."[27]

WAVAW activists vehemently denied any political connections to Whitehouse's campaign. They carefully tried to differentiate their grassroots drives against pornography from the rightist advocacy of state censorship. At the Leeds conference, papers on pornography uniformly rejected Whitehouse's call for more stringent censorship laws and restricted their political propaganda to feminist direct actions: "If all women decided that porn should not exist and smashed and destroyed it on newsstands, bill-boards, in the windows of sex-shops, on the streets of Soho and demanded their right never to be insulted in public again, then at least it would be driven underground."[28]

Feminists unanimously condemned the media hype that constructed the Ripper story as if it were about an exceptional place and exceptional victims, as well as a crime committed by an exceptional man. They condemned police procedures as unduly influenced by this media hype. Mocking the police's romantic identification with the Ripper's late-Victorian contemporary, Sherlock Holmes, feminists exposed the immersion of the police in a fantasy that positioned them, not women, as the Ripper's principal antagonists (citing such statements as "It's between him and me," which they attributed to the officer in charge of the first hunt).[29]

Feminists also exposed the contradictory messages about male sexual danger beamed at women by police officials and the daily press. Although a Yorkshire doctor hypothesized in the press that the Ripper was a "very controlled aggressive sadistic psychopath," the Catch the Ripper Campaign, orchestrated by the police, emphasized his normal appearance and habits: "I appeal to all members of the public especially to all women," announced the chief constable of Leeds, "to think carefully about all males with whom they come in regular contact including those whom they may be married or related to, and ask themselves: could that man be the man we are seeking?" Although the police told women to distrust *all* men, feminist activists complained, they also instructed women to rely on male escorts before venturing out at night. The police tell "us to stay indoors, passive and frightened, depending on men to protect us. . . . Yet they *know* what happens to women at home at the hands of men they live with—they never act on *that*."[30]

Feminists were most coherent in their denunciation of police and press treatment of the victims. What most outraged them was the tendency of the press and police to distinguish between those women who were "innocent" and those who were prostitutes, and to imply, if prostitutes, that they deserved their fate. "WOMEN WERE ANGRY at the media for . . . Dividing women into the 'pure' and 'the fallen.' The 'fallen'—prostitutes, even 'fun-loving' housewives or students—are asking for it, deserve death, being out late *on their own* . . . the 'pure' are granted respectability and concern, and we're told its more worrying such a woman is killed." With eleven women dead and six seriously injured, West Yorkshire's Acting Assistant Chief Constable John Hobson said, "He has made clear that he hates prostitutes.

Many people do," thus implying, observed Joan Smith in the *New Socialist,* that it is "acceptable to hate prostitutes." Character assassinations of the victims continued into the trial proceedings, despite, as Mandy Merck noted, "early and constant criticism from feminists and prostitute groups." "Wilma McCann," intoned Sir Michael Havers (the prosecution) "drank too much, was noisy and sexually promiscuous—she distributed her favours widely." Well before Sutcliffe was apprehended, feminists challenged the assumption that he was primarily a "perverted kind of moralist" and prostitute killer like the Ripper of legendary fame, instead of a "woman killer" who found prostitutes easy prey. Their own political refusal to divide the "odd female" from the innocent ones led WAVAW to deny that prostitutes were special targets of Ripper hatred or even exceptional victims of male violence: "We mourn for all Victims of the Ripper and all women victims of murder, rape, assault . . . by men. The attacks of the Ripper are an extreme example of the sort of attacks that are made on women all the time."[31]

One extraordinary feature of the Yorkshire Ripper case was the emergence of prostitutes as political actors in their own right. Feminists and prostitutes protested together at Sutcliffe's trial. Feminists supported the political agenda of the English Collective of Prostitutes, which demanded: public inquiry into the police handling of investigation; an end to bias and discrimination by police and the courts; the apology by the attorney general to the families of prostitute victims; compensation for the victims and their families. The ECP's slogans reminded the public that prostitutes were mothers "fighting to make ends meet" and that the Ripper had orphaned twenty-three children. Its emphasis on motherhood served diverse purposes: by insisting on the relationship of "sex work" to other domestic labors of women, it stressed the multiple identity of the victims and sought sympathy for them as women who engaged in "good," i.e. desexualized roles. Ironically, as they deemphasized the sexual nature of the job, ECP privileged another female identity, motherhood, that has traditionally naturalized women as a "sex."[32]

Feminists also united in their anger at the way women were put on trial during the judicial proceedings against Sutcliffe in May 1981. They attacked the authoritative male discourses of law and medicine that, in the end, blamed women for provoking the murders. They responded with contempt and disbelief at the jesuitical logic of the prosecution's case that seemed to imply, first of all, that religious and sexual motivations were necessarily different or that "prostitute" was an unambiguous and guilty category. The attorney general's argument that Sutcliffe's vicious attacks were sexually motivated rested on an unexamined conflation of sexuality and violence that, they believed, also informed commonplace models of "natural male sexuality."[32]

Feminist discussions of the Yorkshire Ripper did not escape some of the contradictions that riddled other attempts to extract meaning from the murders. Even as they defended prostitutes as the victims of the Ripper, and protested together with them at the trial, feminists articulated considerable ambivalence about prostitution, a topic generally neglected by the contemporary women's movement. At the WAVAW conference, radical feminists attacked the state repression of prostitutes and endorsed decriminalization, despite considerable uneasiness about the sexual politics of prostitution. In the context of prostitute killing and callous public statements against the prostitute victims, all feminists were anxious to express their solidarity for "all women." Nonetheless conference papers tended to treat prostitution as a degraded site of male violence, a condition more defined by men's sexual needs than women's economic choices. "Studying prostitutes to explain prostitution," declared Sheila Jeffrys, "is as useful as examining the motives of factory workers to explain the existence of capitalism. We must ask who benefits and in whose interests the institution is maintained." Still, they were anxious not to reproduce the division between good and bad women so offensively touted in the press. "We have to work out ways in which to attack the institution of prostitution as we attack all other ways in which male supremacy is supported, while positively supporting women who work as prostitutes against unjust laws, the police, and pimps."[34]

On the mad/bad debate, feminists remained uncertain and divided, partially because they too were entrapped in the dichotomous thinking employed by medical and legal authorities at Sutcliffe's trial. Radical feminists, bent on exposing normative male sexuality as pathological, with no mediating thoughts on the conflictual nature of *human* sexuality, often replayed the anxious logic underwriting both the medical and legal discourses about male sexuality. They too struggled to reconcile voluntarist and determinist models of explanation. When they tried to pronounce upon the meaning of Sutcliffe's acts and their relation to the "masculine norm," they ran into serious difficulties. Calling the Ripper bad, some feminists argued, erroneously assumed that other men, who controlled their "perfectly natural urge to flatten women," are good. Many more objected to the insanity plea on the grounds that it diminished Sutcliffe's responsibility and distanced him from other men. "If he was 'mad' this makes him quantitatively different from other men," wrote Wendy Holloway. "If he was 'bad' it is more difficult to exonerate others: what made him different?"[35]

In "Mad or Bad It's Men who are Violent and Women who are Victims," Jill Tweedie, writing in the woman page of the *Guardian,* dismissed the mad/bad debate as a narrowly legalistic concern that ignored widespread violent misogyny. "I am overwhelmingly aware of one thing:—whether or not Peter Sutcliffe was egged on by his God or acted of his own free will and enjoyed himself, what he did was kill women." Sutcliffe, Tweedie insisted, "gets his star billing for excess," a point widely endorsed by feminist commentators across the political spectrum who insisted that Sutcliffe's killings could only be understood as an extreme expression of entrenched misogyny. WAVAW had made it a central—*the central*—point of its political analysis that male sexuality was violent and deployed to control women: "the attacks of the Ripper are an extreme example of the sort of attacks that are made on women all the time." The hunt for the Ripper was part of a larger "battle against sexual violence." Socialist feminists, who had been previously reticent in polemical debates over male violence (although active in rape-crisis and battered-women centers), also spoke out against male violence as general and endemic. "[W]omen's experience of sexual violence is a core experience of the subordination of women, not a sordid piece of *News of the World* marginalia that healthy socialists need not worry about," declared Elizabeth Wilson. The editors of *Feminist Review* condemned the media for "glossing over" the continuity of Sutcliffe's behavior "with 'normal' male behavior towards women in our society."[36]

Yet without some qualifications, these statements ran the risk of universalizing misogyny, of ignoring social divisions among men, and of collapsing all forms of male violence into single causes and effects. Although feminists insisted that Sutcliffe's actions were symptomatic of a wider social problem, they remained vague about the material and cultural factors that produced these effects. Strikingly missing was the discussion of class or any other social division that might shape more localized cultures of masculinity. Reticence about class reflects the degree to which the feminist discourse of sexual violence had been shaped by radical feminists, who tend to highlight sexual difference over other social divisions, and to underplay differences among men (as well as among women) because they prefer to implicate all men equally in an all-encompassing patriarchal system of violence. Feminists were also influenced by progressive criminology of the 1970s that also tended to deny class patterns in an effort to democratize violence.

If feminists overgeneralized when they tried to use the case of the Yorkshire Ripper to speak about masculinity and violent misogyny, equally troubling problems of establishing cause and effect surfaced in the work of one feminist commentator who focused on the local class conditions that gave rise to serial sex murder. In *"The Streetcleaner"* (1986), Nicole Ward Jouve, a feminist academic living in Yorkshire, interprets Sutcliffe as less a "poseur" who tried to live up to the legend the media was creating around him than a man driven by the contradictory imperatives of a northern working-class culture "in which contempt for women and violence to women" are the norm.[37] In presenting her case, Jouve draws heavily on doctors and investigative reporters for evidence. Although she often works against the grain of their interpretations, she is still bound by the narrative logic of their script. She accepts the scenarios of family melodrama set out by the doctors and the journalists, including their view that the provocative actions of Sutcliffe's mother and wife precipitated attacks on prostitutes. Drawing explicitly on psychoanalytic writings that locate the genesis of paranoid schizophrenia in repressed homosexuality, she even speculates that Sutcliffe was a latent homosexual.[38] Jouve ingeniously tries to invert the meanings attached to these themes; she refuses to blame his homosexuality for his violent misogyny but indicts instead the homophobic culture that would not allow him to "come out" and thus find "release" for the self-hatred that erupted in violence against women.

Jouve's psychoanalytic speculations run perilously close to reproducing the same errors of essentialism about masculinity, femininity, and homosexuality that she denounces in working-class male culture. She presents the gender system in northern working-class environments as producing uniform, unchallenged identities rather than multiple and contested ones. Although she condemns the media conflation of the original Ripper crimes with the Yorkshire murders, her own evocations of the "depressed" Northern landscapes echo an argument from geography: "You couldn't help wondering what connections there were between the socioeconomic dereliction which much of the geography expressed and the type of violence which was at work in the nooks and crannies of those landscapes."[39] Her effort to specify the climate that gave rise to these serial murders is marred by a surprising naiveté about other forms of misogyny in other class cultures.[40] She simply assumes that aggressive macho values do not appear "so conspicuously or so viciously among the middle class or privileged classes,"[41] thus closing off exploration of the "hidden violence" against women in other classes and the cultural and social mechanisms that encourage elite men to commit, albeit less frequently, the same forms of violence—such as wife battering, prostitute bashing—that may be more prevalent in working-class milieus. In the end, both *"The Streetcleaner"* and WAVAW flounder in their effort to conceptualize serial murder as a social crime. Even if responses to the murders may be socially legible and paradigmatic, this may not be true of the acts of serial murder themselves.

Whereas copycat activities usually follow well-established patterns of male violence (such as street harassment and wife-beating), serial sex murders may represent such a gross violation of social boundaries that they exceed the paradigms for socially recognizable behavior.

More than any other case of lust murder, the Yorkshire Ripper murders provoked a forceful feminist intervention against the press coverage of male violence. Feminists of all persuasions united in their denunciation of press and legal discourses around the murders and Sutcliffe's trial; many others, who did not engage in direct actions, vicariously identified with the call to take command of the streets and welcomed the attack on the public media.

Beneath this public unity were profound theoretical differences, generational struggles, and conflicting political priorities that divided British feminists in the early 1980s. Only six weeks after Sutcliffe's trial, at the Communist University summer program (an annual set of workshops held at London University) in July 1981, the uneasy consensus established by feminists in the face of the Yorkshire Ripper soon began to unravel as feminists confronted the issue of pornography as well as the politics of prostitution. The academic and geographic location of the British dispute and its political context are noteworthy: it was held in the south, at the University of London, where feminists remained relatively untouched by the daily terror of the Yorkshire Ripper that had gripped northern women. In this detached atmosphere, discussion could more comfortably shift away from actual violence to the theoretical explorations of violent representation. The political setting, as part of a nonsectarian socialist gathering, under the auspices of the Communist party, was equally telling: testifying to the left's determination at last to give some "air time" to issues of sexuality and sexual violence, but also signaling how much disputes within British feminism —among socialist, "theoretical," and "revolutionary" feminists—were disputes within the left.[42]

By the early 1980s, socialist and "theoretical" feminists (many of whom were academics) who had always regarded themselves as the powerful militant edge of British feminism, found themselves losing political ground to self-styled "revolutionary" feminists (a slightly exaggerated militant version of radical feminism) who dominated WAVAW and operated for the most part outside of the academy. Whereas these "new Angry Women"[43] advocated lesbian separatism, a full, unremitting assault on the institution of heterosexuality, and a coherent feminist sexual politics that could speak for all women against men, their opponents in the pornography debate saw themselves defending a second-stage agenda for feminism: the exploration of difference and diversity among women and the importance of retaining "female sexual pleasure" as the starting point for cultural struggle. This power struggle within feminism, together with the real strategic and theoretical differences between the two sides, partially accounts for the bitterness with which the pornography issue would be debated by feminists in Britain.

Before a large audience at the Communist University, Rosalind Coward acknowledged that pornographic codes are designed for "male arousal" "and *in our culture male arousal is a real social problem.*" She nonetheless expressed serious doubts about an antipornography movement that prioritized "aggressive male sexuality" as the main political problem facing women, to the exclusion of other important issues, and that implied that "male sexuality is in fact 'almost always violent'."[44]

Coward tried to shift the discussion from pornography as a fixed set of images to pornography as a "regime of representations." Pornography, Coward explained, is a practice that corresponds closely with "the whole regime by which sexuality is organized and experienced in our culture." It is historically variable; its representations have no intrinsic meanings but depend on the "context, use of arrangements of elements for male arousal." This does not imply that the representation of women in pornography is "benign"; on the contrary, pornography puts into circulation images of sexuality that represent sexual pleasure for men as "initiation and domination" and "for women submission to men's depersonalized needs."

For women concerned about male violence and the disempowering effect of misogynist representations of women, Coward proposed three lines of attack. Rather than presenting pornography as a separate problem, feminists should concentrate instead on sexual relations generally. In addition, they could support the introduction of positive legislation against sexist speech, similar to existing legislation in France (and comparable to legislation against racist speech in England). Finally, feminists need to define what is "sexist," what is "offensive," and what is "degrading."

WAVAW activists in the audience were disarmed by Coward's presentation, most particularly by her qualified acknowledgment of certain tenets of their own argument: that male sexual arousal was a problem and that feminist intervention against sexist imagery was justified. This did not prevent individual disputes from erupting in surrounding spaces of the University of London student center—one famous angry exchange actually transpired in the "loo line." Nor did it end the debate among feminists over violence and representation.

On the contrary, the confrontation at the Communist University between feminist advocates of antipornography politics and their feminist critics precipitated a decade of debate among British feminists about commercialized sex, sexual representation, and male violence. In the 1980s, feminists continued to debate whether antipornography propaganda empowered women or produced a politics of fear, frustration, and rage.[45] They continued to dispute whether male sexuality is "almost always violent," whether pornography has any mimetic relation to "real" violence, whether it is "deliberate propaganda for men" and a "true representation of what men think female sexuality is."[46] They further disputed whether pornography is a "fixed set of images" or a "regime of representation," or a fantasy that stimulates psychic multiplicity rather than a single and coherent subject position.[47] Nor could feminists agree on the appropriate political interventions around pornography.

The 1980s witnessed no resolution to these debates, although the interpretive systems mobilized by each side could shift over time. In the early 1980s, for example, feminist critics of WAVAW, scornful of WAVAW's assumptions about pornography's mimetic relation to violence against women, took comfort in occupying the high ground of cultural theory. By the end of the decade, works by some feminist cultural critics in Britain who were sympathetic to the antipornography position challenged theoretical feminists on their own grounds: authors like Suzanne Kappeler, Deborah Cameron, and Kathleen Fraser deployed their own version of discourse analysis, mostly derived from a narrow reading of Foucault, to defend a semiotics that still ends up saying that power for men is nothing less than the power of victimizing women.[48]

Against a unified picture of male social power and misogynist cultural production, feminist critics of the antipornography campaign increasingly invoked a world shaped less by unities and binary divisions than by gaps, fragmentations, and contradictions; a world peopled by historically constructed shifting selves with no fixed gender-identity of subject or object. This feminist vision posits a world of complex cultural meanings where perhaps the most strenuous task facing feminists would be to shape representation. Yet the apparent elusiveness and embeddedness of sexist representation have placed feminist critics of the 1990s in a difficult position, as they and others focus increasingly on the power of popular cultural meanings to shape people's experience of themselves and the world.

In good measure, these intellectual debates incited the cultural and historical inquiry resulting in *City of Dreadful Delight*. Like the feminist debates of the 1980s, this book has not resolved the moral and political dilemmas related to representation, violence, and commercialized sex. It has returned to a formative moment in the production of feminist politics and of popular narratives of sexual danger. It has tried to show how late-

Victorian sexual politics and narratives existed in dynamic relation to each other, both articulating and managing, in different ways, challenges to class, gender, and ethnic relations. These late-Victorian formations provided a polyvalent cultural legacy that continues to inform public debates and understandings into the late twentieth century.[49]

Like their counterparts of the 1980s, London feminists of the 1880s forcefully contributed to the politicization of sexuality. They too seized the opportunity to tell the story of sexual danger, focusing on prostitution as a story of sexual victimization and seduction. Through their tale, they articulated their own grievances against men, they inserted themselves into the public discussion of sex to an unprecedented extent, and they gained new entrée to public spaces and to journalistic practices. Their ability to speak about sex opened up a world of new possibilities for them, but fewer possibilities for the objects of their solicitude, the "daughters of the people." Despite their unprecedented political intervention, feminists did not operate as autonomous cultural actors, as interrogatory voices existing outside of power or outside the system of cultural production that generated mythic stories of male danger. On the contrary, late-Victorian feminists participated in a cultural dynamic that circulated and amplified stories of sexual danger in a market culture with contradictory political effects. On the one hand, oppositional feminist politics and the social practice of "New Women" helped to provoke cautionary tales of sexual danger such as the Ripper narrative; on the other hand, feminists themselves refined the same media fantasies to produce their own meanings and narrations.

Today, as in the past, feminists struggle to devise an effective strategy to combat sexual violence and humiliation in our society, where violent misogyny seems so deeply rooted. Similarly, the media continues to amplify the terror of male violence, as it did during the sexual scandals of the 1880s, persuading women that they are helpless victims. In this cultural milieu, we feminists have to come to grips with the painful historic contradictions of feminist sexual strategies, not only for the sex workers who still regard commercialized sex as the "best-paid industry," but also for ourselves. To be sure, the current women's movement has generated a range of responses that transcend the mythic fatality embedded in a narrative like the Ripper story: self-defense techniques, take-back-the-night marches, antirape hotlines, battered women's shelters, antipornography demonstrations, prostitutes' rights coalitions, as well as demands that law enforcement agencies be responsive to female complaints of male assault, offer diverse and contradictory strategies against a false notion of universal female passivity. But feminists also need to recognize the degree to which we participate in and help to circulate cultural scripts that represent male violence or female victimization as the product of single causes and effects. Reliance on an iconography of female victimization can undercut the political impact of feminists' own public initiatives. As publicists and political actors, we need to take care not to play into the hands of the forces of political reaction, who are only too delighted to cast women in the roles of victims requiring male protection and control, and who desire to turn feminist protest into a politics of repression.

NOTES

Abbreviations

NEWSPAPERS AND JOURNALS

BMJ   *British Medical Journal*
DC   *Daily Chronicle*
DN   *Daily News*
DT   *Daily Telegraph*
ELA   *East London Advertiser*
ELO   *East London Observer*
ES   *Evening Standard*
LWN   *Lloyd's Weekly Newspaper*
MP   *Morning Post*
PMG   *Pall Mall Gazette*

RN   *Reynolds Newspaper*
SJG   *Saint James Gazette*
WPP   *Woman's Penny Paper*

ARCHIVES AND LETTERS

E.C.   Elizabeth Cobb
H.O.   Home Office Papers
M.S.   Maria Sharpe
Mepo.   Metropolitan Police Papers
K.P.   Karl Pearson
O.S.   Olive Schreiner

Introduction

1. "London's Horror Chamber Gets a New Look," *Natal Witness* (1980); "Press clippings," Madame Tussaud's Archives, London; Pauline Chapman, *Chamber of Horrors* (London: Constable, 1984), p. 248.

2. In her influential article "Visual Pleasure and Narrative Cinema," *Screen* 16, no. 3 (Autumn 1975): 6–18, Laura Mulvey argues that classic film narrative, epitomized by the work of Alfred Hitchcock, projects woman as an indispensable element of spectacle, passive raw material for the active "male gaze." These films produce a "structure of looking," so that the spectator identifies with the actions of the male protagonist who controls events. Both the "voyeuristic gaze" and the "sadistic will" are male prerogatives directed towards "the woman as the object of both." For the ability of female spectators to "masquerade" and inhabit the male gaze, see Mary Ann Doane, "Film and the Masquerade: Theorising the Female Spectator," *Screen*, 23, nos. 3/4 (Sept./Oct. 1982): 74–87. For Mulvey's own revision of the binary extremism of her premises, see "Afterthoughts on Visual Pleasure and Narrative Cinema," *Frameworks* 15/17 (1981): 12–15. For a consideration of female visual narratives, which do not completely bind women to the objectification of the "male gaze," see Tania Modleski, *Loving with a Vengeance: Mass-Produced Fantasies for Women* (Hamden, Conn.: Archon Books, 1982), and Ien Ang, *Watching Dallas* (London and New York: Methuen, 1985); Teresa de Lauretis, *Alice Doesn't: Feminism, Semiotics, Cinema* (Bloomington: Indiana University Press, 1984).

3. Abigail Solomon Godeau, "The Legs of the Countess," *October* 39 (Winter 1986): 66–108. Linda Williams, "When the Woman Looks," in Mary Ann Doane,

Patricia Mellencamp, Linda Williams, eds., *Revision: Essays in Feminism Art Criticism* (Frederick, Md.: University Publications of America, 1984), pp. 83–99; T. J. Clark, *The Painting of Modern Life: Paris in the Art of Manet and His Followers* (New York: Knopf, 1984), chap. 2.

4. Chapman, *Chamber of Horrors*, pp. 99, 96; "London's Horror Chamber."

5. Spokesman for Madame Tussaud's, quoted in "Madame Tussaud Bows to Demands for More Gore," *Victoria Times*, 5 April 1980, Tussaud Archives. The new exhibit was path-breaking, not only for including the Ripper, but also for introducing the figure of a prostitute into its hallowed chambers for the first time. Tussaud's was "family entertainment," the archivist explained to me; this evidently meant that violence, but not sex, was appropriate "family fare." Madame Tussaud's air of propriety, her "point," to quote Charles Dickens (Chapman, *Chamber of Horrors*, p. 65), that the nastiest murderers were not necessarily "shifty, furtive types, but looked no more sinister . . . than the man sitting opposite on the daily journey to work," had become too subtle for generations accustomed to more explicit presentation of violence in contemporary films and television.

6. Roland Barthes, "Myths Today," in *Mythologies*, trans. Annette Lavers (St. Albans, Herts: Paladin, 1973), pp. 109–59.

7. Leonard W. Matters, *The Mystery of Jack the Ripper* (London: Hutchinson, 1929), pp. 43, 44; *PMG*, 8 Sept. 1888.

8. Maev Kennedy, "Ripping Yarns," *Guardian*, 7 Dec. 1987.

9. Matters, *Mystery of Jack the Ripper*, p. 16; Frayling, "The House that Jack Built," in Sylvia Tomaselli and Roy Porter, eds., *Rape* (Oxford: Basil Blackwell, 1986), p. 267n.

10. Frayling, "The House that Jack Built," p. 177. Following Mulvey ("Visual Pleasure"), many feminist film critics interpret Hitchcock films as the epitome of "classic film narrative" and its pleasures, at the expense of women. See Tania Modleski, ed., *The Women Who Knew Too Much: Hitchcock and Feminist Theory* (New York: Methuen, 1988).

11. For a discussion of the "golden age of Ripper theories" in the late 1960s and early 1970s, see Alexander Kelly, "Bibliography: A Hundred Years of Ripperature," in Colin Wilson and Robin Odell, *Jack the Ripper: Summing Up and Verdict* (London: Bantam Press, 1987), pp. 282, 283. Feminist interpretations of the Ripper legacy include Jane Caputi, *The Age of Sex Crime* (Bowling Green, Ohio: Bowling Green State University Popular Press, 1987), p. 36; Deborah Cameron and Elizabeth Fraser, *Lust to Kill: A Feminist Investigation of Sexual Murder* (New York: New York University Press, 1987).

12. Discussions of Victorian values include James Walvin, *Victorian Values* (London: Penguin, 1988), pp. 3–6; Jeffrey Weeks, *Sexuality and Its Discontents: Meanings, Myths, and Modern Sexualities* (London: Routledge and Kegan Paul, 1985), pp. 15, 41; Lynne Segal, *Is the Future Female? Troubled Thoughts on Contemporary Feminism* (London: Virago, 1987), p. 36. For a discussion of the "poetics" of transgression that accompanies the extreme binarism of class society, see, Peter Stallybrass and Allon White, *The Politics and Poetics of Transgression* (Ithaca: Cornell University Press, 1986). Ripper books that feature an "overworld" Ripper include Michael Harrison, *Clarence: The Life of the Duke of Clarence and*

Avondale, KG 1864–1892 (London: W. H. Allen, 1972); Stephen Knight, *Jack the Ripper: The Final Solution* (London: Harrap, 1976). Studies of Victorian sexuality that follow an underworld/overworld structure include Steven Marcus, *The Other Victorians: A Study of Sexuality and Pornography in Mid-Nineteenth Century England* (New York: Meridian, 1974), p. ix. Other works on the history of sexuality informed by the overworld/underworld dichotomy include Cyril Pearl, *The Girl with the Swansdown Seat* (Indianapolis: Bobbs-Merrill, 1955); Ronald Pearsall, *The Worm in the Bud: The World of Victorian Sexuality* (New York: Macmillan, 1969); Peter T. Cominos, "Late-Victorian Sexual Respectability and the Social System," *International Review of Social History* 8 (1963): 18–48, 216–50; Ben Barker-Benfield, *The Horrors of the Half-Known Life: Male Attitudes towards Women and Sexuality in Nineteenth-Century America* (New York: Harper and Row, 1976). Works critical of this interpretation include Peter Gay, *The Bourgeois Experience: Victoria to Freud* (New York: Oxford University Press, 1984), vol. 1, *The Education of the Senses;* Carl Degler, "What Ought to Be and What Was: Women's Sexuality in the Nineteenth Century," *American Historical Review* 79 (1974): 1467–90; M. Jeanne Peterson, *Family, Love, and Work in the Lives of Victorian Gentlewomen* (Bloomington: Indiana University Press, 1989); Pat Jalland, *Women, Marriage and Politics 1860–1914* (New York: Oxford University Press, 1986). One the whole, these latter works present bourgeois marriages of the nineteenth century as erotically satisfying and happy for both partners. They want "to give the nineteenth century a better name," to quote one reviewer (Lisa Duggan, "History Between the Sheets: Politics Go Under Cover," *Village Literary Supplement,* Sept. 1986, p. 13). Unfortunately these revisions tend to ignore or minimize the operation of class and gender power in the construction of sexuality.

13. Weeks, *Sexuality and Its Discontents,* pp. 11, 18.

14. Woolley, "Pick Your Ripper," *The Listener,* 17/24 Dec. 1987.

15. John D'Emilio and Estelle B. Freedman, *Intimate Matters: A History of Sexuality in America* (New York: Harper and Row, 1988).

16. Thomas Laqueur, *Making Sex: Body and Gender from the Greeks to Freud* (Cambridge, Mass: Harvard University Press, 1990), p. 11. One could extend this observation to other social categories, particularly race and class: dangerous female sexualities not only seemed to "unsex" women but also to render them déclassé and racially degenerate.

17. R. D. French, *Antivivisection and Medical Science in Victorian Society* (Princeton: Princeton University Press, 1975), chap. 11; Coral Lansbury, *The Old Brown Dog: Women, Workers, and Vivisection in Edwardian England* (Madison, Wisconsin: University of Wisconsin Press, 1985); Mary Ann Elston, "Women and Antivivisection in Victorian England, 1870–1900," in Nicholas Rupke, ed., *Vivisection in Historical Perspective* (London: Croom Helm, 1987), pp. 258–89.

18. Jürgen Habermas, *The Structural Transformation of the Public Sphere,* trans. Thomas Burger (Cambridge, Mass.: MIT Press, 1989). See feminist critiques and appropriations of Habermas's theory of the bourgeois public sphere: Mary P. Ryan, *Women in Public: Between Banners and Ballots, 1825–1880* (Baltimore: Johns Hopkins University Press, 1990); Nancy Fraser, "Rethinking the Public Sphere," *Social Text* 25/26 (1990): 56–80.

19. These volatile political conditions would include the further extension of manhood suffrage, the realignment of middle-class party loyalties, the growth of extraparliamentary politics, increased trade union activities, the revival of socialism, the formation of mixed discussion clubs, the campaigning practices of the New Journalism, street corner politicking, and sensational public demonstrations.

20. Linda Gordon and Ellen Dubois, "Seeking Ecstasy on the Battlefield," *Feminist Studies* 9 (Spring 1983): 7–26; Judith R. Walkowitz, "Male Vice and Feminist Virtue: Feminism and the Politics of Prostitution in Nineteenth-Century Britain," *History Workshop Journal* 13 (Spring 1982): 77–93.

21. Judith R. Walkowitz, *Prostitution and Victorian Society: Women, Class, and the State* (New York: Cambridge University Press, 1980).

22. For an excellent application of poststructuralist analysis to Victorian cultural history, see Mary Poovey, *Uneven Developments: The Ideological Work of Gender in Mid-Victorian England* (Chicago: University of Chicago Press, 1988). See also Joan W. Scott, "Deconstructing Equality-Versus-Difference: or the Uses of Poststructuralist Theory for Feminism," *Feminist Studies* 14, no. 1 (Spring 1988): 34.

23. John Toews, "Intellectual History Takes a Linguistic Turn: The Autonomy of Meaning and the Irreducibility of Experience," *American Historical Review* 92, no. 4 (1987): 879–907.

24. For feminist critiques and adaptations of Foucault, see Irene Diamond and Lee Quinby, eds., *Feminism and Foucault: Reflections on Resistance* (Boston: Northeastern University Press, 1988); Naomi Schor, "Dreaming Dyssymmetry: Barthes, Foucault, and Sexual Difference," in Alice Jardine and Paul Smith, eds., *Men in Feminism* (New York: Methuen, 1987), pp. 98–110.

25. Michael Foucault, *The History of Sexuality:* vol. 1, *An Introduction;* vol. 2, *The Uses of Pleasure;* vol. 3, *The Care of the Self;* trans. Robert Hurley (New York: Pantheon, 1978–86). See Biddy Martin, "Feminism, Criticism, and Foucault," *New German Critique,* no. 27 (Fall 1982): 6.

26. Kathy Peiss and Christina Simmons, eds., *Passion and Power: Sexuality in History* (Philadelphia: Temple University Press, 1989), p. 3; Linda Gordon, *Woman's Body, Woman's Right: A Social History of Birth Control in America* (Viking: New York, 1976); Carroll Smith-Rosenberg, "Beauty, the Beast, and the Militant Woman: A Case Study of Sex Role and Social Stress in Jacksonian America," *American Quarterly* 23 (1971); idem, *Disorderly Conduct: Visions of Gender in Victorian America* (Knopf: New York, 1985); Nancy F. Cott, "Passionlessness: A Reinterpretation of Victorian Sexual Ideology, 1790–1850," *Signs* 4 (1978): 219–36.

27. Foucault, *History of Sexuality,* 1:115, 148.

28. For examples of feminist historiography, see Lucy Bland, "Marriage Laid Bare: Middle-Class Women and Marital Sex, 1880s–1914," in Jane Lewis, ed., *Labour and Love: Women's Experience of Home and Family, 1850–1940* (Oxford: Basil Blackwell, 1986), pp. 123–48; Cott, "Passionlessness"; Smith-Rosenberg, "Beauty, the Beast, and the Militant Woman"; Gordon, *Woman's Body, Woman's Right,* chap. 5, "Voluntary Motherhood"; Anna Clark, *Women's Silence, Men's Violence: Sexual Assault in England, 1770–1845* (London: Pandora, 1987).

29. Feminist writings on women's culture in the late 1970s and early 1980s have attributed a degree of cultural autonomy to women that later feminist work

has challenged. See, for example, Smith-Rosenberg, "Female World of Love and Ritual," *Disorderly Conduct;* Temma Kaplan, "Women and the Communal Strikes in the Crisis of 1917–1922," in Renate Bridenthal and Claudia Koonz, eds., *Becoming Visible: Women in European History,* 2d ed. (1987). For a critical evaluation of this tradition, see Linda Kerber, "Seperate Spheres, Female Worlds, Women's Place: The Rhetoric of Women's History," *Journal of American History* 75, no. 1 (June 1988): 9–39; Joan Scott, "Gender: A Useful Category of Historical Analysis," in Scott, *Gender and the Politics of History,* pp. 28–50; Jane Flax, "Postmodernism and Gender Relations in Feminist Theory," *Signs* 12, no. 4 (Summer 1987): 621–43.

30. Judith Newton, "History as Usual?" *Cultural Critique* (Spring 1988): 99.

31. Gabrielle Spiegel, "History, Historicism, and the Social Logic of the Text," *Speculum* 65, no. 1 (January 1990): 59–86.

32. See, for example, Lynn Hunt, ed., *The New Cultural History* (Berkeley: University of California Press, 1989).

Chapter One

1. Henry James, "London," in *Essays in London and Elsewhere* (Freeport, N.Y.: Books for Libraries, 1922 [first pub. 1893]) pp. 27, 32. See "City of Dreadful Delight," review of James's "London," in *PMG* (London), 15 Sept. 1888.

2. Henry James, *The Complete Notebooks of Henry James,* ed. Leon Edel (New York: Oxford University Press, 1987), pp. 215–18; James, "London," pp. 7, 14.

3. Richard Sennett, *The Fall of Public Man* (Cambridge: Cambridge University Press, 1973), pp. 135–37; Peter Stallybrass and Allon White, *The Politics and Poetics of Transgression* (Ithaca: Cornell University Press, 1986), p. 139; Griselda Pollock, "Vicarious Excitements: *London: A Pilgrimage* by Gustave Doré and Blanchard Jerrold, 1872," *New Formations* 2 (Spring 1988): 28.

4. Jane Flax, "Postmodernism and Gender Relations in Feminist Theory," *Signs* 12, no. 4 (Summer 1987): 624.

5. Susan Buck-Morss, "The Flaneur, the Sandwichman, and the Whore: The Politics of Loitering," *New German Critique* 13, no. 39 (1986): 106; Walter Benjamin, quoted in ibid., 106; ibid., 105.

6. James, "London," p. 27.

7. Gareth Stedman Jones, *Outcast London: A Study in the Relationship Between Classes in Victorian Society* (Oxford: Clarendon Press, 1971); Frank Miller Turner, *Between Science and Religion: The Reaction to Scientific Naturalism in Late-Victorian England* (New Haven: Yale University Press, 1974); Colin Ford and Brian Harrison, *A Hundred Years Ago: Britain in the 1880s in Words and Photographs* (Cambridge: Harvard University Press, 1983); Norman MacKenzie and Jeanne MacKenzie, *The Fabians* (New York: Simon and Schuster, 1977); T. J. Jackson Lears, *No Place of Grace: Anti-modernism and the Transformation of American Culture, 1880–1920* (New York: Pantheon, 1981); Richard Wightman Fox and T. J. Jackson Lears, eds., *The Culture of Consumption: Critical Essays in American History, 1880–1980* (New York: Pantheon, 1983).

8. This norm involved the merger of aristocratic and middle-class norms; it was a secularized version of "muscular Christianity" with a decidedly greater em-

phasis on the muscular than the Christian. As historians note, it may have subjected men to a greater degree of emotional deprivation than the moral strictures of evangelical Christianity, which at least offered an outlet of intense emotion in religious expression. See J. A. Mangan and James Walvin, eds., *Manliness and Morality: Middle-Class Masculinity in Britain and America, 1800–1940* (New York: St. Martin's Press, 1987); Ronald Hyam, *Empire and Sexuality: The British Experience* (Manchester: Manchester University Press, 1990), pp. 71–73; Janet Oppenheim, *"Shattered Nerves": Doctors, Patients, and Depression in Victorian England* (New York: Oxford University Press, 1991), pp. 146–51.

9. On Tom and Jerry, see Deborah Epstein Nord, "The City as Theater: From Georgian to Early Victorian London," *Victorian Studies* 31, no. 2 (Winter 1988): 159–88. On reading the city, see William Sharpe and Leonard Wallock, "From 'Great Town' to 'Nonplace Urban Realm': Reading the Modern City," in *Visions of the Modern City: Essays in History, Art, and Literature,* ed. William Sharpe and Leonard Wallock (Baltimore: Johns Hopkins University Press, 1987), p. 9.

10. Peter Keating, ed., Introduction, *Into Unknown England, 1866–1913: Selections from the Social Explorers* (Glasgow: William Collins and Sons, 1976), p. 16; Pollock, "Vicarious Excitements," p. 28; George R. Sims, *My Life: Sixty Years' Recollections of Bohemian London* (London: Eveleigh Nash, 1917), p. 101; James Greenwood, *The Wilds of London* (1874; rpt., New York: Garland, 1985).

11. See Deborah Epstein Nord, "The Social Explorer as Anthropologist: Victorian Travellers among the Urban Poor," in *Visions of the Modern City,* ed. Sharpe and Wallock, pp. 122–34; George W. Stocking, *Victorian Anthropology* (New York: The Free Press, 1987); Adam Kuper, *The Invention of Primitive Society* (London and New York: Routledge and Kegan Paul, 1988).

12. They did not always sustain this separation throughout the texts: as Mayhew detailed the lives of his street folk, observes Catherine Gallagher, "these charges evaporate." Mayhew's ethnography of wandering tribes conflicted with what Gareth Stedman Jones describes as Mayhew's understanding "in embryo" of the "specificity of the London economy," its prevalence of casual trades, low wages, underemployment, that explained the "improvident" habits of the London worker. Catherine Gallagher, "The Body versus the Social Body in the Works of Thomas Malthus and Henry Mayhew," in *The Making of the Modern Body: Sexuality and Society in the Nineteenth Century,* ed. Catherine Gallagher and Thomas Laqueur (Berkeley: University of California Press, 1987), pp. 83–106; Jones, *Outcast London.*

13. "By condensing the 'abnormal' practices of the slum in the figure of the savage Irishman," Engels attempted to protect the English proletariat from conflation with the filth and squalor of their environment (Stallybrass and White, *Politics and Poetics of Transgression,* p. 132). As Gertrude Himmelfarb observes, Mayhew imagined the costermongers more as "a species in the Darwinian sense than a class in the Marxian." As urban primitives, they were likened to the Bushmen and Hottentots of Africa, subjected to the same anthropological scrutiny and classification as subhuman. Commentators often fixed on their animalistic bodies; in Mayhew's case, on the unnaturally robust health of the street traders who parasitically lived off the labor of the productive poor; or, in the cases of Engels and Dickens, the starving, enfeebled bodies of the industrial classes. Gertrude Himmelfarb, "The Culture

of Poverty," in *The Victorian City: Images and Realities*, 2 vols., ed. H. J. Dyos and Michael Wolff (London and Boston: Routledge and Kegan Paul, 1973), 2:712; Gertrude Himmelfarb, *The Idea of Poverty: England in the Early Industrial Age* (New York: Vintage, 1985).

14. James Greenwood, *Low Life Deeps: An Account of the Strange Fish to be Found There* (London: Chatto and Windus, 1876); Henry Mayhew, *London Labour and the London Poor*, four vols. (1861; rpt, New York: Dover, 1968), 3:233, quoted by Jones, *Outcast London*, p. 30.

15. Visual interpretations like *London: A Pilgrimage* helped to sustain nostalgic and anachronistic representations of London in the last decades of the century. See Pollock, "Vicarious Excitements."

16. Stallybrass and White, *Politics and Poetics of Transgression*, pp. 5–6.

17. Urban explorers' efforts to marginalize the "low-Other" reveals an "operative ambivalence," akin to the psychological conflict manifested by the imperialist towards the colonial Other. Stallybrass and White, *Politics and Poetics of Transgression*, p. 5. See also Edward Said, *Orientalism* (New York: Vintage Books, 1979), pp. 3, 7. "Orientalism," the myth of the Middle East constructed by Europe to justify its authority, explains Said, "depends for its strategy on a flexible *positional* superiority, which puts the Westerner in a whole series of possible relationships with the Orient without ever losing him the upper hand."

18. Greenwood, "A Night in the Workhouse" in Keating, *Into Unknown England*, p. 34.

19. This proved to be the sensational climax of his *Morning Chronicle* series in 1849 and 1850. Henry Mayhew, "Second Test—Meeting of needlewomen forced to take to the streets," in *The Unknown Mayhew*, ed. Eileen Yeo and E. P. Thompson (New York: Schocken Books, 1972), p. 168.

20. Mary P. Ryan, *Women in Public: Between Banner and Ballots, 1825–1880* (Baltimore: Johns Hopkins University Press, 1990); Laura Mulvey, "Visual Pleasure and Narrative Cinema," *Screen* 16, no. 3 (Autumn 1975): 6–18.

21. Leonore Davidoff, "Gender and Class in Victorian England: The Diaries of Arthur J. Munby and Hannah Cullwick," *Feminist Studies* 5 (Spring 1979): 87–141.

22. Feminist deconstructionists like Mary Poovey argue that men construct their own identities in opposition to what they have ascribed to women. See Mary Poovey, *Uneven Developments: The Ideological Work of Gender in Mid-Victorian England* (Chicago: University of Chicago Press, 1988), chap. 1.

23. See Judith R. Walkowitz, "Dangerous Sexualities," in *Storia delle Donne*, ed. Michelle Perrot and Georges Duby (Rome: Laterza, 1991).

24. As Deborah Nord observes, early nineteenth-century observers interpreted the solitary prostitute as alter ego for the male spectator, himself an outsider and stranger. De Quincey, for example, has his "Opium Eater" observe: "Being myself at that time of necessity a peripatetic, or a walker of the streets, I naturally fell in more frequently with those female peripatetics who are technically called street walkers." Deborah Epstein Nord, "The City as Theater," p. 181.

25. Charles Dickens, *David Copperfield*, quoted in Lynda Nead, *Myths of Sexuality: Representations of Women in Victorian Britain* (Oxford: Basil Blackwell, 1988), pp. 126–27.

26. Frank Mort, *Dangerous Sexualities: Medico-Moral Politics in England since 1830* (London: Routledge and Kegan Paul, 1987), p. 18; Deborah Epstein Nord, "The Urban Peripatetic: Spectator, Streetwalker, Woman Writer" (unpublished essay), p. 15; Alain Corbin, "Commercial Sexuality in Nineteenth-Century France: A System of Images and Regulations," trans. Katherine Streip, *Representations* 14 (Spring 1986): 212–13. See also "Jack the Ripper," chap. 7 of this book.

27. Judith R. Walkowitz, *Prostitution and Victorian Society: Women, Class, and the State* (New York: Cambridge University Press, 1980).

28. *Parliamentary Papers* (1871) 29, C.408, "Report of the Royal Commission on the Administration and Operation of the Contagious Diseases Acts 1868–69."

29. Cited in Henry Mayhew and Bracebridge Hemyng, "The Prostitute Class Generally," in Mayhew, *London Labour and the London Poor*, 4:205.

30. Robert D. Storch, "Police Control of Street Prostitution in Victorian London: A Study in the Context of Police Action," in *Police and Society*, ed. David H. Bayley (Beverly Hills and London: Sage, 1977), pp. 49–72.

31. Ibid.; Edward J. Bristow, *Vice and Vigilance: Purity Movements in Britain since 1700* (Dublin: Gill and Macmillan, 1977); Judith R. Walkowitz, "Male Vice and Feminist Virtue: Feminism and the Politics of Prostitution in Nineteenth-Century Britain," *History Workshop Journal* 13 (Spring 1982): 77–93; idem, "The Maiden Tribute," chap. 3 in this book.

32. Asa Briggs, *Victorian Cities* (New York and Evanston: Harper and Row, 1963), chap. 8.

33. Gavin Weightman and Steve Humphries, *The Making of Modern London, 1815–1914* (London: Sidgwick and Jackson, 1983).

34. Jones, *Outcast London*, pp. 12–16; chaps. 6, 16.

35. John Morley, quoted in P. J. Waller, *Town, City, and Nation: England, 1850–1914* (Oxford: Oxford University Press, 1983), p. 58; *Daily News*, 1911, quoted in ibid., p. 53.

36. Derek Brewer, Introduction to Henry James, *The Princess Cassamassima* (Harmondsworth, Middlesex: Penguin, 1986), p. 25.

37. James, quoted in ibid., p. 24. Domestic unrest was thus regarded from an imperial perspective; the Home Office and Scotland Yard were rigidly intolerant of lawless political activities, "because imperial responsibilities immediately lent overseas significance to domestic unrest." Ford and Harrison, *One Hundred Years Ago*, p. 178.

38. Greenwood, *Wilds of London*, p. 350; Jerry White, *The Rothschild Buildings: Life in a Tenement Block, 1887–1920* (London: Routledge and Kegan Paul, 1980), pp. 10, 131; John Davis, "Radical Clubs and London Politics," in *Metropolis London: Histories and Representations since 1800*, ed. David Feldman and Gareth Stedman Jones (London and New York: Routledge, 1989), pp. 113–14.

39. David Cannadine, "The Context, Performance, and Meaning of Ritual: The British Monarchy and the Invention of Tradition, c. 1820–1977," in *The Invention of Tradition*, ed. Eric Hobsbawm and Terence Ranger (Cambridge: Cambridge University Press, 1983), pp. 101–65; Thomas Richards, "The Image of

Victoria in the Year of Jubilee," *Victorian Studies* 30, no. 4 (Autumn 1987): 7–32; White, *Rothschild Buildings*, pp. 133–37.

40. Jones, *Outcast London;* P. J. Keating, "Fact and Fiction in the East End," in *The Victorian City,* ed. Dyos and Wolff, 2:585–602; E. P. Hennock, "Poverty and Social Theory in England: The Experience of the Eighteen-Eighties," *Social History* (January 1976): 67–91; George R. Sims, selections from *How the Poor Live,* reprinted in Keating, *Into Unknown England,* p. 85.

41. Frank Mort, *Dangerous Sexualities: Medico-moral Politics in England since 1830* (London and New York: Routledge and Kegan Paul, 1988), p. 15; Anthony S. Wohl, *Endangered Lives: Public Health in Victorian Britain* (Cambridge: Harvard University Press, 1983); Ellen Ross, Introduction, *Love and Labor in Outcast London* (New York: Oxford University Press, forthcoming); Sims, *How the Poor Live,* pp. 69, 68, 77; Jones, *Outcast London,* p. 282.

42. Andrew Mearns, selections from "The Bitter Cry of Outcast London," in Keating, *Into Unknown England,* pp. 94, 97, 92. See also A. J. Wohl's introduction to *The Bitter Cry of Outcast London* (New York: Humanities Press, 1970); Jones, *Outcast London,* pp. 222–23, 282–83.

43. Alan Palmer, *The East End: Four Centuries of London Life* (London: John Murray, 1898).

44. Hennock, "Poverty and Social Theory," pp. 67, 68; Beatrice Webb, quoted in Jones, *Outcast London,* p. 285.

45. Quoted in David Ascoli, *The Queen's Peace: The Origins and Development of the Metropolitan Police 1829–1879* (London: Hamish Hamilton, 1979), p. 161; Octavia Hill, quoted in Ford and Harrison, *One Hundred Years Ago,* p. 196.

46. W. T. Stead, "Government by Journalism," quoted in Michael I. Friedland, *The Trials of Israel Lipski* (London: Macmillan, 1984), p. 127.

47. Keating, "Fact and Fiction," pp. 589–93; James Greenwood, *Undercurrents,* quoted in White, *Rothschild Buildings,* p. 7. While acknowledging that the 1880s witnessed a renewed concern over poverty in the midst of plenty, some historians have disputed the extent to which the political crisis actually provoked innovative social perspectives on poverty: whether collectivist approaches to poverty superseded individualist perspectives, or racialist theories of the urban poor fully displaced "older" moralized interpretations. See, for instance, E. P. Hennock's dispute with Jones's *Outcast London,* in his "Poverty and Social Theory."

48. See Ed Cohen, "Poor London" (unpublished paper, 1991).

49. Keating, "Fact and Fiction," p. 595; Charles Booth, "The Inhabitants of Tower Hamlets (School Board Division), their Condition and Occupations," *Journal of the Royal Statistical Society* 50 (1887); idem, "The Condition of the People of East London and Hackney, 1887," ibid. 51 (1888); idem, *Life and Labour of the People in London,* vol. 1, *East London* (London: Williams and Northgate, 1889); vol. 2, (London, 1891); idem, *Life and Labour of the People in London,* 17 vols. [1st series: Poverty in 4 vols.; 2d series: Industry in 5 vols.; 3d series: Religious Influence in 7 vols.; final volume: *Notes on Social Influences and Conclusions*] (1889–1903; rpt., 3d ed., New York: Macmillan, 1902–3). For Booth's influence,

see Jones, *Outcast London,* and Hugh McLeod, *Class and Religion in Late-Victorian London* (London: Croom Helm, 1974).

50. For both Hennock ("Poverty and Social Theory," p. 70) and David Rubinstein, in "Booth and Hyndman," *Bulletin of the Society for the Study of Labour History* 16 (Spring 1968), 22–24, the assumption that Hyndman's claim precipated Booth's inquiry lacks any evidence other than Hyndman's recall, twenty-five years later. M. S. Simey and M. B. Simey were the first to accept Hyndman's claim: *Charles Booth, Social Scientist* (Oxford: Oxford University Press, 1960), pp. 68–70; it is repeated by Jones, *Outcast London,* p. 306, and others.

51. Booth, "The Inhabitants of Tower Hamlets," p. 375.

52. Ibid.

53. Booth, *Life and Labour,* 3d ed., 1st ser., vol. 1: *East, Central and South London,* p. 39.

54. Ibid., p. 170.

55. See Paul Thompson, *Socialists, Liberals, and Labour: The Struggle for London 1885–1914* (London: Routledge and Kegan Paul, 1967), chap. 1; Dina Copelman, "Where Boundaries Blur: Class and Construction of Gender Identity" (unpublished essay, 1991). According to tables of socioeconomic classification presented in Jones, *Outcast London,* appendix 2, p. 387, 23.5 percent of males over ten in 1861 belong to Class 1 (large employers, merchants, bankers, high officials in shipping and insurance, property owners, and the liberal professions) and Class 2 (small employers, small dealers, wholesalers, retailers, caterers, local government officials, teachers, entertainers, musicians, subordinate officers in insurance and church organizations, clerical occupations). This percentage increases to 25.6 in 1891, due to the increase in lower-middle-class occupations. The percentage of women who were property owners or employed in the middle-class occupations increased from 7.10 in 1861 to 10.6 in 1891.

56. E. P. Hennock, "The Measurement of Urban Poverty: From the Metropolis to the Nation, 1880–1920," *Economic History Review,* 2d ser., 40, no. 2 (1987): 210–12.

57. Asa Briggs, *Victorian Things* (Chicago: University of Chicago Press, 1989).

58. Charles Booth, quoted in Harold Pfautz, *Charles Booth on the City: Physical Pattern and Social Structure* (Chicago: University of Chicago Press, 1967), p. 85.

59. For Booth's relation to the "grand tradition of English empiricism," see Albert Fried and Richard Elman, Introduction, *Charles Booth's London: A Portrait of the Poor at the Turn of the Century Drawn from His "Life and Labour of the People of London"* (Harmondsworth, Middlesex: Penguin, 1971), p. 26. See also, Raymond Williams, *The Country and the City* (New York: Oxford University Press, 1973), p. 222; Booth, "The Inhabitants of Tower Hamlets," p. 327; Booth, "The Condition of the People," p. 278.

60. Booth, "The Inhabitants of Tower Hamlets," p. 362; Booth, *Life and Labour,* 3d ed., 1st ser., 1:66.

61. Quoted in Briggs, "The Human Aggregate," in *Victorian City,* ed. Dyos and Wolff, 1:93–94.

62. Booth, *Life and Labour,* 3d ed., 1st ser., 1:66–68; Fried and Elman, Introduction, p. 21.

63. As E. P. Hennock observes ("Poverty and Social Theory," pp. 77–78), rough versus respectable was a social division already conventionalized by the mid-Victorian period. For a fuller discussion, see Peter Bailey, "Will the Real Bill Banks Please Stand Up?" *Journal of Social History* 12 (1979): 336–53, and Ellen Ross, "'Not the Sort That Would Sit on the Doorstep': Respectability in Pre–World War I London Neighbourhoods," *International Labor and Working Class History* 27 (Spring 1985): 39–59. Patrick Joyce argues that after the Second Reform Bill, all sections of society evidenced a renewed interest in the language of class, but this "renewal of interest took the form of a concern with divisions *within* as much as *between* classes, especially those of a moral-occupational sort." Such categories of rough vs. respectable, or "labour aristocrat" were "rhetorical" rather than "economic" constructs. *Visions of the People: Industrial England and the Question of Class, 1840–1914* (Cambridge: Cambridge University Press, 1991), p. 57.

64. Charles Booth Manuscripts, London School of Economics, series B, vol. 352 ("Police and Publican").

65. Ellen Ross, "'Fierce Questions and Taunts': Married Life in Working-Class London," *Feminist Studies* 8, no. 3 (Fall 1982): 575–76.

66. H. Lllewellyn Smith, "Influx of Population," in Booth, *London Life and Labour,* 3d ed., 1st ser., 3:110.

67. David Englander, "Booth's Jews: The Presentation of Jews and Judaism in *Life and Labour of the People in London,*" *Victorian Studies* 32, no. 4 (Summer 1989): 551–71; Llewellyn Smith, quoted in ibid., p. 555; ibid., p. 565.

68. In his *East London* Booth defended this masquerade as "a touch of colour . . . illuminating the ways of life," an opportunity to gain sufficient insight "into the lives of these people," to counter the "false descriptions of them in the books we read," for the most part as "unlike the truth as are descriptions of aristocratic life in the books they read." Booth, *Life and Labour,* 3d ed., 1st ser., 1:151.

69. Deborah Nord, *The Apprenticeship of Beatrice Webb* (Ithaca: Cornell University Press, 1989), p. 154.

70. "For three separate periods, I have taken up quarters, each time for several weeks, where I was not known, and as a lodger have shared the lives of people who would figure in my schedules as belonging to classes C, D, and E." Booth, *Life and Labour,* 3d ed., 1st ser., 1:158–61; idem, "An Account of Some Houses and Families I have Lodged with—Taken from My Notebooks," reprinted in Mary Macaulay Booth, *Charles Booth: A Memoir* (London: Macmillan, 1918), pp. 105–30.

71. Booth, *Life and Labour,* 3d ed., 1st ser., 1:158.

72. These qualities, according to Ellen Ross, were distinctive of female urban explorers rather than of their male counterparts. See her *Love and Labor in Outcast London: Motherhood, 1870–1918* (New York: Oxford University Press, forthcoming).

73. Booth also acknowledged the social authority of the landlady over her tenants. Class relations between lodger and landlady, he argued, were not very different from those between village and manor. In a spirit of noblesse oblige, the

landlady dispensed patronage, charity, as well as rebukes, all with a "keen sense of social responsibility." Booth, *Life and Labour*, 3d ed., 1st. ser., 1:159.

74. Mary Booth, *Charles Booth*, quoted in Fried and Elman, *Charles Booth's London*, p. 21; Nord, *The Apprenticeship*, pp. 157–59; Beatrice Webb, quoted in ibid., p. 159; Belinda Norman Butler, *Victorian Aspirations: The Life and Labour of Charles and Mary Booth* (London: George Allen and Unwin, 1972).

75. Booth, *Life and Labour*, 3d ed., 1st ser., 1:157.

76. Adrian Poole, *Gissing in Context* (Totowa, N.J.: Rowman and Littlefield, 1975), p. 42.

77. Ibid., p. 21; Stephen Heath, "Psychopathia Sexualis: Stevenson's *Strange Case*," in Colin MacCabe, ed., *Futures for English* (Manchester: Manchester University Press, 1988): 94. Women function as the center of an "erotic triangle," where the bonds between the two male rivals were more intense than the bonds linking either of the rivals to the female object of desire; the prostitute could serve as a displaced object of homoerotic desire. This triangle often masked a suppressed, repudiated, homoeroticism. Sedgwick, *Between Men*, 21–27.

78. These female protagonists differ from the more adventurous sort found in James's problem novels of the 1880s, such as *The Bostonians* (1886; rpt., Harmondsworth, Middlesex: Penguin, 1984) and *The Princess Cassimassima* (1886; rpt., Harmondsworth, Middlesex: Penguin, 1977).

Chapter Two

1. John Davis, "Radical Clubs and London Politics," in *Metropolis London: Histories and Representations since 1800,* ed. David Feldman and Gareth Stedman Jones (London and New York: Routledge, 1989), p. 107; Gwyn Williams, Introduction, in John Gorman, *Banner Bright: An Illustrated History of the Banners of the Trade Union Movement* (London: Allen Lane, 1973), p. 12; Walter Southgate, *That's The Way It Was: A Working-Class Autobiography, 1890–1950* (London: New Clarion Press, 1982), p. 103.

2. David Vincent, *Bread, Knowledge and Freedom: A Study of Nineteenth-Century Working-Class Autobiography* (London and New York: Methuen, 1982), p. 175. See also Hugh McLeod, *Class and Religion in Late-Victorian London* (London: Croom Helm, 1974), and Eric Hobsbawm, "The Labour Aristocracy," in his *Labouring Men* (London: Weidenfeld and Nicholson, 1964).

3. "Travelling by workman's tram from Queen's Road, Battersea, to Waterloo, I was at work [at the Tilbury Docks] by six o'clock. Every weekend I was busy on propaganda work, usually three times on the Sunday—twice in the open air and once indoors. Often the round would be near Bricklayer's Arms, Old Kent Road, at 11 a.m., Victoria in the East End, 3:30 p.m., and indoors at some branch meeting or other public gathering in the evening, rarely reaching home before 11 p.m., to be up at 5 o'clock next morning." Tom Mann, *Tom Mann's Memoirs* (1923; rpt., London: Cox and Wyman, 1967) pp. 25–26.

4. Frederick Rogers, *Labour, Life, and Literature* (London: Smith, Elder, 1913), p. 43. On literacy and workingmen, see Carolyn Steedman, *The Radical Soldier's Tale* (London: Routledge, 1988).

5. Regenia Gagnier, "Social Atoms: Working-Class Autobiography, Subjectivity, and Gender," *Victorian Studies* 30 (Spring 1987): 337. This localized perspective was in part tied to the limited distance workingmen were likely to travel through the city, in search of work. Skilled workers like Mann (approximately 40 percent of the London male labor-force) might be connected to a trade association that guided them to employment in other parts of London. However, unskilled laborers (25 percent of the labor market) could not afford transportation and were generally tied to an area within walking distance from their house, and were thus dependent on local networks for work opportunities. Gareth Stedman Jones, *Outcast London: A Study in the Relationship between Classes in Victorian Society* (Oxford: Clarendon Press, 1971), p. 66. McLeod (*Class and Religion*, p. 9) estimates that 70 percent of the population was made up of the families of manual workers, another 20 percent of the families of shopkeepers, small employers, shop assistants, teachers, and clerks.

6. Jacqueline Bratton, *The Victorian Popular Ballad* (London: Macmillan, 1975), p. 91; Raphael Samuel, ed., *East End Underworld: Chapters in the Life of Arthur Harding* (London, Boston, and Henley: Routledge and Kegan Paul, 1981); Frederick Rogers, *Labour, Life, and Literature;* George Acorn, *One of the Multitude* (London: Heinemann, 1911); Southgate, *That's the Way It Was,* p. 34.

7. Peter Bailey, "Ally Sloper's Half Holiday: Comic Art in the 1880s," *History Workshop Journal* 16 (Autumn, 1983): 4–31; idem, "Champagne Charlie: Performance and Ideology in the Music-Hall Swell Song," in J. S. Bratton, ed., *Music Hall: Performance and Style* (Milton Keynes: Open University Press, 1986). Although young workingmen were more likely than their female counterparts to present themselves in the galleries of West End theaters of variety, on the whole they were more apt to preside "in the Gods" over suburban musical halls.

8. Ellen Moers, *The Dandy: Brummel to Beerbohm,* quoted in Bailey, "Ally Sloper's Half Holiday," p. 13. Two events provoked the literary representation of this new urban type: the extension of the franchise in 1867 to the top echelon of workingmen and the emergence of new patterns of consumption and popular entertainment among the better-paid youth of London's working population. Gareth Stedman Jones, "The 'Cockney' and the Nation, 1780–1988," in Feldman and Jones, *Metropolis London,* pp. 315, 289, 290.

9. Bailey, "Ally Sloper," p. 17.

10. Peter Bailey, "Will the Real Bill Banks Please Stand Up? Towards a Role Analysis of Mid-Victorian Working-Class Respectability," *Journal of Social History* (1979): 336–53; Gagnier, "Social Atoms," p. 341.

11. See Ellen Ross, *Love and Labor in Outcast London: Motherhood, 1870–1918* (New York: Oxford University Press, forthcoming.); "We All Go to Work but Father," in Peter Davison, ed., *Songs of the British Music Hall: Compiled and Edited with a Critical History of the Songs and Their Times* (New York: Oak Publications, 1971), pp. 208–15; Stan Shipley, "Tom Causer of Bermondsey: A Boxer Hero of the 1890s," *History Workshop Journal* 15 (Spring 1983): 28–49; Peter Bailey, "Champagne Charlie," p. 69.

12. Bailey, "Ally Sloper," p. 15. As Jones observes ("The Cockney," p. 274), in

the early 1890s the coster supplanted the swell as the embodiment of cockneydom, continuing the theme of picturesqueness and cheerfulness. Like the class-marginal sham swell, the cockney was not a "maker or producer of things."

13. Mary P. Ryan, *Women in Public: Between Banners and Ballots, 1825–1880* (Baltimore: John Hopkins University Press, 1990), chap. 2.

14. Jane Traies, "Jones and the Working Girl: Class Marginality in Music-Hall Song, 1860–1900," in Bratton, *Music Hall,* p. 29; Peter Bailey, ed., *Music Hall: The Business of Pleasure* (Milton Keynes: Open University Press, 1986), p. xvii.

15. Bailey, "Champagne Charlie," p. 65. Later male impersonators like Vesta Tilley were kinder to the gent; by emulating the dress and privileges of men, they even acknowledged male superiority.

16. The "struggle over the breeches" was a well-entrenched tradition of popular culture. See Anna Clark, "Womanhood and Manhood in the Transition from Plebeian to Working-Class Culture: London, 1780–1845" (Ph.D. diss., Rutgers University, 1988). Jenny Hill, "whose discerning audience was female," centered her act "around a body of material related to the lives of working women" and presented herself as a "strong minded female speaking her mind about the men." J. S. Bratton, "Jenny Hill: Sex and Sexism in the Victorian Music Hall," in Bratton, *Music Hall,* pp. 103–4; *Era,* quoted in ibid., p. 104. In female singers' depiction of the swell, "the clerks, shop assistants and commercial travellers . . . are not simply the butt of satire, but are represented with sympathy and understanding." Traies, "Jones and the Working Girl," p. 47.

17. "Two Lovely Black Eyes," *PMG,* 8 Feb. 1887. The *PMG* reviewer recommended Coburn's realistic performance to strangers to London "who wish to make the acquaintance of a London rough of the Sikes type done to the life."

18. Traies, "Jones and the Working Girl," p. 3. See also Henry James's assessment of the shopgirl, in the person of the "muse of Cockneyism," Millicent Henning: "She stood on her own feet, and she stood very firm." James, *The Princess Cassimassima* (1886; rpt., Harmondsworth, Middlesex: Penguin, 1977), p. 93.

19. Peter Bailey, "Parasexuality and Glamour: The Victorian Barmaid as Cultural Prototype," *Gender and History* 2 (Summer 1990): 1–2, 35, 32.

20. Richard Sennett, *The Fall of Public Man* (Cambridge: Cambridge University Press, 1973), p. 23; Roland Barthes, "Semiology and the Urban," trans. and rpt. in M. Gottdiener and Alexandros Ph. Lagopoulos, eds. *The City and the Sign: An Introduction to Urban Semiotics* (New York: Columbia University Press, 1982), 87–98; Elizabeth Bennett Kubek, "London as Text: Eighteenth-Century Women Writers and Reading the City," *Women's Studies* 17 (1990): 303–39.

21. Leonore Davidoff, *The Best Circles,* p. 67. Quoted in Lisa Tickner, *Spectacle of Women: Imagery of the Suffrage Campaign 1907–1914* (Chicago: University of Chicago Press, 1988), p. 311n.

22. Charles Baudelaire, quoted in Janet Wolff, "The Invisible *Flaneuse:* Women and the Literature of Modernity," *Theory, Culture and Society* 2, no. 3 (1985): 39; Griselda Pollock, "Vicarious Excitements: *London: A Pilgrimage,* by Gustave Doré and Blanchard Jerrold, 1872," *New Formations* 2 (Spring 1988): 39; Walter Besant, *East London* (1901; rpt., New York: Garland, 1980), p. 15.

23. Rosalind H. Williams, *Dream Worlds: Mass Consumption in Late*

Nineteenth-Century France (Berkeley and Los Angeles: University of California Press, 1982), p. 3; *Harrods 1849–1949: A Story of Achievement* (London: Harrods, 1949), p. 23.

24. Alison Adburgham, *Shopping in Style: London from the Restoration to Edwardian Elegance* (London: Thames and Hudson, 1979), pp. 142–44; W. Hamish Fraser, *The Coming of the Mass Market, 1850–1914* (London: Macmillan, 1981), p. 131; Colin Ford and Brian Harrison, eds., *One Hundred Years Ago: Britain in the 1880s in Words and Photographs* (Cambridge, Mass.: Harvard University Press, 1983), p. 117; Adburgham, *Shopping in Style*, p. 144; Alison Adburgham, *Liberty's: A Biography of a Shop* (London: George Allen and Unwin, 1975). Liberty's was even entrusted with organizing an "Indian Village" in Battersea Park in November 1885 (ibid., pp. 59–60).

25. Adburgham, *Shopping in Style*, p. 159. For Molly Thomas and her mother, a morning's shopping was all "we could manage for the day," because most stores lacked restaurants and "conveniences for toilet, however dire the need." In 1884, the Ladies Lavatory Company opened up its first establishment in Oxford Circus, but few such facilities were constructed and ladies worried about being seen entering. Without these facilities, female travelers continued to experience "conventional disabilities" not constraining men, who "may and can . . . make themselves at home anywhere." Quoted in ibid., p. 141. For early developments of the culture of shopping, see Neil McKendrick, "The Commercialization of Fashion," in Neil McKendrick, John Brewer, J. H. Plumb, *The Birth of a Consumer Society: The Commercialization of Eighteenth-Century England* (Bloomington: Indiana University Press, 1985).

26. Richard Wightman Fox and T. J. Jackson Lears, *The Culture of Consumption: Critical Essays in American History, 1880–1980* (New York: Pantheon, 1983), p. xiv; Jean Christophe Agnew, "The Consuming Vision of Henry James," in ibid., pp. 67–100; Rachel Bowlby, *Just Looking: Consumer Culture in Dreiser, Gissing, and Zola* (London and New York: Methuen, 1985), p. 20; William R. Leach, "Transformations in a Culture of Consumption: Women and Department Stores, 1890–1925," *Journal of American History* 7, no. 2 (September 1984): 319–42 (passage quoted on p. 337).

27. Lady Jeune, "The Ethics of Shopping," *Fortnightly Review* (January 1895): 125–32.

28. *Women's Gazette* 3 (July 1878): 100 (thanks to Anna Davin for this citation); Suzanna Shonfield, *The Precariously Privileged: A Professional Family in Victorian London* (Oxford: Oxford University Press, 1987), p. 44; M. V. Hughes, *A London Child of the 1870s* (Oxford: Oxford University Press, 1977), p. 46.

29. Lynda Nead, *Myths of Sexuality: Representations of Women in Victorian Britain* (Oxford: Basil Blackwell, 1988), p. 180. When repeal campaigners complained that police wrongfully accused respectable women of being common prostitutes, defenders of regulation insisted that it was always possible to tell who was and was not a prostitute, by the way she looked: "it was more a question of mannerism than anything else," insisted one witness before a parliamentary committee. Quoted in ibid., p. 102. See also Lisa Tickner, *The Spectacle of Women: Imagery of the Suffrage Campaign 1907–14* (Chicago: University of Chicago Press, 1988), p.

151; Mariana Valverde, "The Love of Finery: Fashion and the Fallen Woman in Nineteenth-Century Social Discourse," *Victorian Studies* 32, no. 2 (Winter 1989): 168–88; Eric Trudgill, "Prostitution and Paterfamilias," in *The Victorian City: Images and Reality*, ed. H. J. Dyos and Michael Wolff, 2 vols. (London: Routledge and Kegan Paul, 1973), 2:696.

30. On the "Girl of the Period," see Nead, *Myths of Sexuality*, pp. 181, 180. On the professional and literary man's view of the market as "feminine," see Elaine M. Hadley, "Melodramatic Tactics: The Social Function of the Melodramatic Mode, 1800–1885" (Ph.D. diss., Johns Hopkins University, 1991), chap. 5.

31. Shonfield, *Precariously Privileged*, pp. 46, 51; Jeannette Marshall, quoted in ibid., p. 51; Elizabeth Robins, *Both Sides of the Curtain* (London: Heinemann, 1940), p. 167; C. S. Peel, quoted in David Rubinstein, *Before the Suffragettes: Women's Emancipation in the 1890s* (Brighton: Harvester Press, 1986), p. 76.

32. Marshall quoted in Shonfield, *Precariously Privileged*, p. 51; *Girl's Own Paper*, 6 December 1890.

33. Shonfield, *Precariously Privileged*, pp. 44, 50, 51.

34. Helena M. Swanwick, *I Have Been Young* (London: Victor Gollancz, 1935), p. 82; *Queen* (London), 6 September 1879, p. 207 (thanks to Anna Davin for this citation); Robins, *Both Sides*, p. 164. Lady Grey recounted how she discovered a strange man looking in at her at her cottage window. "What did he do?" "He looked at me." "What did you do?" "I looked at him." "And what happened?" "He went away." Quoted in Robins, *Both Sides*, p. 166. "There has been only one Dorothy Grey," insisted Robins, "but she must have given a strength of fearlessness to many" (ibid.).

35. Martha Vicinus, *Independent Women: Work and Community for Single Women 1850–1920* (Chicago: University of Chicago Press, 1985), p. 220; Margot Asquith, *The Autobiography of Margot Asquith*, ed. and intro. Mark Bonham Carter (1962; rpt., London: Methuen, 1985), p. 45. Actually, Asquith was freer and more anonymous in the East End than in the West End, where she was recognized and addressed (by a duchess and her footman) while window-shopping. Asquith never mentions any problems of being "annoyed" in her excursions through London, in good part because such interference with her freedom would violate her presentation of self as fearless and independent. In any case, she and her sisters enjoyed considerably more freedom of movement than most upper-class girls, who were more strictly chaperoned. Asquith's parents, she explained, had allowed her siblings to grow up unrestrained—"we were wild children," she explained, "and, left to ourselves, had the time of our lives" (ibid., p. 16). Mary Gladstone blamed Asquith's parents for gross dereliction of duty in bringing daughters up, "never dreaming any kind of protection or guard was necessary, expecting them to run about London all by themselves." Quoted in Pat Jalland, *Women, Marriage, and Politics, 1860–1914* (Oxford: Clarendon Press, 1986), p. 104.

36. Asquith, *Autobiography*, p. 42; Mark Bonham Carter, in ibid., p. xiii; Asquith, in ibid., pp. 43, 44.

37. Patricia Hollis, *Ladies Elect: Women in English Local Government 1865–1914* (Oxford: Clarendon Press, 1987), p. 11.

38. Octavia Hill, quoted in Hollis, *Ladies Elect*, p. 13.

39. Anne Summers, "A Home from Home—Women's Philanthropic Work in the Nineteenth Century," in *Fit Work for Women,* ed. Sandra Burman (New York: St. Martin's Press, 1979), pp. 33–64; p. 53; C. E. Edmund Maurice, *Life of Octavia Hill as Told in Her Letters* (London: Macmillan, 1913); Charles L. Mowat, *The Charity Organization Society, 1869–1913: Its Ideas and Works* (London: Methuen, 1961); A. S. Wohl, "Octavia Hill and the Homes of the London Poor," *Journal of British Studies* 10 (1971): 105–31; Nancy Boyd, *Three Victorian Women Who Changed Their World* (New York: Oxford University Press, 1982).

40. Octavia Hill, *District Visiting* (London: Longman, 1877), p. 6; Ellen Chase, *Tenant Friends in Old Deptford* (London: Williams and Norgate, 1929), p. 125. Octavia Hill, "A More Excellent Way of Charity," in *Our Common Land and Other Short Essays* (London: Macmillan, 1877), p. 75. As Eileen Yeo has observed, female philanthropists exhibited the hectoring, punishing, and protective side of mothering towards the poor: treating the adult poor as childlike, in need of protection, as against the gentle nurturing face of mother-love that they directed to women of their own class (unpublished paper, 1987).

41. Anthony S. Wohl, *Endangered Lives: Public Health in Victorian Britain* (Cambridge: Harvard University Press, 1983), pp. 36–38, 67–69, 78–79; F. K. Prochaska, "Body and Soul: Bible Nurses and the Poor in Victorian London," *Historical Research* 60 (1987): 336–48; Frank Mort, *Dangerous Sexualities: Medico-Moral Politics in England since 1830* (London and New York: Routledge and Kegan Paul, 1987), pp. 53–60.

42. Mort, *Dangerous Sexualities,* p. 57; Margaret McMillan, *The Life of Rachel McMillan* (London: J. M. Dent and Sons, 1927), p. 103; Hill, "A More Excellent Way"; idem, *Open Spaces for Deptford . . . An Appeal* (1892); Margaret Harkness, *In Darkest London,* quoted in Deborah Nord, "The Social Explorer as Anthropologist: Victorian Travellers among the Urban Poor," in *Visions of the Modern City: Essays in History, Art, and Literature,* ed. William Sharpe and Leonard Wallock (Baltimore: Johns Hopkins University Press, 1987), p. 126.

43. Hollis, *Ladies Elect,* p. 13.

44. Carol Dyhouse, *Feminism and the Family in England 1880–1939* (Oxford: Blackwell, 1989), pp. 57–64, 74–81; Walkowitz, chap. 5 below; Polly Beals, "Fabian Feminism: Gender, Politics, and Culture, 1880–1930" (Ph.D. diss., Rutgers University, 1989), chap. 2.

45. Helen Denby, "Marriage in East London," in Bernard Bosanquet, ed., *Aspects of the Social Problem* (London: Macmillan, 1895), and the "Children of Working London," quoted in Ellen Ross, Introduction, *Love and Labor in Outcast London,* pp. 14, 15. In advancing a feminine perspective on poverty, late-Victorian charity workers were articulating a tension and contradiction between male professionals and female philanthropists already articulated by Ellen Ranyard in the 1850s: when Ranyard insisted that Bible Women gained their knowledge of the poor in "a womanly way," she implicitly challenged the routine method of male investigators supported by statutory coercion and the apparatus of the state. Quoted in Mort, *Dangerous Sexualities,* p. 57.

46. When female rent collectors took the side of abused wives, husbands vehemently protested. In Katherine Buildings, one man gave notice: "me and the missus

can't have a row in any peace. All the neighbors come a-knocking and a-fussing at the door and a-carrying their tales to you ladies," he told Margaret Nevinson. Margaret Nevinson, *Life's Fitful Fever, A Volume of Memories* (London: A. and C. Black, 1926), p. 91.

47. Ross, Introduction, pp. 14, 15.

48. Norman MacKenzie and Jeanne MacKenzie, eds., *The Diary of Beatrice Webb*, vol. 1: *Glitter Without and Darkness Within* (Cambridge, Mass.: Belknap Press, 1982), p. 186; Webb, quoted in Deborah Epstein Nord, *The Apprenticeship of Beatrice Webb* (Amherst, Mass.: University of Massachusetts Press, 1985), p. 159.

49. "A Lady Resident," "Sketch of Life in Buildings," *Life and Labour of the People in London*, 17 vols., ed. Charles Booth (London: Macmillan, 1902–4; rpt., New York: AMS Press, 1970), 1st series, 3:45. The lady resident's "finely honed eavesdropping," observes Ellen Ross, "suggests the importance of gossip in the building's ecology. In one day, a gossip network wrongfully maligned one hard-working matron as lazy, detailed the bad temper of another woman's daughter, but alerted the landing to the serious illness of a neighbor in need of assistance." Ellen Ross, "Survival Networks: Women's Neighborhood Sharing in London Before World War I," *History Workshop Journal* 15 (Spring 1983): 10.

50. Webb, *Diary*, 1:137.

51. Vicinus, *Independent Women*, chap. 1.

52. Chase, *Tenant Friends*, pp. 57, 61, 106; Nevinson, *Life's Fitful Fever*, p. 82.

53. Chase, *Tenant Friends*, pp. 10, 25; Nevinson, *Life's Fitful Fever*, p. 29; Beatrice Webb, *My Apprenticeship* (1926; rpt., Cambridge: Cambridge University Press, 1979), p. 264.

54. Nevinson, *Life's Fitful Fever*, p. 91; Chase, *Tenant Friends*, p. 106.

55. Living in rooms, under the control of a central office and superintendent, the district nurse was free of the tedium and disciplinary regime of hospital work.

56. "One Who Has Tried It," "Sick Nursing," *WPP*, 5 Jan. 1889, p. 6; Mrs. Humphry [Mary Arnold] Ward, *Marcella* (1894; rpt., New York: Viking Penguin, 1985), p. 353; Nurse William at the parish house of St. Matthew's Church, Bethnal Green, Booth Manuscripts, Parish Notes, district 9 (1900).

57. Barnett's settler, observes Martha Vicinus, possessed qualities similar to those of the ideal Victorian woman. Observers often noted Barnett's feminine qualities: Beatrice Webb regarded Barnett as being like a "strong woman" and his wife as the "more masculine of the two." Quoted in Vicinus, *Independent Women*, p. 216.

58. H. O. R. Barnett, *Canon Barnett: His Life, Work, and Friends*, 2 vols. (Boston and New York: Houghton Mifflin, 1919), 2:42.

59. Ibid., 2:75, 76; Seth Koven, "From Rough Lads to Hooligans: Boy Life, National Culture and Social Reform," in Andrew Parker et al., eds., *Nationalisms and Sexualities* (London: Routledge, forthcoming); Alan Crawford, *C. R. Ashbee, Architect, Designer, and Romantic Socialist* (New Haven: Yale University Press, 1985), p. 85.

60. George Lansbury, quoted in Vicinus, *Independent Women*, p. 215; Koven, "From Rough Lads."

61. Octavia Hill, quoted in Wohl, "Octavia Hill," p. 119; Carolyn Heilbrun, "Sacrificed to Art," *Women's Review of Books* 5, no. 12 (September 1988): 5.

62. "Aesculapius Scalpel," *St Bernard's: The Romance of a Medical Student* (London: Swan Sonnenschein, 1887).

63. Walter Besant, *All Sorts and Conditions of Men: An Impossible Story* (New York: Harper and Row, 1929). The Palace of Delight actually inspired a major philanthropic undertaking: the construction of a People's Palace (1887), a center of culture for the East End.

64. Walter Besant, *The Revolt of Man* (London: Collins, 1887).

65. Beatrice Webb to Richard Potter, quoted in Webb, *Diary,* 1:142; Nord, *The Apprenticeship of Beatrice Webb,* chaps. 5 and 6; Vicinus, *Independent Women,* chap. 6.

66. Walkowitz, "Dangerous Sexualities"; "The Manly Young Woman," *WPP,* 26 Jan. 1889, p. 5; "Who are the World's Greatest Women?" *PMG,* 30 Nov. 1888. See Anna Clark, "Womanhood and Manhood," chap. 5.

67. "The Glorified Spinster," *Macmillan's Magazine* 58 (1888): 374, 371, 373. Webb paraphrased the article in her diary: " 'A new race of women not looking for or expecting marriage.' 'Self-dependent, courageous and cool-headed.' Ah poor things." Webb, *Diary,* 1:261. Here she was evoking her own sadness at choosing a craft and career instead of love and marriage with politician Joseph Chamberlain, whom she believed would have suppressed her individuality and intellectual ambition.

68. "The Glorified Spinster," p. 372.

69. M. V. Hughes, *A London Girl of the 1880s* (London: Oxford University Press, 1977), p. 18; Sara Burstall, *Retrospect and Prospect: Sixty Years of Women's Education* (London: Longmans, 1911), p. 24; Swanwick, *I Have Been Young,* pp. 16, 73.

70. They have also noted the link between the provision of higher education and "the emergence of a 'women's industry' [teaching], complete with discriminatory wages and for the most part controlled by men." Rita McWilliams-Tullberg, quoted in Joyce Senders Pederson, *The Reform of Girls' Secondary and Higher Education* (New York and London: Garland, 1987), p. vii.

71. "The Glorified Spinster," p. 55.

72. Richard Allen Soloway, *Birth Control and the Population Question* (Chapel Hill: University of North Carolina Press, 1982), pp. 140, 141. According to Ellen Ross (*Love and Labor,* table 2.2), 30 percent of women residing in Hampstead in 1881, aged 40–59, were unmarried, as compared to 7 percent of the same age group in Bethnal Green.

73. Deborah Epstein Nord, " 'Neither Pairs Nor Odds': Beatrice Webb, Margaret Harkness, Amy Levy, and the Promise of Female Community," *Signs* 15, no. 4 (Summer 1990): 733–54; Walkowitz, chap. 5 below.

74. In addition, newspaper articles were continually interviewing and heralding the singular accomplishments of *the* female stockbroker, *the* female solicitor, *the* female landscape designer, etc. See, for example, "Miss Amy E. Bell, Stockbroker," *WPP,* 22 Dec. 1888; "Type-Writing Offices," ibid., 17 Nov. 1888.

75. "Report by Miss Collet on the Statistics of Employment of Women and Girls," *Parliamentary Papers* 1894, vols. 91–92, c.7564, p. 7.

76. Karl Pearson, "Sex and Socialism," in his *Ethic of Freethought* (London: A. and C. Black, 1888), p. 431.

77. Mary Lyndon Shanley, *Feminism, Marriage, and the Law in Victorian England, 1850–1895* (Princeton: Princeton University Press, 1989), p. 124; Alex Owen, *The Darkened Room: Women, Power, and Spiritualism in Late Victorian England* (London: Virago Press, 1989), p. 3; Pat Thane, "Late-Victorian Women," in Gourvish, ed., *Later Victorian Britain, 1867–1900* (Houndsmill, Basingstoke: Hampshire Macmillan Education, 1988); Hollis, *Ladies Elect*, p. 81. See also Anne Marie Turnball, " 'So Extremely like Parliament': The Work of the Women Members of the London School Board, 1870–1904," in *Sexual Dynamics of History*, ed. London Feminist History Group (London: Pluto, 1983), pp. 120–33. Of the twenty-nine women who served on the LSB from 1870 to 1904, four-fifths were single or widowed, most of them were anxious to advance the claims of women to public life as well as to help poor children (Hollis, *Ladies Elect*, p. 87), and a few were already national figures looking for elected office.

78. Hollis, *Ladies Elect*, chap. 2; Elizabeth Cobb to Karl Pearson, 17 Oct. 1885, Pearson Papers, University College, London, 663/1; "Women on Public Boards," *PMG*, 29 Jan. 1884.

79. Hollis, *Ladies Elect*, p. 100; Rosemary Van Arsdel, "Victorian Periodicals Yield Their Secrets: Florence Fenwick Miller's Three Campaigns for the London School Board," *Warwick's Year Studies in English*, 1985.

80. *Lady's Pictorial*, 17 Dec. 1881, quoted in Van Arsdel, "Victorian Periodicals."

81. Frederick Rogers, *Labour, Life, and Literature*, pp. 51, 72; Tom Mann, *Tom Mann's Memoirs*, p. 8; Beals, "Fabian Feminism," chap. 1; George Bernard Shaw, quoted in Michael Holroyd, *Bernard Shaw*, vol. 1: *The Search for Love* (New York: Random House, 1988), p. 177. Elizabeth Robins, writing in 1936, pronounced Besant a "spiritual mother" to the militant suffragettes. Her only difference was that, whereas the militants had no male ally apart from Pethick Lawrence, "even in her more quiet and personal forays," Besant "always had a man at her side." Robins, "Annie Besant" (unpublished paper, 1936), Robins Collection, New York University, series 7, folder 5. Besant was a "born actress," Shaw recalled. Quoted in Rosemary Dinnage, *Annie Besant* (London: Penguin, 1986), p. 78.

82. "Platform Women," *Nineteenth Century* 85 (March 1884): 411, 414; Webb, *Diary*, 1:223. Eleanor Marx registered a similar pleasure in the gift of speech: "I can move an audience." Quoted in Yvonne Kapp, *Eleanor Marx*, 2 vols. (New York: Pantheon, 1976), 2:105.

83. *WPP*, 16 March 1889.

84. Webb, *Diary*, 1:208.

85. "Chaperones," *WPP*, 2 March 1889, excerpted in E. S. Riemer and John Fout, eds., *European Women: A Documentary History* (New York: Schocken, 1980), p. 37.

86. Julia Mitchell to the editor, *WPP*, 9 March 1889; Elizabeth Robins,

"Annie Besant"; Edward Carpenter, quoted in Ruth First and Anne Scott, *Olive Schreiner* (New York: Schocken, 1980), p. 161.

87. Webb, *Diary,* 1:87; *PMG,* 8, 12 Oct. 1883. Annie Besant, smarting over the defection of Edward Aveling to Eleanor Marx, complained that Aveling "fell into the company of Bohemian elements, male and female, who flourish there." Quoted in Susan Budd, *Varieties of Unbelief: Atheists and Agnostics in English Society, 1850–1960* (London: Heinemann, 1977), p. 68.

88. See Norman MacKenzie and Jeanne MacKenzie, *The Fabians* (New York: Simon and Schuster, 1977); Beals, "Fabian Feminism," chap. 1.

89. Marion Meade, *Madame Blavatsky: The Woman Behind the Myth* (New York: G. P. Putnam's Sons, 1980), p. 277.

90. Annie Besant, quoted in Dinnage, *Anne Besant,* p. 67.

91. Jenny Marx to Eleanor Marx, in Olga Meier, ed., *The Daughters of Karl Marx: Family Correspondence 1866–1898* (New York: Harcourt Brace Jovanovich, 1982), p. 152; Nevinson, *Life's Fitful Fever,* p. 60; Hughes, *A London Girl,* p. 233.

92. Eleanor Marx to Jenny Marx, in Meier, *The Daughters,* p. 210; "Women Who Work," *PMG,* 1 April 1884; McMillan, *Rachel McMillan,* p. 34.

93. McMillan, *Rachel McMillan,* p. 35; George Gissing, *In The Year of the Jubilee,* quoted in Dina Copelman, MS (1989), pp. 61, 62.

94. Adburgham, *A Punch History of Manners and Modes, 1841–1940* (London: Hutchinson, 1961); "The Lives that Girton Girls Lead," *Tit-Bits,* 2 March 1888; George Romanes, "The Capacity of Women," *Nineteenth Century* 21 (May 1887): 654–67.

95. Lawrence Lerner, "Olive Schreiner and the Feminists," in Cherry Clayton, ed. *Olive Schreiner* (Johannesburg: McGraw-Hill, 1983).

96. *Maud: The Illustrated Diary of a Victorian Woman,* adapted by Flora Fraser, Introduction by Elizabeth Longford (London: Secker and Warburg, 1987), pp. 9, 157; Turnball, " 'So Extremely like Parliament'," p. 133; Kirsten Drotner, *English Children and Their Magazines, 1751–1945* (New Haven and London: Yale University Press, 1989), pp. 133, 151, 152; Nanette Mason, "How Working Girls Live in London," *Girl's Own Paper* 10 (1889): 422, 531, 763, 823.

97. David Rubinstein, *Before the Suffragettes* (Brighton: Harvester Press, 1986), pp. xiii, xiv.

98. In "Toilers of London," an 1888 investigation into working conditions for men and women, Margaret Harkness found "independent minded young women" among the matchbox makers, women of considerable "self-reliance" "who . . . do not find marriage *per se* attractive." These women may well have been the prototype for a "labour mistress," a "strong-minded spinster," in Harkness' novel *Captain Lobe,* who would "attend women's rights meetings if she knew where they took place." John Law [pseud.], *Captain Lobe: A Story of the Salvation Army* (London: Hodder and Stoughton, 1989).

99. Olive Anderson, "Women Preachers in Mid-Victorian Britain: Some Reflections on Feminism, Popular Religion, and Social Change," *Historical Journal* 12, no. 3 (1969): 482, 483.

100. "Rowdy Religion," *Saturday Review* (31 May 1884): 700; ibid., "Dancing Dervishes," 61 (26 June 1886): 873. The *Saturday Review,* for instance, condemned the Army for its street disorders and "shameless alliance between quackery and hysterics," provoking disgust on the part of "all decent and self-respecting people." Clergymen roundly condemned the Army for disrupting the patriarchal and sexual order of the family: parents complained "of the bonds of filial obedience being weakened and immorality [resulting] from the meetings in which the young mingle and excitement runs high."

101. "Women who Work," *PMG*, 2 May 1884; Josephine Butler, "Catherine Booth," *Contemporary Review* (November 1890): 648. Butler acknowledged, however, that the marks of class still persisted (working-class women were less mutable than their female counterparts who masqueraded down): "As a rule," she concluded, "the manners of the Salvation Lasses are beautiful, in spite of occasional h's, provincial accents, and other such defects."

102. Mrs. General Booth, "Women as Preachers," *PMG*, 31 Jan. 1886.

103. Pamela Walker, " 'Pulling the Devil's Kingdom Down': Gender and Popular Culture in the Salvation Army, 1865–1895" (Ph.D. diss., Rutgers University, 1991). I am grateful to Walker for all her many insights into the cultural strategies of the Salvation Army.

104. Robert Sandall, *The History of the Salvation Army* (New York: Nelson, 1950), vol. 2, p. 14. Kate Shepherd, another female "preacheress," adopted a similar strategy: renowned for her "boisterously high spirits," she roused towns by marching through the streets after the usual advertising had failed to draw a crowd. "Denizens of the slums and public houses," reported the *War Cry* in 1885, forsook their "ale pots" and "street brawls" "to have a look at the wide-mouthed, loud-voiced fearless preacheress who had rushed like a whirlwind through their haunts and who evidently understood so well their language and their habits." "Hallelujah Lasses," *War Cry,* 8 Aug. 1885.

105. "Another Midnight Visit to the West of London," *War Cry,* 4 Sept. 1886, p. 3. One subheading read "Our Dress Spoke for Us."

106. Mrs. General Booth, "Women as Preachers."

107. Ibid.; Mrs. Booth, quoting General Booth, in Sandall, *History of the Salvation Army,* p. 4; Railton, *Heathen England,* p. 90. As a member of the Salvation Army said to Charles Booth, "Conversion has a wonderful effect on a man; he is very soon decently clothed, his home becomes better, and although he still remains a working man outwardly he might pass with the clerks." Quoted in Victor Bailey, "Salvation Army Riots, the 'Skeleton Army,' and Legal Authority in the Provincial Town," in A. P. Donajgrodzki, ed., *Social Control in Nineteenth-Century Britain* (London: Croom Helm, 1979), p. 139. On the Salvation Army and masculinity, see Pamela Walker, " 'I Live but Not Yet I for Christ Liveth in Me': Men and Masculinity in the Salvation Army, 1865–1890," in Michael Roper and John Tosh, eds. *Manfull Assertions: Masculinities in Britain since 1800* (London: Routledge, 1991), p. 6.

108. Quoted to Mildred Duff, in Noel Hope, *Mildred Duff: A Surrendered Life* (London: Salvationist Pub. and Supplies, 1933), p. 64; "Capt. Bessie Wilkins of Seven Dials Slum Post," *War Cry,* 20 Oct. 1888.

109. Clara Collet, quoted in E. Royston Pike, *Human Documents of the Age of Forsythes* (London: Allen and Unwin, 1969), p. 78; William J. Fishman, *East End 1888: Life in a London Borough among the Labouring Poor* (Philadelphia: Temple University Press, 1988), p. 81.

110. "A Great and Notable Victory," *PMG*, 18 July 1888; Beatrice and Sidney Webb, *History of Trade Unions*, quoted in Briggs, *Victorian Things*, p. 204.

111. Barbara Drake, *Women in Trade Unions* (London: George Allen and Unwin, 1920), p. 26.

112. "White Slavery in London," *Link* (London), 23 June 1888.

113. Fishman, *East End*, p. 184; Sarah Boston, *Women Workers and the Trade Unions* (London: Lawrence and Wishart, 1980), p. 48; "The Revolt of the Matchmakers," *Link,* 7 July 1888.

114. "Revolt of the Matchmakers"; Briggs, *Victorian Things*, p. 202.

115. "Match Girls on Strike," *Star*, 6 July 1888; 7 July 1888.

116. Mrs. Davis, Booth Manuscripts, B.177.

117. "The Match Girl's Strike," *Echo*, 16 July 1888.

118. "Victory of the Match Girls," *PMG*, 18 July 1888; "The Revolt of the Match-Makers," *Link,* 7 July 1888.

119. "There is . . . a union among the match girls, which was started by assistance from outside, and seems to be growing in favour. It appears to have already taught its members the advantages of organization and discipline, and it's far from unlikely that the improvement lately noticed as regards both cleanliness and regularity of attendance is, to a considerable extent, due to the originators of the movement, who are teaching the girls that a 'feather club' is not all that combination can do for them." Booth, *Life and Labour*, Industry Series, vol. 2, p. 107. Cited in Anna Davin, "Notes and Extracts from Contemporary Reports and Sources relating to the Matchmakers," Local History Collection, Tower Hamlets Library, London, England. LP 4155, 670.1.

Chapter Three

1. *PMG*, 4 July 1885. "The Maiden Tribute of Modern Babylon" appeared in the *PMG* on 6, 7, 8, 10 July 1885.

2. *Maiden Tribute*, p. 3. "Maiden Tribute" was reissued in *The Maiden Tribute of Modern Babylon (The Report of the "Pall Mall Gazette's" Secret Commission* (London: Pall Mall Gazette, 1885). Except where noted, the quotations from the "Maiden Tribute" are taken from the reprint.

3. *PMG*, 9 July 1885. George Bernard Shaw to W. T. Stead, quoted in F. Whyte, *The Life of W. T. Stead*, 2 vols. (London: Jonathan Cape, 1925), 1:175.

4. H. A. D. Phillips, "Offenses against Marriage and the Relations of the Sexes," *Law Quarterly Journal* (London) (Oct. 1885): 471–86.

5. Raymond L. Schults, *Crusader in Babylon: W. T. Stead and the Pall Mall Gazette* (Lincoln: University of Nebraska Press, 1972), pp. 148–49; Edward Bristow, *Vice and Vigilance: Purity Movements in Britain Since 1700* (Totawa, N.J.: Rowman and Littlefield, 1977), p. 157; Whyte, *The Life*, 1:117; *Saint James Gazette*, quoted in Horace Wyndham, *Victorian Sensations* (London: Jarrolds, 1933), pp. 63, 135; *PMG*, 7 Aug. 1885.

6. For background to the social purity movement, see Judith R. Walkowitz, *Prostitution and Victorian Society: Women, Class, and the State* (New York: Cambridge University Press, 1980); Bristow, *Vice and Vigilance;* Judith R. Walkowitz, "The Politics of Prostitution," *History Workshop Journal,* no. 13 (Autumn 1980); Frank Mort, *Dangerous Sexualities: Medico-moral Politics in England since 1830* (London and New York: Routledge and Kegan Paul, 1987). Stead's revelations greatly aided a number of other fledgling organizations, including the child welfare movement, which insisted that "justice for the young took precedence over the claims of parenthood." This was done without challenging the strict boundaries of the private family. As George Behlmer notes, the men and women who created this vision "would do so by arguing that the security of the home demanded it. The Englishman's castle was to be breached for the good of the castle." George Behlmer, *Child Abuse and Moral Reform in England, 1870–1908* (Stanford: Stanford University Press, 1982), p. 16. The Armstrong trial also did the Salvation Army "a great deal of good," wrote Bramwell Booth. It gained the Army "friends in political circles" and propelled it into rescue work and social services, into a more developed and institutionalized policy of winning souls. Bramwell Booth, quoted in Alison Plowden, *The Case of Eliza Armstrong: 'A Child of 13 Bought for £5'* (London: BBC, 1974), p. 139.

7. Mrinalini Sinha, "Gender and Imperialism: Colonial Policy and the Ideology of Moral Imperialism in Late-Nineteenth Century Bengal," in M. S. Kimmel, ed., *Changing Men: New Directions in Research on Men and Masculinity* (Beverly Hills: Sage, 1987), pp. 217–31; Dagmar Engels, "The Limits of Gender Ideology, Bengali Women, the Colonial State, and the Private Sphere, 1890–1930," *Women's Studies International Forum* 12, no. 4 (1989): 425–37; Ronald Hyam, *Empire and Sexuality: The British Experience* (Manchester and New York: Manchester University Press, 1990).

8. Authors concerned with the truth of the "Maiden Tribute" include Michael Pearson, *The Age of Consent: Victorian Prostitution and Its Enemies* (Newton Abbott: David and Charles, 1972); Alison Plowden, *The Case of Eliza Armstrong: 'A Child of 13 Bought for £5'* (London: BBC, 1974); Charles Terrot, *The Maiden Tribute: A Study of the White Slavery Traffic of the Nineteenth Century* (London: Frederick Muller, 1959). For Stead's sexual psychology, see Havelock Ellis, quoted in Whyte, *The Life,* vol. 2, app. 3, "Stead's Obsession with Sex," p. 341; Hugh Kingsmill, *After Puritanism* (London: Methuen, 1952). On the political implications of the "Maiden Tribute," see Deborah Gorham, "'The Maiden Tribute of Modern Babylon' Re-Visited," *Victorian Studies* (Spring 1976): 353–79; Bristow, *Vice and Vigilance;* Jeffrey Weeks, *Sex, Politics, and Society* (London: Longmans, 1981).

9. All the available statistics on the age of prostitutes drawn from venereal disease hospitals, police reports, rescue homes, workhouses, and prisons indicate very few young females on the streets below the age of sixteen. These institutions, of course, were selective in their recruitment of inmates, but their processes of selection were different. See Walkowitz, *Prostitution and Victorian Society,* chap. 1; Ann Higginbotham, "The Unmarried Mother and Her Child in Victorian London, 1834–1914" (Ph.D. diss., Indiana University, 1985); idem, "Respectable Sinners:

Salvation Army Rescue Work with Unmarried Mothers, 1884–1941," in Gail Malmgreen, ed., *Religion in the Lives of English Women, 1760–1930* (London: Croom Helm, 1980), pp. 216–33.

10. Lisa Duggan, "Uncontrollable Impulses: Sex, Science and Sensationalism in Turn-of-the-Century America," (Ph.D. diss., University of Pennsylvania, 1992), chap. 2, p. 2; Hayden White, "The Value of Narrativity in the Representation of Reality," in W. J. T. Mitchell, ed., *On Narrative* (Chicago: University of Chicago Press, 1988), pp. 1–23.

11. Fredric Jameson, "Magical Narratives: Romance as Genre," *New Literary History* 7 (1975): 157. Quoted in Jean Radford, Introduction, Jean Radford, ed., *The Progress of Romance: The Politics of Popular Fiction* (London: Routledge and Kegan Paul, 1986), p. 11.

12. Stead, from unproofed galleys of *Josephine Butler: A Life Sketch;* Evelyn March Phillips, quoted in Stephen Koss, *The Rise and Fall of the Political Press,* vol. 1, *The Nineteenth Century* (Chapel Hill: University of North Carolina Press, 1981), p. 342.

13. Iain McCalman, *Radical Underworld: Prophets, Revolutionaries and Pornographers in London, 1795–1840* (Cambridge: Cambridge University Press, 1988), chap. 10.

14. For Victor Turner, social dramas are significant events for the production of social meanings. They "arouse consciousness of ourselves as we see ourselves," and they consolidate new systems of meanings by converting "particular values and ends, distributed over a range of actors into a system . . . of shared or consensual meaning." Victor Turner, "Social Dramas and Stories about Them," *Critical Inquiry* 7, no. 1 (Autumn 1980): 156.

15. Jürgen Habermas, "The Public Sphere: An Encyclopedia Article (1964)," *New German Critique* 5, no. 2 (1974): 49–55; Simon Watney, *Policing Desire: Pornography, AIDS, and the Media* (Minneapolis: University of Minnesota Press, 1989), p. 42; W. T. Stead, "Government by Journalism," *The Contemporary Review* 49 (1886): 654–74.

16. Peter Brooks, *The Melodramatic Imagination: Balzac, Henry James, Melodrama and the Mode of Excess* (New Haven: Yale University Press, 1976), p. xiii. See also Michael R. Booth, *English Melodrama* (London: Herbert Jenkins, 1956); David Grimsted, *Melodrama Unveiled: American Theater and Culture, 1800–1850* (Chicago: University of Chicago Press, 1968); Gilbert Cross, *Next Week East Lynne* (Lewisburg: Bucknell University Press, 1977); Martin Meisel, *Realisations: Narrative, Pictorial and Theatrical Arts in Nineteenth-Century England* (Princeton: Princeton University Press, 1983).

17. Thanks to Laura Mulvey for these insights.

18. See Anna Clark, "Rape or Seduction? A Controversy over Sexual Violence in the Nineteenth Century," in *The Sexual Dynamics of History,* ed. London Feminist History Group (London: Pluto Press, 1983).

19. Gareth Stedman Jones, *Languages of Class: Studies in English Working-Class History, 1832–1982* (Cambridge: Cambridge University Press, 1983); Joan Scott, "On Language, Gender and Working-Class History," *Gender and the Politics of History* (New York: Columbia University Press, 1986), pp. 53–67; Patrick

Joyce, *Visions of the People: Industrial England and the Question of Class, 1840–1914* (Cambridge: Cambridge University Press, 1991), chap. 2.

20. Quoted in Barbara Taylor, *Eve and the New Jerusalem: Socialism and Feminism in the Nineteenth Century* (New York: Pantheon, 1983), p. 201.

21. See also Christine Stansell, *City of Women: Sex and Class in New York, 1789–1860* (New York: Knopf, 1986), chap. 3.

22. Martha Vicinus, "'Helpless and Unfriended': Nineteenth-Century Domestic Melodrama," *New Literary History* 13 (1981–82): 127–43; E. Ann Kaplan, "The Political Unconscious in the Maternal Melodrama: Ellen Wood's *East Lynne* (1861)," in Derek Longhurst, ed., *Gender, Genre and Narrative Pleasure* (Hemel Hempstead: Unwin Hyman, 1988), pp. 31–50; Nina Auerbach, *Woman and the Demon: The Life of a Victorian Myth* (Cambridge, Mass: Harvard University Press, 1982); Sally Mitchell, "Sentiment and Suffering: Women's Recreational Reading in the 1860s," *Victorian Studies* 21, no. 1 (Autumn 1977): 29–45.

23. Josephine Butler, *Recollections of George Butler* (Bristol: Arrowsmith, 1892), pp. 97–98. See Nancy Boyd, *Three Victorian Women Who Changed Their World: Josephine Butler, Octavia Hill, Florence Nightingale* (New York: Oxford University Press, 1982), chap. 1.

24. Josephine Butler, *Josephine H. Butler: An Autobiographical Memoir*, ed. George W. and Lucy A. Johnson (London: Arrowsmith, 1928), pp. 58, 60, 64.

25. Josephine Butler, "The Dark Side of English Life: Illustrated in a Series of True Stories," *The Methodist Protest*, Jan. 1877, Feb. 1877, March 1877, April 1877, May 1877. Thanks to Elinor Riemer for this citation.

26. Ibid., "No. 1—Marion," Jan. 1877; "No. 4—Laura," May 1877. Of Marion, Butler wrote, "She loved much, this woman, who had been five years 'on the streets' and her spirit became that of a purified saint," gifted with the power of prophecy. "Marion had 'prophesied' to me, before she died, of hard days and a sad heart which were in store for me in contending against the evil to which she had fallen victim." The dying Emma simply assured Butler, "we shall be together. . . . I will look out for you."

27. Ibid., "No. 4—Emma," April 1877.

28. Ibid., "No. 3—Margaret," March 1877.

29. Coral Lansbury, *The Old Brown Dog: Women, Workers, and Vivisection in Edwardian England* (Madison: University of Wisconsin Press, 1985), chap. 6; Auerbach, *Woman and the Demon*, pp. 163–65.

30. Judith R. Walkowitz, *Prostitution and Victorian Society: Women, Class, and the State* (New York: Cambridge University Press, 1980).

31. Josephine Butler, testimony before the Royal Commission of 1871, quoted in Glen Petrie, *A Singular Iniquity: The Campaigns of Josephine Butler* (New York: Viking Press, 1971), p. 115.

32. Mrs. Kell of Southampton, quoted in Walkowitz, *Prostitution*, p. 170; *National League Journal* (London), 1 Sept. 1870.

33. Josephine Butler to W. T. Stead, n.d. [1886]. Stead Papers. Thanks to Professor Joseph O. Baylen for access to the Stead Papers. Nancy Boyd, *Three Victorian Women*, pp. 61–65.

34. Josephine Butler, *Personal Reminiscences of a Great Crusade* (London: Horace Marshall & Son, 1911; rpt., Westport: Hyperion Press, 1976), p. 49.

35. Ibid., p. 31.

36. Ibid.

37. Quoted in Josephine Butler, "The Garrison Towns of Kent," *Shield,* 9 May 1870.

38. Josephine Butler, speech before the annual meeting of the Ladies National Association, Plymouth, 1872. Quoted in *Western Daily Mercury* (Plymouth), 6 Sept. 1872.

39. A registered woman, quoted in a letter from Josephine Butler to J. J. Garth Wilkinson, quoted in Walkowitz, *Prostitution,* p. 109.

40. "A Woman," "A Protest against the Contagious Diseases Acts," letter to the editor, *RN,* 15 May 1870.

41. Martin Meisel, *Shaw and the Nineteenth-Century Theater* (Princeton: Princeton University Press, 1963); I. M. Britain, *Fabianism and Culture: A Study in British Socialism and the Arts, 1884–1918* (Cambridge: Cambridge University Press, 1982); Catherine Gallagher, *The Industrial Reformation of English Fiction* (Chicago: University of Chicago Press, 1985); Gareth Stedman Jones, *Language of Class.*

42. Joyce, *Visions of the People,* pp. 65, 59.

43. The definitive biography of W. T. Stead awaits the publication of Joseph O. Baylen's study. Existing studies include Whyte, *The Life;* J. W. Robertson Scott, *Life and Death of a Newspaper* (London: Methuen, 1952); Kingsmill, *After Puritanism;* Stephen Koss, *Rise and Fall of the Political Press,* vol. 1, *The Nineteenth Century* (Chapel Hill: University of North Carolina Press, 1981).

44. Pearson, *Age of Consent,* p. 126.

45. Stead to John Morley, quoted in Whyte, *The Life,* vol. 1, p. 72.

46. Ibid.

47. Harold Frederic, quoted in Whyte, *The Life,* vol. 1, p. 115. As Koss remarks, Gladstone, who did not assiduously follow newspapers, followed the *Pall Mall Gazette* very closely. The *PMG* was clearly influential among progressive intellectuals as well: many correspondents writing to Karl Pearson about the issues of the Men and Women's Club commented on Stead's escapades.

48. Michel Foucault, *The History of Sexuality,* vol. 1, *An Introduction,* trans. Robert Hurley (New York: Pantheon, 1978); Stead, quoted in Joseph O. Baylen, "Oscar Wilde Redivivus," *The University of Mississippi Studies in English* 6 (1965): 77–86.

49. Stead, unproofed galleys of *Josephine Butler: A Life Sketch.*

50. Simultaneously with these initiatives against the traffic in girls, a grass-roots purity campaign, spearheaded by Ellice Hopkins, focused on educating workingmen in chastity and in recruiting them into White Cross Leagues. See Bristow, *Vice and Vigilance,* chap. 5; Mort, *Dangerous Sexualities,* pp. 117–26.

51. Stead, *Josephine Butler: A Life Sketch;* Josephine Butler, quoted in Judith R. Walkowitz, "Politics of Prostitution," *History Workshop Journal* (Autumn 1980): 248; A. J. Milner, quoted in Plowden, *The Case,* p. 111.

52. Thanks to Laura Mulvey for her stimulating insights into the connections between melodrama and pornography. See her "Visual Pleasure and Narrative Cinema," *Screen* 16, no. 3 (Autumn 1975): 6–18; E. Ann Kaplan, "Is the Gaze Male?" in *Powers of Desire*, ed. Ann Snitow, et al. (New York: Monthly Review Press, 1983), 309–27; Lansbury, *The Old Brown Dog,* chap. 7.

53. Duncombe, for example, published pornography as well as a vast corpus of popular theater and melodrama, including the works of Douglas Jerrold, author of the immensely popular *Black-Eyed Susan.* McCalman, *Radical Underworld*, p. 211.

54. Kingsmill, *After Puritanism*, p. 208.

55. Thanks to Elaine Showalter for this suggestion.

56. *PMG*, 4, 6, 7, 8, 10 July 1885.

57. *Maiden Tribute*, p. 1. For Victorian literary uses of the monster and the maid theme, see William C. Devane, "The Virgin and the Dragon," *Yale Review* (1947): 33–46. For representations in Victorian high art of the St. George/Perseus story, see Susan Casteras, *The Substance and the Shadow: Images of Victorian Womanhood* (New Haven: Yale Center for British Art, 1982).

58. Thanks to Margaret Homans for this observation.

59. Thanks to Gillian Brown for suggestions about Ariadne's craft.

60. *Maiden Tribute*, p. 2; W. T. Stead, quoted in "The Town Meeting," *PMG*, 24 Aug. 1885; *DT* (London), 4 Nov. 1885; "From One in the Crowd," *PMG*, 24 Aug. 1885. For the democratization of chivalry, see Mark Girouard, *The Return to Camelot: Chivalry and the English Gentleman* (New Haven and London: Yale University Press, 1981), chap. 16. For the tradition of the counterfeit swell, see Peter Bailey, "Champagne Charlie: Performance and Ideology in the Music-Hall Swell Song," in J. S. Bratton, ed., *Music Hall: Performance and Style* (Milton Keynes: Open University Press, 1984), chap. 3.

61. *PMG*, 6 July 1885; *Maiden Tribute*, pp. 12, 13.

62. Surveys of Victorian pornography have noted the shifting themes of "clandestine literature" over the course of the century, from a focus on "straightforward" heterosexual copulation, the "right true end of love," to an obsession with the infliction of pain and corruption of the immature. Surveys of Victorian pornography include Lansbury, *Old Brown Dog,* chap. 7; Peter Fryer, *The Man of Pleasure's Companion* (London: A. Barker, 1968); Peter Fryer, *Forbidden Books of the Victorians* (London: Odyssey Press, 1970); Donald Thomas, *A Long Time Burning* (London: Routledge and Kegan Paul, 1969). Increasingly, pornography concentrated on "coitus atrox," "a mode of intercourse that is extraordinarily violent and sadistic, employing the birch and the whip, straps and knives to break the victim." Lansbury, *Old Brown Dog*, p. 114.

63. "The State's New Duty: An Old Ballad upon the Proposed Extension of The Contagious Diseases Acts to the Civil Population," *The Pearl* (rpt., New York: Grove Press, 1968), pp. 159–62.

64. Women occasionally administered the discipline, such as the governess (whom men actually impersonated in flagellant brothels) and the midwife (who would conduct an intrusive examination, although lacking the gynecological paraphernalia of the doctor), but the figure supervising the punishment and pain was male. Lansbury, *Old Brown Dog,* chap. 7.

65. *Maiden Tribute*, p. 5; *PMG*, 8 July 1885.

66. *Maiden Tribute*, p. 4; *PMG*, 6 July 1885.

67. *Maiden Tribute*, p. 4; *PMG*, 6 July 1885.

68. *Maiden Tribute*, pp. 8, 4. The administration of chloroform during the outrages on violated virgins fully realized the "rape" motif implicit in the earlier debates over the use of chloroform during childbirth. See Mary Poovey, " 'Scenes of an Indelicate Character': The Medical 'Treatment' of Victorian Women," *Representations* 14 (Spring 1986): 137–68.

69. *Maiden Tribute*, pp. 4, 8, 5.

70. Ibid.

71. Ibid.

72. Ibid.

73. "The Stead Case," *Saturday Review of Politics, Literature, Science and Art* (London) (14 Nov. 1885): 631.

74. Reginald Brett, quoted in Whyte, *The Life*, vol. 1, p. 177; *Justice*, quoted in *PMG*, 20 July 1885; *RN* (London), 2 Aug. 1885. The sympathies of *Reynolds* lay wholeheartedly with the working-class paterfamilias whose property—his daughter—had been expropriated by the idle rich; "Not only do they [the rich] rob workers of the fruit of their labour, but the idle classes also regard the daughters of the workers as born and bred to minister to their passions." Other progressive organs tried to accommodate their class protest to the more scientific political discourse of the 1880s or to express their skepticism of the puritanical revival that would result. The Fabians, for example, although endorsing Stead's campaign, looked on the "Maiden Tribute" as but one "result of the exploitation of man by man which is the curse of modern society" (*PMG*, 20 July 1885). Both William Morris and Karl Pearson worried that the revelations would stimulate a puritanical revival. William Morris to Stead, 12 Aug. 1885, Stead Papers.

75. *PMG*, 20 July 1885, 18 July 1885, 10 Aug. 1885; E. Ray Lankester to Stead, 11 July 1887. A barely disguised incest motif was contained in the "Saunterer" letter (*PMG*, 18 July 1885). For Lewis Carroll's outraged response to the "Maiden Tribute," see "Whoso Shall Offend One of These Little Ones," *SJG*, 22 July 1885.

76. Sir Richard Cross, quoted in George Behlmer, *Child Abuse and Moral Reform in England, 1870–1908* (Stanford: Stanford University Press, 1982), p. 75; *Hansard Parliamentary Debates* (Commons), 3d ser., 300 (30 July 1885), cols. 579–85.

77. Quoted in Gibson, *English Vice*, p. 158. *Times*, 31 Aug. 1885; Josephine Butler, "To the Demonstration Committee," *PMG*, 20 Aug. 1885; Ian Gibson, *The English Vice: Beating, Sex, and Shame in Victorian England and After* (London: Duckworth, 1978), p. 158.

78. W. T. Stead, "The Town Meeting," *PMG*, 24 Aug. 1885; Schults, *Crusader in Babylon*, p. 161. See also Benedict Anderson, *Imagined Communities: Reflections on the Origins and the Spread of Nationalism* (London: Verso, 1983).

79. The *Daily News* further characterized the assemblage as "essentially a working men and women's demonstration." "The Press on the Demonstration," *PMG*, 25 Aug. 1885.

80. See John Gorman, *Banner Bright: An Illustrated History of the Banners of the Trade Union Movement* (London: Allan Lane, 1973); "From One in the Crowd," *PMG*, 24 Aug. 1885.

81. A part of the East End contingent had marched through Pall Mall's club-land, where they saw youthful "mashers" assemble at the doorstep of their club; some claimed to have pointed an accusing finger "of scorn" at Cavendish Bentinck, ensconced "in a window at the Carlton." At Hyde Park, hawkers sold fruit and nuts, "prints, cheap and nasty," and "democratic organs" like *Justice,* which detailed how the "working classes are robbed by landlords and capitalists." Schults, *Crusader,* p. 161; Bristow, *Vice and Vigilance,* p. 113; *PMG,* 24 Aug. 1885.

82. Other studies of the Armstrong trial include Wyndham, *Victorian Sensations;* Plowden, *The Case;* Pearson, *Age of Consent,* Madge Unsworth, *Maiden Tribute: A Study in Voluntary Social Service* (London: Salvationist Publisher and Supplies, 1949).

83. "Crying bitterly, she told [the magistrate] how Eliza had left home with an old friend of her neighbours to go into service. The child's employer had said that she would write regularly, but she had not heard from her since the day she left." Quoted in Pearson, *Age of Consent,* p. 171.

84. *LWN* (London), 12 July 1885. This article was also noted in the evening edition of the *PMG.*

85. For a discussion of the tendency of "characters" in newspaper scandals to dispute the meanings produced by both newspaper and courtroom narratives, see Lisa Duggan, "Uncontrollable Impulses."

86. For differing views of the guilt or innocence of the Armstrongs, see Plowden, *The Case,* Unsworth, *Maiden Tribute,* or Pearson, *Age of Consent.* Rebecca Jarrett, unpublished memoir, n.d., p. 12, Salvation Army Archives.

87. *DT,* 24 Oct. 1885; Eliza Armstrong, testimony before Central Criminal Court, *Central Criminal Court Session Papers* (12th session, 1884–85), pp. 900, 896; *DT,* 24 Oct. 1885.

88. *LWN,* quoted in Plowden, *The Case,* p. 24; Mrs. Armstrong, quoted in ibid., p. 29; Mrs Armstrong, quoted in Wyndham, *Victorian Sensations,* p. 143; *DT,* 26 Oct. 1885; *Times,* 9 Nov. 1885.

89. *LWN,* 13 Sept. 1885.

90. Quoted in Ellen Ross, "Survival Networks: Women's Neighborhood Sharing in London Before World War One," *History Workshop Journal* 15 (Spring 1983): 14.

91. Mrs. Armstrong challenged Mrs. Broughton's sexual reputation. "She called me everything," explained Mrs. Broughton in her testimony, "she called me whore and prostitute and said I had been a prostitute all my lifetime; and I was not married to the man I was living with." Mrs. Broughton, testimony at Central Criminal Court, *Session Papers,* p. 924. According to the *PMG,* Mrs. Broughton claimed that Mrs. Armstrong called her a "bloody cow." In an unpublished paper on sexual reputation in early nineteenth-century London, Anna Clark discusses the complex issues involved in neighborhood sexual slanders, including class tensions, competition, and the ambiguous status of common-law marriage (see Anna Clark, unpublished paper, 1986).

92. Mrs. Armstrong, testimony before Central Criminal Court, *Sessions Papers*, p. 915.

93. *PMG*, 15 Sept. 1885; Mr. Armstrong, testimony at Central Criminal Court, *Session Papers*, p. 945; Mrs. Armstrong, testimony at Central Criminal Court, *Session Papers*, p. 904; Mr. Armstrong, testimony at Central Criminal Court, *Sessions Papers*, p. 942; *PMG*, 15 Sept. 1885; *RN*, 8 Nov. 1885. After the Armstrong trial, *Reynolds* ultimately judged Stead "deservedly punished."

94. Mrs. Armstrong, testimony at Central Criminal Court, *Sessions Papers*, p. 904; Plowden, *The Case*, p. 75.

95. Plowden, *The Case*, p. 75.

96. *DT*, 29 Oct. 1885.

97. *DT*, 31 Oct. 1885; Plowden, *The Case*, p. 98.

98. Jarrett, testimony at Central Criminal Court, quoted in Plowden, *The Case*, p. 97; *DT*, 13 Nov. 1885.

99. Sir Charles Webster, quoted in Plowden, *The Case*, p. 121.

100. W. T. Stead, *The Armstrong Case: Mr. Stead's Defense Told in Full* (London: H. Vickers, 1885); *DT*, 5 Nov. 1885; Stead, quoted in Plowden, *The Case*, p. 37.

101. W. T. Stead to Elizabeth Cobb, 5 Aug. 1885. Fawcett Autograph Collection, Fawcett Library, London. Vol. 11; Stead, quoted in Wyndham, *Victorian Sensations*, p. 129; Stead, *Armstrong Case*, p. 12; ibid.

102. Jarrett, unpublished memoir, p. 15; *PMG*, 9 Nov. 1885; *DT*, 3 Nov. 1885; *PMG*, 2 Nov. 1885, 9 Nov. 1885; Stead, testimony at Central Criminal Court, *Sessions Papers*, pp. 999, 1001.

103. *DT*, 4 Nov. 1885.

104. *National Reformer* (London), 30 Aug. 1885; *PMG*, 25 Aug. 1885.

105. Stead, Diary Entries, 3 March–28 July 1886. Stead Papers. According to Robertson Scott, these entries were transcripts of shorthand notes dictated by Stead to his secretary Underhill.

106. Ibid., 6 March 1886, 7 April 1886.

107. Ibid., 3 March 1886.

108. *Maiden Tribute*, pp. 3, 11.

109. For discussions of Freud's role as narrator in the Dora case, see the introductions and articles by Charles Bernheimer and Claire Kahane and the articles by Steven Marcus, Toril Moi, and Madelon Sprengnether in Charles Bernheimer and Claire Kahane, eds., *In Dora's Case: Freud-Hysteria-Feminism* (New York: Columbia University Press, 1985).

110. *DT*, 9 Nov. 1885; Stead, quoted in Wyndham, *Victorian Sensations*, pp. 161, 162; Plowden, *The Case*, p. 141.

111. *PMG*, 9 Nov. 1885; Josephine Butler, *Rebecca Jarrett* (London: Morgan and Scott, 1985), p. 55; Jarrett, unpublished memoir, pp. 15, 12, 13.

112. Jarrett, unpublished memoir, p. 3.

113. Ibid., p. 1.

114. Ibid., p. 9, 8. Arriving at the Salvation Army refuge in Hanbury Street, Whitechapel, (a "place I had never been in my life," for her haunts were in the more prosperous West End) she was greeted by a "lovely young Mother with red jersey on [Salvation Army uniform] [.] She rose up and *kissed* me said I have been waiting for

you dear." Jarrett was stunned and grateful for this intimacy: "I was one of London['s] kept women living a life of impurity getting my living by it [.]" "The kitchen was a poor little back kitchen but its memory is very sacred to me" (pp. 6, 7). Jarrett characterized herself as a "scullery maid" to "show up the dirt" or "to do the dirty work" (pp. 15, 16). For a discussion of maternal ideology and the Salvation Army, see Pamela Walker, "The Hallelujah Lasses," unpublished paper, 1990.

115. Jarrett, unpublished memoir, pp. 11, 12. See Ross, " 'Not the Sort that Would Sit on the Doorstep': Respectability in Pre–World War I London Neighborhoods," *ILWCH*, no. 27 (Spring 1985): 39–59.

116. Jarrett, unpublished memoir, p. 12; Jarrett, testimony at Central Criminal Court, *Sessions Papers*, p. 991. Unsworth (*Maiden Tribute*, p. 30) comments: "A recollection of a similar event in her childhood must have come painfully to Rebecca."

117. Butler, *Rebecca Jarrett*, pp. 43, 44.

118. Ibid., pp. 21, 22, 23, 25, 32. In this pamphlet, Butler attempted to explain why Jarrett lied in court to protect her old associates, whom she had promised not to harm.

119. Amanda Sebestyn, "Two Women from Two Worlds," *Spare Rib* (London), no. 155 (June 1985).

120. Butler to Stead, n.d. [1885]. Stead Papers.

121. In this comparison, I am drawing on Butler's repeal propaganda as well as on her biography of Jarrett.

122. Josephine Butler to Vernon Lushington, P.R.O., Admiralty Papers, Adm.1/6148, 12 Jan. 1870. See Eugene L. Rasor, *Reform in the Royal Navy: A Social History of the Lower Deck, 1850 to 1889* (Hamden, Conn.: Archon, 1976), pp. 98, 99.

123. *PMG*, 6 July 1885. In his diary entry, 3 March 1886, Stead included observations from his nocturnal walk around Hyde Park: "Around the Marble Arch, I found some few women; no boys." A homosexual prototype of the "Maiden Tribute," complete with an upper-class rake who seduces a bootblack boy and then sells him into prostitution in Paris, was published in 1881 as *Sins of the Cities of the Plain or, Confessions of a Maryanne*. Oscar Wilde bought a copy in a bookshop in Coventry Street, Leicester Square. Neil Bartlett, *Who Was That Man? A Present for Mr. Oscar Wilde* (London: Serpent's Tail, 1988), pp. 102, 103. See Stead's rather sympathetic response to the Wilde case (where he judged the Marquess of Queensbury as a far greater villain than Wilde and worried about the chilling effect of the Wilde case on friendship between men [*Review of Reviews* (London) 11 (June 1895): 491, 492]). However marginal, the homosexual theme would surface in the clauses of the Criminal Law Amendment Act itself. An antiaristocratic bias may have prompted its inclusion in the bill (reformers accepted its inclusion but did not themselves propose it), as homosexuality was associated with the corruption of working-class youth by the same upper-class profligates, who, on other occasions, were thought to buy the services of young girls. Jeffrey Weeks, *Coming Out: Homosexual Politics in Britain from the Nineteenth Century to the Present* (London: Quartet Books, 1977), pp. 18–20. *Reynolds News* (19 July 1885), ever vigilant about the perverse practices of the aristocracy, openly addressed the homosexual

subtext that provided a shadow discourse to female outrage. It reminded its readers that there are "offenses which, if less harmful in their immediate physical effects, have yet a horrible degrading influence on childhood and manhood." Whereas the "sated voluptuaries" of the metropolis were never "called to account," at "every country assize there are sure to be several poor ignorant rustics charged with kindred offenses."

124. On child pornography, see Graham Ovenden and Robert Melville, *Victorian Children* (New York: St. Martin's Press, 1972); Ronald Pearsall, *The Worm in the Bud: The World of Victorian Sexuality* (New York: Macmillan, 1969).

125. Josephine Butler, *Personal Reminiscences of a Great Crusade* (London: Horace Marshall and Son, 1911), p. 49.

126. Beatrice Webb, quoted in Gareth Stedman Jones, *Outcast London: A Study in the Relationship between Classes in Victorian Society* (Oxford: Clarendon Press, 1971), p. 285; Anthony Wohl, ed., *The Bitter Cry of Outcast London* (New York: Humanities Press, 1970).

127. Stead, *Armstrong Case*, p. 15. Stead emphasized the degraded environment of Charles Street, hinting at incest: Eliza was "taken from a single room in a Marylebone slum, where eight people lived and slept, and from which she was most anxious to go, and placed in a situation in a comfortable middle-class family." Stead's opponents also manipulated the themes and motifs of "Outcast London": they blamed Stead for unleashing the destructive energies of the street by encouraging and disseminating pornography; and they objected to curtailing elite male sexual prerogatives in the vain attempt to protect girls who had already been corrupted by their environment.

128. On the "endowment of motherhood," see Jane Lewis, *The Politics of Motherhood: Child and Maternal Welfare in England, 1900–1939* (London: Croom Helm, 1980); Ellen Ross, "Response to Hal Benenson," *ILWCH* no. 25 (Spring 1984): 34; Anna Davin, "Imperialism and Motherhood," *History Workshop Journal* 5 (Spring 1978): 9–66.

129. Lewis, *Politics of Motherhood*, pp. 80, 81, 166; Pat Ayers and Jan Lambertz, "Marriage Relations, Money, and Domestic Violence in Working-Class Liverpool, 1919–39," in Jane Lewis, ed., *Labour and Love: Women's Experience of Home and Family, 1850–1940* (Oxford: Blackwell, 1986), pp. 196–202; Carolyn Steedman, *Landscape for a Good Woman: A Story of Two Lives* (New Brunswick, N.J.: Rutgers University Press, 1987).

Chapter Four

1. Jeffrey Weeks, *Sexuality and Its Discontents: Meanings, Myths and Modern Sexualities* (London: Routledge and Kegan Paul, 1985), p. 45. Cited in Simon Watney, *Policing Desire: Pornography, AIDS, and the Media* (Minneapolis: University of Minnesota Press, 1989), p. 40; ibid., p. 43.

2. Richard Altick, *Victorian Sensations: Studies in Scarlet* (New York: W. W. Norton, 1970); Stephen Koss, *Rise and Fall of the Political Press. The Nineteenth Century* (Chapel Hill: University of North Carolina Press, 1981), 1:262.

3. William Coote (quoting Stead's critics), quoted in *PMG*, 29 Aug. 1885.

4. "Indecent Literature," *DT*, 2 Sept. 1885, 10 Sept. 1885.

5. Ibid.

6. Bristow, *Vice and Vigilance*, pp. 47–50, 200, 201.

7. *Town Talk* pretended to be concerned with the exposure of scandalous abuses, deploring the "heinous practices" of the aristocracy in great detail, crying out against the "terrible crime of the streets" while guiding readers to the centers of "youthful depravity." *Town Talk* (London), 4 July 1885–21 July 1888. *Town Talk* had a decidedly mixed-class readership: it listed distributors in Deptford and in the Whitechapel Road as well as in the Strand. It was published sporadically in the late 1870s and in the 1880s, and was closed down in 1888 under Commissioner Warren's orders. The publisher was periodically jailed under obscenity charges.

8. *RN*, 2 Aug. 1885; *PMG*, 9 July 1885; *DT*, 26 Aug. 1885; Ellice Hopkins to Stead, n.d. [1885], Stead Papers. In a letter to the editor of the *Daily Telegraph* (28 Aug. 1885), "Hermes" proposed the formation of a philanthropic association to aid orphans—to "assist them by selling matches, newspapers or flowers," rather than "the vile street literature they were currently vending."

9. *DT*, 26 Aug. 1885.

10. *SJG*, 11 Aug. 1885.

11. J. W. Robertson Scott, *Life and Death of a Newspaper* (London: Methuen, 1952), p. 132; *PMG*, 16 July 1885; *RN*, 19 July 1885; "The Stead Case," *Saturday Review* (14 Nov. 1885), p. 631. *National Reformer*, 2 Aug. 1885. On class, politics, and pornography, see Iain McCalman, *Radical Underworld: Prophets, Revolutionaries, and Pornographers in London, 1795–1840* (Cambridge: Cambridge University Press, 1988), chap. 10.

12. *DT*, 25 Aug. 1885; *PMG*, 10 Aug. 1885; *PMG*, 31 Sept. 1885.

13. *DT*, 25 Aug. 1885.

14. On September 1, Thomas Duggan was charged with selling obscene publications in Fleet Street. He was hawking *Aristotle's Masterpiece*, whose cover contained "twenty headlines of an abominable nature." The defendant objected, all to no avail, that if the outside was "objectionable" the inside was "intended to enlighten and not degrade." *DT*, 2 Sept. 1885.

15. Bristow, *Vice and Vigilance*, pp. 201–7. As Bristow notes (p. 207), this new campaign against obscenity was an "epoch-making departure" for using the law of obscene libel against serious literature. Henry Vizetelly, the English publisher of Zola, was a libertarian pressman in the tradition of radical journalism of the Regency years. McCalman, *Radical Underworld*, p. 237.

16. In 1884, before Stead had interested himself in sexual violence, only one assault on a woman was reported over a six-month period. In contrast, between July and December 1885, 45 cases of criminal assault under the "Old Law" were reported, as compared to 93 cases charged under the new categories of sexual crimes introduced by the Criminal Law Amendment Act (criminal assault against girls under sixteen, prosecution of disorderly houses, procuration, abduction, drugging, and retaining of girls' clothes, for example). Four hundred additional news items about sexual violence and the "New Crusade" were reported in the *PMG* for these months, ranging from testimonies at the "Armstrong trial" to "Miscellaneous Facts" that documented other cases of "Mothers Selling Daughters." Although coverage of sexual crime abated somewhat after 1885, Stead continued

to publish numerous accounts of "assaults on women" until he left the *PMG* in 1889. *Index to the Pall Mall Gazette*, January–June 1884; July–December 1884; January–June 1885; July–December 1885; January–June 1886; July–December 1886; January–June 1887; July–December 1887; January–June 1888; July–December 1888. Historians of crime have noted that at a time when "crimes against the person," including physical assaults on women, were declining, "sex crimes" were the notable exception to the trend, in good part because of the new categories of sex crimes introduced by the Criminal Law Amendment Act and increased police surveillance. V. A. C. Gatrell, "The Decline of Theft and Violence in Victorian and Edwardian England," in V. A. C. Gatrell, et al., eds., *Crime and the Law: The Social History of Crime in Western Europe since 1500* (London: Europa Publications, 1980).

17. *PMG*, 20 July 1885; "A Servant Drugged in Liverpool," *PMG*, 31 Aug. 1885; "An Alleged Minotaur in Birmingham," *PMG*, 26 Sept. 1885; "Shocking Assault on a Child," *PMG*, 14 July 1886; "Alleged Abduction by a Gentleman," *PMG*, 19 Aug. 1886; "The Charge of Abduction Against an Officer," *PMG*, 9 May 1887.

18. Stead to Mr. Yates Thompson, quoted in Robertson Scott, *Life and Death*, pp. 143–44. Much to the chagrin of some of his libertarian allies, Stead soon departed from his previous position against singling out individuals for condemnation and punishment, rather than attacking an organized system.

19. Discussions of Stead and the Dilke affair may be found in Roy Jenkins, *Victorian Scandal: A Biography of the Right Honourable Gentleman Sir Charles Dilke* (New York: Chilmark Press, 1965); Betty Askwith, *Lady Dilke: A Biography* (London: Chatto and Windus, 1969); J. O. Baylen, "Oscar Wilde Redivivus," *University of Mississippi Studies in English* 6 (1965): 77–86. Some of Stead's publications on Dilke include: "Should Scandals in High Life be Hushed Up?" *PMG*, 5 Feb. 1886; *PMG*, Feb. and March, 1886, passim; "Sins of Ananias and Sapphira," *Review of Reviews* 5 (Feb. 1892): 140–42; "Character Sketch, Sir Charles Dilke," *Review of Reviews* 6 (Aug. 1892): 127–41; *Has Sir Charles Dilke Cleared His Name? An Examination of the Alleged Commission?* (London: Review of Reviews, 1891).

20. Donald Crawford, quoting his wife, in Jenkins, *Victorian Scandal*, p. 219.

21. Whyte, *The Life of W. T. Stead*, vol. 2 (London: Jonathan Cape, 1925), p. 16.

22. Askwith, *Lady Dilke*, p. 151.

23. *Has Sir Charles Dilke Cleared His Name?* By comparison, Parnell, whose career was also ruined through adultery, had committed a minor offense: "Mr. Parnell did not initiate Mrs. O'Shea in all the mysteries of 'French Vice'; nor did Mr. Parnell force Mrs. O'Shea to endure the humiliation of passing the night with an Irish Fanny."

24. Raymond L. Schults, *Crusader in Babylon: W. T. Stead and the Pall Mall Gazette* (Lincoln: University of Nebraska Press, 1972), pp. 212, 213. Leaders on the Langworthy case appeared regularly in the *PMG* from 18 April 1887 to 24 May 1887.

25. Michael I. Friedland, *The Trials of Israel Lipski* (London: Macmillan,

1984); Gilbert Cross, *Next Week East Lynne* (Lewisburg: Bucknell University Press, 1975), pp. 99, 147.

26. In *The Armstrong Case* (p. 14), Stead had entitled a crossheading, "Ineptitude of the Police." He had already denounced police corruption in the failure to prosecute Mrs. Jeffries, a notorious brothel-keeper, who catered to "aristocratic" patrons and who was ultimately prosecuted in the late 1880s.

27. On Stead and the unemployed, see *PMG*, Feb. 1886, Oct., Nov. 1887, passim; Schults, *Crusader*, pp. 227–32; Arthur H. Nethercot, *The First Five Lives of Annie Besant* (Chicago: University of Chicago Press, 1960), pp. 246–57.

28. On general press reaction to police repression, see Robert Storch, "Police Control of Street Prostitution in Victorian London: A Study in the Context of Police Action," in *Police and Society,* ed. David H. Bayley (Beverly Hills: Sage, 1977), p. 55. Stead began to voice his concern with police mistreatment of prostitutes in November 1885 (*PMG*, 11 Nov. 1885).

29. "Police Outrage on a Lady," *PMG*, 5 Jan. 1886; *PMG*, 6 Jan. 1886; 5 Jan. 1886. See also Ruth First and Ann Scott, *Olive Schreiner* (New York: Schocken Books, 1980), p. 157.

30. See Index of the *PMG*, January–June 1887, July–December 1887, January–June 1887, July–December 1888. Between January and June 1887, for instance, the *PMG's* index listed fifteen items under the heading, "Assaults on Women (involving police)."

31. Between 30 June and 31 July 1887, the *PMG* carried 37 items devoted to the Cass case.

32. *Daily News* (London), 6 July 1887.

33. See Storch, "Police Control," pp. 55, 56.

34. Butler to Stead, n.d. [July 1887], Stead Papers. In "How the Police Abuse Their Power" (*PMG*, 7 July 1885) Stead acknowledged the effect of the Criminal Law Amendment Act, as a bill "not so much . . . for raising the age of consent and increasing the stringency of the provisions against procuration and the traffic in English girls as a bill for the arbitrary power of the police in the street." The metropolitan police campaign against streetwalkers began, under the pressure of local vigilance committees, in 1884, but like the rest of the purity mobilization gained momentum after the "Maiden Tribute" in 1885.

35. "The Police Outrage in Regent Street," *PMG*, 5 July 1887; "How Ladies are Annoyed on the Streets," *PMG* 19, 21, 22, 27, 30 July 1887.

36. *PMG*, 30 July 1887. See also E. Ray Lankester to Karl Pearson, 21 July 1887, Pearson Papers, 10/29.

37. Peter Bailey, "Parasexuality and Glamour: The Victorian Barmaid as Cultural Prototype," *Gender and History* 2, no. 2 (Summer 1990): 148–72; "What the Male Pests Have to Say for Themselves," *PMG*, 30 July 1887.

38. On the Gothic, see Rosemary Jackson, *Fantasy: The Literature of Subversion* (London and New York: Methuen, 1981), p. 25; Nina Auerbach, *Woman and the Demon: The Life of a Victorian Myth* (Cambridge: Harvard University Press, 1982); Elaine Showalter, "Sexuality, Syphilis and the Fiction of the Fin de Siècle," in Ruth Yeazell et al., eds., *Sex, Politics, and Science, in the Nineteenth Century*

(Baltimore: Johns Hopkins University Press, 1986), pp. 88–115; Eve Kosofsky Sedgwick, "The Beast in the Closet: James and the Writing of the Homosexual Panic," in Yeazell, *Sex, Politics, and Science*, pp. 148–86; Ed Block, "Evolutionary Psychology and Late-Victorian Gothic Fiction," *Victorian Studies* 25, no. 4 (Summer 1982): 443–65.

39. W. E. Henley to Robert Louis Stevenson, 9 July 1885, Stevenson Papers, Beinecke Library, Yale University, #4841. "Have you received the three copies of the *PMG*? There was never such indignation before as over this new feat of Stead." Henley later derisively referred to Stead as "Bed Stead" (Robertson Scott, *Life and Death*, p. 132), but he initially gave mocking credence to the "revelations": "What we all want to know is who's Dr. D—the hero of the three maids per fortnight. and who, o who! is the Minotaur, the devourer of the 2000 virginities at five pounds a piece. . . . Somehow I don't think the government can or rather will interfere. If Stead has really been exploring, he has probably got hold of facts which would upset a good many applecarts."

40. Dennis Porter, *The Pursuit of Crime: Art and Ideology in Detective Fiction* (New Haven: Yale University Press, 1981), p. 123. See also Stephen Knight, *Form and Ideology in Crime Fiction* (Bloomington: Indiana University Press, 1980).

41. See Judith R. Walkowitz, "Jack the Ripper and the Myth of Male Violence," *Feminist Studies* 8 (Fall 1982): 542–74.

42. Cobb to Pearson, 17 July 1885, Pearson Papers; Maria Sharpe, "Autobiographical Memoir," 1889, p. 5, Pearson Papers.

43. Henrietta Muller, quoted in *PMG*, 22 Aug. 1885; Mary Priestman to the editor, *PMG*, 24 July 1885. "There was no place of absolute safety, neither in the streets, nor parks, nor railways, nor in the houses, where the procuresses were often known to enter as charwomen, nor indeed in the very churches and chapels," one speaker announced at a meeting of middle-class women. "The Crusade against the Crimes of Modern Babylon," *PMG*, 23 July 1885. They were supported here by Stead. When, in 1885, a judge callously dismissed an assault charge on the grounds that the woman did not have a corroborating witness, and that "no man's liberty was safe if women were allowed to give men into custody under such circumstances," Stead was outraged. Such statements, duly reported in police court news, could make "women become more bitter and men more brutal."

44. Susan Edwards, "Sex Crimes in the Nineteenth Century," *New Society* 49 (13 Sept. 1979): 52–53; Anna Clark, *Women's Silence, Men's Violence: Sexual Assault in England, 1770–1845* (London: Pandora, 1987); Linda Gordon, commentary on session on "Family Violence," Berkshire Conference on Women's History, Vassar College, May 1981; Jan Lambertz, "Male-Female Violence in Late Victorian and Edwardian England," (B.A. diss., Harvard University, 1979).

45. I am following Nancy Cott's use of the concept of passionlessness as representing a "cluster of ideas about the comparative weight of women's carnal nature." "Passionlessness: An Interpretation of Victorian Sexual Ideology, 1790–1850," *Signs* 4 (1978): 220.

46. Victor Bailey and Sheila Blackburn, "The Punishment of Incest Act 1908: A Case Study of Law Creation," *Criminal Law Review* (1979): 708–18; Sheila

Jeffreys, *The Spinster and Her Enemies: Feminism and Sexuality, 1880–1930* (London: Pandora Press, 1986).

47. Carroll Smith-Rosenberg and Esther Newton, "The Mythic Lesbian and the New Woman: Power, Sexuality and Legitimacy," presented at the Berkshire Conference, May 1981. In a private letter to Edward Carpenter, at the time of the Wilde trial in 1895, Stead argued that the undefined status of female homosexuals afforded them more safety than their male counterparts: because the "law is absolutely indifferent to any amount of indecent familiarity taking place between two women . . . many women given themselves up to this kind of thing without any consciousness of it being wrong." Quoted in Baylen, "Oscar Wilde," p. 84.

48. *PMG*, 14 Aug. 1885; Margaret McMillan, *The Life of Rachel McMillan* (London and Toronto: J. M. Dent and Sons, 1927), p. 26; Olive Schreiner, quoted in Ruth First and Ann Scott, *Olive Schreiner*, p. 156; Elizabeth Cobb to Karl Pearson, Pearson Papers, 18 July 1885, 663/1.

49. *Maiden Tribute*, p. 5; Gorham, "Maiden Tribute," pp. 372, 373; Walkowitz, *Prostitution and Victorian Society*, p. 249; John Gillis, *Youth and History* (New York: Academic Press, 1974). For reformers, "girlhood" was a stage in life marked by dependency but not by any specific psychosexual development. Accordingly, debates over the age of consent rarely included reference to the actual sexual development of the girls to be protected. The age of consent was arbitrary; indeed many reformers wanted to raise it to eighteen, some to twenty-one. Moreover, many of the same assumptions about protecting and controlling female adolescents ultimately led to the definition and incarceration of sexually active girls as "sex delinquents." Respectable working-class parents certainly shared many of the same sentiments towards female adolescents. Despite the fact that they often sent their own daughters out to work at thirteen, they nonetheless took pains to restrict their social independence and sexual knowledge and experience. Gorham, "Maiden Tribute." For workingmen and workingwomen's response to social purity, see Walkowitz, "Politics of Prostitution," pp. 86, 87.

50. Emma Brooke, "Notes on a Man's View of the Woman Question," 1885, Pearson Papers, 10/2.

51. "Minute Book of the Men and Women's Club," pp. 119–24, Pearson Papers, 10/1.

Chapter Five

1. This chapter is an expanded and extensively revised version of "Science, Feminism, and Romance: The Men and Women's Club, 1885–1889," *History Workshop Journal* (April 1986): 37–59, used here by permission of Oxford University Press. Other discussions of the Men and Women's Club are in Phyllis Grosskurth, *Havelock Ellis* (New York: Knopf, 1980), pp. 93–106; Ruth First and Ann Scott, *Olive Schreiner* (New York: Schocken Books, 1980), pp. 144–72; Daniel J. Kevles, *In the Name of Eugenics: Genetics and the Uses of Human Heredity* (New York: Knopf, 1985); Lucy Bland, "Marriage Laid Bare: Middle-Class Women and Marital Sex c. 1880–1914," in Jane Lewis, ed., *Labour and Love* (Oxford: Basil Blackwell, 1986); Carol Dyhouse, *Feminism and the Family in England 1880–1939* (Oxford: Basil Blackwell, 1989), pp. 159–66, 171–74; Ruth Brandon,

The New Women and the Old Men: Love, Sex, and the Woman Question (New York: W. W. Norton, 1990); Janet Oppenheim, *"Shattered Nerves": Doctors, Patients, and Depression in Victorian England* (New York: Oxford University Press, 1991), pp. 219–22.

2. In other contexts, a more heterodox and adventurous investigation of sexual variation and sexual identity was undertaken, but in such settings women were rarely present or vocal. See Sheila Rowbotham and Jeffrey Weeks, *Socialism and the New Life: The Personal and Sexual Politics of Edward Carpenter and Havelock Ellis* (London: Pluto, 1977); Phyllis Grosskurth, *The Woeful Victorian: A Biography of John Addington Symonds* (New York: Longmans, 1964).

3. Gertrude Himmelfarb, *The Idea of Poverty: England in the Early Industrial Age* (New York: Vintage Books, 1985), chap. 16; I. M. Britain, *Fabianism and Culture: A Study in British Socialism and the Arts, 1884–1918* (Cambridge: Cambridge University Press, 1982).

4. Michel Foucault, *The History of Sexuality,* vol. 1, *An Introduction* (New York: Pantheon, 1978); Rowbotham and Weeks, *Socialism;* Jeffrey Weeks, *Sex, Politics, and Society* (London: Longman, 1981). For a critical revision of the Foucauldian formulation, see Judith R. Walkowitz, "Male Vice and Feminist Virtue: Feminism and the Politics of Prostitution in Nineteenth-Century Britain," *History Workshop Journal,* 13 (Spring 1982), p. 89; "Dangerous Sexualities," in Georges Duby and Michelle Perrot, eds., *Storia delle Donne* (Rome: Laterza, 1991), vol. 4; Jonathan Katz, ed., *Gay/Lesbian Almanac: A New Documentary* (New York: Harper and Row, 1983); John D'Emilio and Estelle Freedman, *Intimate Matters: A History of Sexuality in America* (New York: Harper and Row, 1988).

5. Sixteen thousand items are collected in the Pearson Papers, University College, London. Citations to the manuscript letters and records are indicated by "Pearson Papers"; citations to the typed transcripts of documents from the collection by Pearson's daughter, Helen Sharpe Hacker, are indicated by "Pearson Transcripts." In addition, another ten thousand items related to Maria Sharpe's family have recently been made available in the Sharpe Papers, University College, London.

6. See Ruth Yeazell, "Nature's Courtship Plot in Darwin and Ellis," *Yale Journal of Criticism* 2, no. 2 (1989): 35; Leila J. Rupp, "Public Prudery, Private Passion," review of Karen Lystra, *Searching the Heart: Women, Men and Romantic Love in Nineteenth-Century America, Women's Review of Books* 7, no. 7 (April 1990): 20.

7. Grosskurth, *Havelock Ellis,* p. 98. Pearson had a habit of "roving into other people's preserves": he studied mathematics in Cambridge, but also read papers on Spinoza; he studied civics in Heidelberg, but also metaphysics; and he read law in Berlin, but also attended lectures on Darwinism. In London in the early 1880s, in addition to his professional pursuits, he lectured on heat in Barnes, on Luther in Hampstead, and on Marx and Lassalle in revolutionary clubs in Soho. He even contributed a hymn or two to the socialist songbook. Egon Pearson, *Karl Pearson: An Appreciation of Some Aspects of His Life and Work* (Cambridge: University Press, 1938), p. 7. On the intellectual tendencies of the late-Victorian period, see Beatrice Webb, *My Apprenticeship,* quoted in First and Scott, *Schreiner,* p. 108; Gareth Stedman Jones, *Outcast London: A Study in the Relationship between Classes in Victorian Society* (Oxford: Clarendon Press, 1971). On Pearson's free thought and

scientism, see D. Mackenzie, "Karl Pearson and the Professional Middle Class," *Annals of Science* 36, no. 22 (March 1979): 124–44; K. P. to E. C., 2 April 1927 (but never sent), Pearson Papers, 9/6.

8. Mrs. W. K. Clifford to Olive Schreiner, quoted in Betty McGinnis Fradkin, "Olive Schreiner and Karl Pearson," *Quarterly Bulletin of the South African Quarterly Library* (Capetown) 31, no. 4 (1977): 85; O. S. to K. P., 18 Oct. 1886, Pearson Typescripts, D. 2,3; Joan Evans, *The Conways, A History of Three Generations* (London: Museum Press, 1966), p. 67; O. S., quoted in Kevles, *Eugenics*, p. 29; E. C. to Bryan Donkin, Dec. 1886, Pearson Transcripts, D.2.

9. Thanks to Nina Auerbach for this insight.

10. Kevles, *Eugenics*, pp. 23, 24; Karl Pearson, *The Ethic of Freethought* (London: A. and C. Black, 1888); idem, *The Chances of Death and Other Studies in Evolution*, 2 vols. (London: E. Arnold, 1897); Mackenzie, "Karl Pearson and the Professional Middle Class": 125–44; Harold Perkin, *The Rise of Professional Society: England Since 1880* (New York: Routledge, 1989).

11. Pearson, "The Woman's Question," in *Ethic*, p. 376.

12. E. C. to K. P. (quoting Pearson), Sept. 1884, Pearson Papers, 663/1; See Jonathan Ned Katz, "The Invention of Heterosexuality," *Socialist Review* 20, no. 1 (January–March 1990): 7–34.

13. Kevles, *Eugenics*, p. 21; Karl Pearson, *The Life, Letters, and Labours of Francis Galton* (Cambridge: Cambridge University Press, 1914–30), vol. III A, pp. 327–28.

14. Pearson, quoted in Kevles, *Eugenics*, p. 24; K. P. to M. S., 21 March 1887, Pearson Transcripts, D.2,3.

15. K. P. to M. S., 10 Aug. 1889, Pearson Transcripts, D.13.

16. Pearson maintained a warm but condescending relationship with his afflicted mother; he contemptuously regarded his other female relatives as "shopping dolls." See, for example, K. P. to Fanny Pearson, 1 Feb. 1880; Fanny Pearson to K. P., 28 Nov. 1874; K. P. to William Pearson, 5 May 1882; K. P. to M. S., 6 Jan. 1888, Pearson Transcripts, D.1,2,3. For a theoretical discussion of men's resentment towards women that might be appropriate to the kind of bourgeois family life and culture from which Pearson emerged, see Dorothy Dinnerstein, *The Mermaid and the Minotaur: Sexual Arrangements and Human Malaise* (New York: Harper and Row, 1976).

17. In a letter to Betty Fradkin (n.d.), Helga Sharpe Hacker claimed that Pearson recoiled from Olive Schreiner after "she had in word and deed thrown herself at [him] with passionate sexual desire." Pearson Transcripts. For a different reading of Schreiner's behavior towards Pearson, see First and Scott, *Schreiner*, pp. 166–88.

18. Deidre David, "Ideologies of Patriarchy, Feminism, and Fiction in *The Odd Women*," *Feminist Studies* 10 (Spring 1984): 117–40.

19. In a 1889 letter, Pearson recounted how important women's friendships had been to him, despite the danger of misunderstood intimacy and sexual interest: "Believe me I have found it, especially in the years gone by, so hard to do without women's friendship and yet seen that, however cautious and self-controlled one might be oneself, there was danger, perhaps evil, produced which one would have

done anything to avoid." K. P. to M. S., 8 Sept. 1889, Pearson Transcripts, D.13.

20. Hacker to Fradkin, Pearson Transcripts; E. C. to K. P., 25 March 1885, Pearson Papers, 663/1.

21. On Schreiner, see First and Scott, *Olive Schreiner*, p. 184; Olive Renier, "A South African Rebel," in Cherry Clayton, ed., *Olive Schreiner* (Johannesburg: Mc Graw-Hill, 1983), p. 53. On Eleanor Marx Aveling, see Beatrice Webb, *The Diaries of Beatrice Webb*, vol. 1, *1873–1892*, ed. Norman MacKenzie and Jeanne MacKenzie (Cambridge, Mass: Belknap Press, 1982), p. 88.

22. Hacker to Fradkin, Pearson Transcripts; E. C. to K. P., 26 June 1885, 17 Oct. 1885, Pearson Papers, 663/1.

23. On Wollstonecraft, see M. S. to R. J. Parker, 20 July 1885; Sharpe, "Autobiographical Notes," p. 15, Pearson Papers, 10/1. On Marx Aveling, see Eleanor Marx Aveling to Bryan Donkin, 8 Feb. 1886; K. P. to M. S., 10 Feb. 1886, 17 March 1886, Pearson Transcripts, D.2,3. For a discussion of the "Hintonian Imbroglio," see Grosskurth, *Havelock Ellis,* chap. 6; First and Scott, *Schreiner,* pp. 125–29; 152, 153.

24. O. S. to K. P., 11 Oct. 1885, Pearson Transcripts, D.2. In a letter to Maria Sharpe of 12 Feb. 1888, Pearson enclosed a letter from another correspondent. He was quite certain the writer underestimated the physical incapacity of women; he asked Sharpe whether her experience "with servants and others would lead you to confirm it." This piece of "field work" later was incorporated into Pearson's discussion of the cultural and class variations of female sexual response. See Karl Pearson, "Thoughts suggested by the papers and discussion at the meeting of the Club on 9 May," Pearson Papers, 10/11. As Thomas Laqueur observes, although medical authorities might disagree about the degree of female sexual responsiveness, hardly any systematic survey had been undertaken of women's sexual feelings before the 1890s. That is, a knowledge of sexual responsiveness among women in general (not to speak of the sexual responsiveness and habits of men), systematically collected and organized to meet Pearson's specifications, did not then exist. *Making Sex: Body and Gender from the Greeks to Freud* (Cambridge: Harvard University Press, 1990), pp. 190, 191.

25. For discussions of radical heterodox London, see William Sylvester Smith, *The London Heretics 1870–1914* (London: Constable, 1967); Yvonne Kapp, *Eleanor Marx*, vol. 2 (New York: Pantheon Books, 1976); Norman MacKenzie and Jeanne MacKenzie, *The Fabians* (New York: Simon and Schuster, 1977).

26. "Glorified Spinster" to the editor, *DT,* London, 17 Sept. 1888; "The Glorified Spinster," *Macmillan's Magazine* 58 (Sept. 1888): 371–76; Sharpe, "Autobiographical Notes," p. 37, Pearson Papers; Maria Sharpe, "Secretary's Conclusion," in Minute Book of the Men and Women's Club, p. 285, Pearson Papers, 10/1. There is no complete discussion of metropolitan feminism in this period, but see Diana Burford, "Theosophy and Feminism," in Pat Holden, ed., *Women's Religious Experience* (London: Croom Helm, 1983), pp. 27–56; Martha Vicinus, *Independent Women: Work and Community for Single Women, 1850–1920* (Chicago: University of Chicago Press, 1985).

27. Emma Brooke to K. P., 14 Dec. 1888, Pearson Papers, 10/28; Annie Besant to K. P., 12 Jan. 1887, quoted in Scott and First, *Olive Schreiner,* p. 146;

Karl Pearson, "The Enthusiasm of the Marketplace and of the Study," in *The Ethic of Freethought and Other Addresses and Essays* (London: A. and C. Black, 1901), pp. 103–24; Emma Brooke to K. P., 14 March 1886; 11 March 1886; 14 Dec. 1888, Pearson Papers, 10/28. Havelock Ellis and Bernard Shaw were two men rejected for club membership. Pearson may have had numerous reasons for objecting to their candidacy. Ellis had bohemian associations and a personal connection to Schreiner that might have excited Pearson's jealousy. Shaw was undoubtedly too irreverent and ungenteel for the club. Pearson may have also regarded both as threatening intellectual competitors.

28. Kevles, *Eugenics*, chap. 2; Penny Boulmelha, *Thomas Hardy and Women: Sexual Ideology and Narrative* (Brighton, Sussex: Harvester, 1982), p. 21; Frances Power Cobbe, quoted in Olive Banks, *Becoming a Feminist: The Social Origins of 'First Wave' Feminism* (Brighton, Sussex: Wheatsheaf, 1986), p. 74.

29. Janet E. Courtney, *An Oxford Portrait Gallery* (London: Chapman and Hall, 1931), p. 184.

30. M. S. to R. J. Parker, 27 April 1889, Pearson Papers, 10/1; M. S. to R. J. Parker, 10 Nov. 1885, Pearson Papers, 10/1.

31. Sharpe, "Autobiographical Notes," excerpt for Feb. 1886, Pearson Transcript, D.2,3; Egon Pearson, *Karl Pearson: An Appreciation of Some Aspects of His Life and Work* (Cambridge: The University Press, 1938); E. C. to K. P., 28 Dec. 1881, Pearson Papers, 663/1; Loetitia Sharpe, "Recollections of Lucy Sharpe," Sharpe Papers, 133.

32. When, in 1889, Karl Pearson read her "commonplace book," he was impressed with the tepid, abstract sentiments filling the pages in the 1870s and early 1880s: a "pale enthusiasm of loving work for others because such was pleasing to the Deity," he summed up. K. P. to M. S., 4/9/1889, Pearson Transcripts, D. 13.

33. Sharpe, "Autobiographical Notes," pp. 1–3, Pearson Papers, 10/1.

34. M. S. to K. P., 15 Jan. 1888, Pearson Papers, 793. "I cannot help feeling very young and very romantic," Lina Eckenstein wrote to Sharpe in 1884. "My mind sees you in the brim bonnet with the lace neatly arranged in a curve . . . the velvet sleets closing about those good kind hands, and lace ribbons . . . about with feminine daintiness and puritanical quaintness. . . ." "When I say certain things to you you take them as the outcome of momentary infatuation, whereas [if I write them] you must grant them more than the transitory existence of words crafted to oblivion. . . . When I say you are beautiful, do you think I do so just because your hair is especially luminous against a dark wallpaper." 22 June 1884, 3 Feb. 1884, Sharpe Papers, 139/5. On Boston marriages, see Lillian Faderman, *Surpassing the Love of Men: Romantic Friendships and Love Between Women from the Renaissance to the Present* (New York: William Morrow, 1981); John D'Emilio and Estelle Friedman, *Intimate Matters: A History of Sexuality in America* (New York: Harper and Row, 1988), p. 125; Emma Willard, "Companionships," reprinted in Jonathan Katz, *Gay/Lesbian Almanac: A New Documentary* (New York: Harper & Row, 1983), pp. 216–18.

35. Sharpe, "Autobiographical Notes," p. 1; M. S. to K. P., 19 July 1885, Pearson Transcripts, D. 2,3.

36. E. C. to K. P., 17 July 1885, 25 March 1885, 19 July 1885, Pearson Papers, 663/1.

37. O. S. to M. S. 24 Nov. 1887, Pearson Transcripts, D.2,3; Sharpe, "Autobiographical Notes," p. 1, Pearson Papers, 10/1; Emma Brooke, "Notes on a Man's View of the Woman's Question," Pearson Papers, 10/2.

38. On the eclipse of state medicine, see Frank Mort, *Dangerous Sexualities: Medico-Moral Politics in England since 1830* (London: Routledge and Kegan Paul, 1987). On Pearson's fear of female temptresses, see Lucy Bland, "Rational Sex or Spiritual Love? The Men and Women's Club of the 1880s," *Women's Studies International Forum* 13, nos. 1/2 (1990): 46. On Darwinism, see Charles Darwin, citing Schopenhauer, in *The Descent of Man,* quoted in Gillian Beer, *Darwin's Plots: Evolutionary Narrative in Darwin, George Eliot, and Nineteenth-Century Fiction* (London: Ark Paperbacks, 1985), p. 211; Yeazell, "Nature's Courtship Plot."

39. "Rules," "Minute Book of the Men and Women's Club," Pearson Transcripts, D.2,3.

40. For instance, Bryan Donkin was the rejected suitor and consulting physician for Olive Schreiner; Karl Pearson was Maria Sharpe's suitor and tutor. Elizabeth Cobb wrote to Pearson in December 1886, having received a "stormy letter" from Schreiner. "She was telling me how passionately she loved me, in such a way as to distress me." E. C. to K. P., 15 Dec. 1886, Pearson Transcripts, Olive Schreiner Transcripts. A year later, Schreiner herself wrote Pearson: "I have had a curious kind of feeling attracting me to Mrs. Cobb, such as I have not felt for another woman." O. S. to K. P., 30 Jan. 1887, Pearson Papers, 840/4.

41. O. S. to K. P., 4 March 1886, Pearson Transcripts, D.2,3.

42. Sharpe, "Autobiographical Notes," p. 24, Pearson Papers, 10/1.

43. "Rules," Pearson Transcripts, D.2,3; Karl Pearson, *The Grammar of Science* (New York: Meridian Library, 1957 [rpt. of 1911 ed.]), p. 9; K. P. to M. S., 21 Sept. 1889, Pearson Transcripts, Box 13.

44. M. S. P. to Loetitia Sharpe, 25 Nov. 1889, Pearson Papers, 142/5.

45. Sharpe, "Secretary's Conclusion," pp. 284, 281, 286; M. J. to R. J. Parker, 10 Nov. 1885, Pearson Papers, 10/1.

46. Schopenhauer, quoted in Charles Darwin, *Descent of Man,* quoted in Beer, *Darwin's Plots,* p. 210.

47. Beer, *Darwin's Plots,* p. 125; Flavia Alaya, "Victorian Science and the 'Genius' of Woman," *Journal of the History of Ideas* 38 (April–June 1977): 261–80; Lorna Duffin, "Prisoners of Progress: Women and Evolution," in Sara Delamont and Lorna Duffin, eds., *The Nineteenth-Century Woman, Her Cultural and Physical World* (London: Croom Helm, 1978), pp. 57–91; Elizabeth Fee, "Science and the Woman Problem: Historical Perspectives," in Michael Teitelbaum, ed., *Sex Differences: Social and Biological Perspectives* (New York: Anchor Press, 1976), pp. 175–223.

48. E. C. to K. P., 20 Sept. 1886, Sept. 1885, Pearson Papers, 663/1.

49. Lawrence Birken, *Consuming Desire: Sexual Science and the Emergence of a Culture of Abundance, 1871–1914* (Ithaca: Cornell University Press, 1988), chap. 3; Cynthia Eagle Russett, *Sexual Science: The Victorian Construction of*

Womanhood (Cambridge: Harvard University Press, 1989), pp. 40–42, 90–91.

50. Sharpe, "Secretary's Conclusion," p. 280.

51. The following is based on the version of Pearson's "Woman's Question," read at the first club meeting. Pearson Papers, 10/2. It was revised and reprinted in *Ethic of Freethought*, 354–78.

52. These would include the physiological division of labor; the recapitulation of ontogeny indicated by women's inherited capacity; and the relation of sexual instinct to race survival. See Russett, *Sexual Science*.

53. Excerpts of letters from Miss Mills and Mrs. John Brown to E. C., included in a letter to K. P., 1885, Pearson Papers, 663/1.

54. O. S. to K. P., n.d. [July 1885], Pearson Transcripts; O. S. to K. P., circa 14 July 1885, Pearson Transcripts, D.2,3; Emma Brooke to K. P., 14 March 1886, Pearson Papers, 10/28; Brooke, "Notes on a man's view of the woman's question," Pearson Papers, 10/2. Brooke's defiance in tone was contrasted to her personal timorousness over the circulation of her letters. She asked him several times not to show her letters to anyone.

55. Charlotte Wilson to K. P., 8 Aug. 1885, Pearson Papers, 900; Pearson, "Sex and Socialism," in *Ethic of Freethought*, p. 427.

56. Henrietta Muller, "The other side of the question," Pearson Papers, 10/3.

57. E. C. to K. P., 17 Oct. 1885, Pearson Papers, 663/1; "Second Meeting of the Club, 12 Oct. 1885," "Third Meeting of the Club, 9 Nov. 1885," "Minute Book," Pearson Papers, 10/1.

58. M. S. to K. P., 29 Oct. 1885, Pearson Papers, 793.

59. On the sexual plot of Darwinism, see Ruth Yeazell, "Nature's Courtship Plot." On Pearson's use of case studies, see Pearson, "Note on the sexual feeling," Pearson Transcripts, D.4.

60. K. P. to M. S., 13 April 1887, Pearson Transcripts; Pearson, "Note," K. P. to M. S., 14 Nov. 1885; R. J. Parker to K. P., 23 Sept. 1887; K. P. to M. S., 14 Jan. 1885, Pearson Transcripts, D.2,3.

61. M. S. to K. P., 15 Nov. 1885, Pearson Transcripts, D.2,3.

62. O. S. to K. P., 5 Nov. 1888, Pearson Transcripts, D. 2,3.

63. Sharpe, "Autobiographical Notes," excerpt for 8 Feb. 1886, Pearson Transcripts, D.2,3; Pearson, "Sketch of Sexual Relations in Primitive and Medieval Germany," reprinted in *Ethic of Freethought*, pp. 379–410.

64. See Elizabeth Fee, "The Sexual Politics of Victorian Social Anthropology," in Mary Hartman and Lois Banner, eds., *Clio's Consciousness Raised: New Perspectives on the History of Women* (New York: Harper and Row, 1974), p. 101.

65. "Report of Lecture by Professor Carl [sic] Pearson," 20 Dec. 1890, Pearson Transcripts, D.14; Pearson, "Sketch of Sexual Relations." "The student of the history of civilization will find that there was a time when the woman *physically* was practically on a par with the man while *mentally* she was his superior." Pearson, "Sex and Socialism," p. 441.

66. "Minute Book," pp. 104–24, 127–34, Pearson Papers, 10/1.

67. "Women's Sphere in Modern Society" was later read before the Fabian Society and published, in revised form, under the pseudonym of "E. Fairfax Brynne"

in Besant's *Our Corner* (1888): 5–13, 65–73. Direct quotations are from the printed version.

68. Women's wages, Brooke argued, were "low" because of the "sexual value" men attached to "women's personality." Because women's sexuality was a marketable quantity (with prostitution and marriage constituting two sides of the same commercial coin), the value of all women's labor was depressed, for it was assumed that women had recourse to alternative sources of support. The only solution to women's bleak economic condition was the simultaneous introduction of the following reforms: political and social equality; easy divorce; abolition of the regulation and licensing of prostitution; education reform; the free education of children in state institutions under the guidance of the state; and the state support of motherhood. Ibid., pp. 6–9, 66, 67.

69. Ibid., pp. 67, 68.

70. Ibid., p. 71. For Bebel's discussion of the population question, see August Bebel, *Women in the Past, Present, and Future* (London: Zwan, 1988 [rpt. of 1885 translation]), pp. 237–56, 262.

71. Beals, "Fabian Feminism," p. 127.

72. "Minute Book," pp. 133–35.

73. "Sex and Socialism," pp. 426–46.

74. K. P. to M. S., 14 Dec. 1886, quoted in Brandon, *The New Women and the Old Men* (New York: W. W. Norton, 1990), p. 76.

75. In an earlier letter to Sharpe, Pearson laid out the sexual basis of home duties. After decrying the inertness and laziness of home-bound women, he asked "how far do these home services go—and if they touch or include the services of friendship, possibly those of sex, are you not, dangerously near making the finest human relation a matter of pecuniary arrangement. . . . The 'home duties' are generally but a poor excuse, the real payment is for providing bodily service to an individual either in the form of 'home duties' or more physically in the matter of sex." K. P. to M. S., 14 Dec. 1886, Pearson Papers, 793.

76. Olive Schreiner, *Woman and Labour* (London: T. Fisher Unwin, 1911), chap. 1.

77. K. P. to M. S., 21 March 1887, Pearson Papers, 793.

78. Ralph Thicknesse, quoted by M. S. to K. P., 20 March 1887, Pearson Papers, 793.

79. Pearson added, "*Personally*, we do not feel this struggle, but in treating long periods of human development, it seems to me clearly enough marked." K. P. to M. S., 25 March 1887, Pearson Papers, 793.

80. K. P. to M. S., 16 Dec. 1886, Pearson Papers, 793; M. S. to K. P., 31 March 1887, Pearson Papers, 793.

81. "14th Meeting, 18 Jan. 1887," "Minute Book," pp. 119–24, Pearson Papers, 10/1.

82. Anon [Kathleen Mills], "Checks to Population"; Abstract of Henrietta Muller, "The Limitation of the Family"; Karl Pearson, "Thoughts Suggested by the Papers and Discussion at the Meeting of the Club on May 9th," Pearson Transcripts, D.4. See also Bland, "Laid Bare."

83. Sharpe, "Autobiographical Notes," Pearson Transcripts, D.2,3; "Comments on Karl Pearson's Thoughts suggested in the Papers and Discussion," Pearson Transcripts, D.4.

84. See First and Scott, *Olive Schreiner*, pp. 164–71; E. C. to K. P., 11 May 1887, Pearson Papers, 663/1.

85. Linda Gordon and Ellen Dubois, "Seeking Ecstasy on the Battlefield: Danger and Pleasure in Nineteenth-Century Feminist Sexual Thought," *Feminist Studies* 9 (Spring 1983): 7–26.

86. Elizabeth Pleck, "Feminist Responses to 'Crimes against Women,' 1868–1896," *Signs* 8, no. 3 (1983): 451–70.

87. K. P. to M. S., 24 Nov. 1886, 14 Feb. 1888, Pearson Transcripts, D. 2, 3; Sharpe, "Autobiographical Notes," pp. 59–76, Pearson Papers, 10/1; R. J. Parker, "The Contagious Diseases Act," read on 12 Dec. 1887 and 9 Jan. 1888, Pearson Papers, 10/13; "Notes" by Loetitia Sharpe, Annie Eastty, Maria Sharpe, and Lina Eckenstein, read on 12 March 1888, Pearson Papers, 10/14.

88. Ralph Thicknesse, "Some social aspects of the regulation of prostitution," read on 13 Feb. 1888, Pearson Papers, 10/14.

89. There is no record of Muller organizing such a group. Instead, she went on to found the *Woman's Penny Paper*, the first women's newspaper in London, and to join theosophy, where women were much more at the center of knowledge and power.

90. K. P. to M. S., 14 Feb. 1888; Sharpe, "Autobiographical Notes," p. 60, Pearson Papers, 10/1; First and Scott, *Schreiner*, p. 154.

91. Sharpe, "Autobiographical Notes," p. 2, Pearson Papers, 10/1.

92. M. S. to K. P., 15 Jan. 1888, Pearson Papers, 793; Sharpe, "Autobiographical Notes," pp. 48–64.

93. "The various 'early society' books which I have read since I joined the club have made a stronger impression on me than anything else." M. S. to K. P., 11 June 1887, Pearson Papers, 793.

94. Sharpe, "Autobiographical Notes," p. 65.

95. Sharpe, "Note on the Woman's Movement," read on 10 Dec. 1888, Pearson Transcripts, D.4; "Autobiographical Notes," p. 87, Pearson Papers, 10/1; M. S. to R. J. Parker, 27 April 1889, Pearson Papers, 10/1; M. S. to K. P., 22 Oct. 1887, 26 March 1890; Pearson Transcripts, D.2,3; Oppenheim, "*Shattered Nerves*," p. 222. On psychological and literary realism, see Elaine M. Hadley, "Melodramatic Tactics: The Social Function of the Melodramatic Mode, 1800–1885" (Ph.D. diss., Johns Hopkins University, 1991), chap. 5.

96. K. P. to M. S., 30 July 1889, Pearson Transcripts, D. 13; M. S. to K. P. 25 Oct. 1891, Pearson Transcripts, D. 14.

97. See, for example, E. C. to K. P., 14 April 1882; 14 Sept. 1885, 13 March 1886, 6 June 1886, 27 March 1927, Pearson Papers, 663/1. See also O. S. to K. P. [20 June 1886], in Richard Rive, ed., *Olive Schreiner Letters*, vol. 1: *1871–1899* (Oxford: Oxford University Press, 1988), p. 84.

98. Schreiner's overidentification and lack of "scientific" distance must have appalled (if perhaps intrigued) Pearson. "I . . . am long past the stage in which one

only 'studies' human beings. They all seem like part of myself." In one letter, Schreiner could propose something outlandish, like bringing Pearson together with a prostitute, "a woman with sweet blue eyes and a loveable child's face," and then invent "Professor K.P."'s "priggish response": "Ill-regulated mind." O. S. to K. P., 5 March 1886, 20 June 1886, reprinted in Rive, *Olive Schreiner*, pp. 73, 84.

99. K. P. to M. S., 6 July 1885, Pearson Transcripts, D.2,3.

100. "28th Meeting, 15 Oct. 1888," "Minute Book," K. P. to M. S., 19 March 1888; Sharpe, "Autobiographical Notes," excerpts for 15 Oct. 1888, 13 Nov. 1888, Pearson Transcripts, D.2,3.

101. M. S. to K. P., 20 Oct. 1888; K. P. to M. S., 21 Oct. 1888; M. S. to K. P., 9 Nov. 1888, Pearson Transcripts, D.2,3.

102. M. S. to K. P., 21 March 1889; K. P. to M. S., 24 March 1889; M. S. to K. P., 26 March 1889, Pearson Transcripts, D.2,3.

103. Sharpe, "Autobiographical Notes," excerpts for 18 Dec. 1888, 13 Feb. 1888, Pearson Transcripts, D.2,3; E. C. to K. P., 6 June 1889, Pearson Papers, 663/1.

104. "Author of 'A Superfluous Woman,'" [Emma Brooke], "The Position of Woman: Its Origin and History," *The Woman's Signal* (London), 12 April 1894; 29 March 1894. Like Maria Sharpe, Brooke's imagination was fired by the Mother-age "findings" that challenged "the deeply-rooted idea of the natural subordination of women to men." Quoted in Dyhouse, *Feminism and the Family*, p. 71.

105. Pearson, observes Beals, was the most frequently cited writer on the Woman's Question by Fabian feminists. Beals, "Fabian Feminism," pp. 121, 122. See also Sally Alexander, ed., *Women's Fabian Tracts* (London: Routledge, 1989).

106. Vera Brittain, quoted in First and Scott, *Olive Schreiner*, p. 265.

107. Lina Eckenstein, *Woman under Monasticism: Chapters on Saint-Lore and Convent Life between A.D. 500 and A.D. 1500* (Cambridge: Cambridge University Press), 1896.

108. M. S. to Loetitia Sharpe, 4 Sept. 1890, Pearson Transcripts; M. S. to K. P., 26 March 1890, Pearson Papers, 793; E. C. to K. P., 10 Oct. 1889, Pearson Papers, 663/1; M. S. to K. P., 30 May 1889, Pearson Transcripts, D.2,3; K. P. to E. C., 2 March 1927, Pearson Papers, 9/6.

109. Schreiner, quoted in Brandon, *New Women*, p. 30; Edith Lees, quoted in MacKenzie and MacKenzie, *The Fabians*, p. 168.

110. G. Udny Yule, "Karl Pearson," *Obituary Notices of Fellows of the Royal Society* 2 (1936–38), p. 100.

111. Mona Caird, "Marriage," *Westminster Review* 130 (Aug. 1888).

112. *DT,* 9 Aug.–29 Sept. 1888; Harry Quilter, ed., *Is Marriage a Failure?* (London: Swan Sonnenschein, 1888).

113. E. C. to K. P., 2 Oct. 1889, Pearson Papers, 663/1; Sharpe, "Auto-biographical Notes," excerpt for 13 Nov. 1888, Pearson Transcripts, D.2,3; *PMG*, 29 Sept. 1888; *DT*, 8 Sept. 1888, 14 Sept. 1888.

114. See Judith Walkowitz, "Jack the Ripper and the Myth of Male Violence," *Feminist Studies* 8 (Fall 1982): 543–74; "Jack the Ripper," chap. 7 below.

Chapter Six

1. This is a revised version of "Science and the Séance: Transgressions of Gender and Genre in Late-Victorian London," *Representations* 22 (Spring 1988): 3–29, © 1988 by the Regents of the University of California. On the marriage debates, see Lucy Bland, "Marriage Laid Bare: Middle-Class women and Marital Sex, c. 1880–1914," in Jane Lewis, ed., *Labour and Love: Women's Experience of Home and Family, 1820–1940* (Oxford: Basil Blackwell, 1986), pp. 123–48; Philip Treherne, *A Plaintiff in Person* (London: William Heinemann, 1923), p. 97.

2. Peter McCandless, "Dangerous to Themselves and Others: The Victorian Debate over the Prevention of Wrongful Confinement," *Journal of British Studies* 23 (Fall 1983): 84–104; idem, "Liberty and Lunacy: The Victorians and Wrongful Confinement," *Journal of Social History* 11 (1978): 366–86.

3. Attendance at séances became a popular craze for the well-heeled in the late 1860s and 1870s, when even Charles Darwin and Francis Galton participated in drawing-room sessions. See Janet Oppenheim, *The Other World: Spiritualism and Psychical Research in England, 1850–1914* (New York: Cambridge University Press, 1985); Ruth Brandon, *The Spiritualists: The Passion for the Occult in the Nineteenth Century* (New York: Knopf, 1983); Alex Owen, "The Other Voice: Women, Children, and Nineteenth-Century Spiritualism," in Carolyn Steedman et al., eds., *Language, Gender, and Childhood* (London: Routledge and Kegan Paul, 1985), pp. 31–73; S. E. D. Shortt, "Physicians and Psychics: The Anglo-American Medical Response to Spiritualism, 1870–90," *Journal of the History of Medicine and Allied Sciences* 39 (1984): 339–55.

4. Judith R. Walkowitz, *Prostitution and Victorian Society: Women, Class, and the State* (New York: Cambridge University Press, 1980), chaps. 4, 5; R. D. French, *Antivivisection and Medical Science in Victorian Society* (Princeton: Princeton University Press, 1975), chap. 9; R. M. McLeod, "Law, Medicine and Public Opinion: The Resistance to Compulsory Health Legislation 1870–1901," *Public Law* (1967): 189–211. F. B. Smith, *The People's Health 1830–1910* (New York: Holmes and Meier, 1979), pp. 158–68.

5. Crookes, for example, extended his patronage to an attractive young test medium (provoking considerable gossip) and published findings that, he claimed, verified the physical phenomena produced by mediums. See Brandon, *The Spiritualists*, pp. 113–26; Oppenheim, *The Other World*, pp. 16–21.

6. Shortt, "Physicians and Psychics," pp. 345, 354.

7. William Clifford, quoted in Oppenheim, *The Other World*, p. 240; "Spiritualism and Science," *Lancet* 2 (1876): 431–33.

8. Carpenter published a scathing critique of Crookes, "Some Recent Converts to Spiritualism," *Quarterly Review* 131 (October 1871): 301; *Lancet* 2 (1876): 832.

9. He claimed to have snatched a slate away from Slade with a spirit message written on it even before the spirit communication had begun. Mr. Flowers, the police-court magistrate, sentenced Slade to three months' hard labor. The decision was overturned because of a technicality, but Slade fled the country anyway. Oppenheim, *The Other World*, pp. 23, 241; *Lancet* 2 (1876): 474.

10. "Mesmeric visions and prophecies, clairvoyances, spirit rappings, tableturnings and liftings," declared Sir Henry Holland, could best be explained as "morbid or anomalous states of the brain." Quoted in Oppenheim, *The Other World*, p. 244.

11. George Savage, quoted in Jane Marcus, "Mothering, Madness and Music," in Elaine K. Ginsberg and Laura Moss Gotlieb, *Virginia Woolf: Centennial Essays* (Troy, N.Y.: Whitston, 1983), p. 33; Alexandra Owen, *The Darkened Room: Women, Power, and Spiritualism in Late-Victorian England* (London: Virago, 1989), pp. 144–46.

12. L. Forbes Winslow, *Recollections of Forty Years* (London: John Ouseley, 1910); Obituary, *Lancet* 1 (1913): 1704; Obituary, *BMJ* 1 (1913): 1302; Dr. A. L. Wyman, "Why Winslow? The Winslows of Sussex House," *Charing Cross Hospital Gazette* 64 (1966–67): 143–46. The *Lancet*'s obituary coldly described him as one "who was well known in lay circles as an alienist," while the *British Medical Journal* peremptorily dismissed him as a publicity hound: "His opinion in any case that happened to interest the public was apparently highly valued by some newspapers, but with his own profession it carried less weight." Quoted in Wyman, "Why Winslow?"

13. L. S. Jacyna, "Somatic Theories of Mind and the Interests of Medicine in Britain, 1850–1879," *Medical History* 26 (1982): 233–58; Michael Clark, "The Rejection of Psychological Approaches to Mental Disorder in Late Nineteenth-Century British Psychiatry," in Andrew Scull, ed., *Madhouses, Mad-Doctors, and Madmen: The Social History of Psychiatry in the Victorian Era* (Philadelphia: University of Pennsylvania Press, 1981), pp. 271–312; Shortt, "Physicians and Psychics," p. 353; W. F. Bynum, "Themes in British Psychiatry: J. C. Prichard (1786–1918) to Henry Maudsley (1835–1918)," in Michael Ruse, ed., *Nature Animated* (Dordrecht: Reidel, 1983), pp. 225–42.

14. Winslow's record was to testify at three murder trials in a week (*Recollections*, p. 139). L. Forbes Winslow, *Fasting and Feeding Psychologically Considered* (London: Balliere, Tindall and Cox, 1881); idem, *Insanity of Passion and Crime, with 43 Photographic Reproductions of Celebrated Cases* (London: John Ouseley, 1912), p. 205. His writings claimed a somatic basis for disease yet identified the signs of criminal insanity in terms of behavioral symptoms: "external signs of speech behavior and acts," a failure of the rational will, that displayed a want of "prudence and foresight." Winslow also presented himself as an expert on "the borderlands," that newly identified twilight region where personal eccentricities shaded off into mental disorder. Winslow had a penchant for alarmist prediction of a "Mad Humanity": "Insanity is advancing by progressive leaps," he wrote in 1912, as "is shown by the official annual reports during the last fifty years." *Insanity of Passion*, p. 205.

15. Winslow, *Recollections*, p. 60.

16. L. Forbes Winslow, *Spiritualistic Madness* (London: n.p., 1877), p. 32. He coupled this "sensationalism" with a scientific explanation of spiritualist madness as a "physiological" condition of the "nervous system," once again following the lead of more prestigious scientists like Lankester and Maudsley.

17. In response, spiritualists organized defense funds and stepped up their

own campaign against the lunacy laws. Owen, "Subversive Spirit, chaps. 5, 6; S. E. Gay, *Spiritualistic Sanity: A Reply to Dr. Forbes Winslow's 'Spiritualistic Madness'* (London: Falmouth, 1879); "A Vigilance Committee," *The Spiritualist* (London) (10 Dec. 1880): 287.

18. Over 400 patients had been placed in his asylums through lunacy certification. *The Times* (London), 11 July 1884.

19. Winslow, quoted in *The Times,* 28 Nov. 1884.

20. Treherne, *Plaintiff;* Edward Grierson, *Storm Bird: The Strange Life of Georgina Wilson* (London: Chatto and Windus, 1959); "Mrs. Weldon's Orphanage," *Spiritualist* (21 Sept. 1877).

21. Mrs. Weldon, quoted in Grierson, *Storm Bird,* pp. 26, 27.

22. She was a well-known figure in society circles, a frequent visitor to Little Holland House and friend of the pre-Raphaelites. Ibid., p. 43.

23. "Mrs. Weldon's Orphanage."

24. Ibid.

25. Mrs. Weldon was not an isolated pioneer in this kind of undertaking. During the 1860s and 1870s a number of women opened small, private, rescue homes for prostitutes; their "personal style of philanthropy," to quote Josephine Butler, was a self-conscious challenge to the impersonal and repressive regimes of evangelical penitentiaries that had been founded and administered by men in the early Victorian period. By and large, these female philanthropists were middle-class Quakers and nonconformists, not members of fashionable society. If they engaged in personal charity at all, society ladies of the 1870s generally restricted themselves to home-visiting of the poor, not importing "street arabs" into their own residences. See Josephine Butler, *An Autobiographical Memoir,* ed. by G. W. Johnson and L. A. Johnson (Bristol: Arrowsmith, 1928), pp. 81–83.

26. Middle-class Victorian conventions called for the rigid segregation of children from adults and their training in self-restraint rather than self-expression. Middle-class observers expected poor children to be even more regimented.

27. Georgina Weldon, *The History of My Orphanage, or the Outpourings of an Alleged Lunatic* (London: Mrs. Weldon, 1878); Grierson, *Storm Bird,* pp. 147, 148.

28. Grierson, *Storm Bird,* p. 148.

29. Georgina Weldon, *How I Escaped the Mad Doctors* (London: Mrs. Weldon, 1882), p. 6; Grierson, *Storm Bird,* p. 233.

30. Logie Barrow, "Socialism in Eternity: Plebian Spiritualists 1853–1913," *History Workshop* 9 (Spring 1980): 56.

31. "Printed Allegations against Mrs. Weldon," *Spiritualist,* 19 April 1878; "Notes and Comments," *The Medium and Daybreak* (London), 17 Oct. 1879.

32. "Topics of the Day be the Heroes of the Hour," *Pall Mall Budget* (London), 21 March 1884. On social leveling and spiritualism, see Morell Theobald, *Spirit Workers in the Home Circle: An Autobiographic Narrative of Psychic Phenomena in Family Daily Life Extending over a Period of Twenty Years* (London: F. Fisher Unwin, 1887); Owen, "The Other Voice," pp. 55–57; *Light* (London), 26 March 1887.

33. *Medium and Daybreak,* 24 Aug. 1888, 7 Sept. 1888.

34. Miss March, a healing and trance medium, observed a lady in pain at her séance in 1887, "brought her into the center of the room and placing her hand on her back and chest, indicated the whereabouts of her pains" to the woman's evident surprise. On other female healers, see also *Medium and Daybreak*, 7 Oct. 1887, 13 July 1888; Owen, *Darkened Room*, chap. 5.

35. Mrs. Henry Sidgwick, "Results of a Personal Investigation into the Physical Phenomena of Spiritualism," *Proceedings of the Society for Psychical Research* 4 (1886–87): 45.

36. Owen, "The Other Voice," pp. 45, 47; Florence Marryat, *There Is No Death* (London: Kegan Paul, Trench, Trubner & Co., 1891), pp. 202–4; George Sitwell, to the editor of *The Times*, reprinted in *Spiritualist*, 16 Jan. 1880; R. Laurence Moore, "The Spiritualist Medium: A Study of Female Professionalism in Victorian America," *American Quarterly* 27 (1975): 207, 214.

37. Moore, "Spiritualist Medium," p. 202.

38. According to a spirit census conducted by psychical researchers in the 1880s, 58 percent of the mediums were women, while 63 percent of the spirit controls were male. Spiritualists explained the tendency of female mediums to be possessed by a "masculine spirit force" on the grounds that men were most likely to experience a violent death, and these earthbound spirits were most likely to communicate at séances. Ostensibly a defense of individuality, since it insisted that spirits preserved their own identity even after death, spiritualism also demonstrated the fragility of the holistic, undivided self and of gendered subjectivity in particular. Vieda Skultans, "Mediums, Controls and Eminent Men," in Pat Holden, ed., *Women's Religious Experience* (London: Croom Helm, 1983), p. 17.

39. Owen, "The Other Voice," pp. 37, 38, 67, 68.

40. Mrs. Weldon first attended séances in France, at a fashionable drawing room, where she tried to communicate with dead friends and received some "test messages" spelled out through rappings on the table. *Spiritualist*, 23 June 1876.

41. Owen, "The Other Voice," p. 35.

42. *Spiritualist*, 23 June 1876. Mrs. Weldon's spiritual taste reflected her class position. According to Logie Barrow, there were notable class differences in religious practice among spiritualists: plebian spiritualists tended to be vehemently anti-Christian, less mystical, more empiricist and materialist than their middle-class counterparts. Treherne, *Plaintiff*, p. 208; Logie Barrow, *Independent Spirits: Spiritualism and English Plebeians, 1850–1910* (London: Routledge and Kegan Paul, 1986), chap. 5.

43. Weldon, *How I Escaped*; "Printed Allegations."

44. Mrs. Weldon repeated her version of the "plot that failed" (Treherne, *Plaintiff*, p. 58) in a wide array of articles, pamphlets, newspaper interviews, and courtroom testimonies. See for example, Mrs. Weldon, quoted in "Some Medical Men at their Work," *Spiritualist*, 17 May 1878; *The Times*, 15 March 1884.

45. Mrs. Weldon, quoted in "Some Medical Men." The visitors took copious notes on her description of visions, including one featuring a shower of stars and Christ on the cross.

46. Ibid.

47. *How I Escaped*, p. 13.

48. Mrs. Weldon, quoted in "Some Medical Men." Sir Charles Dilke and William Gladstone were among her correspondents.

49. Louisa Lowe, quoted in Treherne, *Plaintiff*, p. 61. For other discussions of Mrs. Lowe's activities on behalf of lunacy law reform, see Peter McCandless, "Build, Build: The Controversy over the Care of the Chronically Insane in England, 1855–70," *Bulletin of the History of Medicine* (1979): 87; Owen, *Darkened Room*, chap. 7.

50. Louisa Lowe, *The Bastilles of England: or the Lunacy Laws at Work* (London: Crookenden, 1883).

51. Mrs. Weldon, quoted in "Some Medical Men."

52. Ibid.

53. Ibid.

54. Weldon, *How I Escaped*, pp. 17, 19; *The Times*, 28 Nov. 1884; Winslow, quoted in Treherne, *Plaintiff*, p. 63.

55. Mr. Flowers, quoted in "Mrs. Weldon and the Lunacy Laws," *Spiritualist*, 18 Oct. 1878.

56. *BMJ* 1 (1879): 39. *Truth* demanded a "searching inquiry" (quoted in *Spiritualist*, 18 Oct. 1878). The *British Medical Journal* further castigated Winslow for improperly trying to confine Mrs. Weldon in the hope of deriving pecuniary profits.

57. Treherne, *Plaintiff*, p. 119.

58. Weldon, quoted in "Some Topics of the Day."

59. Grierson, *Storm Bird*, p. 176. In the early 1880s, Mrs. Weldon temporarily reconstituted her orphanage. By 1884, however, the orphanage was defunct and the children dispersed. Grierson, *Storm Bird*, p. 245.

60. See Reginia Gagnier, "Mediums and the Media," *Representations* 22 (Spring 1988).

61. Brandon, *Spiritualists*, pp. 113–26; Oppenheim, *The Other World*, pp. 16–21; Owen, *The Darkened Room*, chap. 3.

62. Mrs. Weldon, quoted in Treherne, *Plaintiff*, p. 98; Lowe, *Bastilles of England*.

63. Wilkie Collins, *The Woman in White* (London, 1859–60; rpt., Harmondsworth, Middlesex: Penguin, 1974); Charles Reade, *Hard Cash: A Matter-of-Fact Romance* (London: Chatto and Windus, 1895; rpt., Collier, New York, 1970).

64. Winifred Hughes, *Maniac in the Cellar* (Princeton: Princeton University Press, 1980).

65. Lowe, *Bastilles of England; My Outlawry; A Lecture Delivered in the Cavendish Room* (London, 1874); *My Story: Exemplifying the Injurious Working of the Lunacy Laws and the Undue Influence Possessed by Lunacy Experts* (London, 1878); Dr. Maudsley, testimony before the Select Committee on the Lunacy Laws, *Parliamentary Papers*, 1877 (373), 13, Q. 7328; Dr. Fox, Q.7642.

66. *Spiritualist*, 26 April 1878.

67. For a discussion of melodramatic themes, see Hughes, *Maniac*, passim; Peter Brooks, *The Melodramatic Imagination: Balzac, Henry James, Melodrama, and the Mode of Excess* (New Haven: Yale University Press, 1976); Michael R. Booth, *English Melodrama* (London: Herbert Jenkins, 1965).

68. "Mrs. Georgina Weldon," *Medium and Daybreak*, 17 Oct. 1879.

69. *Medium and Daybreak*, 22 Aug. 1879.

70. Mystery was structured into Mrs. Weldon's narrative order. In her first account, she introduced her story *in media res*, making the invasion of the mad housekeeper and his assistants initially appear as a mysterious act of violence. See "Some Medical Men."

71. In stage dramas this climax would be visually fixed into a dramatic tableau.

72. "Mrs. Georgina Weldon."

73. *Spiritualist*, 4 July 1879. As a result of this interview, Mr. Weldon, who insisted the idea of marrying de Bathe's daughter never entered his head, successfully sued the *Figaro*'s publisher, Mr. Mortimer, for libel. For our purposes, the veracity of her accusation is less important than her loyal adhesion to a conspiratorial representation of sexual danger.

74. Gayle Rubin, "The Traffic in Women: Notes on the 'Political Economy' of Sex," in Rayna Reiter, ed., *Toward an Anthropology of Women* (New York: Monthly Review Press, 1975), pp. 157–210.

75. This triangular relationship echoed Freud's famous Dora case. See Charles Bernheimer and Claire Kahane, eds. *In Dora's Case: Freud-Hysteria-Feminism* (New York: Columbia University Press, 1985).

76. The " 'mad doctors' method of hurting their prey is exciting and truly sportsmanlike," *Medium and Daybreak* observed sarcastically ("Mrs. Georgina Weldon"). For the response of the medical press, see "Lunacy Law Reform: The Power of the Keys," *BMJ* 1 (1879): 245. Notice that the spiritualists focus on the sexual perversions of the doctors, while the medical press concentrated on the husband.

77. Mrs. Weldon united in herself both the victim and the detective/heroine.

78. Grierson, *Storm Bird*, p. 206; "Married Women's Property Act 1882 . . . Right of Married Woman to Sue Alone," *Law Times* (London) 77 (9 Aug. 1884): 267; Mrs. Weldon, quoted in Treherne, *Plaintiff*, p. 95; "Some Topics of the Day."

79. *The Times*, 30 July 1884; *Law Times* 77 (4 Oct. 1884): 373; (11 Oct. 1884): 386: 78 (21 Feb. 1885): 296; "The Lunacy Laws," *Law Quarterly Review* 1 (1885): 150–60; McCandless, "Build, Build."

80. He cut a pathetic figure; now "aged and bald," a striking contrast from the "slim, skipjack clerk with plenty of hair on his head," as Mrs. Weldon remembered him in their first encounter. "Some Topics of the Day."

81. Quoted in Grierson, *Storm Bird*, p. 108.

82. "The Sanity of Great Men," *PMG*, 15 March 1884; *The Times*, 20 April 1884; Dr. Edmunds, quoted in "The Sanity of Great Men"; *The Times*, 11 July 1884.

83. *The Times*, 29 Nov. 1884; *The Times*, 1 Dec. 1884.

84. "The Medical Risks of Certifying Lunacy," *Lancet* 1 (1881): 932.

85. "The Risk of Certifying Lunatics," *BMJ* 2 (1884): 1149. The *British Medical Journal* wondered aloud whether doctors had not "saddled themselves with a thankless office" (p. 1138).

86. "Juries have been deeply impressed . . . with the idea of the law is defec-

tive and that it is administered with culpable laxity." *The Times*, 19 Aug. 1885. Medical correspondents to *The Times* reiterated this point and acknowledged that the practical difficulties were compounded by the "uncertainty" of diagnosis and treatment of the insane. Dr. Bucknill, to the editor, *The Times*, 21 Aug. 1885.

87. Mrs. Weldon, quoted in "Some Topics of the Day."

88. "Ladies-No X. Mrs. Georgina Weldon," *Vanity Fair* 31 (3 May 1884): 243; F. C. Philips, quoted in Treherne, *Plaintiff*, pp. 93, 94; "Some Topics of the Day."

89. Treherne, *Plaintiff*, p. 96.

90. Mrs. Weldon, quoted in Grierson, *Storm Bird*, p. 227.

91. Junior members of the bar had dubbed her the "Portia of the New Law Courts" and undoubtedly took some pleasure in her triumph against the eminent senior counsels for the defense. A number of presiding judges graciously endeavored to instruct her in the best way to proceed with her case. On the other hand, the fiercely misogynist Fitzjames Stephens severely rebuked her to "argue in a legal manner." Grierson, *Storm Bird*, p. 227.

92. William Joseph Reader, *Professional Men: The Rise of the Professional Class in Nineteenth-Century England* (New York: Basic Books, 1966), pp. 150, 151, 174–8; Daniel Duman, *The English and Colonial Bars in the Nineteenth Century* (London: Croom Helm, 1983), pp. 48, 49, 114–16.

93. "Mrs. Georgina Weldon," *Vanity Fair*.

94. *The Times*, 23 Sept. 1885.

95. Patrick Joyce, *Visions of the People: Industrial England and the Question of Class, 1840–1914* (Cambridge: Cambridge University Press, 1991), p. 104.

96. Grierson, *Storm Bird*, p. 233. Barrow, *Independent Spirits*, chap. 5, notes the triangular relation among secularists, spiritualists, and socialists, all of whom were competing for the same constituency. Victor Bailey argues for a similar congruence between socialism and the Salvation Army: "'In Darkest England and the Way Out': the Salvation Army, Social Reform and the Labour Movement, 1885–1910," *International Review of Social History* 29 (1984): 135. Mrs. Weldon blissfully ignored the ambiguities and animosities among these groups, as she heralded Mrs. Booth and Annie Besant as her two favorite heroines.

97. "Some Topics of the Day."

98. Grierson, *Storm Bird*, p. 245.

99. Mrs. Weldon, quoted in "Some Topics of the Day." She did, however, dress up as "Sergeant Fuzbuz" (a senior member of the bar), as one of her satirical turns on the stage.

100. Philips, quoted in Treherne, *Plaintiff*, p. 94.

101. "Mrs. Georgina Weldon," *Vanity Fair*, p. 243.

102. Ibid.

103. Anna Clark, "The Struggle for the Breeches" (unpublished paper, 1987).

104. "Days with Celebrities: A Women's Rightess," *Moonshine* (10 May 1884): 217.

105. Sarah Maitland, *Vesta Tilley* (London: Virago Press, 1986), pp. 78–103; Ellen Ross, "'Fierce Questions and Taunts': Married life in Working-Class London, 1870–1914," *Feminist Studies* 8, no. 3 (Fall 1982): 593–95; Gareth Stedman

Jones, "Working-Class Culture and Working-Class Politics in London," 1870–1900: Notes on the Remaking of a Working Class," in *Languages of Class: Studies in English Working-Class History 1832–1982* (Cambridge: Cambridge University Press, 1983), pp. 225–27.

106. Historians have noted a high degree of gender conflict and gender consciousness among different classes in late-Victorian society; but they have yet to compare their different meanings or to explore the relationship among the cultural forms they took.

107. Treherne, *Plaintiff*, p. 118.

108. For a discussion of nineteenth-century women and spectacle, see Abigail Solomon Godeau, "The Legs of the Countess," *October* 39 (Winter 1986): 66–108.

109. Grierson, *Storm Bird*, p. 223.

110. See Marion Meade, *Madame Blavatsky: The Woman Behind the Myth* (New York: G. P. Putnam's Sons, 1980); Diana Burford, "Theosophy and Feminism," in Pat Holden, ed., *Women's Religious Experience* (London: Croom Helm, 1983), pp. 27–56; Edward Maitland, *Anna Kingsford: Her Life, Letters, Diary and Work* 2 vols. (London: G. Redway, 1896); Joy Dixon, "Theosophy and Feminism in Late-Nineteenth Century and Early Twentieth Century England (unpublished paper, 1987).

111. Shortt, "Physicians and Psychics," pp. 354, 355.

112. Owen, *The Darkened Room*, p. 167, argues for the abatement of medical antagonism toward "mediumship pathology" because, by the 1890s, British psychiatrists themselves had begun to use hypnosis. At the time of Mrs. Weldon's campaign, articles in the *Law Times* emphasized the practical lessons in self-restraint doctors had begun to draw from the Winslow and Semple trials: "The Lunacy Laws," 77 (1884): 373; "The Reform of the Lunacy Laws," 8 (1885): 296.

113. Coral Lansbury, *The Old Brown Dog: Women, Workers, and Vivisection in Edwardian England* (Madison: University of Wisconsin Press, 1985).

114. Winslow, *Recollections*, pp. 251, 252. According to Donald McCormick (*The Identity of Jack the Ripper*), "All the detectives working on the case knew [Winslow] and at one time his ubiquity at the scene of the crimes caused them to check up on his movements." Quoted in Tom Cullen, *Autumn of Terror: Jack the Ripper, His Crimes and Times* (London: Bodley Head, 1965), p. 91.

115. "The Spirits on the Whitechapel Murders," *Medium and Daybreak*, 5 Oct. 1888; "Mrs. Nichols Controls," 12 Oct. 1888; "Notes and Comments," 19 Oct. 1888.

Chapter Seven

1. This is an extensively revised version of an article, "Jack the Ripper and the Myth of Male Violence," *Feminist Studies* 8 (Fall 1982): 542–74. *PMG*, 1 Oct. 1888. Quoted in Jerry White, *Rothschild Buildings: Life in an East End Tenement Block, 1887–1920* (London: Routledge and Kegan Paul, 1980), p. 26.

2. The number of murder victims credited to Jack the Ripper was contested at the time and is still subject to dispute. During the "autumn of terror," two earlier murders of prostitutes were initially connected retrospectively with the five murders; two subsequent murders in 1889 and 1891 were subsequently linked to the

Ripper. However, two official reports, one by Police Commissioner McNaghton and another by a forensic specialist, Dr. Thomas Bond, asserted that only these five homicides bore the marks of a single killer. See, Mepo 3/141, 10 Nov. 1888; Sir Melville McNaghton letter, quoted in full in Donald Rumbelow, *The Complete Jack the Ripper* (New York: New American Library, 1975), pp. 132–33.

3. Dozens of books have been written on Jack the Ripper. They include Leonard W. Matters, *The Mystery of Jack the Ripper* (London: Hutchinson, 1929); Daniel Farson, *Jack the Ripper* (London: Sphere Book Limited, 1973); Tom Cullen, *Autumn of Terror: Jack the Ripper His Crimes and Times* (London: Bodley Head, 1965); Elwyn Jones, ed., *Ripper File* (London: Barker, 1975). A whole new crop of Ripper books appeared in honor of the 1988 Ripper centenary, many of them new editions of books first published in the 1970s. They include Martin Howell and Keith Skinner, *The Ripper Legacy: The Life and Death of Jack the Ripper* (London: Sidgwick and Jackson, 1987); Colin Wilson and Robin Odell, *Jack the Ripper: Summing Up the Verdict* (London: Bantam Press, 1989); Donald Rumbelow, *Complete Jack the Ripper;* Terence Starkey, *Jack the Ripper: 100 Years of Investigation: The Facts, the Fiction, the Solution* (London: Ward Lock, 1987); Martin Fido, *The Crimes, Detection, and Death of Jack the Ripper* (London: Weidenfeld and Nicolson, 1987). A few cultural critics have attempted a more serious exploration of the Ripper story. They include Christopher Frayling, "The House that Jack Built," in Sylvia Tomaselli and Roy Porter, eds., *Rape* (Oxford: Basil Blackwell, 1986), pp. 174–215; Deborah Cameron and Elizabeth Fraser, *Lust to Kill: A Feminist Investigation of Sexual Murder* (New York: New York University Press, 1987); Jane Caputi, *The Age of Sex Crime* (Bowling Green: Bowling Green State University Popular Press, 1987).

4. Quoted in White, *Rothschild Buildings,* p. 7.

5. W. J. Fishman, *East End 1888: Life in a London Borough among the Laboring Poor* (Philadelphia: Temple University Press, 1988); David Widgery, "History without its Aitches" [review of *East End 1888*], *New Statesman & Society* (17 June 1988): 39, 40; White, *Rothschild Buildings,* p. 26.

6. "The East End Atrocities," *London City Mission Magazine* (1 Dec. 1888): 258–60; Chaim Bermant, *Point of Arrival: A Study of London's East End* (London, Methuen, 1975), p. 188; Charles Booth, *Life and Labour of the People in London,* 17 vols., 1st series: *Poverty,* in 4 vols. (1889–1903; rpt., 3d ed., New York: Macmillan, 1902–3), 1:66–68.

7. *DT,* 10 September 1888; *ELO,* 27 July 1889; Quoted in White, *Rothschild Buildings,* p. 8; Arthur Harding, quoted in *East End Underworld: Chapters in the Life of Arthur Harding,* ed. Raphael Samuel (London: Routledge and Kegan Paul, 1981), p. 110.

8. *The Times,* 2 Oct. 1888; *DC,* 19 Sept. 1888.

9. On an "argument from geography," see Mandy Merck, "Sutcliffe: What the Papers Said," *Spare Rib* no. 108 (July 1981): 17. On Lamarckian interpretations of the murder site, see *The Times,* quoted in Farson, *Jack the Ripper,* p. 100, and *The Curse upon Mitre Square,* quoted in ibid., p. 99.

10. *The Times,* quoted in Farson, *Jack the Ripper,* p. 100; *DT,* quoted in ibid., p. 101.

11. *LWN*, 7 Oct. 1888; Rosemary Jackson, *Fantasy: The Literature of Subversion* (London and New York: Methuen, 1981), pp. 25, 26.

12. *RN*, 1 Oct. 1888; *Echo*, 19 Oct. 1888; *ELA*, 15 Sept. 1888.

13. *DT*, 2 Oct. 1888; *Star*, 14 Sept. 1888.

14. "Murder—And More to Follow," *PMG*, 8 Oct. 1888; *DT*, 1 Oct. 1888; *Star*, 4 Oct. 1888; Walter Dew, *I Caught Crippen* (London: Blackie and Son, 1938); *DC*, 11 Sept. 1888.

15. For a discussion of the "sex beast," see Cameron and Fraser, *Lust to Kill*, pp. 35–44. For Gothic images in the press, see *LWN*, 7 Oct. 1888; *DC*, 10 Sept. 1888; *DT*, 2 Oct. 1888. For "talk" of black magic, see Dew, *I Caught Crippen*, p. 125.

16. Cameron and Fraser, *Lust to Kill*, p. 127; Michel Foucault, *The History of Sexuality*, vol. 1, *An Introduction*, translated by Robert Hurley (New York: Pantheon, 1985), p. 56.

17. "The Whitechapel Murders," *Lancet* (29 Sept. 1888): 637.

18. Peter Stallybrass and Allon White, *The Politics and Poetics of Transgression* (Ithaca, N.Y.: Cornell University Press, 1986), pp. 20–23.

19. Marina Warner, *Monuments and Maidens: The Allegory of the Female Form* (New York: Atheneum, 1985); Nancy Armstrong, "The Occidental Alice," *Differences* 2, no. 2 (Summer 1990): 14; *The Times*, quoted in *Ripper File*, p. 49; Stallybrass and White, *Politics and Poetics*, p. 23.

20. Alain Corbin, "Commercial Sexuality in Nineteenth-Century France: A System of Images and Regulation," in *The Making of the Modern Body: Sexuality and Society in the Nineteenth Century*, ed. Catherine Gallagher and Thomas Laqueur (Berkeley: University of California Press, 1987), pp. 209–18; *ES*, 9 Nov. 1888; *RN*, 2 Sept. 1888; *PMG*, quoted in Farson, *Jack the Ripper*, p. 47.

21. Elaine Showalter, *Sexual Anarchy: Gender and Culture at the Fin de Siècle* (New York: Viking, 1990), p. 127; Judith R. Walkowitz, *Prostitution and Victorian Society: Women, Class, and the State* (New York: Cambridge University Press, 1980); R. M. McLeod, "Law, Medicine, and Public Opinion: The Resistance to Compulsory Health Legislation, 1870–1901," *Public Law* (1967): 189–211; R. D. French, *Antivivisection and Medical Science in Victorian Society* (Princeton: Princeton University Press, 1975), chap. 11; Coral Lansbury, *The Old Brown Dog: Women, Workers, and Vivisection in Edwardian England* (Madison: University of Wisconsin Press, 1985); Mary Ann Elston, "Women and Antivivisection in Victorian England, 1870–1900," in Nicholas Rupke, ed., *Vivisection in Historical Perspective* (London: Croom Helm, 1987), pp. 259–89.

22. All the letters are collected in Mepo. 3/142. Sir Robert Anderson, *The Lighter Part of My Official Life* (London: Hodder and Stoughton, 1910), p. 138; H.O. 144/A49301C/8a, 23 Oct. 1888; Mepo. 3/142; Sir Melville McNaghton, *Days of My Years* (London: Edward Arnold, 1915), pp. 58, 59; *Star*, quoted in Rumbelow, *The Complete Jack the Ripper*, p. 93; Caputi, *Age of Sex Crime*, p. 21.

23. Ironically, the assumption of a "familiar" pattern was made at the time of a 1889 murder inquest when the homicide was incorrectly associated with the serial crimes of the Ripper. *ELA*, Aug. 1889; *Daily Chronicle*, Nov. 10, 1888; *DT*, 24 Sept. 1888; *PMG*, 10 Sept. 1888.

24. *PMG,* 19 Sept. 1888; *DC,* 10 Sept. 1888.

25. *Commonweal,* 13 Nov. 1888; *The Times,* 18 Sept. 1888; 1 Oct. 1888; 12 Oct. 1888; Judith R. Walkowitz, "The Politics of Prostitution," *Signs* 6 (Autumn 1980): 124–27.

26. Ruth Harris, "Melodrama, Hysteria and Feminine Crimes of Passion in the Fin-de-Siècle," *History Workshop* 25 (Spring 1988): 32, 33.

27. *The Times,* 1 Sept. 1888; *Star,* 1 Sept. 1888; *Penny Illustrated News* and *The Times,* quoted in Harris, *Jack the Ripper,* pp. 18, 19; Howells and Skinner, *Ripper Legacy,* p. 4. In the two previous homicides, for example, Emma Smith lived to tell her story of being beaten, robbed, and assaulted by four men, while Martha Tabram received 39 bayonet wounds, rather than knife wounds to the abdomen, as suffered by Nicholls and some later Ripper victims. Nonetheless, both the *Star* and the *PMG* stressed the "SIGNIFICANT SIMILARITY" between the Nicholls murder and the "two mysterious murders of women." *Star,* 1 Sept. 1888; *PMG,* 3 Sept. 1888. Thanks to Jennifer Pugh for these observations.

28. H.O. 144/220/A49301c/8a, 23 Oct. 1888.

29. Bermant, *Point of Arrival,* chap. 9; White, *Rothschild Buildings,* chap. 1; *Jewish Chronicle,* 5 Oct. 1888.

30. For a summary of contemporary parliamentary discussion on restricting immigration, see Fishman, *East End,* pp. 144–47. For press coverage of Leather Apron, see *Star,* 7 Sept. 1888; "The Horrors of the East End," *PMG,* 8 Sept. 1888; *LWN,* 9 Sept. 1888.

31. It is significant that Pizer, the man accused of being Leather Apron, used the occasion of Annie Chapman's inquest to vindicate himself—an example of the way the poor used legal occasions and spaces for their own purposes and to obtain a public hearing. See Jennifer Davis, "A Poor Man's System of Justice: The London Police Courts in the Second Half of the Nineteenth Century," *The Historical Journal* 27 (no. 2) (1984): 309–35.

32. Bermant, *Point of Arrival,* pp. 110–18.

33. *ELO,* 15 Sept. 1888.

34. Michael I. Friedland, *The Trials of Israel Lipski* (London: Macmillan, 1984).

35. It was also generalized into a term of abuse applied to threatening husbands.

36. *DC,* 10 Sept. 1888.

37. After the *Illustrated Police News* published a woodcut of Leather Apron, one man resembling the picture found himself surrounded by a menacing crowd. Into the nineties, children still taunted strangers with being Leather Apron; Leather Apron toffee became a local East End specialty. Farson, *Jack the Ripper,* p. 25.

38. Fido, *The Crimes,* p. 63; *Jewish Chronicle,* 5 Oct. 1888; Samuel Montagu to the Editor, *PMG,* 15 Oct. 1888.

39. H.O. 144/220/A49310C/8C and 15; A49301D/5; *Ripper File,* p. 135; Bermant, *Point of Arrival,* pp. 111–18.

40. *DT,* quoted in Farson, *Jack the Ripper,* p. 101; "The Nemesis of Neglect," *Punch,* 29 Sept. 1888; "Undiscovered Crimes," *Star,* 10 Sept. 1888; "Crime in Whitechapel," *Star,* 14 Sept. 1888; "The Insecurity of Our Streets," *DC,* 14 Sept.

1888; "S.G.O." to the Editor, *The Times*, 22 Sept. 1888. See discussion of model-dwelling plans in letters on "A Safe Four Percent," *DT*, 22 Sept. 1888.

41. "Murder and More to Follow," *PMG*, 8 Sept. 1888; Robert Louis Stevenson, *Doctor Jekyll and Mr. Hyde*, with an introduction by Abraham Rothberg (New York: Bantam, 1967; first edition, 1886), p. 78 (all citations from the novel come from this edition); Paul Wilstach, *Richard Mansfield, the Man and the Actor* (New York: Charles Scribner's Sons, 1908); Harry M. Geduld, Introduction, in Harry M. Geduld, ed., *The Definitive "Dr. Jekyll and Mr. Hyde" Companion* (Garland: New York and London, 1983), p. 12; "Richard Mansfield, vol. 8," Robinson Locke Collection, New York Public Library.

42. "Murder and More to Follow," *PMG*, 8 Sept. 1888.

43. "Occasional Notes," *PMG*, 10 Sept. 1888.

44. *Star*, 16 Sept. 1888; *DT*, 22 Sept. 1888. The *East London Advertiser* pronounced the Jekyll and Hyde theory an "enduring theory" (13 Oct. 1888). On the closing down of the play, see Rumbelow, *Complete Jack the Ripper* (1975), p. 124.

45. Frayling, "The House," p. 197.

46. Cameron and Fraser, *Lust to Kill*, p. 127.

47. *Psychopathia Sexualis* grew from 45 case histories and 110 pages in 1886 to 238 histories and 437 pages by the twelfth edition in 1903. See Jeffrey Weeks, *Sexuality and Its Discontents: Meanings, Myths, and Modern Sexualities* (London: Routledge and Kegan Paul, 1985), p. 67.

48. Weeks, *Sexuality and Its Discontents*, p. 67.

49. Thanks to Susan Maslin for these observations.

50. Dr. R. von Krafft-Ebing, *Psychopathia Sexualis: With Especial Reference to Contrary Sexual Instinct: A Medico-Legal Study*, trans. Charles Gilbert Chaddock (Philadelphia: F. A. Davis, 1892), pp. 1, 56.

51. Ibid., p. 378. As Sander Gilman observes, Krafft-Ebing's view of perversion as intrinsic to modern life differed from the evolutionary view of earlier sexologists, who tended to treat sexual perversions as throwbacks to an earlier sexual primitivism, as "ambiguous eddies" within a linear history of progress. "Sexology and Psychoanalysis," in J. Edward Chamberlain and Sander Gilman, eds., *Degeneration: The Dark Side of Progress* (New York: Columbia University Press, 1985), pp. 75–79.

52. Krafft-Ebing, *Psychopathia Sexualis*, p. 57.

53. Ibid., pp. 13, 60.

54. Forbes Winslow to the Editor, *The Times*, 12 Sept. 1888; *Recollections of Forty Years* (London: J. Ousley, 1910), p. 270.

55. *Lancet*, excerpted in Jones, *Ripper File*, p. 26; Coroner Baxter, excerpted in ibid., p. 31.

56. Baxter, excerpted in Jones, *Ripper File*, pp. 31, 24, 25.

57. "The Whitechapel Murders," *Lancet*, Sept. 29, 1888: 637; "The Whitechapel Murders," *EN*, 17 Sept. 1888.

58. Antivivisection was a campaign with no "landmarks," that reached no great climax, that was fought in the hearts and minds of Victorians with few institutional and legal results. Nonetheless, the amount of propaganda literature churned out by Cobbe's organization is staggering: in 1885 alone, Victoria Street put out

81,672 books, pamphlets, and leaflets (French, *Anti-Vivisection*, pp. 255, 256). Though the press remained overwhelmingly hostile to Cobbe and her fellow agitators, antivivisection tropes and iconography pervaded popular journalism and fiction. Indignant opponents of the "Maiden Tribute," for example, accused Stead of "moral vivisection" for imposing the gynecological examination of Eliza Armstrong. Stead himself made ready use of antivivisectionist rhetoric in his crusades against sexually dangerous men. In 1887, he introduced Edwin Langsworthy to his readers as a privileged sadist who amused himself by torturing cats before he extended his "cruel sport" to his bride, a "refined and cultivated lady." Quoted in Raymond L. Schults, *Crusader in Babylon: W. T. Stead and the Pall Mall Gazette* (Lincoln, Nebraska: University of Nebraska Press, 1972), pp. 212, 213.

59. Frances Power Cobbe, *Life of Frances Power Cobbe*, 2 vols. (Boston: Houghton Mifflin, 1895), 2:607.

60. Authored by Edward Berdoe, an East End doctor and close collaborator of Cobbe, *St. Bernard's* was a thinly disguised autobiographical account of Berdoe's own training at the London Hospital. Its publication caused quite a sensation: over fifty reviews of the novel appeared, some denouncing it as a "gross calumny" upon the medical profession, others concerned and appalled by its exposé of doctors as "monsters of cruelty" and of hospitals as "hotbeds of corruption and cruelty." Edward Berdoe, *St. Bernard's: The Romance of a Medical Student* (London: Swan, Sonnenschein, 1887); Edward Berdoe, *Dying Scientifically: A Key to St. Bernard's* (London: Swan Sonnenschein, 1888); Coral Lansbury, *The Old Brown Dog: Women, Workers, and Vivisection in Edwardian England* (Madison: University of Wisconsin Press, 1985), chap. 10.

61. Orvilla Moscucci, *The Science of Woman: Gynecology and Gender in England 1800–1929* (Cambridge: Cambridge University Press, 1990). Already stung by public criticism over lunacy confinement and the medical "rape" of registered prostitutes, doctors responded to this propagandist assault by defending animal experimentation as a sacred cause to be upheld against quacks and religious fanatics. They also countered with their own interpretation of the medical invasion of innocent "feminized" bodies. Medical publicists acknowledged the experimental link between women's bodies and those of laboratory animals, but they defended the violation of the latter to preserve the health of the former. It was precisely *because* the "public" demanded such medical intervention into female bodies that animal experimentation was necessary, declared one gynecologist, Mr. Spencer Wells, who pointed to surgical advances in ovariotomy gained from animal experimentation. Wells complained of public ingratitude: "the public demands of us to save the lives of their wives and daughters and forces upon us operations undreamt of from their very severity even a few years ago" ("Vivisection and Ovariotomy," *BMJ*, 22 Jan. 1881, p. 133). The symbolic struggle between antivivisectionists and their medical opponents escalated significantly in the 1880s, as did the statistics on antivivisection experiments: in 1879, there were 270 vivisections in Great Britain; ten years later there were 1,417.

However, some doctors remained uneasy about the link between vivisection and ovariotomy. Because the ovaries were deemed the "grand organs" of female identity, medical spokesmen expressed fears that their surgical removal would lead to the "unsexing" of women: there was a widespread feeling, argued the *British Medical Journal* in 1887, that the ovaries of women should be respected because they were "the organs of sexual life, making a woman what she is, fitted for the duties of womanhood, including childbearing." "Normal Ovariotomy: Battey's operation: Tait's operation," *BMJ*, 1 (1887): 576–77. Moscuccci, *Science of Woman*, pp. 134, 157.

62. Archibald Forbes to the Editor, *DN*, 3 Oct. 1888.

63. This venereal anxiety also coincided with a more explicit thematizing of the danger of "syphilis of the innocents," as expressed in works like Ibsen's *Ghosts* and the New Women novels of the 1890s. Showalter, *Sexual Anarchy*; Alain Corbin, *Women for Hire: Prostitution and Sexuality in France after 1850*, trans. Alan Sheridan (Cambridge, Mass: Harvard University Press, 1990), p. 249.

64. Alex Comfort, *The Anxiety Makers: Some Curious Preoccupations of the Medical Profession* (London: Nelson, 1967).

65. Dr. Phillips, testimony at Chapman's inquest, excerpted in Jones, *Ripper File*, p. 25.

66. D. G. Halsted, *Doctor in the Nineties* (London: Christopher Johnson, 1959), p. 48.

67. Foucault, *History of Sexuality*, vol. 1.

68. As Ludmilla Jordanova observes, because doctors regularly executed tasks which would "in normal circumstances be taboo or emotionally repugnant," they had to renegotiate "body taboos" by presenting themselves "as rational, scientific, in alliance with polite culture and clean." Ludmilla Jordanova, *Sexual Visions* (Madison: University of Wisconsin Press, 1989), p. 138. Thanks to Andrew Bragen and Kim Thompson for some of these observations.

69. In addition, later media coverage "democratized" knowledge by reporting on the extent and nature of the mutilations. *Star*, 1 Oct. 1888; Fido, *The Crimes*, pp. 70–80.

70. George Bernard Shaw, "Blood Money to Whitechapel," letter to the Editor, *Star*, 24 Sept. 1888.

71. *DT*, 4 Oct. 1888.

72. H.O. 144/220/A49301C/8a, 23 Oct. 1888; *Echo*, 14 Sept. 1888.

73. Frederick Porter Wensley, *Detective Days* (London: Cassell, 1931), p. 128; Halsted, *Doctor in the Nineties*, p. 45.

74. *DC*, 15 Sept. 1888; *DT*, 2, 4 Oct. 1888; *DN*, 9 Oct. 1888; Halsted, *Doctor in the Nineties*, p. 48.

75. "The East End Murders: Detailed Lessons," *BMJ* (6 Oct. 1888): 769.

76. Walkowitz, "Politics of Prostitution," pp. 129–30; Josephine Butler to Miss Priestman, 5 Nov. 1896, Butler Collection, Fawcett Library, City of London Polytechnic, London; Mrs. H. O. R. Barnett, *Canon Barnett: His Life, Work, and Friends by His Wife*, 2 vols. (London: Murray, 1921), 2:305–8.

77. *The Times*, 6 Oct. 1888; Dew, *I Caught Crippen*, p. 107; *ELO*, 15 Sept. 1888; Halsted, *Doctor in the Nineties*, pp. 54, 55; Mepo. 3/140; *ELO*, 13 Oct. 1888; *DN*, 6, 15 Oct. 1888; *ES*, 6 Oct. 1888.

78. Victor Turner, "Social Dramas and Stories about Them," *Critical Inquiry* 7, no. 1 (1980): 141–68.

79. John Kelly, testimony at Catherine Eddowes' inquest, excerpted in Jones, *Ripper File*, p. 51.

80. *DC*, 10 Nov. 1888; *DT*, 10 Nov. 1888.

81. "The Terrible Crime," *Echo*, 10 Nov. 1888; *DC*, 10 Nov. 1888; "The Whitechapel Horrors," *ELO*, 13 Oct. 1888.

82. Quoted in Howells and Skinner, *Ripper Legacy*, p. 112.

83. "Reign of Terror in the East End," *ELO*, 15 Sept. 1888.

84. "East End Horrors," *LWN*, 7 Oct. 1888; *DT*, 4 Oct. 1888; Harris, *Jack the Ripper*, pp. 23, 24; Rumbelow, *The Complete Jack the Ripper*, pp. 74, 75.

85. Matters, *Mystery of Jack the Ripper*, p. 243. "I knew Marie quite well by sight," declared Walter Dew, who had been a constable in Whitechapel in 1888. "Often I had seen her parading along Commercial Street . . . in the company of two others of her kind, fairly neatly dressed and invariably wearing a clean white apron, but no hat." Dew, *I Caught Crippen*.

86. "Whitechapel: Important Evidence at the Inquest Today," *Star*, 12 Nov. 1888.

87. Rumbelow, *Complete Jack the Ripper*, pp. 88, 89. The transition to the East End always proved a difficult narrative move: "By some means, however, at present not exactly clear, she suddenly drifted into the East End." "Whitechapel," *Star*, 12 Nov. 1888.

88. George Hutchinson, deposition, reproduced in Wilson and Odell, *Jack the Ripper*, p. 63; Fido, *The Crimes*, p. 178.

89. *Star*, 8 Sept. 1888.

90. *ES*, 9 Nov. 1888; *DC*, 18 Sept. 1888; *Police Illustrated News*, 3 Nov., 1 Dec. 1888; *WPP*, 6 Nov. 1888; "G.S.O." to the Editor, *The Times*, 22 Sept. 1888; letter to the Editor, *SJG*, 12 Nov. 1888.

91. It should be noted that male libertarians came to the defense of prostitutes in the pages of the *Personal Rights Journal* (Nov. 1888), pp. 69, 76, 84.

92. *The Times*, 12 Nov. 1888.

93. Cullen, *Autumn of Terror*, p. 78; *Echo*, 1, 2, 3 Oct. 1888; *ELO*, 6 Oct. 1888; *MP*, 4 Oct. 1888.

94. On marital cruelty in middle-class households, see A. James Hammerton, "Victorian Marriage and the Law of Matrimonial Cruelty," *Victorian Studies* 33, no. 2 (Winter 1990): 269–92.

95. *The Times*, 1 Oct. 1888; Cullen, *Autumn of Terror*, p. 79; *Echo*, 3 Oct. 1888.

96. Criminal Court, *Sessions Papers*, London, 109, (1888–89), pp. 76–78. Thanks to Ellen Ross for this citation.

97. Ellen Ross, "'Fierce Questions and Taunts': Married Life in Working-Class London, 1870–1914," *Feminist Studies*, 8, no. 3 (Fall 1982): 575–602.

98. Helen Corke, *In Our Infancy: An Autobiography*, Part 1, *1882–1912* (Cambridge: Cambridge University Press, 1975), p. 25 (thanks to Dina Copelman for this citation); Mrs. Bartholemew, interview (thanks to Anna Davin for the transcript).

99. Letter to the Editor, *SJG*, 16 Nov. 1888.

100. Leonard Ellisden, "Starting from Victoria," #229, Burnett Collection, Brunel University; Leonard Woolf, *Sowing: An Autobiography of the Years 1880 to 1904* (New York: Harcourt Brace, 1960), pp. 60–62; Sylvia Pankhurst, *The Suffragette Movement . . .* , pp. 110, 111; Compton Mackenzie, *My Life and Times: Octave One 1883–1891* (London: Chatto and Windus, 1963), pp. 164, 165.

101. Montagu Williams, *Round London: Down East and Up West* (London: Macmillan, 1892), p. 12; *PMG*, 18 Oct. 1888; *DN*, 4 Oct. 1888.

102. *DT*, 4 Oct., 10 Sept. 1888; *RN*, 9 Sept. 1888; Mepo. 3/142, 5 Oct. 1888.

103. Dew, *I Caught Crippen*, p. 95; "Ready for Whitechapel Fiend: Women Secretly Armed," *Police Illustrated News*, 22 Sept. 1888; *DT*, 2 Oct. 1888; *War Cry*, 1 Dec. 1888.

104. *War Cry*, 1 Dec. 1888; Barnett, *Canon Barnett*, p. 306.

105. Quoted in White, *Rothschild Buildings*, p. 125.

106. In interviews conducted in East London in July 1983, four informants, three women and one man, told this story as their family history. As far as I can discern, this story has not entered print culture.

107. Lynda Nead, *Myths of Sexuality: Representations of Women in Victorian Britain* (Oxford: Basil Blackwell, 1988), pp. 176–80; Ellen Ross, "'Not the Sort that Would Sit on the Doorstep,': Respectability in Pre–World War I London Neighborhoods," *International Labor and Working-Class History* 27 (Spring 1985): 39–59.

108. In 1966, a woman who, as a young woman, had lived in Jubilee Road, "in the heart of the area terrorised by Jack the Ripper," remembered her father taking part in nightly patrols to protect the women. She herself came close to stumbling on the murderer as she walked along Hanbury Street one night at dark. When, the next morning, she found out a "42-year old widow" (Annie Chapman) had been murdered, "I was terrified to put my head outside the house for days." "R. J. Lees—the Jack the Ripper Case," Society for Psychical Research Archives, London.

109. Rumbelow, *Complete Jack the Ripper*, p. 86; "The Whitechapel Murders," *Medium and Daybreak* (London), 2 Nov. 1888. On R. J. Lees, see the reprint of an article in the *Chicago Sunday Times-Herald* of 1895, in Jones, *Ripper File*, p. 166; Nandor Fodor, *Encyclopedia of Psychic Science* (1933; rpt., New Jersey: Citadel Press, 1974), p. 193; "R. J. Lees—the Ripper Case"; Harris, *Jack the Ripper*, chaps. 18, 19.

110. Quoted in McCormick, *Identity*, p. 81; Quoted in Rumbelow, *Complete Jack the Ripper*, p. 101.

111. On women who resisted the terror, see Margot Asquith, *The Autobiography of Margot Asquith*, ed. and intro. Mark Bonham Carter (London: Methuen, 1985; rpt. from 1962 ed.), pp. 43, 44; Margaret Nevinson, *Life's Fitful Fever: A Volume of Memories* (London: A. and C. Black, 1926), p. 106. On the effects of the terror, see M. V. Hughes, *A London Girl of the 1880s* (London: Oxford University Press, 1978), p. 218.

112. *Personal Rights Journal*, Nov. 1888, pp. 69, 76, 84; *Dawn*, 1 Nov. 1888; *Sentinel*, Dec. 1888, p. 145.

113. Jan Lambertz, "Feminists and the Politics of Wife-Beating," in Harold L.

Smith, ed., *British Feminism in the Twentieth Century* (Amherst: University of Massachusetts Press, 1990), pp. 25–46; Frances Power Cobbe to the Editor, *The Times*, 11 Oct. 1888; *DN,* 2 Oct. 1888.

114. *DN,* 4, 6, 9, 11 Oct. 1888.

115. *Star,* 4 Oct. 1888. On other responses of Radicals and socialists, see *Justice,* 6 Oct. 1888 and 17 Nov. 1888; *Star,* 1 Oct. 1888; Ben Tillett, quoted in William J. Fishman, *East End Jewish Radicals, 1875–1914* (London: Duckworth, 1975), p. 236.

116. Peter Keating, "Fact and Fiction in the East End," in *The Victorian City,* ed. H. J. Dyos and M. Wolff, 2 vols. (London: Routledge and Kegan Paul, 1973), 1:585–603; Bailey, "Dangerous Classes in Late-Victorian England"; *The Times* leader, quoted in "Murder as an Advertisement," *PMG,* 19 Sept. 1888.

117. White, *Rothschild Buildings,* chap. 1. See, for example, *The Times,* 22 Sept.; 2, 11, 18, 26, 29, 30 Oct.; 6, 16 Nov. 1888. See the series of letters in the *Daily Telegraph* on the "Safe Four Percent," 21, 24, 26 Sept. 1888.

118. Thomas Hancock Nunn and Thomas Gardner to the Editor, *The Times,* 6 Oct. 1888. Both Nunn and Gardner were members of the National Vigilance Association, a social purity group.

119. *The Times,* 16 Nov. 1888.

120. White, *Rothschild Buildings,* chap. 1.

121. Jones, *Outcast London,* chap. 17; Keating, "Fact and Fiction," pp. 595, 596; *Star,* 20 July 1889. However, the East End retained its reputation as a "Ripperland" for decades. This reputation lingers on, as indicated by the recent release of *The Krays,* a film that features the mobster twins from Bethnal Green as contemporary incarnations of Jack the Ripper.

122. Dr. Thomas Bond, to the Commissioner of the Metropolitan Police, 10 Nov. 1888, Mepo. 3/141. See the letter from Arthur Mc Donald, requesting the "medical reports on the bodies of the victims," for publication in "American Blue Books" and in a French publication. 15 Oct. 1892, H.O. 144/A49301/219. See a similar request from Dr. Gustave Ollive of Nantes, requesting a copy of Dr. Bond's report. 8 Nov. 1894, H.O. 144/A49301/C/36.

123. James G. Kiernan, "Sexual Perversion and the Whitechapel Murders," *Medical Standard* 4, no. 5 (Nov. 1888), 129–30; no. 6 (Dec. 1888), 170–71; E. C. Spitzka, "The Whitechapel Murders: Their Medico-Legal and Historical Aspects," *The Journal of Nervous and Mental Diseases,* 13, no. 12 (Dec. 1888), 765–78. On Jack the Ripper as a medical case, see also "The Whitechapel Murders," appearing contemporaneously in the *British Medical Journal* (8 Dec. 1888): 1302, as well as a letter to the editor from "A Medical Man," "A Theory of the Whitechapel Murders," in the *Evening News,* 15 Oct. 1888. The "mere existence of anthropophagy, necrophilism, or sexual perversion when unaccompanied by other evidences of nervous or mental disease, is not sufficient proof of insanity," declared Spitzka ("the Whitechapel Murders," p. 775).

Epilogue

1. *News of the World,* 24 May 1981. Special thanks to Mandy Merck for an opportunity to read her clipping file on the Yorkshire Ripper.

2. As other commentators have noted, this was a pattern that became established in other twentieth-century cases of serial "sex murders" like the Boston and Hillside stranglers, Ted Bundy, and the Son of Sam. But the explicit cultural frame of reference was the Whitechapel killer. See Jane Caputi, *The Age of Sex Crime* (Bowling Green: Bowling Green State University Popular Press, 1987).

3. Caputi, *Age of Sex Crime*, pp. 5, 6.

4. *Maclean's*, for example, proclaimed the Yorkshire murderer "Jack the Ripper's latest disciple." Quoted in ibid., p. 27.

5. After Peter Sutcliffe was apprehended as the mass murderer, journalists persisted in transforming him into a Gothic Victorian monster. "A suitably ghoulish past, complete with odd goings-on in grave yards, was unearthed to prove he was some sort of monster." Joan Smith, "Getting Away with Murder," *New Socialist* (May/June 1982): 10. Journalists continued to historicize Sutcliffe, exposing him as a rather old-fashioned sadist, who eschewed hardcore pornography or "books about Nazism and torture" (*Guardian*, 19 May 1981), but who drew inspiration instead from regular visits to a macabre waxwork exhibit in Blackpool that featured a Victorian "Museum of Anatomy," "the local version of Tussaud's, where headless female wax torsos illustrated the 'nine stages of pregnancy.' In addition, models of diseased male sexual organs in various stages of putrefaction represented "the awful results of men leading immoral lives before marriage." Gordon Burns, . . . *Somebody's Husband, Somebody's Son: The Story of Peter Sutcliffe* (London: Heinemann, 1984), p. 115.

6. *Evening News Magazine*, 7 Dec. 1979, quoted in Mandy Merck, "Sutcliffe: What the Papers Say," *Spare Rib* (July 1981): 16.

7. Guy Martin, "The Ripper," *Esquire* 95 (Jan. 1981): 60. For an excellent discussion of the media manipulation of the Ripper myth, see Merck, "Sutcliffe," pp. 16–18.

8. Roland Barthes, "Myths Today," in *Mythologies*, trans. Annette Lavers (St. Albans, Herts: Paladin, 1973), pp. 109–59.

9. Smith, "Getting Away with Murder," p. 1.

10. "The Shy Man Who Brought Fear to the North," *The Times*, 23 May 1981.

11. "Letters," *Spare Rib* (Sept. 1981): p. 110. Seventy percent of Leeds women answering a questionnaire "had been kerb-crawled or flashed on." Forty percent never went out at night. *Spare Rib* (June 1979): 6.

12. Burns, *Somebody's Husband*, p. 260, *Guardian*, 7 May 1981, Wendy Holloway, "'I Just Wanted to Kill Women.' Why? The Ripper and Male Sexuality." *Feminist Review* 9 (Autumn 1981): 39.

13. Michael Ignatieff, Review of Roger Smith, *Trial by Medicine: Insanity and Responsibility in Victorian Trials*, *London Review of Books* 3 (1981): 22.

14. *Guardian*, 19 May 1981, quoted in Holloway, "'I Just Wanted to Kill'," p. 35; "Is the System Fair to the Likes of Peter Sutcliffe?" *Guardian*, May 1981.

15. Burns, *Somebody's Husband*, p. 260; Sutcliffe, quoted in Holloway, "'I Just Wanted to Kill'," p. 39.

16. New trends in horror films certainly facilitated the Ripper's comeback. While the violation of the female body has always been a "convenient" prop in hor-

ror movies, a number of critics, including Roger Ebert and Linda Williams, have noted something "different" about the psychopathic horror films of the early eighties: some "basic changes" in the level of violence, the cynical manipulation of audience, and the representation of women as independent, active sexual agents, "looking to be killed." Roger Ebert, "Why Movie Audiences Aren't Safe Anymore," *American Film* 16, no. 5 (March 1981): 54–56; Linda Williams, "When the Woman Looks," in Mary Ann Doane, Patricia Mellencamp, Linda Williams, eds., *Revision: Essays in Feminist Art Criticism* (Frederick, Md.: University Publications of America, 1984), pp. 83–99. In the new brand of "woman-in-danger" films like *Dressed to Kill* and *Friday the Thirteenth* a nameless, dreaded, faceless, "nonspecific male killing force" assaults and mutilates women who are increasingly punished for the threatening nature of their sexuality. The "recognition and affinity between woman and monster of the classic horror film gives way to pure identity: she *is* the monster, her mutilated body is the only visible horror." Williams, "When the Woman Looks," p. 96.

17. "The Shy Man Who Brought Fear to the North."

18. Lucy Bland, "The Case of the Yorkshire Ripper: Mad, Bad, Beast or Male?" in *Cases for Concern: Questions of Law and Justice* (Penguin, 1984), p. 198.

19. Joan Smith and Anita Bennett, "Women on Trial," *Spare Rib* (July 1981): 18.

20. For critical responses to the Ripper books, see Maev Kennedy, "Ripping Yarns," *Guardian*, 7 Dec. 1987; Matthew Coady, "A Better Class of Suspect," *Guardian*, 16 Oct. 1987; Benjamin Woolley, "Pick Your Ripper," *The Listener*, 17/24 Dec. 1987.

21. Ruth Wallgrove, "Women against Violence against Women," *Spare Rib* (Feb. 1981): 26.

22. Ibid.

23. Hilary Rose, Eileen Noxon, Gill Sidel, to the Editor, *The Times*, 3 Dec. 1980. Quoted in Burns, *Somebody's Husband*, p. 209.

24. "Men off the Streets," *Spare Rib* (Jan. 1981): 11.

25. Dusty Rhodes and Sandra McNeill, eds. *Women Against Violence Against Women* (London: Only Woman Press, 1985), p. 12; "March Women," "Our Demo," *Yorkshire Evening Post*, 24 Nov. 1980; Burns, *Somebody's Husband*, p. 209; Wallgrove, "Women against Violence," p. 25.

26. "Girls in Ripper Riot Fury," *Daily Mirror* (London), 23 Nov. 1980.

27. Mary Whitehouse, to the Editor, *The Times*, 9 Dec. 1980. Even in the pages of *The Times*, Whitehouse's comments did not go unanswered. Gerald Boner, in another letter to the editor (13 Dec. 1980), suggested that since "we have no knowledge of the identity of the Leeds murderer, let alone his motivation," it was by no means clear he is inspired by "indecent films." It was just as "conceivable," but equally "hypothetical," "that he could be a religious maniac inspired by certain passages in the bible."

28. *Women Against Violence Against Women*, p. 70.

29. Rose et al., to the editor.

30. Quoted in *Yorkshire Evening Post*, 19 Nov. 1980; Wallgrove, "Women Against Violence," p. 24.

31. Wallgrove, "Women against Violence," p. 24; Smith, "Getting Away with Murder," p. 10; Merck, "Sutcliffe," p. 17; Havers, quoted in Smith and Bennett, "Women on Trial," p. 18; *Women Against Violence Against Women*, pp. 14, 15.

32. Selma James to the editor, *Guardian*, 13 July 1981; "Thirteen Women-Victims of Terrorism," English Collective of Prostitutes, Leaflet, July 1981.

33. Merck, "Sutcliffe," p. 18.

34. Sheila Jeffreys, in *Women Against Violence Against Women*, p. 61, 70. This is a worrying statement that trivializes female experience and silences women; if carried to its logical conclusion it would also undermine the validity of women's history, except as the study of gender oppression. From a socialist feminist perspective, Elizabeth Wilson also tied prostitution to "economic" violence in her 1982 *What Is to Be Done about Violence Against Women* (Harmondsworth, Middlesex: Penguin, 1983), p. 206. She also speculated about the reluctance of contemporary feminists to take up prostitution as a political issue: whereas nineteenth-century feminists understood prostitution to be a vital aspect of the organization of female sexuality, a direct parallel to marriage, twentieth-century feminists "have found it easier to protest against rape and pornography, perhaps because we feel it affects us all." Whereas nineteenth-century feminists felt little self-consciousness about being a group of bourgeois women "saving" the fallen working-class sister, contemporary feminists are acutely aware of the danger of patronizing working-class women. The result is a confusion over the issue, due in part to reluctance to take up the issue of customer exploitation of prostitutes, to caution about attacking people's freedoms and rights, and to fear of restricting sexual behavior. "At the same time, the prostitute's relationship with her client may seem mysterious and repugnant. After all, part of the struggle of contemporary feminists is to retain sexual love as an area of pleasure and to extend our autonomy and control over this dark and disputed area."

35. For the radical feminist view on male sexuality, see, in particular, *Women Against Violence Against Women*. For a similar perspective articulated in socialist and in socialist/feminist journals, see Sally Vincent, "Women Who Ask for It," *New Statesman*, 19/26 Dec. 1980; Holloway, " 'I Just Wanted to Kill,' " p. 35.

36. Jill Tweedie, "Mad or Bad It's Men Who Are Violent and Women Who Are Victims," *Guardian*, 21 May 1981; Wilson, *What Is to Be Done about Violence*, pp. 38, 39; Editorial, *Feminist Review* 9 (Autumn 1981): 1.

37. Nicole Ward Jouve, *"The Streetcleaner": The Yorkshire Ripper Case on Trial* (London: Marion Boyars, 1986), p. 91.

38. There is a certain degree of irresponsibility in these public musings: Jouve fails to acknowledge the highly compromised and homophobic lineage of a post-Freudian theory of "sex crime" as an expression of homosexual misogyny, as it has filtered through the media and mainstream psychiatry in the twentieth century: how, according to historian Estelle Freedman ("'Uncontrolled Desires': The Response to the Sexual Psychopath, 1920–1960," in Kathy Peiss and Christina Simmons, eds., *Passion and Power: Sexuality in History* [Philadelphia: Temple University Press, 1989], pp. 199–225), Freudian theory helped to mobilize political support for the passage of sexual psychopath laws against nonconforming individuals during the sex-crime panics of the mid-twentieth century.

39. Jouve, *"Streetcleaner,"* p. 18.

40. A *Spare Rib* reviewer complained of Jouve's "virtual separation of working-class people from the rest of England." M. J. Whitlock, review of *"The Streetcleaner," Spare Rib* (January 1987): 28.

41. On pp. 65, 75, 79, and 145 Jouve cites Dobash and Dobash (*Violence against Wives*) and Tolson (*The Limits of Masculinity*), yet the Dobashs offer no evidence about class and Tolson makes no statement about violence against women and different class cultures of masculinity.

42. An earlier session of the conference was devoted to discussing my book *Prostitution and Victorian Society: Women, Class, and the State* (New York: Cambridge University Press, 1980). I was a participant in the conference.

43. Sue O'Sullivan, "Passionate Beginnings: Ideological Politics: 1969–1982," *Feminist Review* 11 (1982): 84, 85.

44. Versions of Coward's presentation were published as "Sexual Violence and Sexuality," *Feminist Review* 11 (Summer 1982): 9–22, and in "What Is Pornography?" *Spare Rib* (June 1982): 53–55.

45. Ann Snitow, "Retrenchment versus Transformation: The Politics of the Anti-Pornography Movement," in Varda Burstyn, ed., *Women against Censorship* (Vancouver and Toronto: Douglas and McIntyre, 1985).

46. WAVAW, "What Is Pornography," *Spare Rib* (June 1982): 54, 55.

47. Cora Kaplan, *"The Thorn Birds:* Fiction, Fantasy, Femininity," in *Sea Changes: Essays on Culture and Feminism* (London: Verso, 1986), pp. 117–46; Judith Butler, "The Force of Fantasy: Feminism, Mapplethorpe and Discursive Excess," *Differences* 2, no. 2 (Summer 1990).

48. Susanne Kappeler, *The Pornography of Representation* (Minneapolis: University of Minnesota Press, 1986); Deborah Cameron and Elizabeth Fraser, *Lust to Kill: A Feminist Investigation of Sexual Murder* (New York: New York University Press, 1987).

49. The press reception in the United States of Paul West's novel *The Women of Whitechapel and Jack the Ripper* illustrates the dynamic and politically ambiguous interaction between feminist discourses and narratives of sexual danger. On the one hand, *The Atlantic* refused to publish a favorable review of the book, claiming that "we cannot publish something that asks us to admire the literary merit of a book about chopping women up . . . when so many of them [women] are being chopped up all over this terrible anarchy we are living in." On the other hand, Andrea Dworkin, in the pages of *Ms.*, recommended the novel as summer reading for feminists, praising West as an elegant, intelligent novelist, who does not "lie" about "the sadism of men" or the "complicity of the decent man in acts of atrocity." Roger Cohen, "Book Notes," *New York Times,* 3 July 1991; "What Writers are Reading," *Ms.* 2, no. 2 (July/August 1991): 82.

SELECTED BIBLIOGRAPHY

Archival Sources

Booth Manuscripts, London School of Economics, British Library of Political and Economic Science, Archives, London
Pearson Papers, University College, London.
Public Record Office, London
    Admiralty Papers, Adm. 1
    Home Office Papers, H.O. 144
    Metropolitan Police Papers, Mepo. 3
Robins Collection, Fales Library, New York University, New York
Robinson Locke Collection, New York Public Library, New York
Sharpe Papers, University College, London
Local History Collection, Tower Hamlets Library, London
Salvation Army Archives, Salvation Army, London
Society for Physical Research Archives, Society for Psychical Research, London
Stead Papers. Thanks to Professor J. O. Baylen. Now housed at Churchill College, Cambridge University, Cambridge
Tussaud's Archives, Madame Tussaud's, London
Stevenson Papers, Beinecke Library, Yale University, New Haven

Parliamentary Papers

"Report by Miss Collett on the Statistics of Employment of Women and Girls," *P.P.* 1894, vols. 91–92, C.7564.
"Report of the Royal Commission on the Administration and Operation of the Contagious Diseases Acts, 1868–9," *P.P.* (1871), 29, C. 408.
"Report of the Select Committee on the Lunacy Laws," *P.P.* (1877), C.323.

Newspapers and Periodicals (substantially consulted)

British Medical Journal, 1879, 1884, 1887, 1888.
Commonweal, 1885, 1888.
Daily Chronicle, 1888.
Daily Mirror, 1980.
Daily News, 1883, 1887, 1888.
Daily Telegraph, 1885–1888.
East London Advertiser, 1886–1891.
East London Observer, 1888, 1889.
Echo, 1887, 1888.
Evening News, 1888.
Evening Standard, 1888.
Feminist Review, 1981, 1982.

Girl's Own Paper, 1887–1890.
Guardian, 1980, 1981, 1987.
Jewish Chronicle, 1888.
Justice, 1885, 1887, 1888.
The Lancet, 1876, 1881, 1887, 1888.
Light, 1887.
The Link, 1888.
Lloyd's Weekly Newspaper, 1885, 1888.
Medium and Daybreak, 1879, 1887, 1888.
Moonshine, 1884.
National Reformer, 1885.
New Statesman, 1980.
Our Corner, 1888.
Pall Mall Gazette, 1883–1889.
Penny Illustrated Magazine, 1888.
Police Illustrated News, 1885, 1888.
Proceedings of the Society for Psychical Research, 1886–1887.
Punch, 1885–1888.
Review of Reviews, 1891, 1892.
Reynolds Newspaper, 1870, 1885, 1887, 1888.
Saturday Review of Politics, Literature, Science, and Art, 1884, 1885, 1888.
Spare Rib, 1979–1982.
Spiritualist, 1876, 1878, 1879.
Star, 1888, 1889.
The Times, 1884, 1885, 1888, 1980, 1981.
Town Talk, 1885–1888.
Yorkshire Evening Post, 1980.
Tit-Bits, 1888.
War Cry, 1885, 1886, 1888.
Woman's Penny Paper, 1888.

Printed Sources

Acorn, George. *One of the Multitude*. London: Heinemann, 1911.
Adburgham, Alison. *Liberty's: A Biography of a Shop*. London: George Allen and Unwin, 1975.
———. *A Punch History of Manners and Modes, 1841–1940*. London: Hutchinson, 1961.
———. *Shopping in Style: London from the Restoration to Edwardian Elegance*. London: Thames and Hudson, 1979.
Alaya, Flavia. "Victorian Science and the 'Genius' of Woman." *Journal of the History of Ideas* 38 (April–June 1977): 261–80.
Alexander, Sally, ed. *Women's Fabian Tracts*. London: Routledge, 1989.
Altick, Richard. *The Shows of London*. Cambridge: Harvard University Press, 1978.
———. *Victorian Sensations: Studies in Scarlet*. New York: W. W. Norton, 1970.

Anderson, Benedict. *Imagined Communities: Reflections on the Origins and Spread of Nationalism.* London: Verson, 1983.

Anderson, Olive. "Women Preachers in Mid-Victorian Britain: Some Reflections on Feminism, Popular Religion, and Social Change." *Historical Journal* 12, no. 3 (1969): 467–84.

Anderson, Sir Robert. *The Lighter Part of My Official Life.* London: Hodder and Stoughton, 1910.

Ang, Ien. *Watching Dallas.* London and New York: Methuen, 1985.

Armstrong, Nancy. "The Occidental Alice." *Differences* 2, no. 2 (Summer 1990): 3–40.

Ascoli, David. *The Queen's Peace: The Origins and Development of the Metropolitan Police, 1829–1879.* London: Hamish Hamilton, 1979.

Askwith, Betty. *Lady Dilke: A Biography.* London: Chatto and Windus, 1969.

Asquith, Margot. *The Autobiography of Margot Asquith,* edited by Mark Bonham Carter. 1962. Reprint. London: Methuen, 1985.

Auerbach, Nina. *Woman and the Demon: The Life of a Victorian Myth.* Cambridge: Harvard University Press, 1982.

Bailey, Peter. "Ally Sloper's Half Holiday: Comic Art in the 1880s." *History Workshop Journal* 16 (Autumn 1983): 4–31.

———. "Champagne Charlie: Performance and Ideology in the Music-Hall Swell Song." In J. S. Bratton, ed., *Music Hall: Performance and Style.* Milton Keynes: Open University Press, 1986.

———, ed. *Music Hall: The Business of Pleasure.* Milton Keynes: Open University Press, 1986.

———. "Parasexuality and Glamour: The Victorian Barmaid as Cultural Prototype." *Gender and History* 2, no. 2 (Summer 1990): 148–72.

———. "Will the Real Bill Banks Please Stand Up? Towards a Role Analysis of Mid-Victorian Working-Class Respectability." *Journal of Social History* 12 (1979): 336–53.

Bailey, Victor. "'In Darkest England and the Way Out': The Salvation Army, Social Reform and the Labour Movement, 1885–1910." *International Review of Social History* 29 (1984): 133–71.

———. "Salvation Army Riots, the 'Skeleton Army', and Legal Authority in the Provincial Town." In A. P. Donajgrodzki, ed., *Social Control in Nineteenth-Century Britain.* London: Croom Helm, 1979.

Bailey, Victor, and Sheila Blackburn. "The Punishment of Incest Act 1908: A Case Study of Law Creation." *Criminal Law Review* (1979): 708–18.

Banks, Olive. *Becoming a Feminist: The Social Origins of "First Wave" Feminism.* Brighton, Sussex: Wheatsheaf, 1986.

Barker-Benfield, Ben. *The Horrors of the Half-Known Life: Male Attitudes Towards Women and Sexuality in Nineteenth-Century America.* New York: Harper and Row, 1976.

Barnett, Mrs. H. O. R. *Canon Barnett: His Life, Work, and Friends by his Wife.* 2 volumes. London: Murray, 1921.

Barrow, Logie. *Independent Spirits: Spiritualism and English Plebians, 1850–1910.* London: Routledge and Kegan Paul, 1986.

_____. "Socialism in Eternity: Plebian Spiritualists, 1853–1913." *History Workshop* 9 (Spring 1980): 37–69.

Barthes, Roland. "Myths Today." In *Mythologies*. Translated by Annette Lavers. St. Albans, Herts.: Paladin, 1973.

Bartlett, Neil. *Who Was That Man? A Present for Mr. Oscar Wilde*. London: Serpent's Tail, 1988.

Baylen, Joseph O. "Oscar Wilde Redivivus." *The University of Mississippi Studies in English* 6 (1965): 77–86.

Beals, Polly. "Fabian Feminism: Gender, Politics, and Culture, 1880–1930." Ph.D. dissertation, Rutgers University, 1989.

Bebel, August. *Women in the Past, Present, and Future*. 1885. Reprint, London: Zwan, 1988.

Beer, Gillian. *Darwin's Plots: Evolutionary Narrative in Darwin, George Eliot, and Nineteenth-Century Fiction*. London: Ark Paperbacks, 1985.

Behlmer, George. *Child Abuse and Moral Reform in England, 1870–1908*. Stanford: Stanford University Press, 1982.

Berdoe, Edward. *St. Bernard's: The Romance of a Medical Student*. London: Swan, Sonnenschein, 1888.

_____. *Dying Scientifically: A Key to St. Bernard's*. London: Swan, Sonnenschein, 1888.

Bermant, Chaim. *Point of Arrival: A Study of London's East End*. London: Methuen, 1975.

Bernheimer, Charles, and Claire Kahane, eds. *In Dora's Case: Freud-Hysteria-Feminism*. New York: Columbia University Press, 1985.

Besant, Walter. *All Sorts and Conditions of Men: An Impossible Story*. New York: Harper and Row, 1929.

_____. *East London*. 1910. Reprint, New York: Garland, 1980.

_____. *The Revolt of Man*. London: Collins, 1887.

Birken, Lawrence. *Consuming Desire: Sexual Science and the Emergence of a Culture of Abundance, 1871–1914*. Ithaca: Cornell University Press, 1988.

Bland, Lucy. "The Case of the Yorkshire Ripper: Mad, Bad, Beast or Male?" In *Cases for Concern: Questions of Law and Justice*. Penguin, 1984.

_____. "Marriage Laid Bare: Middle-Class Women and Marital Sex c. 1880–1914." In Jane Lewis, ed., *Labour of Love: Women's Experience of Home and Family, 1850–1940*. Oxford: Basil Blackwell, 1986.

Block, Ed. "Evolutionary Psychology and Late-Victorian Gothic Fiction." *Victorian Studies* 25, no. 4 (Summer 1982): 443–65.

Booth, Charles. "The Condition of the People of East London and Hackney, 1887." *Journal of the Royal Statistical Society* 51 (1888): 276–331.

_____. "The Inhabitants of Tower Hamlets (School Board Division), Their Condition and Occupations." *Journal of the Royal Statistical Society* 50 (1887): 326–91.

_____. *Life and Labour of the People in London*. 17 volumes. 1892–97. Reprint, New York: AMS Press, 1970.

Booth, Mary Macaulay. *Charles Booth: A Memoir*. London: Macmillan, 1918.

Booth, Michael R. *English Melodrama*. London: Herbert Jenkins, 1956.

Boston, Sarah. *Women Workers and the Trade Unions*. London: Lawrence and Wishart, 1980.

Boulmelha, Penny. *Thomas Hardy and Women: Sexual Ideology and Narrative*. Brighton, Sussex: Harvester, 1982.

Bowlby, Rachel. *Just Looking: Consumer Culture in Dreiser, Gissing, and Zola*. London and New York: Methuen, 1985.

Boyd, Nancy. *Three Victorian Women Who Changed Their World: Josephine Butler, Octavia Hill, Florence Nightingale*. New York: Oxford University Press, 1982.

Brandon, Ruth. *The New Women and the Old Men: Love, Sex, and the Woman Question*. New York: W. W. Norton, 1990.

_____. *The Spiritualists: The Passion for the Occult in the Nineteenth Century*. New York: Knopf, 1983.

Bratton, Jacqueline. *The Victorian Popular Ballad*. Totowa, N.J.: Rowman and Littlefield, 1978.

_____., ed. *Music Hall: Performance and Style*. New York: Taylor and Francis, 1987.

Briggs, Asa. *Victorian Cities*. New York and Evanston: Harper and Row, 1963.

_____. *Victorian Things*. Chicago: University of Chicago Press, 1989.

Bristow, Edward J. *Vice and Vigilance: Purity Movements in Britain Since 1700*. Totowa, N.J.: Rowman and Littlefield, 1977.

Britain, I. M. *Fabianism and Culture: A Study in British Socialism and the Arts, 1884–1918*. Cambridge: Cambridge University Press, 1982.

Brooks, Peter. *The Melodramatic Imagination: Balzac, Henry James, Melodrama and the Mode of Excess*. New Haven: Yale University Press, 1976.

Buck-Morss, Susan. "The Flaneur, the Sandwichman, and the Whore: The Politics of Loitering." *New German Critique* 13, no. 39 (1986): 99–142.

Budd, Susan. *Varieties of Unbelief: Atheists and Agnostics in English Society, 1850–1960*. London: Heinemann, 1977.

Burford, Diana. "Theosophy and Feminism." In Pat Holden, ed., *Women's Religious Experience*. London: Croom Helm, 1983.

Burns, Gordon. . . . *Somebody's Husband, Somebody's Son: The Story of Peter Sutcliffe*. London: Heinemann, 1984.

Burstall, Sara. *Retrospect and Prospect: Sixty Years of Women's Education*. London: Longmans, 1911.

Butler, Belinda Norman. *Victorian Aspirations: The Life and Labour of Charles and Mary Booth*. London: George Allen and Unwin, 1972.

Butler, Josephine. *Josephine H. Butler: An Autobiographical Memoir*. George W. Johnson and Lucy A. Johnson, eds. London: Arrowsmith, 1928.

_____. "The Dark Side of English Life: Illustrated in a Series of True Stories." *The Methodist Protest* (January–May 1877).

_____. "The Garrison Towns of Kent." *Shield* (9 May 1870).

_____. *Personal Reminiscences of a Great Crusade*. London: Horace Marshall and Son, 1911. Reprint, Westport: Hyperion Press, 1976.

_____. *Rebecca Jarrett*. London: Morgan and Scott, 1985.

_____. *Recollections of George Butler*. Bristol: Arrowsmith, 1892.

Butler, Judith. "The Force of Fantasy: Feminism, Mapplethorpe, and Discursive Excess." *Differences* 2, no. 2 (Summer 1990): 105–25.

Bynum, W. F. "Themes in British Psychiatry: J. C. Prichard (1786–1918) to Henry Maudsley (1835–1918)." In Michael Ruse, ed. *Nature Animated*. Dordrecht, Holland: Reidel, 1983.

Cameron, Deborah, and Elizabeth Fraser. *Lust to Kill: A Feminist Investigation of Sexual Murder*. New York: New York University Press, 1987.

Cannadine, David. "The Context, Performance, and Meaning of Ritual: The British Monarchy and the Invention of Tradition, c. 1820–1977." In Eric Hobsbawm and Terence Ranger, eds., *The Invention of Tradition*. Cambridge: Cambridge University Press, 1983.

Caputi, Jane. *The Age of Sex Crime*. Bowling Green: Bowling Green State University Popular Press, 1987.

Casteras, Susan. *The Substance and the Shadow: Images of Victorian Womanhood*. New Haven: Yale Center for British Art, 1982.

Central Criminal Court, Sessions Papers. London, 1880–88.

Chapman, Pauline. *Madame Tussaud's Chamber of Horrors: Two Hundred Years of Crime*. London: Constable, 1984.

Chase, Ellen. *Tenant Friends in Old Deptford*. London: Williams and Norgate, 1929.

Clark, Anna. "Queen Caroline and the Sexual Politics of Popular Culture in London, 1820." *Representations* 31 (Summer 1990): 47–68.

———. "Rape or Seduction? A Controversy over Sexual Violence in the Nineteenth-Century." In London Feminist History Group, ed., *The Sexual Dynamics of History*. London: Pluto Press, 1983.

———. "The Struggle for the Breeches." Unpublished paper, 1987.

———. "Womanhood and Manhood in the Transition from Plebeian to Working-Class Culture: London, 1780–1845." Ph.D. dissertation, Rutgers University, 1988.

———. *Women's Silence, Men's Violence: Sexual Assault in England, 1770–1845*. London: Pandora, 1987.

Clark, Michael. "The Rejection of Psychological Approaches to Mental Disorder in Late-Nineteenth Century British Psychiatry." In Andrew Scull, ed., *Madhouses, Mad-Doctors, and Madmen: The Social History of Psychiatry in the Victorian Era*. Philadelphia: University of Pennsylvania Press, 1981.

Clark, T. J. *The Painting of Modern Life: Paris in the Art of Manet and His Followers*. New York: Knopf, 1985.

Clayton, Cherry, ed. *Olive Schreiner*. Johannesburg: McGraw Hill, 1983.

Cobbe, Frances Power. *Life of Frances Power Cobbe*. 2 volumes. Boston: Houghton Mifflin, 1985.

Cohen, Ed. "Poor London." Unpublished paper, 1991.

Collins, Wilkie. *The Woman in White*. London, 1859–60. Reprint, Harmondsworth, Middlesex: Penguin, 1974.

Comfort, Alex. *The Anxiety Makers: Some Curious Preoccupations of the Medical Profession*. London: Nelson, 1967.

Cominos, Peter. "Late-Victorian Sexual Respectability and the Social System." *International Review of Social History* 8 (1963): 18–48.

Copelman, Dina. "Where Boundaries Blur: Class and Construction of Gender Identity." Unpublished paper, 1991.

Corbin, Alain. *Women for Hire: Prostitution and Sexuality in France after 1850.* Translated by Alan Sheridan. Cambridge: Harvard University Press, 1990.

Corke, Helen. *In Our Infancy: An Autobiography,* Part I, *1882–1912.* Cambridge: Cambridge University Press, 1975.

Cott, Nancy F. "Passionlessness: An Interpretation of Victorian Sexual Ideology, 1790–1850." *Signs* 4 (1978): 219–36.

Courtney, Janet E. *An Oxford Portrait Gallery.* London: Chapman and Hall, 1931.

Coward, Rosalind. "Sexual Violence and Sexuality." *Feminist Review* 11 (Summer 1982): 9–22.

Crawford, Alan. *C. R. Ashbee: Architect, Designer, and Romantic Socialist.* New Haven: Yale University Press, 1985.

Cross, Gilbert. *Next Week East Lynne.* Lewisburg: Bucknell University Press, 1975.

Cullen, Tom. *Autumn of Terror: Jack the Ripper, the Crimes and Times.* London: Bodley Head, 1965.

David, Deidre. "Ideologies of Patriarchy, Feminism, and Fiction in *The Odd Women.*" *Feminist Studies* 10 (Spring 1984): 117–40.

Davidoff, Leonore. "Gender and Class in Victorian England: The Diaries of Arthur J. Munby and Hannah Cullwick." *Feminist Studies* 5 (Spring 1979): 87–141.

Davin, Anna. "Imperialism and Motherhood." *History Workshop Journal* 5 (Spring 1978): 9–66.

Davis, Jennifer. "A Poor Man's System of Justice: The London Police Courts in the Second Half of the Nineteenth-Century." *The Historical Journal* 27, no. 2 (1984): 309–35.

Davison, Peter. *Songs of the British Music Hall: Compiled and Edited With a Critical History of the Songs and Their Times.* New York: Oak Publications, 1971.

Degler, Carl. "What Ought to Be and What Was: Women's Sexuality in the Nineteenth-Century." *American Historical Review* 79 (1974): 1467–90.

De Lauretis, Teresa. *Alice Doesn't: Feminism, Semiotics, Cinema.* Bloomington: Indiana University Press, 1984.

D'Emilio, John, and Estelle Freedman. *Intimate Matters: A History of Sexuality in America.* New York: Harper and Row, 1988.

Denby, Helen. "Marriage in East London." In Bernard Bosanquet, ed., *Aspects of the Social Problem.* London: Macmillan, 1895. Reprint, New York: Krause Reprint Company, 1968.

Devane, William. "The Virgin and the Dragon." *Yale Review* (1947): 33–46.

Dew, Walter. *I Caught Crippen.* London: Blackie and Son, 1938.

Diamond, Irene, and Lee Quinby, eds., *Feminism and Foucault: Reflections on Resistance.* Boston: Northeastern University Press, 1988.

Dinnage, Rosemary. *Annie Besant.* London: Penguin, 1986.

Dinnerstein, Dorothy. *The Mermaid and the Minotaur: Sexual Arrangements and Human Malaise*. New York: Harper and Row, 1976.

Dixon, Joy. "Theosophy and Feminism in Late-Nineteenth Century and Early Twentieth-Century England." Unpublished paper, 1987.

Doane, Mary Ann. "Film and the Masquerade: Theorising the Female Spectator." *Screen* 23, nos. 3/4 (September/October 1982): 74–87.

Dobash, R. Emerson, and Russell Dobash. *Violence against Wives: A Case against the Patriarchy*. New York: The Free Press, 1979.

Drake, Barbara. *Women in Trade Unions*. London: George Allen and Unwin, 1920.

Drotner, Kirsten. *English Children and Their Magazines, 1751–1945*. New Haven and London: Yale University Press, 1989.

Duman, Daniel. *The English and Colonial Bars in the Nineteenth Century*. London: Croom Helm, 1983.

Duffin, Lorna. "Prisoners of Progress: Women and Evolution." In Sara Delamont and Lorna Duffin, eds., *The Nineteenth-Century Woman, Her Cultural and Physical World*. London: Croom Helm, 1978.

Dyhouse, Carol. *Feminism and the Family in England, 1880–1939*. Oxford: Basil Blackwell, 1989.

Ebert, Roger. "Why Movie Audiences Aren't Safe Anymore." *American Film* 16, no. 5 (March 1981): 54–56.

Eckenstein, Lina. *Woman under Monasticism: Chapters on Saint-Lore and Convent Life between A.D. 500 and A.D. 1500*. Cambridge: Cambridge University Press, 1986.

Elston, Mary Ann. "Women and Antivivisection in Victorian England, 1870–1900." In Nicholas Rupke, ed., *Vivisection in Historical Perspective*. London: Croom Helm, 1987.

Engels, Dagmar. "The Limits of Gender Ideology, Bengali Women, the Colonial State, and the Private Sphere, 1890–1920." *Women's Studies International Forum* 12, no. 4 (1989): 425–37.

Englander, David. "Booth's Jews: The Presentation of Jews and Judaism in *Life and Labour of the People in London*." *Victorian Studies* 32, no. 4 (Summer 1989): 551–71.

Evans, Joan. *The Conways, A History of Three Generations*. London: Museum Press, 1966.

Faderman, Lillian. *Surpassing the Love of Men: Romantic Friendships and Love Between Women from the Renaissance to the Present*. New York: William Morrow, 1981.

Fairbanks, Jenty. *Booth's Boots: Social Services in the Salvation Army*. London: General of the Salvation Army, 1983.

Farson, Daniel. *Jack the Ripper*. London: Sphere Books, 1973.

Fee, Elizabeth. "Science and the Woman Problem: Historical Perspectives." In Michael Teitelbaum, ed., *Sex Differences: Social and Biological Perspectives*. New York: Anchor Press, 1976.

Feldman, David, and Gareth Stedman Jones, eds., *Metropolis London: Histories and Representations Since 1800*. London and New York: Routledge, 1989.

Fido, Martin. *The Crimes, Detection, and Death of Jack the Ripper.* London: Weidenfeld and Nicolson, 1987.

First, Ruth, and Ann Scott. *Olive Schreiner.* New York: Schocken Books, 1980.

Fishman, William J. *East End 1888: Life in a London Borough Among the Labouring Poor.* Philadelphia: Temple University Press, 1988.

———. *East End Jewish Radicals, 1875–1914.* London: Duckworth, 1975.

Flax, Jane. "Postmodernism and Gender Relations in Feminist Theory." *Signs* 12, no. 4 (Summer 1987): 621–43.

Ford, Colin, and Brian Harrison, eds. *One Hundred Years Ago: Britain in the 1880s in Words and Photographs.* Cambridge: Harvard University Press, 1983.

Foucault, Michel. *The History of Sexuality.* 3 volumes. Translated by Robert Hurley. New York: Pantheon, 1978–86.

Fox, Richard Wightman, and T. J. Jackson Lears, eds. *The Culture of Consumption: Critical Essays in American History, 1880–1980.* New York: Pantheon, 1983.

Fradkin, Betty McGinnis. "Olive Schreiner and Karl Pearson." *Quarterly Bulletin of the South African Quarterly Library* (Capetown) 31, no. 4 (1977): 83–93.

Fraser, Flora. *Maud: The Illustrated Diary of a Victorian Woman.* London: Secker and Warburg, 1987.

Fraser, Nancy. "Rethinking the Public Sphere." *Social Text* 25/26 (1990): 56–80.

Fraser, W. Hamish. *The Coming of the Mass Market, 1850–1914.* London: Macmillan, 1981.

Frayling, Christopher. "The House that Jack Built." In Sylvia Tomaselli and Roy Porter, eds., *Rape.* Oxford: Basil Blackwell, 1986.

French, Richard D. *Antivivisection and Medical Science in Victorian Society.* Princeton: Princeton University Press, 1975.

Fried, Albert, and Richard Elman. *Charles Booth's London: A Portrait of the Poor at the Turn of the Century Drawn from His "Life and Labour of the People of London."* Harmondsworth, Middlesex: Penguin, 1971.

Friedland, Michael I. *The Trials of Israel Lipski.* London: Macmillan, 1984.

Fryer, Peter. *Forbidden Books of the Victorians.* London: Odyssey Press, 1970.

———. *The Man of Pleasure's Companion.* London: A. Barker, 1968.

Gagnier, Regenia. "Mediums and the Media." *Representations* 22 (Spring 1988): 29–36.

———. "Social Atoms: Working-Class Autobiography, Subjectivity, and Gender." *Victorian Studies* 30 (Spring 1987): 335–63.

Gallagher, Catherine. *The Industrial Reformation of English Fiction.* Chicago: University of Chicago Press, 1985.

Gatrell, V. A. C. "The Decline of Theft and Violence in Victorian and Edwardian England." In V. A. C. Gatrell et al., eds., *Crime and the Law: The Social History of Crime in Western Europe since 1500.* London: Europa Publications, 1980.

Gay, Peter. *The Bourgeois Experience: Victoria to Freud.* 2 volumes. New York: Oxford University Press, 1984.

Gay, Susan Elizabeth. *Spiritualistic Sanity: A Reply to Dr. Forbes Winslow's "Spiritualistic Madness."* London: Falmouth, 1879.

Geduld, Harry M., ed. *The Definitive "Dr. Jekyll and Mr. Hyde" Companion.* New York and London: Garland, 1983.

Geertz, Clifford. "Blurred Genres: The Refiguration of Social Thought." In *Local Knowledge: Further Essays in Interpretive Anthropology.* New York: Basic Books, 1983.

Gibson, Ian. *The English Vice: Beating, Sex, and Shame in Victorian England and After.* London: Duckworth, 1978.

Gillis, John. *Youth and History.* New York: Academic Press, 1974.

Gilman, Sander, and J. Edward Chamberlain, eds. *Degeneration: The Dark Side of Progress.* New York: Columbia University Press, 1985.

Girouard, Mark. *The Return to Camelot: Chivalry and the English Gentleman.* New Haven and London: Yale University Press, 1981.

"The Glorified Spinster." *Macmillan's Magazine* 58 (1888): 371–76.

Godeau, Abigail Solomon. "The Legs of the Countess." *October* 39 (Winter 1986): 66–108.

Gordon, Linda. *Woman's Body, Woman's Right: A Social History of Birth Control in America.* New York: Viking, 1976.

Gordon, Linda, and Ellen Dubois. "Seeking Ecstasy on the Battlefield: Danger and Pleasure in Nineteenth-Century Feminist Sexual Thought." *Feminist Studies* 9 (Spring 1983): 7–26.

Gorham, Deborah. "'The Maiden Tribute of Modern Babylon' Re-Visited." *Victorian Studies*(Spring 1976): 353–79.

Gorman, John. *Banner Bright: An Illustrated History of the Banners of the Trade Union Movement.* London: Allen Lane, 1973.

Gottdiener, M., and Alexandros Ph. Lagopoulos, eds. *The City and the Sign: An Introduction to Urban Semiotics.* New York: Columbia University Press, 1982.

Greenwood, James. *Low Life Deeps: An Account of the Strange Fish to Be Found There.* London: Chatto and Windus, 1876.

———. *The Wilds of London.* London: Chatto and Windus, 1874. Reprint, New York: Garland, 1985.

Grierson, Edward. *Storm Bird: The Strange Life of Georgina Weldon.* London: Chatto and Windus, 1959.

Grimsted, David. *Melodrama Unveiled: American Theater and Culture, 1800–1850.* Chicago: University of Chicago Press, 1968.

Grosskurth, Phyllis. *Havelock Ellis: A Biography.* New York: Knopf, 1980.

———. *The Woeful Victorian: A Biography of John Addington Symonds.* New York: Longmans, 1964.

Habermas, Jürgen. "The Public Sphere: An Encyclopedia Article (1964)." *New German Critique* 5, no. 2 (1974): 49–55.

———. *The Structural Transformation of the Public Sphere.* Translated by Thomas Burger. Cambridge, MIT Press, 1989.

Hadley, Elaine M. "Melodramatic Tactics: The Social Function of the Melodramatic Mode, 1800–1885." Ph.D. dissertation, Johns Hopkins University, 1991.

Haley, Bruce. *The Healthy Body and Victorian Culture*. Cambridge: Harvard University Press, 1978.

Halsted, D. G. *Doctor in the Nineties*. London: Christopher Johnson, 1959.

Hammerton, A. James. "Victorian Marriage and the Law of Matrimonial Cruelty." *Victorian Studies* 33, no. 2 (Winter 1990): 269–92.

Hansard Parlimentary Debates (Commons). Third Series, 300 (30 July 1885).

Harris, Ruth. "Melodrama, Hysteria, and Feminine Crimes of Passion in the Fin-de-Siècle." *History Workshop* 25 (Spring 1988): 31–63.

Harrison, Michael. *Clarence: The Life of the Duke of Clarence and Avondale, KG, 1864–1892*. London: W. H. Allen, 1972.

Hartman, Mary, and Lois Banner, eds. *Clio's Consciousness Raised: New Perspectives on the History of Women*. New York: Harper and Row, 1974.

Heath, Stephen. "Psychopathia Sexualis: Stevenson's *Strange Case*." In Colin McCabe, ed., *Futures for English*. Manchester: Manchester University Press, 1988.

Hennock, E. P. "The Measurement of Urban Poverty: From the Metropolis to the Nation, 1880–1920." *Economic History Review*, 2d ser., 40, no. 2 (1987): 208–27.

———. "Poverty and Social Theory in England: The Experience of the Eighteen-Eighties." *Social History* (January 1976): 67–91.

Higginbotham, Ann. "Respectable Sinners: Salvation Army Rescue Work with Unmarried Mothers, 1884–1941." In Gail Malmgreen, ed., *Religion in the Lives of English Women, 1760–1930*. London: Croom Helm, 1980.

———. "The Unmarried Mother and Her Child in Victorian London, 1834–1914." Ph.D. dissertation, Indiana University, 1985.

Hill, Octavia. *District Visiting*. London: Longman, 1877.

———. "A More Excellent Way of Charity." In *Our Common Land and Other Short Essays*. London: Macmillan, 1877.

———. *Open Spaces for Deptford . . . An Appeal*, 1892.

Himmelfarb, Gertrude. "The Culture of Poverty." In H. J. Dyos and Michael Wolff, eds., *The Victorian City: Images and Realities*. 2 volumes. London and Boston: Routledge and Kegan Paul, 1973.

———. *The Idea of Poverty: England in the Early Industrial Age*. New York: Vintage Books, 1985.

Hobsbawm, Eric. *Labouring Men*. London: Weidenfeld and Nicolson, 1964.

Hollis, Patricia. *Ladies Elect: Women in English Local Government 1865–1914*. Oxford: Clarendon Press, 1987.

Holloway, Wendy. " 'I Just Wanted to Kill a Woman' Why? The Ripper and Male Sexuality." *Feminist Review* 9 (Autumn 1981): 33–40.

Holroyd, Michael. *Bernard Shaw*. Vol. 1, *The Search for Love, 1856–1898*. New York: Random House, 1988.

Hope, Noel. *Mildred Duff: A Surrendered Life*. London: Salvationist Publications and Supplies, 1933.

Howell, Martin, and Keith Skinner. *The Ripper Legacy: The Life and Death of Jack the Ripper*. London: Sidgwick and Jackson, 1987.

Hughes, M. V. *A London Girl of the 1880s.* Oxford: Oxford University Press, 1978.

Hughes, Winifred. *Maniac in the Cellar.* Princeton: Princeton University Press, 1980.

Hunt, Lynn, ed., *The New Cultural History.* Berkeley: University of California Press, 1989.

Hyam, Ronald. *Empire and Sexuality: The British Experience.* Manchester: Manchester University Press, 1990.

Israel, Kali. "Drawing from Life: Art, Work, and Feminism in the Life of Emilia Dilke." Ph.D. dissertation, Rutgers University, 1991.

Jackson, Rosemary. *Fantasy: The Literature of Subversion.* London and New York: Methuen, 1981.

Jacyna, L. S. "Somatic Theories of Mind and the Interests of Medicine in Britain, 1850–1879." *Medical History* 26 (1982): 233–58.

Jalland, Pat. *Women, Marriage and Politics, 1860–1914.* New York: Oxford University Press, 1986.

James, Henry. *The Complete Notebooks of Henry James,* ed. Leon Edel and Lyall H. Powers. New York: Oxford University Press, 1987.

———. "London." In *Essays in London and Elsewhere.* 1893. Reprint, Freeport, N.Y.: Books for Libraries, 1922.

———. *The Princess Cassimassima.* 1886. Reprint, Harmondsworth, Middlesex: Penguin, 1986.

Jeffreys, Sheila. *The Spinster and Her Enemies: Feminism and Sexuality, 1880–1930.* London: Pandora, 1986.

Jenkins, Roy. *Victorian Scandal: A Biography of the Right Honourable Gentleman Sir Charles Dilke.* New York: Chilmark Press, 1965.

Jeune, Lady. "The Ethics of Shopping." *The Fortnightly Review* (January 1895): 125–32.

Jones, Elwyn, ed. *Ripper File.* London: Barker, 1975.

Jones, Gareth Stedman. *Outcast London: A Study in the Relationship between Classes in Victorian Society.* Oxford: Clarendon Press, 1971.

———. *Languages of Class: Studies in English Working-Class History, 1832–1982.* Cambridge: Cambridge University Press, 1983.

Jordanova, Ludmilla. *Sexual Visions.* Madison: University of Wisconsin Press, 1989.

Jouve, Nicole Ward. *"The Streetcleaner": The Yorkshire Ripper Case on Trial.* London: Marion Boyars, 1986.

Joyce, Patrick. *Visions of the People: Industrial England and the Question of Class, 1840–1914.* Cambridge: Cambridge University Press, 1991.

Kaplan, Cora. *Sea Changes: Essays on Culture and Feminism.* London: Verso, 1986.

Kaplan, E. Ann. "Is the Gaze Male?" In Ann Snitow et al., eds., *Powers of Desire.* New York: Monthly Review Press, 1983.

———. "The Political Unconscious in the Maternal Melodrama: Ellen Wood's *East Lynne* (1861)." In Derek Longhurst, ed., *Gender, Genre and Narrative Pleasure.* Hemel Hempstead: Unwin Hyman, 1988.

Kaplan, Temma. "Women and the Communal Strikes in the Crisis of 1917–1922." In Renate Bridenthal and Claudia Koonz, eds., *Becoming Visible: Women in European History.* Boston: Houghton Mifflin: 1987.

Kapp, Yvonne. *Eleanor Marx.* Vol. 2, *The Crowded Years, 1884–1898.* New York: Pantheon, 1976.

Kappeler, Susanne. *The Pornography of Representation.* Minneapolis: University of Minnesota Press, 1986.

Katz, Jonathan Ned. "The Invention of Heterosexuality." *Socialist Review* 20, no. 1 (January–March 1990): 7–34.

_____, ed. *Gay/Lesbian Almanac: A New Documentary.* New York: Harper and Row, 1983.

Keating, Peter. "Fact and Fiction in the East End," In H. J. Dyos and M. Wolff, eds., *The Victorian City.* 2 volumes. London: Routledge and Kegan Paul, 1973.

_____. *Into Unknown England, 1866–1913: Selections from the Social Explorers.* Glasgow: William Collins and Sons, 1976.

Kerber, Linda. "Separate Spheres, Female Worlds, Women's Place: The Rhetoric of Women's History." *Journal of American History* 75, no. 1 (June 1988): 9–39.

Kevles, Daniel J. *In the Name of Eugenics: Genetics and the Uses of Human Heredity.* New York: Knopf, 1985.

Kiernan, James G. "Sexual Perversion and the Whitechapel Murders." *Medical Standard* 4, no. 5 (November 1888): 129–30 and (December 1888): 170–71.

Kijinski, John L. "John Morley's 'English Men of Letters' Series and the Politics of Reading." *Victorian Studies* 34, no. 2 (Winter 1991): 205–25.

Kingsmill, Hugh. *After Puritanism.* London: Methuen, 1952.

Knight, Stephen. *Form and Ideology in Crime Fiction.* Bloomington: Indiana University Press, 1980.

_____. *Jack the Ripper: The Final Solution.* London: Harrap, 1976.

Koss, Stephen. *The Rise and Fall of the Political Press.* Vol. 1, *The Nineteenth Century.* Chapel Hill: University of North Carolina Press, 1981.

Koven, Seth. "From Rough Lads to Hooligans: Boy Life, National Culture and Social Reform." In Andrew Parker et al., eds., *Nationalisms and Sexualities,* London: Routledge, forthcoming.

Krafft-Ebing, R. *Psychopathia Sexualis: With Especial Reference to Contrary Sexual Instinct: A Medico-Legal Study.* Translated by Charles Gilbert Chaddock. Philadelphia: F. A. Davis, 1892.

Kubek, Elizabeth Bennett. "London as Text: Eighteenth-Century Women Writers and Reading the City." *Women's Studies* 17 (1990): 303–39.

Kuper, Adam. *The Invention of Primitive Society.* London and New York: Routledge and Kegan Paul, 1988.

Lambertz, Jan. "Feminists and the Politics of Wife-Beating." In Harold L. Smith, ed., *British Feminism in the Twentieth Century.* Amherst: University of Massachusetts Press, 1990.

_____. "Male-Female Violence in Late-Victorian and Edwardian England." B.A. dissertation, Harvard University, 1979.

Lansbury, Coral. *The Old Brown Dog: Women, Workers, and Vivisection in Edwardian England.* Madison: University of Wisconsin Press, 1985.

Laqueur, Thomas. *Making Sex: Body and Gender from the Greeks to Freud*. Cambridge: Harvard University Press, 1990.

Law, John [pseud.]. *Captain Lobe: A Story of the Salvation Army*. London: Hodder and Stoughton, 1989.

Leach, William R. "Transformations in a Culture of Consumption: Women and Department Stores, 1890–1925." *Journal of American History* 7, no. 2 (September 1984): 319–42.

Lears, T. J. Jackson. *No Place of Grace: Anti-modernism and the Transformation of American Culture, 1880–1920*. New York: Pantheon, 1981.

Lewis, Jane, ed. *Labour and Love: Women's Experience of Home and Family, 1820–1940*. Oxford: Basil Blackwell, 1986.

———. *The Politics of Motherhood: Child and Maternal Welfare in England, 1900–1939*. London: Croom Helm, 1980.

Lowe, Louisa. *The Bastilles of England: or The Lunacy Laws at Work*. London: Crookenden, 1883.

———. *My Outlawry; A Lecture Delivered in the Cavendish Room, Mortimer Street on the 17th of July 1873*. London: Lunacy Law Reform Association Offices, 1874.

———. *My Story: Exemplifying the Injurious Working of the Lunacy Laws and the Undue Influence Possessed by Lunacy Experts*. London: Lunacy Law Reform Association Offices, 1878.

Mackenzie, Compton. *My Life and Times: Octave One, 1883–1891*. London: Chatto and Windus, 1963.

Mackenzie, D. "Karl Pearson and the Professional Middle Class." *Annals of Science* 36, no. 22 (March 1979): 124–44.

MacKenzie, Norman, and Jeanne MacKenzie. *The Diary of Beatrice Webb*. Vol. 1, *Glitter Without and Darkness Within*. Cambridge, Mass.: Belknap Press, 1982.

———. *The Fabians*. New York: Simon and Schuster, 1977.

Maitland, Edward. *Anna Kingsford: Her Life, Letters, Diary and Work*. 2 volumes. London: G. Redway, 1896.

Maitland, Sarah. *Vesta Tilley*. London: Virago, 1986.

Mangan, J. A., and James Walvin, eds. *Manliness and Morality: Middle-Class Masculinity in Britain and America, 1800–1940*. New York: St. Martin's Press, 1987.

Mann, Tom. *Tom Mann's Memoirs*. London: The Labor Publishing Company, 1923. Reprint, London: Cox and Wyman, 1967.

Marcus, Jane. "Mothering, Madness, and Music." In Elaine K. Ginsburg and Laura Moss Gotlieb, eds., *Virginia Woolf: Centennial Essays*. Troy, N.Y.: Whitson, 1983.

Marcus, Steven. *The Other Victorians: A Study of Sexuality and Pornography in Mid-Nineteenth Century England*. New York: Meridian, 1974.

Marryat, Florence. *There Is No Death*. London: Kegan Paul, Trench, Trubner and Co., 1891.

Martin, Guy. "The Ripper." *Esquire* (January 1981): 58–68.

Matters, Leonard W. *The Mystery of Jack the Ripper*. London: Hutchinson, 1929.

Maurice, C. E. Edmund. *Life of Octavia Hill as Told in Her Letters*. London: Macmillan, 1913.

Mayhew, Henry. *London Labour and the London Poor*. 4 volumes. 1861. Reprint, New York: Dover, 1968.

McCalman, Iain. *Radical Underworld: Prophets, Revolutionaries, and Pornographers in London, 1795–1840*. Cambridge: Cambridge University Press, 1988.

McCandless, Peter. "Build, Build: The Controversy over the Care of the Chronically Insane in England, 1855–70." *Bulletin of the History of Medicine* 4 (1979): 553–74.

———. "'Dangerous to Themselves and Others': The Victorian Debate over the Prevention of Wrongful Confinement." *Journal of British Studies* 23 (Fall 1983): 84–104.

———. "Liberty and Lunacy: The Victorians and Wrongful Confinement." *Journal of Social History* 11 (1978): 366–86.

McKendrick, Neil, John Brewer, and J. H. Plumb. *The Birth of a Consumer Society: The Commercialization of Eighteenth-Century England*. Bloomington: Indiana University Press, 1985.

McLeod, Hugh. *Class and Religion in Late-Victorian London*. London: Croom Helm, 1974.

McLeod, R. M. "Law, Medicine, and Public Opinion: The Resistance to Compulsory Health Legislation, 1870–1901." *Public Law* (1967): 189–211.

McMillan, Margaret. *The Life of Rachel McMillan*. London and Toronto: J. M. Dent and Sons, 1927.

McNaghton, Sir Melville. *Days of My Years*. London: Edward Arnold, 1915.

Meacham, Standish. *Toynbee Hall and Social Reform, 1880–1914: The Search for Community*. New Haven and London: Yale University Press, 1987.

Meade, Marion. *Madame Blavatsky: The Woman Behind the Myth*. New York: G. P. Putnam's Sons, 1980.

Meier, Olga, ed. *The Daughters of Karl Marx: Family Correspondence, 1866–1898*. New York and London: Harcourt Brace Jovanovich, 1982.

Meisel, Martin. *Realisations: Narrative, Pictorial and Theatrical Arts in Nineteenth-Century England*. Princeton: Princeton University Press, 1983.

———. *Shaw and the Nineteenth-Century Theater*. Princeton: Princeton University Press, 1963.

Mitchell, Sally. "Sentiment and Suffering: Women's Recreational Reading in the 1860s." *Victorian Studies* 21, no. 1 (Autumn 1977): 29–45.

Modleski, Tania. *Loving with a Vengeance: Mass-Produced Fantasies for Women*. Hamden, Conn.: Archon Books 1982.

———. *The Women Who Knew Too Much: Hitchcock and Feminist Theory*. New York: Methuen, 1985.

Moore, R. Laurence. "The Spiritualist Medium: A Study of Female Professionalism in Victorian America." *American Quarterly* 27, no. 2 (1975): 200–221.

Mort, Frank. *Dangerous Sexualities: Medico-Moral Politics in England since 1830*. London: Routledge and Kegan Paul, 1987.

Mosucci, Orvilla. *The Science of Woman: Gynecology and Gender in England, 1800–1929*. Cambridge: Cambridge University Press, 1990.

Mowat, Charles L. *The Charity Organization Society, 1869–1913: Its Ideas and Works*. London: Methuen, 1961.

Mulvey, Laura. "Afterthoughts on Visual Pleasure and Narrative Cinema." *Frameworks* 15/17 (1981): 12–15.

———. "Visual Pleasure and Narrative Cinema." *Screen* 16, no. 3 (Autumn 1975): 6–18.

Nead, Lynda. *Myths of Sexuality: Representations of Women in Victorian Britain*. Oxford: Basil Blackwell, 1988.

Nethercot, Arthur H. *The First Five Lives of Annie Besant*. Chicago: University of Chicago Press, 1960.

Nevinson, Margaret. *Life's Fitful Fever, A Volume of Memories*. London: A. and C. Black, 1926.

Nord, Deborah Epstein. *The Apprenticeship of Beatrice Webb*. Ithaca: Cornell University Press, 1989.

———. "The City as Theater: From Georgian to Early Victorian London." *Victorian Studies* 31, no. 2 (Winter 1988): 159–88.

———. " 'Neither Pairs Nor Odds': Beatrice Webb, Margaret Harkness, Amy Levy, and the Promise of Female Community." *Signs* 15, no. 4 (Summer 1990): 733–54.

———. "The Urban Peripatetic: Spectator, Streetwalker, Woman Writer." Unpublished essay.

Oppenheim, Janet. *The Other World: Spiritualism and Psychical Research in England, 1850–1914*. New York: Cambridge University Press, 1985.

———. *"Shattered Nerves": Doctors, Patients, and Depression in Victorian England*. New York: Oxford University Press, 1991.

O'Sullivan, Sue. "Passionate Beginnings: Ideological Politics: 1969–1982," *Feminist Review* 11 (1982): 70–86.

Ovenden, Graham, and Robert Melville. *Victorian Children*. New York: St. Martin's Press, 1972.

Owen, Alex. *The Darkened Room: Women, Power, and Spiritualism in Late Victorian England*. London: Virago Press, 1989.

———. "The Other Voice: Women, Children, and Nineteenth-Century Spiritualism." In Carolyn Steedman et al., eds., *Language, Gender, and Childhood*. London: Routledge and Kegan Paul, 1985.

Palmer, Alan. *The East End: Four Centuries of London Life*. London: John Murray, 1898.

Pankhurst, Christabel. *The Great Scourge and How to End It*. London: E. Pankhurst, 1913.

Pearl, Cyril. *The Girl with the Swansdown Seat*. Indianapolis: Bobbs-Merrill, 1955.

Pearsall, Ronald. *The Worm in the Bud: The World of Victorian Sexuality*. New York: Macmillan, 1969.

Pearson, Egon. *Karl Pearson: An Appreciation of Some Aspects of His Life and Work*. Cambridge: University Press, 1988.

Pearson, Karl. *The Chances of Death and Other Studies in Evolution*. 2 volumes. London: E. Arnold, 1897.

_____. *The Ethic of Freethought: and Other Addresses and Essays*. London: A. and C. Black, 1888.

_____. *The Life, Letters, and Labours of Francis Galton*. Cambridge: Cambridge University Press, 1914–30.

Pearson, Michael. *The Age of Consent: Victorian Prostitution and Its Enemies*. Newton Abbott: David and Charles, 1972.

Pederson, Joyce Senders. *The Reform of Girls' Secondary and Higher Education*. New York and London: Garland, 1987.

Peiss, Kathy, Christina Simmons, eds., *Passion and Power: Sexuality and History*. Philadelphia: Temple University Press, 1989.

Perkin, Harold. *The Rise of Professional Society: England since 1880*. New York and London: Routledge, 1989.

Peterson, Jeanne. *Family, Love, and Work in the Lives of Victorian Gentlewomen*. Bloomington: Indiana University Press, 1989.

Petrie, Glenn. *A Singular Iniquity: The Campaigns of Josephine Butler*. New York: Viking Press, 1971.

Pfautz, Harold, ed. *Charles Booth on the City: Physical Pattern and Social Structure*. Chicago: University of Chicago Press, 1967.

Phillips, H. A. D. "Offenses against Marriage and the Relations of the Sexes." *Law Quarterly Journal* (October 1885): 471–86.

Pike, E. Royston, ed. *Human Documents of the Age of Forsythes*. London: Allen and Unwin, 1969.

Pleck, Elizabeth. "Feminist Responses to 'Crimes Against Women,' 1868–1896." *Signs* 8, no. 3 (1983): 451–70.

Plowden, Alison. *The Case of Eliza Armstrong: "A Child of 13 Bought for £5."* London: BBC, 1974.

Pollock, Griselda. "Vicarious Excitements: *London: A Pilgrimage* by Gustave Doré and Blanchard Jerrold, 1872." *New Formations* 2 (Spring 1988): 25–50.

Poole, Adrian. *Gissing in Context*. Totowa, N.J.: Rowman and Littlefield, 1975.

Poovey, Mary. *Uneven Developments: The Ideological Work of Gender in Mid-Victorian England*. Chicago: University of Chicago Press, 1988.

Porter, Dennis. *The Pursuit of Crime: Art and Ideology in Detective Fiction*. New Haven: Yale University Press, 1981.

Prochaska, F. K. "Body and Soul: Bible Nurses and the Poor in Victorian London." *Historical Research* 60 (1987): 336–48.

Quilter, Harry, ed. *Is Marriage a Failure?* London: Swan Sonnenschein, 1888.

Radford, Jean. *The Progress of Romance: The Politics of Popular Fiction*. London: Routledge and Kegan Paul, 1986.

Railson, George. *Heathen England*. London: Salvation Army Book Deposit, 1886; first edition, 1878.

Rasor, Eugene L. *Reform in the Royal Navy: A Social History of the Lower Deck, 1850–1889*. Hamden, Conn.: Archon, 1976.

Reade, Charles. *Hard Cash: A Matter-of-Fact Romance*. 1882. Reprint, New York: Collier and Son, 1970.

Reader, William Joseph. *Professional Men: The Rise of the Professional Class in Nineteenth-Century England*. London: Weidenfeld and Nicolson, 1966.

Rhodes, Dusty, and Sandra McNeil, eds. *Women Against Violence Against Women*. London: Only Woman Press, 1985.

Richards, Thomas. "The Image of Victoria in the Year of Jubilee." *Victorian Studies* 30, no. 4 (Autumn 1987): 7–32.

Riemer, E. S., and John Fout, eds. *European Women: A Documentary History*. New York: Schocken, 1980.

Rive, Richard, ed. *Olive Schreiner Letters*. Vol. 1, *1871–1899*. Oxford: Oxford University Press, 1988.

Robins, Elizabeth. "Annie Besant." Unpublished paper, 1936.

————. *Both Sides of the Curtain*. London: Heinemann, 1940.

Rogers, Frederick. *Labour, Life, and Literature*. London: Smith, Elder, 1913.

Romanes, George. "The Capacity of Women." *Nineteenth Century* 21 (May 1887): 654–67.

Ross, Ellen. "'Fierce Questions and Taunts': Married Life in Working-Class London, 1870–1914." *Feminist Studies* 8, no. 3 (Fall 1982): 575–76.

————. *Love and Labour in Outcast London: Motherhood, 1870–1918*. New York: Oxford University Press, forthcoming.

————. "'Not the Sort That Would Sit on the Doorstep': Respectability in Pre–World War I London Neighborhoods." *International Labor and Working-Class History* 27 (Spring 1985): 39–59.

————. "Survival Networks: Women's Neighborhood Sharing in London before World War One." *History Workshop Journal* 15 (Spring 1983): 4–27.

Rowbotham, Sheila, and Jeffrey Weeks. *Socialism and the New Life: The Personal and Sexual Politics of Edward Carpenter and Havelock Ellis*. London: Pluto, 1977.

Rubin, Gayle. "The Traffic in Women: Notes on the 'Political Economy' of Sex." In Rayna Reiter, ed., *Towards an Anthropology of Women*. New York: Monthly Review Press, 1975.

Rubinstein, David. *Before the Suffragettes: Women's Emancipation in the 1890s*. Brighton: Harvester Press, 1986.

————. "Booth and Hyndman." *Bulletin of the Society for the Study of Labour History* 16 (Spring 1968): 22–24.

Rumbelow, Donald. *The Complete Jack the Ripper: A New and Completely Revised Edition of a Classic Case History of Murder*. London: W. H. Allen, 1987.

Russett, Cynthia Eagle. *Sexual Science: The Victorian Construction of Womanhood*. Cambridge: Harvard University Press, 1989.

Ryan, Mary P. *Women in Public: Between Banners and Ballots, 1825–1880*. Baltimore: Johns Hopkins University Press, 1990.

Said, Edward. *Orientalism*. New York: Vintage Books, 1979.

Samuel, Raphael. *East End Underworld: Chapters in the Life of Arthur Harding*. London, Boston, and Henley: Routledge and Kegan Paul, 1981.

Sandall, Robert. *The History of the Salvation Army*. New York: T. Nelson, 1947–73.

Schor, Naomi. "Dreaming Dissymmetry: Barthes, Foucault, and Sexual Difference." In Alice Jardine and Paul Smith, eds., *Men in Feminism*. New York: Methuen, 1987.

Schreiner, Olive. *Women and Labour*. London: T. Fisher Unwin, 1911.

Schults, Raymond L. *Crusader in Babylon: W. T. Stead and the Pall Mall Gazette*. Lincoln: University of Nebraska Press, 1972.

Scott, J. W. Robertson. *Life and Death of a Newspaper*. London: Methuen, 1952.

Scott, Joan W. "Deconstructing Equality-Versus-Difference: or the Uses of Post-structuralist Theory for Feminism." *Feminist Studies* 14, no. 1 (Spring 1988): 33–38.

———. *Gender and the Politics of History*. New York: Columbia University Press, 1986.

Sedgwick, Eve Kosofsky. *Between Men: English Literature and Male Homosocial Desire*. New York: Columbia University Press, 1988.

Segal, Lynne. *Is the Future Female? Troubled Thoughts on Contemporary Feminism*. London: Virago, 1987.

Sennett, Richard. *The Fall of Public Man*. Cambridge: Cambridge University Press, 1973.

Shanley, Mary Lyndon. *Feminism, Marriage, and the Law in Victorian England, 1850–1895*. Princeton, Princeton University Press, 1989.

Sharpe, William, and Leonard Wallock, eds. *Visions of the Modern City: Essays in History, Art, and Literature*. Baltimore: Johns Hopkins University Press, 1987.

Shipley, Stan. "Tom Causer of Bermondsey: A Boxer of the 1890s." *History Workshop Journal* 15 (Spring 1983): 28–49.

Shonfield, Suzanna. *The Precariously Privileged: A Professional Family in Victorian London*. Oxford: Oxford University Press, 1987.

Shortt, S. E. D. "Physicians and Psychics: The Anglo-American Medical Response to Spiritualism, 1870–90." *Journal of the History of Medicine and Allied Sciences* 39 (1984): 339–55.

Showalter, Elaine. *Sexual Anarchy: Gender and Culture at the Fin de Siècle*. New York: Viking, 1990.

Simey, M. S., and M. B. Simey. *Charles Booth, Social Scientist*. Oxford: Oxford University Press, 1960.

Sims, George R. *My Life: Sixty Years' Recollections of Bohemian London*. London: Eveleigh Nash, 1917.

Sinha, Mrinalini. "Gender and Imperialism: Colonial Policy and the Ideology of Moral Imperialism in Late-Nineteenth Century Bengal." In M. S. Kimmel, ed., *Changing Men: New Directions in Research on Men and Masculinity*. Beverly Hills: Sage, 1987.

Skultans, Vieda. "Mediums, Controls, and Eminent Men." In Pat Holden, ed., *Women's Religious Experience*. London: Croom Helm, 1983.

Smith, Francis Barrymore. *The People's Health, 1830–1910*. New York: Holmes and Meier, and London: Croom Helm, 1979.

Smith, Harold L., ed., *British Feminism in the Twentieth Century*. Amherst: University of Massachusetts Press, 1990.

Smith, Joan. "Getting Away with Murder." *New Socialist* (May/June 1982): 10–12.

Smith, William Sylvester. *The London Heretics, 1870–1914*. London: Constable, 1967.

Smith-Rosenberg, Carroll. *Disorderly Conduct: Visions of Gender in Victorian America.* New York: Knopf, 1985.

Smith-Rosenberg, Carroll, and Esther Newton. "The Mythic Lesbian and the New Woman: Power, Sexuality, and Legitimacy." Paper presented at the Berkshire Conference on Women's History, Vassar College, May 1981.

Snitow, Ann, Christine Stansell, and Sharon Thompson, eds., *Powers of Desire: The Politics of Sexuality.* New York: Monthly Review Press, 1983.

Snitow, Ann. "Retrenchment versus Transformation: The Politics of the Anti-Pornography Movement." In Varda Bustyn, ed., *Women against Censorship.* Vancouver and Toronto: Douglas and McIntyre, 1985.

Soloway, Richard Allen. *Birth Control and the Population Question.* Chapel Hill: University of North Carolina Press, 1982.

Southgate, Walter. *That's The Way It Was: A Working-Class Autobiography, 1890–1950.* London: New Clarion Press, 1982.

Spiegel, Gabrielle. "History, Historicism, and the Social Logic of the Text." *Speculum* 65, no. 1 (January 1990): 59–86.

Spitzka, E. C. "The Whitechapel Murders: Their Medico-Legal and Historical Aspects," *The Journal of Nervous and Mental Diseases* 13, no. 12 (December 1888): 765–78.

Stallybrass, Peter, and Allon White. *The Politics and Poetics of Transgression.* Ithaca: Cornell University Press, 1986.

Stansell, Christine. *City of Women: Sex and Class in New York, 1789–1860.* New York: Knopf, 1986.

Starkey, Terence. *Jack the Ripper: 100 Years of Investigation: The Facts, the Fiction, the Solution.* London: Ward Lock, 1987.

"The State's New Duty: An Old Ballad Upon the Proposed Extension of the Contagious Diseases Acts to the Civil Population." In *The Pearl.* Reprint, New York: Grove Press, 1968.

Stead, W. T. *The Armstrong Case: Mr. Stead's Defense Told in Full.* London: H. Vickers, 1885.

———. "Government by Journalism." *The Contemporary Review* 49 (1986): 654–74.

———. *Has Sir Charles Dilke Cleared His Character? An Examination of the Alleged Commission.* London: Review of Reviews, 1891.

Steedman, Carolyn. *Landscape for a Good Woman: A Story of Two Lives.* New Brunswick, N.J.: Rutgers University Press, 1987.

———. *The Radical Soldier's Tale.* London: Routledge, 1988.

Stevenson, Robert Louis. *Dr. Jekyll and Mr. Hyde,* with an introduction by Abraham Rothenberg. 1886. Reprint, New York: Bantam, 1967.

Stocking, George W. *Victorian Anthropology.* New York: The Free Press, 1987.

Storch, Robert D. "Police Control of Street Prostitution in Victorian London: A Study in the Context of Police Action." In David H. Bayley, ed., *Police and Society.* Beverly Hills and London: Sage, 1977.

Summers, Anne. "A Home from Home—Women's Philanthropic Work in the Nineteenth-Century." In Sandra Burman, ed., *Fit Work for Women.* New York: St. Martin's Press, 1979.

Swanwick, Helena M. *I Have Been Young.* London: Victor Gollancz, 1935.

Taylor, Barbara. *Eve and the New Jerusalem: Socialism and Feminism in the Nineteenth Century.* New York: Pantheon, 1983.

Terrot, Charles. *The Maiden Tribute: A Study of the White Slavery Traffic of the Nineteenth Century.* London: Frederick Muller, 1959.

Thane, Pat. "Late-Victorian Women." In T. R. Gourvish and Alan O'Day, eds., *Later Victorian Britain, 1867–1900.* Houndsmill, Bastingstoke: Hampshire Macmillan Education, 1988.

Theobald, Morell. *Spirit Workers in the Home Circle: An Autobiographical Narrative of Psychic Phenomena in Family Daily Life Extending over a Period of Twenty Years.* London: F. Fisher Unwin, 1877.

Thomas, Donald. *A Long Time Burning.* London: Odyssey Press, 1970.

Thompson, Paul. *Socialists, Liberals, and Labour: The Struggle for London, 1885–1914.* London: Routledge and Kegan Paul, 1967.

Tickner, Lisa. *Spectacle of Women: Imagery of the Suffrage Campaign, 1907–1914.* Chicago: University of Chicago Press, 1988.

Toews, John. "Intellectual History Takes a Linguistic Turn: The Autonomy of Meaning and the Irreducibility of Experience." *American Historical Review* 92, no. 4 (October 1987): 879–907.

Tolson, Andrew. *The Limits of Masculinity: Male Identity and the Liberated Woman.* New York: Harper and Row, 1977.

Treherne, Philip. *A Plaintiff in Person.* London: William Heinemann, 1923.

Trudgill, Eric. "Prostitution and Paterfamilias." In H. J. Dyos and Michael L. Wolff, eds., *The Victorian City: Images and Reality.* 2 volumes. London: Routledge and Kegan Paul, 1973.

Turnball, Anne Marie. "'So Extremely like Parliament': The Work of the Women Members of the London School Board, 1870–1904." In London Feminist History Group, ed., *Sexual Dynamics of History.* London: Pluto, 1983.

Turner, Frank Miller. *Between Science and Religion: The Reaction to Scientific Naturalism in Late-Victorian England.* New Haven: Yale University Press, 1974.

Turner, Victor. "Social Dramas and Stories about Them." *Critical Inquiry* 7, no. 1 (1980): 141–68.

Underwood, Peter. *Jack the Ripper: One Hundred Years of Mystery.* London: Blandford Press, 1988.

Unsworth, Madge. *Maiden Tribute: A Study in Voluntary Social Service.* London: Salvationist Publisher and Supplies, 1949.

Valverde, Mariana. "The Love of Finery: Fashion and the Fallen Woman in Nineteenth-Century Social Discourse." *Victorian Studies* 32, no. 2 (Winter 1989): 168–88.

Van Arsdel, Rosemary. "Victorian Periodicals Yield Their Secrets: Florence Fenwick Miller's Three Campaigns for the London School Board." *Warwick's Year Studies in English,* 1985.

Vicinus, Martha. "Distance and Desire: English Boarding School Friendships, 1870–1920." In Martin Bauml Duberman, Martha Vicinus, and George Chauncey, Jr., eds., *Hidden From History: Reclaiming the Gay and Lesbian Past.* New York: New American Library, 1989.

————. "'Helpless and Unfriended': Nineteenth-Century Domestic Melodrama." *New Literary History* 13 (1981–82): 127–43.

————. *Independent Women: Work and Community for Single Women, 1850–1920.* Chicago: University of Chicago Press, 1985.

Vincent, David. *Bread, Knowledge and Freedom: A Study of Nineteenth-Century Working-Class Autobiography.* London and New York: Methuen, 1982.

Walker, Pamela. "'I Live but Not Yet I for Christ Liveth in Me': Men and Masculinity in the Salvation Army, 1865–1890." In Michael Roper and John Tosh, eds., *Manfull Assertions: Masculinities in Britain since 1800.* London: Routledge, 1991.

————. "'Pulling the Devil's Kingdom Down': Gender and Popular Culture in the Salvation Army, 1865–1895." Ph.D. dissertation, Rutgers University, 1991.

Walkowitz, Judith R. "Jack the Ripper and the Myth of Male Violence." *Feminist Studies* 8 (Fall 1982): 543–74.

————. "Male Vice and Feminist Virtue: Feminism and the Politics of Prostitution in Nineteenth-Century Britain." *History Workshop Journal* 13 (Spring 1982): 77–93.

————. *Prostitution and Victorian Society: Women, Class, and the State.* New York: Cambridge University Press, 1980.

————. "Science and the Séance: Transgressions of Gender and Genre in Late-Victorian London." *Representations* 22 (Spring 1988): 3–29.

————. "Science, Feminism, and Romance: The Men and Women's Club, 1885–1889." *History Workshop Journal* (April 1986): 37–59.

Waller, P. J. *Town, City, and Nation: England, 1850–1914.* Oxford: Oxford University Press, 1983.

Walvin, James. *Victorian Values.* London: Penguin, 1988.

Ward, Mrs. Humphry [Mary Arnold]. *Marcella.* 1894. Reprint, New York: Viking Penguin, 1985.

Warner, Marina. *Monuments and Maidens: The Allegory of the Female Form.* New York: Atheneum, 1985.

Watney, Simon. *Policing Desire: Pornography, AIDS, and the Media.* Minneapolis: University of Minnesota Press, 1989.

Webb, Beatrice. *The Diaries of Beatrice Webb.* Vol. 1, 1873–1892. edited by Norman MacKenzie and Jeanne MacKenzie. Cambridge, Mass.: Belknap Press, 1982.

Weeks, Jeffrey. *Coming Out: Homosexual Politics in Britain from the Nineteenth Century to the Present.* London: Quartet Books, 1977.

————. *Sex, Politics, and Society.* London: Longman, 1981.

————. *Sexuality and Its Discontents: Meanings, Myths, and Modern Sexualities.* London: Routledge and Kegan Paul, 1985.

Weightman, Gavin, and Steve Humphries. *The Making of Modern London, 1815–1914.* London: Sidgwick and Jackson, 1983.

Weldon, Georgina. *The History of My Orphanage, or the Outpourings of an Alleged Lunatic.* Tavistock Square: Printed and Published by Mrs. Weldon, 1878.

————. *How I Escaped the Mad Doctors.* London: Mrs. Weldon, 1882.

Wensley, Frederick Porter. *Detective Days*. London: Cassell, 1931.

White, Jerry. *The Rothschild Buildings: Life in a Tenement Block, 1887–1920*. London: Routledge and Kegan Paul, 1980.

Whyte, F. *The Life of W. T. Stead*. 2 volumes. London: Jonathan Cape, 1925.

White, Hayden V. "The Value of Narrativity in the Representation of Reality." In W. J. T. Mitchell, ed., *On Narrative*. Chicago: University of Chicago Press, 1988.

Williams, Linda. "When the Woman Looks." In Mary Ann Doane, Patricia Mellencamp, and Linda Williams, eds., *Revision: Essays in Feminist Art Criticism*. Frederick, Md.: University Publications of America, 1984.

Williams, Montagu. *Round London: Down East and Up West*. London: Macmillan, 1892.

Williams, Raymond. *The Country and the City*. New York: Oxford University Press, 1973.

Williams, Rosalind H. *Dream Worlds: Mass Consumption in Late Nineteenth-Century France*. Berkeley and Los Angeles: University of California Press, 1982.

Wilson, Colin, and Robin Odell. *Jack the Ripper: Summing up the Verdict*. London: Bantam Press, 1987.

Wilson, Elizabeth. *What Is to Be Done about Violence Against Women?* Harmondsworth, Middlesex: Penguin, in association with the Socialist Society, 1983.

Wilstach, Paul. *Richard Mansfield, the Man and the Actor*. New York: Charles Scribner's and Sons, 1908.

Winslow, L. Forbes. *Fasting and Feeding Psychologically Considered*. London: Bailliere, Tindall and Cox, 1881.

———. *Insanity of Passion and Crime, with 43 Photographic Reproductions of Celebrated Cases*. London: John Ouseley, 1912.

———. *Recollections of Forty Years*. London: John Ousley, 1910.

———. *Spiritualistic Madness*. London, 1877.

Wohl, Anthony S., ed. *The Bitter Cry of Outcast London*. New York: Humanities Press, 1970.

———. "The Bitter Cry of Outcast London." *International Review of Social History* 13, part 2 (1968): 189–245.

———. *Endangered Lives: Public Health in Victorian Britain*. Cambridge: Harvard University Press, 1983.

———. "Octavia Hill and Homes of the London Poor." *Journal of British Studies* 10 (1971): 105–31.

Wolff, Janet. "The Invisible *Flaneuse:* Women and the Literature of Modernity." *Theory, Culture and Society* 2, no. 3 (1985): 37–16.

Woolf, Leonard. *Sowing: An Autobiography of the Years 1880 to 1904*. New York: Harcourt Brace, 1960.

Wyman, A. L. "Why Winslow? The Winslows of Sussex House." *Charing Cross Hospital Gazette* 64 (1966–67): 143–46.

Wyndham, Horace. *Victorian Sensations*. London: Jarrolds, 1933.

Yeazell, Ruth. "Nature's Courtship Plot in Darwin and Ellis." *Yale Journal of Criticism* 2, no. 2 (1989): 33–53.

———, et al., eds. *Sex, Politics, and Science in the Nineteenth-Century.* Baltimore: Johns Hopkins University Press, 1986.

Yeo, Eileen, and E. P. Thompson. *The Unknown Mayhew.* New York: Schocken Books, 1972.

Yule, G. Udny. "Karl Pearson." *Obituary Notices of Fellows of the Royal Society* 2 (1936–38): 100.

INDEX

Also of interest

SEXUAL ANARCHY: Gender and Culture at the *Fin de Siècle*

Elaine Showalter

'A triumph . . . gleams with wit and wry insight' – *New Statesman & Society*

'Sexual anarchy' – dire predictions, disasters, apocalypse – became the hallmark of the closing decades of the nineteenth century. The New Woman and the Odd Woman threatened male identity and self-esteem; the emergence of feminism and homosexuality meant the redefining of masculinity and femininity. This is the terrain which Elaine Showalter explores with such consummate originality and wit.

Looking at parallels between the ends of the nineteenth and twentieth centuries and their representations in literature, art and film, she ranges over the trial of Oscar Wilde, public furore over prostitution and syphilis, and in our own time, moral outrage over the breakdown of the family, abortion rights, AIDS. High and low culture – from male quest romances to contemporary male bonding movies (*Heart of Darkness* reworked into *Apocalypse Now*), Freud to *Fatal Attraction* – all are part of this scholarly and entertaining study of the *fin de siècle*.

THE SPHINX IN THE CITY: Urban Life, the Control of Disorder and Women

Elizabeth Wilson

'Stimulating . . . I would recommend it to anyone who wants an introduction to the tensions, texture and contradictions of urban life' – *Times Educational Supplement*

In the pre-industrial West, urban life was seen as civilised, sophisticated and harmonious. The nineteenth-century metropolis offered new excitements and pleasures, but strong fears of urban disintegration emerged – the notion of the industrial city as hell on earth. This urban disorder – represented by the figure of the sphinx – continues to haunt many Western writers and planners.

Elizabeth Wilson's elegant, provocative and scholarly study uses fiction, essays, film and art, as well as history and sociology, to look at some of the world's greatest cities – London, Paris, Moscow, New York, Chicago, Lusaka and São Paulo – and presents a powerful critique of utopian planning, anti-urbanism, postmodernism and traditional architecture. For women the city offers freedom, including sexual freedom, but also new dangers. Planners and reformers have repeatedly attempted to regulate women – and the working class and ethnic minorities – by means of grandiose, utopian plans, nearly destroying the richness of urban culture. City centres have become uninhabited business districts, the countryside suburbanised. There is danger without pleasure, consumerism without choice, safety without stimulation. What is urgently needed is a new vision of city life.

SEDUCTIONS: Studies in Reading and Culture

Jane Miller

'An incisive and marvellously timely book bent on retrieving "woman" from the status of metaphor she still has in contemporary political and literary debate. Jane Miller reads the culture – from theoretical models to novels to social documents – consummately, with energy and subtlety and, above all, engagement. Seduction is her metaphor and she uses it to shrewd effect' – *Lorna Sage*

'One of the deadliest of seductions for feminists is their seduction by theorists, by theories.' With this boldly polemical stroke, Jane Miller begins her exploration stealthily, cumulatively, and with a deft and compelling intelligence. In looking at the complex relation of women to culture and literature, and to theory and politics, and in recalling her own coming to feminism, she asks how women experience themselves within ideas and traditions which simultaneously include and exclude them, take their presence for granted and deny it – seducing them in short.

Seductions makes a stunning contribution to feminist theory while tackling issues of importance for education and the study of culture and language.